Olympic Philosophy

The Ideas and Ideals behind the Ancient and Modern Olympic Games

Olympic Philosophy

The Ideas and Ideals behind the Ancient and Modern Olympic Games

Heather L. Reid

Parnassos Press
2020

Copyright © 2020 Fonte Aretusa LLC
All rights reserved. This book or any portion thereof may not be reproduced or used in any manner whatsoever without the express written permission of the author and publisher except for the use of brief quotations in a book review or scholarly journal.

First Printing: 2020
ISBN 978-1-942495-44-4 (hardcover)
ISBN 978-1-942495-34-5 (paperback)

Parnassos Press
Fonte Aretusa Organization
1628 W. Willis Ave.
Sioux City, Iowa 51103

www.fontearetusa.org

Acknowledgments

The essays collected in this book are the fruit of more than 20 years of scholarship supported by a variety of individuals and institutions, only a portion of which can be acknowledged here. The International Olympic Academy in Olympia, Greece has been the primary source of inspiration and support for this work. My home institution, Morningside College, also supported my scholarship in Olympic studies, as has the Exedra Mediterranean Center in Siracusa Sicily, where I am scholar in residence.

In addition, several centers and foundations have supported my work including the William J. Fulbright Foreign Scholarship Board, Harvard Center for Hellenic Studies, Andrew W. Mellon Foundation, National Endowment for the Humanities, and the American Academy in Rome.

Among the myriad colleagues who have encouraged and enriched my thought on the Olympic Games, those who stand out are Susan Brownell, Stamatia Dova, Christos Evangeliou, Warren P. Fraleigh, Paul Gaffney, Kostas Georgiadis, Ren Hai, Elizabeth Hanley, Drew Hyland, Apostolos Kosmopoulos, Emanuele Isidori, Sigmund Loland, Mike McNamee, Greg Nagy, Stephen G. Miller, William J. Morgan, J.S. Russell, Angela Schneider, Charles Stocking, Nathan Sivin, Panos Valavanis, and Ingomar Weiler.

Special thanks are also due to the next generation of Olympic scholars, especially Rafael Mendoza, who collaborated on the organization and revision of the anthology. Georgios Mouratidis, Mateus Nagime, Marjorie Yuri Enya, David Grassi, and Dominick Gusia also offered valuable feedback on the initial draft.

In addition, I thank the publishers of the work reprinted here for their cooperation in granting the appropriate permissions.

Finally, I thank my husband, Larry Theobald, and my extended family for their enduring support of my athletic and philosophical activitie

Ολυμπιακό Πνεύμα

Πνεύμα θεών αθάνατο, το τρισχαριτωμένο,
κάτελθε και προσκύνησε, στη γη σε περιμένω,
της Ολυμπίας την καλή, των αθλητών πατρίδα,
στην ομορφιά πιο ζηλευτή άλλην εγώ δεν είδα!

Με ίδρωτα την πότισαν των αθλητών οι άθλοι!
Της αρετής βλαστήματα, σαν της ελιάς τα άνθη,
καρπό πολύ θα δέσουνε, θα δώσουν νέο λάδι,
τον κότινο των αθλητών κι αγνής αγάπης χάδι.

Της θερινής της πυρκαγιάς οι καυτερές οι φλόγες
δεν ήταν τόσο δυνατές, μαζί κι ας ήρθαν όλες,
να σβήσουνε τη λάμψη σου, την έμπνευση τη θεία.
Σαν Φοίνικας, στην τέφρα σου ζητάς αθανασία!

Πάρε φτερούγες των αετών, των αθλητών μυώνες,
πάρε Διός Ολύμπιου θεόρατες κολόνες,
και πύργωσε την κεφαλή, στύλωσε το κορμί σου,
αγκάλιασε την Αρετή, σαν κόρη κι αδερφή σου!

Χρήστος Κ. Ευαγγελίου

Olympic Spirit

Spirit of immortal gods, most beautiful and blessed!
Descend, for we await you by Cronion's naked crest,
In glorious Olympia, motherland of athletes,
Beauty greater in my life, I've not and never will see.

Irrigated with the sweat from athletes' holy struggles,
Virtue here will bloom again, like your ageless olives,
Fruit will weigh their branches down and they will give new oil,
To massage the athletes' skin and crown the victors' toil.

That summer's cruel inferno, the hottest of her flames,
Never could be strong enough to take away your fame,
Even though they stripped you bare, your godlike spirit shines,
Like Phoenix from the ashes, you beam eternal life!

So take the wings of eagles, your athletes' famous strength,
And like your temple's columns, bear this heavy weight.
Straighten up your back, and raise your head with pride,
Embrace again sweet Virtue, your sister and your child!

Christos C. Evangeliou

Table of Contents

Acknowledgments v

Olympic Spirit vi

Guide to Olympic Studies Topics xi

Introduction 1

PROLOGUE

1. Ancient Ideals and the Modern Olympics 5

SECTION I
HEROIC HERITAGE

2. Pre-Olympic Heroes 21

3. Heracles' Choice: Is Strength Really a Virtue? ... 35

4. Olympic Athletes as Heroes and Role Models ... 47

SECTION II
ANCIENT OLYMPIC PHILOSOPHY

5. Racing toward Truth in Ancient Olympia 67

6. From Aristocracy to Democracy at Olympics ... 79

7. Olympic Sacrifice 97

SECTION III
THE ETHICS OF EXCELLENCE

8. The Soul of an Olympian 115

9. Coaching for Virtue in Olympic Sport 129

10. The Ecstasy of *Aretē* 147

SECTION IV
BEAUTIFUL GOODNESS

11. Athletic Beauty in Ancient Greece: 163

12. Virtuous Viewing of Olympic Athletes 183

13. Olympic Ethics as *Kalokagathia* 195

SECTION V
MODERN OLYMPISM

14. The Philosophy of Olympic Revival 207

15. Olympism: a Philosophy of Sport 221

16. What Counts as an Olympic Sport? 247

SECTION VI
JUSTICE AS FAIR PLAY

17. The Ideal of Justice and Olympic Reality 265

18. Performance Technology and Olympic Fair Play 279

19. Athlete Agency and the Spirit of Olympic Sport 289

SECTION VII
PEACE AND WORLD COMMUNITY

20. The Political Heritage of the Olympic Games 311

21. Olympic Sport and Its Lessons for Peace 331

22. Olympic Sport and Globalization 347

SECTION VIII
OLYMPISM EAST AND WEST

23. Olympic Virtue between East and West 365

24. East to Olympia 379

25. An American Philosopher at the Beijing Olympics .. 403

EPILOGUE

26. Why Olympic Philosophy Matters 415

Glossary of Ancient Greek Terms 433

Bibliography 435

Index 453

About the Author 458

Guide to Olympic Studies Topics

In discussing Olympic philosophy this text addresses many issues in Olympic Studies. Most of these are listed in the subject index. In addition, chapters focused on popular topics are listed here.

Commercialism
Chapter 7. Olympic Sacrifice
Chapter 16. What Counts as an Olympic Sport?

Doping/Performance-Enhancing Technologies
Chapter 15. Performance Technology and Olympic Fair Play
Chapter 16. Athlete Agency and the Spirit of Olympic Sport

Education/Role Models
Chapter 4. Olympic Athletes as Heroes and Role Models
Chapter 9. Coaching for Virtue in Olympic Sport

Globalization/Multiculturalism
Chapter 15. Olympism as a Philosophy of Sport (240-245)
Chapter 22. Olympic Sport and Globalization

Peace/Politics
Chapter 20. The Political Heritage of the Olympic Games
Chapter 21. Olympic Sport and its Lessons for Peace

Religion/Religious Tolerance
Chapter 5. Racing toward Truth in Ancient Olympia
Chapter 7. Olympic Sacrifice

Social Class/Economic Disparity
Chapter 6. From Aristocracy to Democracy at the Olympics
Chapter 17. The Ideal of Justice and Olympic Reality

Spectacle/Spectatorship
Chapter 11. Athletic Beauty in Ancient Greece
Chapter 12. Virtuous Viewing of Olympic Athletes

Women/Gender
Chapter 6. From Aristocracy to Democracy at the Olympics
Chapter 11. Athletic Beauty in Ancient Greece (177-180)

Introduction

My first attempt to explain Olympic philosophy came when I was still in college during the run-up to the 1984 Los Angeles Games. I was a serious cyclist, exasperated with the nationalistic rhetoric in the local newspaper, so I wrote a letter to the editor of the *Santa Barbara News Press* arguing that the Olympic Motto, "*citius, altius, fortius,*" did not mean "faster, higher, stronger," than the USSR, but rather "faster, higher, stronger" than I have ever been before. An athlete's goal, I tried to explain, was the same as her competitors': improvement. We were not trying to destroy one another, but rather to push one another toward the mutual goal of excellence.

Although I made it to the final qualifying races in 1984 and 1988, I never did make the Olympic team. Eventually, I stopped racing and focused full-time on my studies. I never stopped trying to understand and explain Olympic philosophy though. In fact, when I was invited to teach "Olympic Ethics and Philosophy" at the International Olympic Academy in the fall of 2019, I looked back through my publications and realized I had written more than enough to fill a book. This is that book.

My understanding of Olympic philosophy is supported by three pillars: my personal experience as an athlete, my academic expertise in ancient Greek athletics and philosophy, and my enthusiasm for the ideals that inspire the modern Olympic Movement. I believe that the ideas and ideals behind the ancient and modern Olympic Games can imbue sport with meaning and value, not just on a personal level but also socially and globally.

Sport is not intrinsically meaningful and victory has no intrinsic value. What makes the Olympics meaningful and what gives value to sports of all kinds is the ideas and ideals that human beings express through them. The inability to understand or articulate those ideas, furthermore, leaves us with cold, often instrumental explanations for sport. We say it is a way to stay healthy, a form of entertainment, or a means to financial reward. But those of us who love sports, who have lived the life of an athlete, who catch ourselves thinking about games and goals to the exclusion of much more important things, we know that sports—and the Olympic Games in particular—are so much more than that. The essays in this book attempt to explain why.

The initial essays focus on the Olympics ancient Greek heritage. To explain the power of the Modern Games, which have endured for more than 100 years, we need to examine the ancient Olympic festival, which lasted for more than 1,000. It was the rich mythology of heroes, the beautiful poetry of Pindar, the idealistic philosophy of Plato, the potent politics of democracy, and the graceful elegance of athletic sculpture that combined in ancient Greece to create a culture centered on the concept of *aretē* (excellence). Athletics became the centerpiece of that cultural conspiracy and the Olympic Games became its primary celebration.

The founders of the Modern Games, likewise, were trying to promote more than sports and fitness when they revived the Games toward the end of the 19th century. They were trying to revive those ancient Greek ideals in the form of a "philosophy of life" that would come to be called "Olympism." Although their philosophy may better reflect the beliefs of the European Enlightenment than Plato and Aristotle, it engages important and enduring ideas from ancient Greece that not only sustained the 1,000 year history of Olympia's Games, but have also had remarkable success as the guiding principle of such a complex and multicultural organization as the Olympic Movement.

What makes the Olympic Games special as a sporting event is the philosophy that guides them. I have spent the better part of my career trying to understand and explain that philosophy because I believe it can bring the best out of sport and the human beings who practice it. It is my hope that these essays will help others to understand Olympic philosophy and thereby to preserve and promote the positive power of sport today and in the future.

Syracuse, Sicily
October, 2019

Prologue

1. Ancient Ideals and the Modern Olympics[1]

Introduction: Questions of Relevance

As is known, the modern Olympic Games trace their origins to ancient Greece. The Olympic flame is ignited in Olympia by the rays of the same sun that caressed the bodies of ancient athletes. Then the flame is transported by torch from the ancient sanctuary to the Games' modern home—wherever in the world that may be. The torch-relay links the ancient and modern games, but what underlies this symbolic transmission of the Olympic spirit? We know that the 19th century revivalists often idealized or distorted ancient history and literature to suit their goals. Such cherished Olympic ideals as amateurism, sound minds in strong bodies, even the emphasis on participation over victory, are not reflective of ancient reality. Furthermore, the Olympic Movement's 21st century path toward multiculturalism seems to render its ancient heritage an irrelevant relic of its Eurocentric history. Given these past abuses and present aims, the question naturally arises: Should Olympic scholars continue to study the ancient Games?

The answer to this question is an emphatic "Yes." In fact, scholars must do more than study the history and archaeology of the ancient Olympic Games; we must also come to understand and appreciate their philosophical ideals. A more philosophical understanding of the Olympics' Hellenic heritage is especially relevant now as the movement strives for multiculturalism and diversity. We contend that the alleged Eurocentrism of Olympic ideals is itself a product of Eurocentric bias; born of a desire among modern Europeans to claim Classical Greece as their heritage.[2] In fact, the history and geography of ancient Olympia

---

[1] Co-authored with Christos Evangeliou. Originally published in *The Olympic Studies Reader*, eds. H. Ren & L. DaCosta (Beijing Sport University, 2008) 205-216. Reprinted with the authors' permission.

[2] D. Chatziefstathiou and I. Henry, "Hellenism and Olympism: Pierre De Coubertin and the Greek Challenge to the Early Olympic Movement" *Sport in History* 26:1 (March 2007).

place it *between* Europe, Africa, and Asia (and within that triangle, more East than West).[3] The Olympic Games functioned politically to unify and pacify diverse groups of people in that region. Indeed recent research suggests that Hellenic philosophy and athletics stem partly from early contacts with the peoples of Asia and Africa.[4] The specifically Olympic ideals of humanism, justice, and peace derive less from a particular cultural mythology or ethnic heritage than from the communal experience of diverse peoples finding common ground via the practice of sport.

The purpose of this paper is to identify and articulate the philosophical ideals that, in our view, underpinned the ancient Olympic Games and may serve the modern Olympic Movement in its quest for global harmony. Although the claim of the ancient Games to unite the far corners of Hellas may appear quaint when compared with our worldwide festivals, the political and logistical challenges were arguably no less formidable than ours. Furthermore the ancient Games' more than 1,000 year span makes the modern Games' single-century history look like a flash in the pan. Big and strong as the modern Games seem, they should humbly acknowledge their infancy and look to their venerable ancestor for advice as they face an uncertain future. It was the ideals associated with Olympia that secured the ancient Games' long-enduring success. Only if the modern Olympic Movement actively understands and consciously preserves its ancient heritage, can the Games remain a beacon of idealism amid the headlong pursuit of worldly wealth and power.

Idealism and Agōnism

To unleash the power of ancient Olympic ideals, we must first understand the meaning of Hellenic idealism and its connection to Hellenic *agōn* (contest or struggle). Idealism is traditionally

---

[3] For a full discussion see C. Evangeliou, *Hellenic Philosophy Origin and Character* (Burlington, VT: Ashgate, 2006), especially 22-28.

[4] For Philosophy's debt to Egypt and Ionia, see Evangeliou, *Hellenic Philosophy*, 10-30, 173-176. For the athletics, see D. Kyle, *Sport and Spectacle in the Ancient World* (Malden MA: Blackwell, 2007), 23-54.

linked with Plato's "theory of forms," which holds that universal ideas or "forms" such as "the good" exist in a metaphysical realm beyond our worldly reality. Their status is akin to that of numbers, that is, universal concepts that can be grasped by human minds and applied in diverse worldly circumstances, but which nevertheless exist independently and eternally. Beings in this world are always imperfect copies or approximations of corresponding ideas, and they are better or worse according to how they live up to their archetypal ideals.

Thus, for example, a knife is good insofar as it approximates the ideal knife—which is not a knife found in a Japanese kitchen or British museum, but rather a perfect pattern, paradigm, or *idea* that exists in the realm of forms.[5] The knife, however, is just a convenient illustration. There are also moral ideals such as justice, courage, and piety, which stipulate how the ideal character of a human being should be shaped. Close approximation to ideals, for humans and other things, is called *aretē* (excellence, virtue), an important concept in Hellenic ethics as well as athletics. But these ideals are not considered products of a particular culture or authority; they are thought to be applicable to everyone and everywhere. It is the task of ethical agents, therefore, to try to understand these ideals through reason, and then to approximate them as much as possible in their choices and actions.

Olympism, as described in the "Fundamental Principles" of the Olympic Charter, offers its own ideal vision of humanity towards which the Olympic Movement is expected to move and strive.[6] As thinking athletes know, however, the achievement of ideals is rarely easy or automatic. It requires *agōn*, the struggle and striving characteristic of ancient Greek culture in general; which is associated closely with athletics.[7] Indeed the Olympic Games

---

[5] See, for example, Plato, *Parmenides*, 129a-135e.
[6] International Olympic Committee, *Olympic Charter* (Lausanne: IOC, 2004), 9.
[7] For example, J. Burkhardt, *The Greeks and Greek Civilization* (New York: St. Martin's, 1998), 160-213.

were and still are called in Greek *Olympiakoi Agōnes*. Understood in terms of the Hellenic contrast between the human and the divine, *agōn* characterizes the basic human condition. If we were gods, we would already have perfect understanding and strength; so there would be no need for struggle.

Although human beings rarely achieve divine perfection, we are nonetheless encouraged to strive towards an ideal of excellence, whatever the particular endeavor may be. In ancient Greek literature and mythology such strivings are supported and rewarded by the gods themselves. Indeed *agōn* underpins the very concept of heroism. Hellenic heroes, such as Heracles and Pelops, who were associated with Olympia, and even Socrates, the gadfly of Athens, were mortals who achieved semi-divine status through their extraordinary striving for excellence.[8] They were "first in their struggle" or "*prōtagōnistēs*." Like Olympic victors, they came closer to the gods, but only through struggle and striving toward their respective ideals.

Although Hellenic *agōn* is often individual, true idealists strive not only for personal perfection, but also for the *koinon agathon* or common good of the community. Hellenic heroes ultimately are lauded for their social service: Heracles liberates his people from horrible monsters, Pelops frees Elis from a brutal tyrant, and Socrates tries to release Athens from sclerotic modes of thinking. In fact Socrates views his struggles quite explicitly as public service, and asks to be rewarded like an Olympic victor (Plato, *Apology* 36de). This comparison made sense to ancient Hellenes because the Olympic festival, like so many other athletic festivals in the ancient world, was a symbolic form of religious service and sacrifice. Olympic victors were thought to serve their own cities and families, as well as the Panhellenic community, by attracting divine favor and hence answered prayers for harvests, healing, or peace. In this way the Games mixed ethnic rivalry with common benefit. Just as a polytheistic Athenian could worship

---

[8] Heracles and Pelops are both mythological founders of the Olympic Games, see Pindar, *Olympian Odes* 10.27-77 and 1.75-99.

both his patron goddess Athena and the Panhellenic god Zeus, the agonistic struggle for universal ideals can accommodate group and individual rivalry even as it serves a greater common good.

Olympic Ideals

Evidently, then, idealism and agonism are as much a part of the Olympics' Hellenic heritage as the particular ideals of humanism, justice, and peace. It matters little that Olympic reality, ancient or modern, rarely manages to achieve these ideals because in Hellenic idealism, the struggle for victory outweighs the victory itself. Nor does the Hellenic origin of these ideals discount their relevance to the modern Olympic Movement's multicultural mission. This is so because the Olympic ideals derive less from cultural peculiarities than from multicultural challenges, specifically the challenge of bringing together diverse peoples from Asia and Africa as well as Europe to live, eat, and compete together in peace. There were shared linguistic and religious traditions, of course, but the ancient Olympic Games worked primarily to bridge political and cultural differences through the common practice of athletics. Insofar as the ancient Olympic ideals of humanism, justice, and peace reflect the unifying function of Pan-Hellenic athletics rather than a distinctively ethnic mindset, we believe that they can also function as Pan-anthropic models appropriate to the modern Olympic Movement's global aims.

Humanism

In the context of ancient Hellas, our modern Olympic flame recalls the mythical torch of Prometheus and his fiery gift to humanity—the gift that elevated us above mere animals and illuminated a path toward divinity. In our modern world the term 'humanism' is often saddled with the prefix 'secular' and used by certain religious leaders to identify and demonize non-believers who may challenge the powers of the Church. But Hellenic humanism was neither a serious challenge to religion nor a rejection of the supernatural; rather it was an appreciation of the potential of human beings. The ancient Hellenic esteem for humankind was rooted in an understanding of our imperfection with respect to the divine—an understanding that makes our struggle and achievement all the more worthwhile.

Furthermore, they recognized that Prometheus' gift of fire and reason elevated mankind above the animals and made us capable of more than survival and other pragmatic tasks. In other words, it made us capable—and even worthy—of doing things for their own sake.[9] As Aristotle suggests (*Metaphysics* 981b.15-20), it is not those arts invented for utility, but rather those created for recreation that represent humanity's highest achievement. By associating humanity's divine potential with the universal quality of human reason, Hellenic humanism avoids allegiance to any particular culture or religion. Like the playful and tolerant polytheism of ancient Hellas,[10] it simultaneously embraces commonality while it celebrates cultural differences.

Hellenic humanism champions human reason and virtue as tools of liberation from ignorance and servitude to unworthy masters. Ancient athletics and philosophy both reflect this ideal. The pre-Socratic philosophers employed reason to liberate themselves from (often worrying) mythological explanations of the natural world. Next to them, the Platonic Socrates insisted on the rational examination of human life, making reason and not tradition or worldly power the key to piety, ethics, and social reform. Aristotle in his turn classified human beings as rational and political animals, while Cynics and Stoics used reason to liberate themselves from social convention and moral corruption. In short, Hellenic humanism sees reason as the tool of our potential independence from forces that would deny human dignity; it gives us the power and possibility to learn for ourselves about ourselves and about the wrld, and to take control of our lives to be lived in the pursuit of excellence.

---

[9] Allen Guttmann, *From Ritual to Record: the Nature of Modern Sports* (New York: Columbia U.P., 1978), 22-3.

[10] For more on the inherent tolerance of Hellenic polytheism, see Evangeliou, *Hellenic Philosophy*, 175.

Sport, too, developed in the ancient Hellenic world as a means for testing and evaluating human excellence against rational and objective parameters, rather than worldly authorities. For example, in Homer's *Iliad* (23.256-24.6), the funeral games settled questions of social merit,[11] and in Olympia athletic contests selected worthy victors for symbolic sacrifice on the basis of performance rather than social status.[12] This religious function may explain why the impartiality of judging standards and corresponding fairness of results was a key value at ancient Olympia, and crucial for the Games' Pan-Hellenic prestige.[13] It is no accident that athletic contests show structural similarities to Socratic method and to scientific inquiry. After all, to stand on a starting line is to risk the possibility of failure, admitting that the outcome of the contest is unknown and undetermined at that point of time. So, it is akin to the Socratic admission of imperfection that prompts and motivates philosophical inquiry.[14]

Finally, by setting up specific rules and impartial testing conditions that independently validate results, athletic contests respect all contestants' claim to victory. In this sense, the athlete who survives the challenge of his competitors resembles the hypothesis that survives scientific testing. The driving motivation of the athlete and fan, therefore, is not so different from that of the philosopher or scientist. To use Aristotle's phrase (*Metaphysics* 980a22), they all desire *to know,* and they set up rational testing conditions in order to achieve this precious knowledge. Ancient and modern peoples alike are attracted to the Olympics because

---

[11] Ben Brown "Homer, Funeral Contests and the Origins of the Greek City" in *Sport and Festival in the Ancient Greek World*, eds. D.J. Phillips and D. Pritchard (Swansea, The Classical Press of Wales, 2003), 123-162.

[12] D. Sansone, *Greek Athletics and the Genesis of Sport* (Berkeley, CA: U. of California Press, 1988), 82-4.

[13] S. Miller, *Ancient Greek Athletics* (New Haven, CT: Yale University Press, 2004), 84.

[14] For more on this connection, see H. Reid, "Athletic Competition as Socratic Philosophy." AUPO *Gymnika* 35:2 (2006): 73-77.

they want to see what humanity might be capable of achieving. Thus the Olympic Games express Hellenic humanism by using reason and virtue to liberate our potential. They make us dream now as then about what we can achieve as human beings when we compete for the wreath of victory in the pursuit of excellence, whether athletic, artistic, or intellectual.

Justice

The Hellenic heritage of the Olympic Games also exalts an ideal of justice that privileges the authority of reason rather than the worldly rule of "might makes right," and promises the peaceful thriving of diverse human communities. At least since Homer's description of the power struggle between King Agamemnon and the brilliant warrior Achilles, the just and proper distribution of honor and power within communities was a key concern for the ancient Hellenes. So, it is no coincidence that the *Iliad's* athletic games effected the reunification of the Achaean army. According to the logic of sport, might can be "right" when and only when there is equal opportunity and reward according to demonstrated merit. It is perhaps no coincidence either that these fundamental principles of social justice reflect the athletic ideal of fair play.

Despite the social stratification of their societies, the principle of equal opportunity was essential to the Greeks at their athletic competitions.[15] An athlete's strength may win him victory in the wrestling match, but his military rank, social class, and worldly wealth provided no advantage to him under the rules of the games.[16] Reflecting his awareness of such principles, Alexander the Great said he would run in the Olympic Games only if his opponents were limited to other kings (Plutarch, *Life of Alexander*, 4.6.) According to the principles of fair play, an accurate determination of contest-relevant inequalities, i.e. running speed, *depends* on elimination of irrelevant inequalities, such as ethnic

---

[15] Guttman, *From Ritual to Record*, 28.

[16] M. Finley & H. Plecket, *The Olympic Games: The First Thousand Years* (New York: Viking, 1976), 58.

origin, noble birth, and even wealth.¹⁷ Contest rules strive to provide equal opportunity for all competitors, going beyond the basic principle of a common starting line, to the point of drawing lots for particular lanes on the track or switching sides of the playing field. Ancient boxing matches, for example, were held at high noon to be sure that neither competitor would have the sun in his eyes.¹⁸

Most symbolic of all was the fact that ancient athletes were literally stripped of their worldly differences: they competed in the nude without shame. Indeed, entering an athletic contest meant relinquishing any and all social privileges. Although the distinction between a free Greek and a barbarian slave had huge legal consequences in Greek society, a free man who competed as an athlete at the Games had to be willing to accept even the servile punishment of public flogging. Stephen Miller takes this fact to be a paradigmatic example for his argument that Greek athletics actually created the concept of *isonomia* or equality before the law—the foundational principle of democracy.¹⁹ For the Greeks, the need to provide equal opportunity in athletics was directly connected to their religious obligation to select the most worthy victor as a symbolic offering to the god. But the Hellenes also saw athletics as a means of education. The experience of competing on equal terms with one's peers was certainly good preparation for the challenges of citizenship. Competing on equal terms with athletes from around the world is an experience no less valuable in today's globalized society.

This ancient ideal of justice will serve the Olympic Games well as it confronts global diversity in the present era. Modern sports can preserve the educational benefit of equality before the

---

[17] Sigmund Loland, *Fair Play in Sport: A Moral Norm System* (London: Routledge, 2002), 46.
[18] Exceptions to the principle of equal opportunity in modern sport tend only to prove the rule, i.e. handicapping seeks to even out ability differences and achieve a more "equal competition."
[19] See, for example, Miller, *Ancient Greek Athletics*, 18, and 232-234.

Prologue

law among diverse peoples. When we watch an Olympic event, we encounter a group of people who speak different languages, have vastly different personal incomes, live under different legal systems, and are sometimes subject to governments at odds or at war with one another—yet we witness these people competing for a common prize under a single set of rules that treats them all as equals and demands that they treat each other accordingly. At the Olympic Games this world community is guided by a universal ideal of justice expressed in the form of game rules, which are comprehended and freely accepted by a diverse set of competitors. Here justice is simultaneously a right and duty for every member of the community, not a matter of charity or benevolence granted by the most powerful. It may be only a glimpse of the ideal, but it is one that provides much-needed hope and guidance for a better and more humane future.

Peace

Justice is often considered a precondition for peace, which is the Modern Olympic Movement's most venerable goal.[20] The association between Olympic Games and Pan-Hellenic peace is reflected in ancient mythology and rhetoric, but its true source was more likely the effect of athletic competition itself. Who would propose competition as a means to friendship and good will? No other authority than the Delphic Oracle, which was famous for its paradoxical proclamations (Pausanias 5.4.6). Greek city-states were almost constantly at war and the Olympic sanctuary itself was full of captured booty.[21] Nevertheless Olympia in time became a beacon of peace. Orators, including Gorgias, Lysias, and Isocrates, preached Panhellenism to festival

---

[20] The Olympic Charter identifies promotion of "a peaceful society" as a primary goal and "the endeavor to place sport at the service of humanity and thereby to promote peace," in the IOC mission. 11.

[21] Left as thanks to Zeus for victory, as in other sanctuaries. Nigel Crowther, "The Ancient Olympics and Their Ideals" in *Athletika: Studies on the Olympic Games and Greek Athletics* (Hildesheim: Weidemann, 2004) 17.

crowds; Olympic officials were used as ambassadors of peace, and there is evidence of a court being set up at Olympia to mediate disputes among Greek city-states.[22] The Olympics helped the ancient Hellenes to cultivate peace by obliging them to set aside conflict and political disagreements, treat others as equals, and tolerate differences. Since modern Olympic sport requires participants to do the same, there is some hope that these lessons may endure through the 21st century—but first we must strive to understand them.

Although the ancient Olympic Games clearly failed to eradicate war and enmity in the ancient world, they tirelessly declared their truce and regularly brought diverse people together to engage in rule-governed, non-violent competition.[23] The original cause of ancient Olympic festival was religious, but the effects of the gathering transcended that purpose and apparently resulted in feelings of peace and solidarity among those gathered. Like religion, peace develops in "sanctuaries" – spaces and times specifically marked off from the realm of day-to-day life (and hostilities). Athletic space can also be interpreted as a kind of sanctuary, set apart from the everyday. Basketball courts in turbulent neighborhoods often provide an oasis where interpersonal quarrels are suspended, enough at least to make the game possible. The Greeks' ability to compete peacefully, even with their temporary enemies, may have roots in the venerable Hellenic tradition of *xenia* or hospitality. *Xenia* requires that one welcome the stranger and provide for his basic needs—all before knowing anything about him. It reflects the enduring importance of overcoming such common human sentiments as fear and hostility in the face of a total stranger. No doubt inspired by their

---

[22] Crowther, "Ideals," 19.

[23] Here I use the term 'violence' to contrast games with war, in which the objective of the activity is to kill or disable one's opponent. Although such ancient sports as boxing and pankration were brutal, and sometimes resulted in death, death was not the goal of the contest and in some cases the dead man was posthumously awarded the victory, see Pausanias, *Guide to Greece*, 8.40.2-5.

early contact with foreign tribes, the Hellenic practice of *xenia* habitually and effectively creates sanctuaries where the roots of friendship and brotherhood can take hold.

As a Panhellenic event attracting participants from a variety of city-states, the ancient Olympic festival took the religious, athletic, and cultural idea of sanctuary to an "inter-state" level. The vehicle necessary for such a gathering was an official truce, known as *ekecheiria*, which allowed people from all over the Hellenic world to travel safely to and from Olympia. The Olympic truce did not, as is sometimes claimed, put an end to wars permanently. Its main function was the protection of pilgrims traveling to and from the festival. But even this limited function makes it clear that the communal festival was regarded as *more important* than the power politics and worldly conflicts between city-states.[24] The truce shows that the Pan-Hellenic festival effectively trumped war by rendering it a baser activity (at least in the imagined opinion of the-all-watching gods). In practice, the large and diverse gatherings at Olympia provided unparalleled opportunities for social, artistic, and intellectual interaction. Of course the truce was not fail-safe, but violations were notable for their rarity. Therefore the effectiveness and duration of the ancient Olympic Games and their truce stand as a monument to the perennial human struggle for peace on earth.[25]

However, it was not enough to provide a time and space for peaceful gathering; just as it wasn't enough to observe the laws of justice by treating athletes as equals. The Olympic festival also had to respect difference and diversity. Respect for diversity has deep Olympic roots. Long before the first race was run at the site,

---

[24] Finley & Plecket, *Olympic Games*, 98. Those who say the *ekecheiria* stopped wars may be confusing it with the Panhellenic truce of 481 BCE, probably negotiated at Olympia, which did put an end to internal conflicts until the end of the Persian Wars (Crowther, "Ideals," 21).

[25] In 364 BCE, a battle took place within the sanctuary during the games See L. Drees, *Olympia: Gods, Artists and Athletes* (New York: Praeger, 1968), 154 and S. Miller, *Ancient Greek Athletics*, 225.

Olympia hosted altars to a variety of gods and heroes. Further, it was a Panhellenic site, serving not just a single city or region, but the diverse panorama of peoples and cultures within a world that covered the shores of both the Mediterranean and the Black seas. Every four years during the Games, the small valley space was packed with a huge variety of strange visitors. By coming to Olympia for common worship, feasting, and athletic competition, this selected group created a new Panhellenic community—one more culturally and politically diverse than the communities from which they traveled. The Games themselves must have facilitated the unification by dispelling stereotypes and confirming their common Hellenic humanity, but also by helping those gathered to tolerate and even appreciate their differences.

Moderns may call the Olympic community multicultural, but the ancients had their own word for it: "cosmopolitan." The conception of cosmopolitanism or world-citizenship bloomed when the philosophy of Greek Stoicism faced the unprecedented racial and religious diversity of the Roman Empire. Stoic cosmopolitanism, like Pierre de Coubertin's internationalism, did not advocate a withdrawal from particular communities; nor did it encourage insulation from or imposition of one culture over another, rather, it sought to engage different cultures on common ground, forming a higher human community to be held together by the bond of shared habits, ideas and ideals. [26] Athletic arenas are one such common ground, the valley of Olympia was another, our modern Olympic villages are yet one more. It may be daunting to imagine a true worldwide community, but the Olympic Games have been remarkably successful at presenting at least the image of one—especially in the closing ceremonies when athletes abandon national ranks and march as one world made of many diverse individuals united for a precious moment by the bond of the Olympic spirit.

---

[26] W. Morgan, "Cosmopolitanism, Olympism, and Nationalism," *Olympika* IV (1995), 88.

Conclusion

In Plato's allegory of the cave (*Republic* VII.514-518), a fire lit manipulators' puppets and cast shadows on the wall, which the shackled prisoners mistook for reality. Eventually, however, some prisoners escaped the cave and ascended into the authentic light of the sun where they gazed upon true ideal forms. These escapees were obliged to re-enter the cave and inform the other prisoners that the images they were watching were a sham.

One day we may discover that the modern Olympic Movement has worked with political and corporate interests to sell false images of the Olympic ideal to an unsuspecting public. Before that day comes, we escaped philosophers must return to the cave and make sure that the Olympic Movement does its best to understand and promote the ancient Hellenic ideals that fuel its flame in the first place. The Hellenic heritage of agonism and idealism, as well as the ancient Olympic ideals of humanism, justice, and peace are particularly relevant now as the Movement cultivates a multicultural identity consonant with the spirit of our time. Understood in their historical, geographical, and philosophical context, we can see that these ideals belong not just to the West or to Europe, but to humanity as a whole. As long as the Olympic Games keep striving to achieve their own ancient and Hellenic ideals, the Olympic flame can unite the world and live up to its promise to "Celebrate Humanity."

Section I
Heroic Heritage

2. Pre-Olympic Heroes[1]

We might say that the Olympic Spirit is even older than sport itself. Before athletes competed in funeral games, Olympic Games, or any other kind of contest that we would recognize as sport, ancient heroes were celebrated for performing *athla* (ordeals, feats, achievements). They were the original *athletes,* and the virtues and values celebrated in their stories were absorbed the heroic *ethos* that eventually inspired the Olympic Games. Indeed, the activities that would become the ancestors of Greek athletics took root around the ancient Mediterranean among Mesopotamians, Egyptians, Minoans, Hittites and Mycenaeans millennia before the first footrace was run at Olympia. By the time that Homer's epics provide the first literary account of Olympic-style sports, around the 8th c. BCE, athleticism's heroic association with virtue, nobility, divinity, and leadership had already been established

As a matter of fact, in these early cultures, athletic feats were taken as proof—or at least evidence—of virtue. They apparently demonstrated divine favor, personal excellence, mastery over nature, and worthiness to lead. The more astounding or even incredible the feat, the more convincing it seems to have been as evidence that a reputed hero was connected with the divine. After all, belief in a leader's power and divinity would be comforting and reassuring, especially in an uncomfortable and unpredictable world. Ancient skepticism about the truth of the legends is accordingly scarce. Perhaps like modern sports fans who seem blind to their athletic heroes' faults, the ancient subjects avoided contemplating the shortcomings of their kings. Humanity's inquisitive nature, however, couldn't be suppressed forever.

Genuine philosophy exhibits curiosity, love of learning, and critical questioning. The Egyptian and Mesopotamian ancestors of Olympic-style sport seem to run counter to these characteristics;

---

[1] Originally published as "Athletic Heroes" in *Athletics and Philosophy in the Ancient World: Contests of Virtue* (Abingdon: Routledge, 2011), 11-22. Reprinted with permission. All rights reserved.

they apparently tend to sustain existing beliefs and discourage doubt. Likewise, these activities lack some fundamental characteristics of sport, such as open competition and the selection of single winners. Nevertheless, legendary feats of strength and athleticism among Sumerian kings and Egyptian Pharaohs establish a connection between sport and virtue that survives even today. By the time of Homer's epics, not only do the games more closely resemble modern sport, they begin take on philosophical characteristics. Pre-Olympic sport is also pre-philosophical. It affirms rather than challenges authoritarian hierarchies, and preordains answers before questions are ever asked. On the other hand, such activities paved the way for philosophical sport. The true origin of philosophy is human wonder (*thaumazein*)—and wonder there must be about the feats of the earliest athletic heroes.

Gilgamesh & Shulgi

By most accounts Gilgamesh was a historical person, the king of Mesopotamian city called Uruk during the 3rd Millennium BCE. But the story of his life, *The Epic of Gilgamesh*, is a fantastic tale better classified as mythology than history. We learn from the *Epic* that Gilgamesh was endowed by the gods with a perfect body, prodigious beauty, and stout courage. "Two thirds they made him god and one third man," the *Epic* says, "terrifying like a great wild bull."[2] Gilgamesh's outsized virtues seem to have been accompanied by outsized appetites that prevented him from being a good ruler. Indeed he was on his way to forcefully deflower some betrothed virgins when, in a matter of speaking, "sport" made him a better man. Specifically, he was challenged to a wrestling match by Enkidu, a creature the gods had created in response to the prayers of Gilgamesh's battered subjects:

> Mighty Gilgamesh came on and Enkidu met him at the gate. He put out his foot and prevented Gilgamesh from entering the house, so they grappled, holding each other like bulls. They broke the doorposts and the walls shook,

---

[2] N. Sandars, trans., *The Epic of Gilgamesh* (London: Penguin, 1960), 61.

they snorted like bulls locked together. They shattered the doorposts and the walls shook. Gilgamesh bent his knee with his foot planted on the ground and with a turn Enkidu was thrown. Then immediately his fury died. When Enkidu was thrown he said to Gilgamesh, "There is not another like you in the world. Ninsun, who is as strong as a wild ox in the byre, she was the mother who bore you, and now you are raised above all men, and Enlil has given you the kingship, for your strength surpasses the strength of men."[3]

As so often happens in sports, these bitter athletic rivals became the best of friends. Reflecting the enduring belief that sports helps aggressive young men better direct their energies, the two set off on heroic adventures that benefit the community rather than terrorizing it. Gilgamesh, says Poliakoff, "emerges from the contest a more serious and determined leader."[4]

According to H. and H.A. Frankfort, ancient Mesopotamians did not think of cosmic order as something simply given by the gods; rather it had to be achieved by mankind.[5] Unlike in Egypt, where the Pharaoh himself guaranteed stability to society, the divine favor granted to mortal Mesopotamian rulers could be withdrawn at any time.[6] The Gods may have endowed Gilgamesh with great gifts, but their continued favor and the community's welfare seems to depend on the responsible exercise of those virtues. Gilgamesh's heroic striving to become like a god fails to earn him immortality, however. He may transcend the limitations of common men, yet he is not and cannot become a god. Not unlike modern Olympic heroes, however, his exploits become a cause for celebration and inspiration both in his own time and beyond.

---

[3] Sandars, *Epic of Gilgamesh*, 69.
[4] M. Poliakoff, *Combat Sports in the Ancient World* (New Haven: Yale University Press, 1987), 136.
[5] H. and H.A. Frankfort, *The Intellectual Adventure of Ancient Man:* (Chicago: Chicago University Press, 1946), 127.
[6] Frankfort & Frankfort, *Intellectual Adventure*, 366.

I. Heroic Heritage

Gilgamesh's greatest fan may have been an athletic Sumerian sovereign named Shulgi who ruled some 700 years later. Hymns proclaiming Shulgi's sporting heroism were composed and sung during his lifetime. In one, he claims to have run from Nippur to Ur, a distance of nearly 100 miles, in one day:

> I, the runner, rose in my strength, all set for the course,
>   From Nippur to Ur,
> I resolved to traverse as if it were (but a distance) of one
>   "double-hour."
> Like a lion that wearies not of its virility I arose,
> Put a girdle (?) about my loins,
> Swung my arms like a dove feverishly fleeing a snake,
> Spread wide the knees like an Anzu bird with eyes lifted
>   toward the mountain.
> (The inhabitants) of the cities that I had founded in the
>   land swarmed all about me,
> My black headed people, as numerous as ewes,
>   marveled at me.
>
> Like a mountain kid hurrying to its shelter,
> When Utu shed his broad light on man's habitations,
> I entered the Ekishnugal,
> Filled with abundance the great stall, the house of Sin,
> Slaughtered oxen there, multiplied sheep,
> Made resound there the drum and the timbrel,
> Conducted there the tigi-music, the sweet.
>
> I, Shulgi, the multiplier of all things, brought bread
>   offerings there,
> Inspiring fear from my royal seat like a lion,
> In the lofty palace of Ninegal,
> I scoured my knees, I bathed in fresh water,
> Bent the knees, ate bread,
> Like an owl and a falcon I arose,
> Returned triumphantly to Nippur.
>
> On that day, the storm howled, the tempest swirled,

> The North Wind and the South Wind roared violently,
> Lightning devoured in heaven alongside the seven
>   winds,
> The deafening storm made the earth tremble,
> Ishkur thundered throughout the heavenly expanse
> The rains above embraced the waters below
> Its (the storm's) little stones, its big stones,
> Lashed at my back.
>
> (But) I, the king, was unafraid, uncowed,
> Like a young lion I was set for the spring,
> Like a donkey of the steppe I rushed forward,
> My heart full of happiness I sped along the course,
> Racing like a donkey journeying all alone,
> (Like) Utu facing homeward,
> I traversed the journey of fifteen "double hours,"
> My acolytes gazed at me (in wonder),
> As in one day I celebrated the esbesh feast (both) in Ur
> and Nippur.[7]

The feat described links Shulgi with the gods; detailing his pious activities at one religious festival then the other. It also marks his territory and describes the adoration of his subjects. Most important, the run is incredible—in the literal sense of being difficult to believe. The hymn describes great toil and inclement weather. It would seem that the only reasonable explanation is that the poet exaggerates and lies…or perhaps that the gods somehow pushed the king beyond the capacities of a normal man. Ancient Sumerians most likely came to the latter conclusion.

A modern scholar named Dean Lamont sees it differently. Admitting that Sumer's royal poets were "inclined toward exaggeration"[8] and "often used extravagant imagery in an effort to

---

[7] S.K. Kramer, "Hymn of Praise to Shulgi," in *History Begins at Sumer*, (Philadelphia: University of Pennsylvania Press, 1981), 286-287.

[8] D. Lamont, "Running Phenomena in Ancient Sumer," *Journal of Sport History*, 22:3 (1995), 210 n. 20.

create, maintain, or bolster the royal image,"[9] Lamont tests Shulgi's feat against modern standards of ultra-marathon running in similar climates and terrain. He concludes that the feat was indeed possible, adding that it might have been attempted "to please the deities responsible for the seasonal cycles and thus gain their good will with regard to the maintenance of a regular and thus predictable cycle."[10] This explanation applies just as easily to the hypothesis that the feat was embellished or even fabricated in order to make people believe the gods were pleased; it all depends on who the real audience was thought to be: the king's gods or his subjects.

Feats of the Pharaohs

Perhaps the next question to ask is whether failure was even possible for these ancient "athletes." To the modern mind, it is not a real athletic competition unless the outcome is unpredictable. Scripted contests, such as those promoted by World Wrestling Entertainment are not considered sport. In fact, modern sport philosophers sometimes regard the "sweet uncertainty" of contests as one of their primary components and virtues. Not so in ancient Egypt. There, as we noted earlier, the Pharaoh him- or herself guaranteed social stability. Considered the child and image of the Creator, the Pharaoh insured harmonious integration between nature and society at all times.[11] It was accordingly unthinkable that he or she should fail athletically. Or did the gods simply prevent it? Either way, the Pharaoh's victory was never in doubt.

In at least one case success was assured by the relative ease of the "feat." At the Festival of Renewal (Sed), pharaohs made a circuit on foot around posts placed about 55 meters apart in the pyramid complex of Djoser (c. 2600 BCE). There were no competing runners and little exertion. Even the female pharaoh Hatsheptsut performed it. The run was performed 30 years into the ruler's reign, perhaps to demonstrate that his or her divine

---

[9] Lamont, "Running Phenomena in Ancient Sumer," 209.
[10] Lamont, "Running Phenomena in Ancient Sumer,"215.
[11] Frankfort & Frankfort, *Intellectual Adventure*, 366

powers were still intact.[12] Pharaohs also displayed their skills in other "sports," including chariot driving, horsemanship, and archery. But the need for secure outcomes meant few if any rivals. Royal hunts were staged to show the king's mastery of nature and wild animals, but the Pharaoh hunted alone with the help of many assistants. It was like shooting proverbial fish in a barrel. As historian Donald Kyle explains, "A failed royal hunt…would suggest personal weakness or an inability to control nature, so states arranged precautions and procedures to make hunting success convenient and secure."[13] Presumably Egyptian subjects were appropriately satisfied by these performances, but one has to wonder why. Was the Pharaohs' divine virtue so far beyond question that athletic evidence simply wasn't required?

There is evidence of head-to head competition in ancient Egypt, but it does not involve the Pharaoh and there is no indication of a single winner. Tomb excavations near Beni Hasan and elsewhere have revealed scenes of wrestling, and stick fighting; but these most likely were simply military training exercises. Carvings from Medinet Habu, suggest that Egyptian wrestlers might have competed against foreigners…but the Egyptians always won.[14] This is understandable as propaganda, but implausible as sport. According to Frankfort, the way of Egyptian thought was to accept new ideas and incorporate them into existing beliefs without discarding the old.[15] Perhaps this explains the absence of selecting winners through sport. But eventually this kind of thinking leads to internal contradictions: the Pharaoh is the son of god, yet the new Pharaoh is the old Pharaoh's child. Such contradictions eventually lead to doubt, which leads to questions, inquiry, and eventually philosophy.

Indeed, as time goes on in Egypt, doubt seems to surface and sport seems to become more competitive; perhaps as a result of

---

[12] Kyle, *Sport and Spectacle*, 29.
[13] Kyle, *Sport and Spectacle*, 35.
[14] Kyle, *Sport and Spectacle*, 30
[15] Frankfort & Frankfort, *Intellectual Adventure*, 33.

I. Heroic Heritage

contact with diverse cultures. The New Kingdom (c. 1570-1085 BCE) Stela of Tuthomosis III celebrates an incredible archery feat in which the king pierced a small copper target, three fingers thick. But the most interesting thing about the text is this final comment: "I'm telling you what he did, without deception and without lie, in front of his entire army, and there is no word of exaggeration therein."[16] The very fact that the author feels the need to reassure readers suggests the existence of doubt and maybe even fear. In the presence of rival claims to virtue, only open competition can bring true assurance. By the 7th c. BCE, open competition with a special reward for the winner seems to have taken hold. The "Running Stela of Taharqa" describes a military race that the king observes, but doesn't compete in.[17] First prize was a meal with the royal body guards, which may not seem like much. But for the winning soldier it probably represented access to a higher social class; a just reward for demonstrated virtue. Of course by the 7th c. BCE competitive athletics had also taken hold in Greece; featuring prominently in Homer's quintessentially Hellenic epics, *Iliad* and *Odyssey*.

Confirming Aristocracy in Homer's Iliad

Homer's poems purport to describe the Bronze Age Mycenaeans, whose civilization peaked around 1450-1200. We know that they were a competitive and militaristic nation, who had contact with Crete, Egypt, Anatolia, and the Levant. We also know that in describing them, Homer includes many anachronistic details from later times. As a result, we cannot say exactly how much Homeric sport resembles historical Mycenaean practice. Nevertheless, we can see important differences between pre-Hellenic athletic traditions and the relatively open, impartial, and publicly scrutinized games described in Homer. Virtue, leadership, and divine favor are still associated with athletic performance in Homer, but they no longer are they monopolized

---

[16] A. De Buck, trans., "The Armant Stela of Tuthmosis III," in *Egyptian Readingbook* (Chicago: Ares,1948), 65.

[17] Kyle, *Sport and Spectacle*, 32.

by a single king or Pharaoh. Rather, in the *Iliad*, virtue is symbolically transformed into prizes that are contested and distributed to reflect social rank. And in the *Odyssey*, athletic challenges prove a battered leader's virtue to a suspicious and incredulous public. In Homeric sport, virtue is contested, but the games help to negotiate competing claims to honor, thereby unifying and pacifying troubled communities.

Modern abridgements of Homer's *Iliad* often exclude book 23, which describes Patroclos' funeral games. Perhaps this reflects our tendency today to regard sport as gratuitous activity; mere entertainment or recreation. We overlook the epistemological logic of games as unbiased tests of particular virtues, and find it difficult to recognize the pivotal role of the *Iliad*'s games in restoring the lost social order, reconciling rivals, and portending the end of the war with the Trojans. The war, after all, is the overriding contest (*agōn*) of the *Iliad*. Because war was more or less a way of life in the ancient world, military performance figured strongly in their estimation of social worth, virtue (*aretē*) and excellence (*aristeia*).[18] The second contest (*agōn*) of the *Iliad* comes about when Achilles, the best fighter among the Achaeans clashes with King Agamemnon, their leader. As in athletic games, their dispute is over a prize, the battle prize of a slave girl that Agamemnon takes from Achilles. Prizes in this culture were evaluated not by monetary worth, but by the honor inherent in their history and symbolism.[19] They were effectively the currency of social worth and virtue, so by taking his prize Agamemnon deliberately denies Achilles the honor he deserves.

Once Achilles' demonstrated excellence is not properly acknowledged he withdraws and refuses to fight. His actions are not unlike those of the star athlete who stays out of training camp because he is insulted by the team's salary offer. It's not about the money itself, it goes without saying that professional athletes'

---

[18] Arthur Adkins, *Merit and Responsibility: A Study in Greek Values* (Chicago: The University of Chicago Press, 1975), 197.

[19] Ben Brown, "Homer and Funeral Contests," 127.

salaries are more than adequate to cover living expenses. It's about what the money represents: an acknowledgment of the player's worth. Significantly, the entire Achaean community—a loose association of diverse Hellenic tribes--suffers from this conflict. Even his rookie protégée Patroclos cannot replace Achilles' excellence; he goes to battle wearing the hero's armor and is killed by Hector. Now, everyone is suffering. It may seem that Achilles is being greedy and selfish, disregarding the interests of his community. But it's not market value of the prize, it's the honor those prizes represent and the very principle of aristocracy: leadership by the best.

It is the athletic competition staged on the occasion of Patroclos' funeral that re-establishes reason and order to this society. Although some details of the games better reflect the athletic contests of Homer's own time (8th c. BCE), archaeological evidence suggests that funeral games may well have been staged by the Bronze Age Myceneans.[20] Their purpose was not just to honor the deceased and the relevant gods, but also to redistribute his property in a socially appropriate, that is, meritocratic, way.[21] Since property represents honor, the prizes must be generous enough to attract the worthiest competitors, and the system for selecting winners (that is, the contest itself) must reliably reveal their merit. The entire community gathers both to witness and to participate in this redistribution of social honor, thereby validating its results and reinforcing their sense of solidarity.[22]

An unprecedented concern for fairness of competition and accuracy of results emerges in Homer's Games. The contests are not completely open, only social elites take part, but Achilles dips into his own treasury to offer such valuable prizes that no worthy competitor among them would avoid the risk of defeat. Unlike the "sport" of the Egypt and Mesopotamia, much attention is paid to

---

[20] M. Golden, *Sport and Society in Ancient Greece,* (Cambridge, UK: Cambridge University Press, 1998), 68.
[21] Brown, "Homer and Funeral Contests," 136-7.
[22] Brown, "Homer and Funeral Contests," 139.

the principles of fair contest and the spectators cast a critical eye upon the proceedings, voicing their approval and disapproval, and effectively reinforcing the validity of the contest's results. When a dispute erupts over the results of the chariot race, prizes are added and redistributed until the majority is satisfied with the final allocation. And in a symbolic deference to the principle of political authority, Achilles awards the javelin prize to Agamemnon without carrying out the contest. In this way, he demonstrates that he is capable of respecting authority once honor has been redistributed according to social worth. This public act reunites the Achaean army and reconfirms Achilles' *aristeia;* setting them up for victory in the decisive battle.[23]

Proving Identity in Odyssey

Homer's *Odyssey* presents not just a different hero and different setting from the *Iliad*, but also a different function for athletics—one that takes another giant step toward truth-seeking Olympic-style sport. Our hero is the wily Odysseus, known for cleverness if not exactly wisdom, and our story is one of wandering rather than war; discovery rather than dispute. On his circuitous route back home after the Trojan war, the beaten-down and disheveled Odysseus lands in a strange place called Phaeacia, where he is taken to the palace and treated as a guest despite his anonymity. After dinner, King Alcinous offers the stranger a demonstration of athletic feats by the local youth, reminiscent perhaps of the acrobatic and bull-leaping shows of Minoan Crete. Says Ancinous, "Now, let us go outside and make trial of the contests, all of them, so that the stranger [Odysseus] may say to his friends, once he has come home, how much we surpass others in boxing, wrestling, jumping, and racing with our feet" (*Od.* 8.100-103). The games begin as a display of the host city's identity, but they end up as a means for the stranger to demonstrate his identity; more specifically to prove his aristocracy in the face of ignorance and doubt. It all begins with some trash talk.

---

[23] Adkins, *Merit and Responsibility*, 49.

I. Heroic Heritage

After a footrace and wrestling match, there is a contest in boxing won by the king's son, Laodamas. Flush with his victory and perhaps a bit resentful at having been forced to give up his chair to the stranger (*Od.* 7.168-71), Laodamas wonders aloud whether their visitor might be an athlete, pointing out Odysseus' once robust physique, visibly "shattered by many evils." He approaches Odysseus and invites him to compete, noting famously that "no glory is greater for a man while he is alive than what he accomplishes with his hands and feet" (*Od.* 8.146-148). When the homesick Odysseus resists, the wrestling victor Euryalos steps in and taunts him, suggesting that he is a lowly, profit-minded merchant rather than an aristocrat. "You do not look like an athlete," he concludes (*Od.* 8.164). This doubt about his virtue rouses the weary traveler's pride; perhaps he himself had begun to doubt his personal excellence. Odysseus lashes back with a few choice words, then grabs a discus and slings it well beyond the marks made by others. Infused with energy by the proof of his virtue, Odysseus launches his own smug soliloquy, challenging anyone to beat him at any athletic event, except the footrace since his legs have gone weak after all his time lost at sea (*Od.* 8.130-233). Odysseus has proven his nobility, not in ritual reenactment where victory was guaranteed, but in an atmosphere of sincere doubt, stripped of his social status and ravaged by his ordeals at sea. The point seems to be that true excellence reveals itself when tested in open athletic contests.

The message is reinforced near the end of the epic when Odysseus finally does make it home to the land where he is in fact king, but his travels have winnowed him to such a shadow of his former self that only his dog seems able to recognize him. During Odysseus' twenty year absence, an unworthy group of parasitic suitors had gathered at his palace, seeking his queen Penelope's hand. In order to win back his kingdom and household, Odysseus would have to prove his nobility and, again, athletic feats would figure prominently in his doing so. Disguised as a beggar, the king confronts the real palace beggar, Iros, a man notorious for his "incessant eating and drinking," which had given him great size but little strength (*Od.* 18.3-5). Iros challenges Odysseus to a boxing match and, as the suitors look on, the king's superior physique is revealed. Odysseus dispatches the beggar with one skull-crushing punch (*Od.*18.96-7). Of course, defeating one beggar does not a noble man make. In order to finally prove his *aristeia* Odysseus would have to outdo the suitors by stringing the royal bow and shooting an arrow through a row of axe-head sockets. The suitors try to keep him out of this contest since he appears to be a beggar; only the fair-minded Penelope permits him; albeit because he claims to be of noble blood (*Od.* 21.334-5). Odysseus' triumph is not simply a confirmation of his excellence, but also of the idea that athletic feats reveal excellence even when apparent social status does not.

Conclusion

What is different between the *Iliad's* and *Odyssey's* games is the sincerity of the doubt about individual merit and the ability of the contest to sort it out. Both epics illustrate the importance of accurately determining and rewarding social merit. The dangers of relying upon political or perhaps even divine authority for the answering of such questions are made equally evident. Athletic contests, in the form of funeral games, emerge as a relatively accurate, rule-governed, publicly overseen mechanism for finding out these important answers. They go beyond their traditional purpose of redistributing the deceased's wealth and are used to add truth and clarity to the distribution of social worth. Even further, by enabling the Achaean community to resolve its own epistemological problems, the games set the stage for independent truth seeking among communities and individuals in the ancient world.

In Egypt and Mesopotamia, athletic feats—or at least stories about them—were used to affirm the social hierarchy, but there could be no open competition lest the hierarchy be challenged. The kings' and pharaoh's accomplishments seem to have the epistemological status of myth—unquestioned stories that express collectively held beliefs. The Homeric epics, by contrast, suggest

I. Heroic Heritage

that open and fair athletic competition would test and confirm a proper social hierarchy. In *Iliad,* Patroclos' funeral games reconstitute a community disrupted by the conflict between virtue and authority. In *Odyssey,* the true nobility of the king is athletically tested and proven despite the profound doubts of onlookers. Of course, *Iliad* and *Odyssey* are poetry and not history. Nevertheless, the function of sport within them foreshadows the social and political function of the Olympic Games. Homer's heroes are models for Olympic heroes, ancient and modern.

3. Heracles' Choice: Is Strength Really a Virtue?[1]

Heracles (better known by his Latin name, Hercules) reigned as a god of the gymnasium in ancient Greece and Rome. There were altars set up to him, where athletes, presumably asking for strength, prayed and made offerings. In modern times, Heracles' strength-cult seems still to be thriving. Gymnasia, weight-lifting clubs, and strength awards are routinely named after him. His sometimes comical muscular image is emblazoned on t-shirts and supplement packages. There is even Disney movie telling his story.

In ancient and modern times alike, Heracles seems to represent the value of human strength—the idea that physical strength is a virtue. Human virtue was an important topic in ancient Greek philosophy, and Heracles was indeed connected with virtue in ancient Greek mythology. Unlike other gods, he began as a mere mortal and ascended to Mount Olympus upon the completion of his famous labors.[2] But even if mythology states that Heracles, a symbol of physical strength, was deified because of his virtue, does it follow that his strength was his virtue? Is strength really a virtue at all?

Heracles' history as a muscle-bound savior begins, quite literally, in his crib. He was a son of the supreme god Zeus, who seduced the beautiful mortal Alcmene while her husband Amphitryon was away. This infuriated Zeus' immortal wife Hera and, when the boy was ironically named Heracles, which means "glory of Hera," the goddess became angrier still. She sent a pair of snakes to the baby's crib in an effort to kill him and his half-brother Iphicles, but the infant Heracles strangled them, one in

---

[1] Originally published as "Hercules' Dilemma: Is Strength Really a Virtue?" in *Philosophical Reflections on Physical Strength: Does a Strong Mind Need a Strong Body?*, eds. M. Holowchak & T. Todd. (New York: Mellen Press, 2010), 146-160.

[2] Accounts of Heracles' life and labors are found throughout ancient Greek and Roman literature. A good summary, generally followed here, is the website "Hercules: Greece's Greatest Hero," *Perseus Digital Library Project* http://www.perseus.tufts.edu.

each hand, foretelling both his prodigious strength and his protective instinct. One act of juvenile heroism, however, does not amount to virtue.

The ancient Greek word for virtue, *aretē*, is more accurately translated 'excellence'. As discussed in the philosophy of Plato, and Aristotle, it requires not just the performance of good acts, but the intentional cultivation and demonstration of a disposition to perform them consistently. The baby Heracles might have thought that the snakes were merely toys; virtue requires an understanding of right actions and the deliberate choice to do them. It does not come about by fortune or accident. The ideal of virtue touted by philosophers is constant and reliable—a steady state of character.

Unlike his strength, Heracles' virtue is a matter of choice rather than inheritance. "Heracles' Choice" is a myth attributed to Prodicus and recounted by Xenophon (*Memorabilia* 2.1) to make a point about the nature of virtue. The story depicts Heracles as a young man going to a quiet place to choose his future path. He is approached there by two women, both larger than life. One is adorned with make-up and provocatively dressed; the other is simple and modest, wrapped in a pure white robe. The first woman was named Pleasure, the second Virtue. Pleasure rushes up and says, "Heracles, I see that you are in doubt which path to take towards life. Make me your friend; follow me, and I will lead you along the pleasantest and easiest road."[3] She promises a life of indulgence and ease; one in which he would live off the fruits of others' labor and taste all the sweetest things that worldly life can offer. Virtue promises no more than a life of toil and hardship, but one that is dear to the gods. She explains that Heracles must serve the gods and his community in the way that shepherds serve their flocks and farmers serve their land. Virtue concludes that true strength comes when the body serves the mind. Pleasure interrupts and announces that the road to pleasure is much shorter and easier than the long and steep path proposed by Virtue. After much deliberation, Heracles chooses Virtue.

---

[3] Xenophon, *Memorabilia*, 2.1.24, trans. Marchant.

Though Heracles chose the longer road and suffered through the whole of his mortal life, he did earn the favor of the gods and won for himself an immortal place among them. Likewise in Ancient Greece, athletic excellence promised the joys of Olympic victory as well as the praises and prizes that accompany it. Athletic excellence was associated with virtue largely because it was achieved by toil and sweat. But we have seen from the story of the snakes in the crib that Heracles was born with prodigious strength—a genetic gift from his divine father. There are no stories of Heracles training to build himself up; he was never the proverbial 90-pound weakling. To be sure, Heracles chooses a hard road in life—one full of the toil and challenges described by Virtue. But Heracles' prodigious strength is neither the result of virtue, as athletes' strength is assumed to be, nor a virtue itself. Heracles' strength turns out to be his cross to bear. His true virtue is the moral strength that allows him to put his physical strength in the service of humanity; a quality not of body, but of soul.

What Is Virtue?

In ancient Greek philosophy, virtue is understood as a kind of health of the soul. It is the disposition and ability to perform good actions, which, like physical health, requires almost constant training and maintenance. In fact, we might update this metaphor and compare Greek virtue to athletic fitness: The better trained one's soul is, the more reliably and powerfully one will perform good actions. Virtue is understood as excellence because it is an internal state that produces good action. This does not mean that virtue of the soul is unconnected to physical strength and prowess. For the Greeks souls were what animated the body, so physical movement originated in the soul. Because Heracles' strength was the product of birth rather than training, it is not true virtue. But his ability to act on that strength for the good of his fellow humans and to endear himself to the gods is a product of his soul and, therefore, of his virtue. Heracles only achieved immortality because he painstakingly acquired the virtue needed to put his inborn strength to good use. Strength's value, like the value of money, depends entirely upon its proper use. In short, Heracles' strength is a tool for his virtue, rather than virtue itself.

Even the most powerful tool is only as good as its operator. Indeed powerful tools can be dangerous when left to untrained or undisciplined hands. So too it was with Heracles' strength. As a young man, he married Megara and started a happy family, but his divine nemesis Hera sent him into a fit of madness in which he brutally murdered his wife and children. When he regained his senses to behold the horrific deed, he was pierced by unfathomable sorrow and regret. In Euripides' play, the hero's pain is palpable:

> O children! He who begot you, your own father, has been your destroyer, and you have had no profit of my triumphs, all my restless toil to win for you by force a fair name, a glorious advantage from a father. You too, unhappy wife, this hand has slain, a poor return to make you for preserving the honor of my bed so safely, for all the weary watch you long have kept within my house. Alas for you, my wife, my sons! Alas for me, how sad my lot, cut off from wife and child![4]

One can even imagine Heracles resenting the prodigious strength that made his brief bout of madness so destructive. Heracles' strength was anything but a virtue when it was out of his control. But as mortals we are all subject to forces outside our control; Heracles' first step toward virtue was acknowledging that.

Despite his godlike strength, Heracles had the humility to admit his limitations. Though he himself had never wronged the gods, nor had he willingly harmed his wife and children, he recognized that his soul had been polluted by his deed. He took responsibility for it and went to the god Apollo to learn how to expiate his crime. Apollo told Heracles that he would have to complete twelve heroic feats or labors (*athla*) as a servant of King Eurystheus, who had a reputation for being mean and was indeed

---

[4] Euripides, "Heracles," trans. E.P. Coleridge, in *The Complete Greek Drama* (New York. Random House. 1938), lines 1369-1376.

a lesser man than Heracles. It is through his performance of these labors that we see Hercules building up the moral strength to match his physical strength. Through the labors, he demonstrates the virtue touted by the philosophers.

Socratic Humility

At his trial in Athens in 399 B.C.E., the philosopher Socrates compared himself to the hero Heracles (Plato, *Apology* 22a). For philosophers, Socrates is a symbol of virtue primarily because of his intellectual integrity. Just as Heracles' supreme strength is complemented by the honest admission of his weakness with respect to the gods, Socrates' supreme wisdom is complemented by the honest admission of his ignorance with respect to the gods. However, these admissions of imperfection do not merely honor the gods, they have the practical benefit of motivating human beings to continually improve themselves. Socrates embodies that purpose when he "serves the god" by showing those with a reputation for wisdom that they are not wise at all. In this way, he rids the city of demagogues and would-be tyrants who discourage Athenian citizens from thinking for themselves. It is a feat comparable to the Herculean labors, in which the hero rids various communities of fearsome beasts, which terrorize the people.

Indeed, Heracles' first labor was to slay the Nemean Lion, which had been terrorizing the countryside and could not be killed by arrows or spears. The task was considered virtually impossible and Heracles knew that it would be dangerous. When his host Morlorchus offered to pray for a good hunt, Heracles asked him to see instead whether the hero would return alive. The willingness to risk one's life in order to help one's community is another manifestation of virtue shown by Socrates. The philosopher's public interrogation of community leaders predictably got him into trouble. He was tried and convicted on the capital offense of impiety and then sentenced to death by a reluctant jury. Socrates seems to have recognized that his trial and death would make Athens rethink its "values" and perhaps strive again for virtue. At the same time, the philosopher preserved his own virtue by accepting his death sentence and refusing an opportunity to escape by bribing the guard. One might say that Socrates' wisdom was what got him into trouble, but it was wisdom in service of the common good and, thus, it amounted to virtue. Heracles used his strength to strangle the Nemean lion, as well as to dispatch the Lernean hydra, Erymanthian boar, Stymphalian birds, Cretan bull, and finally the man-eating horses of Diomedes. It was the same strength he used to kill his wife and children, but now it was a tool of virtue and, therefore, the good.

Platonic Intelligence

Personified Virtue had warned the young Heracles that true strength is when the body serves the mind and the community. This idea resembles Plato's theory of virtue as the proper ordering and harmonious function of a tripartite soul. In *Republic* and other dialogues, Plato conceives of the human soul as being divided into rational, emotional, and appetitive parts. In a virtuous soul, the rational part leads while emotions and appetites follow and are kept in check. In *Phaedrus*, the tripartite soul is illustrated by the image of a two-horse chariot with a rational charioteer, a strong but unruly horse that represents the appetites, and an obedient horse that represents the spirit or emotions (246ab). The chariot-soul's struggle for *aretē* is described as an upward climb toward truth and divinity that is especially difficult for humans because "the heaviness of the bad horse drags its charioteer toward the earth and weighs him down if he has failed to train it well" (247b). For the chariot to function well, it must be properly guided by the charioteer's understanding, which must pull emotion and appetite in the right direction. Plato thought that people guided by the appetitive desire for food, sex, and money or by the emotional drive for honor and social esteem do not demonstrate virtue. The virtuous person must be guided by reason, which is then aided by emotion, appetite, and, in Heracles' case, prodigious strength, to accomplish great deeds.

Although he is sometimes described, like so many men of strength, as mentally weak, a closer look reveals that several of

Heracles' labors required as much mental as physical power. In order to kill the Nemean lion, he had to figure out how to trap and then strangle the beast, since its pelt was impenetrable. The Lernean Hydra had nine heads, and each time Heracles cut off one, two more would spring up in its place. The hero had the humility and smarts to call for help. His friend Iolaus arrived with a torch and cauterized the neck-stumps to prevent more heads from sprouting back. Displaying forethought, Heracles even had the presence of mind to dip his arrows in the Hydra's poisonous blood. The labor of cleansing the Augean stables showed not only the willingness to do a dirty, smelly job, but also admirable intelligence. Heracles bet the supremely wealthy King Augeas that he could clean the immense stables in a single day. Believing the task impossible, Augeas promised to pay the hero a tenth of his cattle, should he succeed. Bringing Augeas' son as a witness, Heracles cleansed the stables by diverting two nearby rivers to flow through and flush the stalls out. Strength played a part, but foresight and engineering also came into play in that event. Collection of the payment required some intellectual maneuvering, too. The King went back on his promise, but rather than slay him as a monster, Heracles took the case to a judge. With the king's own son as witness to the promise and the deed, the judge ruled in favor of Heracles. There is a sense in which Augeas was another public menace defeated by Heracles, but that monster was defeated with intelligence, not violence.

Moreover, it was Heracles who rescued the symbol and savior of human intelligence, Prometheus. The Titan, whose name means "forethought," was famous for stealing fire from the gods and giving it to humanity. Some interpret this fire in terms of its practical use for cooking and heating, others understand it as symbolic of divine intelligence. Plato's Socrates reckons that Prometheus' gift gave humanity a portion of the divine, which explains not only religion but also our use of language (*Protagoras* 322a). Zeus punished Prometheus for his philanthropy by chaining him to Mount Caucasus and having a giant eagle peck out his liver every day. Every night, it would grow back, only to be pecked out again, until Heracles finally killed the eagle after thirty years of torture. It is significant that Heracles should be the one to rescue "Forethought," the symbol of human intelligence. Not only does Heracles liberate humanity from terrifying beasts and monsters, he symbolically saves our intelligence from eternal torture. This is an act of body serving mind; Heracles' virtue is more than "brute" strength.

Prometheus is also a prominent part of another labor that resembles the theft of divine fire. Heracles was attempting to steal from Zeus the golden apples of the Hesperides, which had been a wedding gift from the hero's arch-nemesis Hera. This truly seemed an impossible task, one that would require all of Heracles' powers, not just his strength. The apples were heavily guarded by a hundred-headed dragon as well as the Hesperides, daughters of Atlas, the Titan who used to hold up the sky. Heracles needed a plan to get the apples and a grateful Prometheus gave him one. The plan was to get Atlas to fetch the golden apples, by offering to relieve him in the meantime of his burden. When Atlas returned with the apples, a battle of strong-men's wits ensued. Atlas offered to take the apples to Eurystheus himself, which would leave Heracles to hold up the earth and sky. Sensing Atlas' plot, Heracles feigned agreement and asked only for a moment's reprieve in order to put some padding on his shoulders. When Atlas put down the golden apples to hoist the earth and sky, Heracles picked them up, escaped, and left Atlas with his eternal burden. Heracles had the strength to hold up the world, but it was cleverness that allowed him to complete his assigned deed. Heracles' strength serves his reason, just as in Plato's theory of virtue.

Of course, a huge part of Heracles' cleverness was the Socratic humility to ask for help: from Iolaos with the Hydra, from Augeas' son with the stables, from Prometheus with the apples, and most importantly, from the gods themselves. In a memorable relief at Olympia depicting the hero's labors, the goddess Athena is shown sharing Heracles' burden as he shoulders the universe. For help in driving off the Stymphalian Birds, Heracles receives special noisemakers from Athena. Athena is a goddess of wisdom and war who is often depicted supporting those engaged in meaningful struggle (*agōn*). In Homer's *Odyssey*, she is almost constantly at Odysseus' side. The Homeric hero is known for his wily intelligence. Heracles too must be loved and aided by the goddess of wisdom for something more than the strength of his muscles. Even Athena could not spare Heracles from the world's injustice. The labor of the Hesperides' apples was demanded after Eurystheus unfairly rejected the labors of the Lernean Hydra and Augean Stables. But Athena is one who supports struggle, aiding in the production of noble deeds, almost as the embodiment of virtue itself.

Aristotelian Integrity

Aristotle endorsed Plato's theory of virtue as order in the soul, but he distinguished virtue of thought from virtue of character, noting that the first requires teaching and experience and the second habituation or training. Says Aristotle, "Virtue of character (*ēthos*) results from habit (*ethos*); hence its name 'ethical', slightly varied from '*ethos*'" (*Nicomachean Ethics*, 1103a15-18). Both rational and non-rational aspects of virtue, then, are achieved through training and practice. Heracles illustrates Aristotle's principle insofar as he is strong from birth, but only achieves his virtue through the process of completing his labors. Indeed his labors become more challenging and complex as they progress. After killing the Nemean Lion singlehandedly, then dispatching the Lernean Hydra with the help of Iolaus, the third labor requires Heracles to capture a deer with golden horns and bronze hooves called the Cerynean hind. This was a delicate task, because the hind was a pet of the goddess Artemis.

The first thing this hunt demanded was patience and endurance; the hero chased the deer for a year before finally shooting it on Mount Artemisius. Heracles put the injured animal over his shoulders and was heading away when he was confronted by the predictably unhappy Artemis and her brother Apollo. Heracles was smart enough to tell these gods the truth about his labor, and, as a result, Artemis healed the deer's wound and allowed the hero to take her back to Eurystheus. This was a not a test of strength, skill, or pure intelligence so much as moral character. Heracles acted virtuously by facing up to the goddess' anger and confessing his deed; she, in turn, corrected his mistake, allowing him to complete his task.

Divine intervention was not always at hand to correct Heracles' errors, however. On his way to the fourth labor, the killing of the Erymanthian boar, Heracles' appetites and political misjudgment cost him dearly. The hero was visiting his friend Pholus, who was a centaur (half-man and half-horse). Heracles asked for food, which Pholus happily offered, but when he asked for wine, Pholus was reluctant to open the jar, since the wine belonged to all of the centaurs in common. Heracles was known for letting his appetites affect his judgment; the comic playwright Aristophanes even ridicules him for it (*Birds* 1565). Rationalizing perhaps that he could dispatch any disgruntled centaurs with his hydra-poisoned arrows, Heracles told Pholus not to worry and helped himself to the wine. Predictably, the centaurs attacked him. Heracles killed several of them, but when Pholus picked up one of the poisonous arrows in wonder that it could kill so easily, he accidentally pricked himself with it and died on the spot. As Heracles mournfully buried his host and friend, he must have reflected again on the danger that comes with great power and the need to moderate one's appetites. Even though the hero was strong enough to handle the battle sparked by his impulsive taking of the wine, he could not control the unfortunate aftermath in which one of his weapons was turned on a friend.

Not only does this story emphasize the importance of self-control and moderation, it illustrates Aristotle's point that we are political animals. What the philosopher means is not that we should all become politicians, but rather that we should see ourselves as members of a community and recognize our dependence on others as well as our obligations toward them. When Heracles selfishly takes the centaur's wine, not only does he violate his relationship with his host (*philoxenia*), he fails to respect common property. His ability to overpower the attacking centaurs—essentially the exercise of the principle that might is right—backfires. Even when physical force prevails, it hardly seems the best solution.

That lesson is reinforced with the Amazons. Charged with capturing the belt of the Amazon queen Hippolyta, Heracles assembles an army and sails away. When he meets the queen on the shore, she kindly agrees to give the belt to him. But meanwhile Hera rousts the Amazon troops and convinces them that Heracles is about to kidnap their queen. When the fierce female fighters charge toward the shore, a bloody battle ensues and Heracles is forced to kill Hippolyta. The hero must have reflected, as he removed the gracious queen's belt, that violent force had not really been necessary. In fact the strongest warrior is the one who never has to draw his sword.

By the time of his twelfth and final labor, Heracles seems to have achieved what Aristotle calls practical wisdom (*phronēsis*), the ability to hit the target set up by reason and skillfully achieve one's ethical goals. Of course, Heracles had shown moments of practical wisdom throughout his labors, but for his final task he was expected to enter the kingdom of Hades, the underworld dwelling of the dead, and to capture Cerberus—the three-headed, serpent-tailed dog that guarded its gates. First, Heracles showed his Socratic integrity and humility by going to Eleusis to learn about the Eleusinian mysteries—religious secrets that promised a life of happiness in the underworld. Heracles understood that his mission might fail, so he prepared himself as best he could. The road to the underworld was studded with beasts and monsters much like those he had learned to defeat during his labors. Upon reaching Hades, the god of the underworld, Heracles simply asked him for Cerberus, as he had done with Artemis and Hippolyta. The god graciously complied—but only if Heracles could capture the creature bare-handed. So Heracles' final labor ends with a task of pure strength, but now that bodily strength is controlled by a rational and honorable soul. Heracles' strength is not his virtue, but rather it is a powerful tool for his virtuous soul.

Conclusion

Heracles is a symbol of strength. One can see why he is worshipped by modern and ancient athletes alike. But we must recognize the moral virtue and community service that makes Heracles' strength something worth worshipping. From the innocent act of saving his infant brother to the deliberate choice to follow the path of Virtue and to the twelve labors, Heracles' story is a human saga about striving to become better. It begins with the humility to acknowledge limitations and the courage to choose the harder, better road. It asks us willingly to serve the wider community and to endure the often-outrageous whims of fortune. It asks us to moderate our appetites and develop our minds and to privilege divine intelligence over animalistic urges. It asks us to organize our talents in a way that achieves good goals with a minimum of force. In short, it epitomizes Olympic values. Through athletic training, we may indeed cultivate some virtue, but we must not confuse mere bodily strength with the holistic nature of true heroic and Olympic virtue. Heracles chose to match the virtue of his strength with the strength of his virtue.

4. Olympic Athletes as Heroes and Role Models[1]

Every summer in the month of June, I make a pilgrimage with a group of fellow cyclists to the tiny hillside town of Castellania, Italy, to visit the tomb of the cycling legend Fausto Coppi. Cyclists come from all over the world to visit the monument, many bringing gifts which are housed in a little museum attached to a church that was built on the site. The village itself is decorated with giant photographs and murals that show the champion in action and at leisure. The the local people greet us and sometimes take us inside their houses to show old pictures and tell tales from when they knew Fausto as children. Some would say that Fausto Coppi is an athletic hero, others may put him up as a role model. For me he is neither, but one thing's for sure: I am always inspired by my visits to this shrine, and my legs always feel lighter as I climb up the hill that leads there.

* * *

A common argument for the social value of Olympic sport is that athletes serve as heroes who inspire people – especially young people – to strive for excellence. This argument has been questioned by sport philosophers at a variety of levels. On the one hand, there are questions about whether athletes deserve such a role. Unlike the soldiers, Samaritans, and emergency response personnel more conventionally referred to as heroes, athletes do not protect innocents, serve the needy, or save lives – much less risk their lives to achieve such goals. Furthermore, the values promoted by sporting heroes have been described as fascist,[2] morally instrumental,[3] or at least undesirable from the point of

---

[1] Originally published as "Athletes as Heroes and Role Models: an Ancient Model" in *Sport, Ethics and Philosophy* 11.1 (2016): 40-51. Reprinted with permission, all rights reserved.
[2] T. Tannsjo, "Is our admiration for sports heroes fascistoid?" *Journal of the Philosophy of Sport* 25.1 (1998): 23–34.
[3] C. Tamburrini, "Sports, Fascism, and the Market," *Journal of the Philosophy of Sport* 25.1 (1998): 35-47.

view of ethical consequentialism.[4] The phenomenon of apparently bad educational consequences, in addition, has raised the question of whether Olympic athletes have special moral responsibilities implied by their status as role models, whether that status is chosen or not.[5] The question has also been raised whether athletes' status as role models justifies the legislation of their moral behavior through, for example, bans on doping.[6]

Philosophers have also questioned exactly what role athletic heroes are expected to be modeling. If a role model is someone who sets an example of excellence in a role we also play, or plan one day to play, then great athletes may be role models for other professional athletes – but it makes little sense for them to be role models for children or even for athletic adults, who have an infinitesimal chance of occupying similar positions.[7] At best, it is unrealistic to encourage children to believe that they will grow up to be sports stars. At worst, it is irresponsible because such dreams may encourage them to neglect opportunities to pursue much more realistic and socially beneficial roles. Athletic heroes are rarely admired for their studiousness and compassion; indeed they are overwhelmingly male and the ideal of masculinity they embody does not always fit well with the world beyond sport. Not only do athletes seem unsuited to be heroes or role models in the

---

[4] Mark Holowchak, "Fascistoid heroism revisited: A deontological twist to a recent debate," *Journal of the Philosophy of Sport* 32.1 (2005.): 96–104.

[5] C. Jones, "Drunken role models: Rescuing our sporting exemplars," *Sport, Ethics and Philosophy* 5.4 (2011): 414–32; R. Simon, *Fair Play: The Ethics of Sport*, (Boulder, CO: Westview Press, 2004) 211–15.

[6] T.S. Petersen, "Good athlete—bad athlete? On the 'role-model argument' for banning performance enhancing drugs," *Sport, Ethics and Philosophy* 4.3 (2010): 332–340.

[7] R. Feezell, "Celebrated athletes, moral exemplars, and lusory objects," *Journal of the Philosophy of Sport* 32.1 (2005) 2-35, argues that famous athletes should be regarded as lusory objects; i.e. models of athletic achievement we would like to obtain, rather than models of general morality.

conventional sense, it is unclear more generally what the social and educational value of athletic excellence could be.[8]

In this essay I construct an argument for the social and educational value of Olympic sport built upon the relationship between athletes, heroes, and poets in archaic Greece. On this model, athletes are neither heroes nor role models in the conventional sense. Rather, athletes, athletics, and the poets who extolled them are part of a cultural conspiracy to celebrate and inspire virtue (*aretē*) by connecting a community with its heroic past. Festivals like the Olympic Games as well as local events like funeral games educated and unified communities by cultivating an aesthetic appreciation for excellence and inspiring youth to strive for it. Athletes aren't heroes but by re-enacting heroic struggles, they experience heroic virtues, and inspire both artists and spectators to bond with the higher ideals of their ancestry. In this way, athletes, athletics, and the media that celebrated them played important social and educational roles. Insofar as modern Olympic sport performs a similar service, its association with heroism and with moral education may ultimately be justified.

Heroes and Athletes in Ancient Greece

Philosophers have observed that any moral understanding of sport must take account of its cultural context and even the extent to which sports form their own communities and cultures. The virtue-ethical values arising from competitive social cultures have been particularly useful in this regard.[9] A closer look at the heroic song-culture of ancient Greece provides an apt illustration of how

---

[8] As Fleming et al., "Role models amongst elite young male rugby league players in Britain," *European Physical Education Review* 11.2 (2005), 65, showed, the main characteristics of athletes admired by youth were technical competence, physical characteristics and temperament, specifically those instrumentally important to the success in the game. Moral and nonathletic characteristics were rarely cited.

[9] McNamee, Jones, and Duda, "Psychology, ethics and sport," *International Journal of Sport and Health Sciences* 1.1 (2003): 27.

I. Heroic Heritage

athletics may function as moral education. Heroes, in this tradition, were human beings (of either sex) from the remote past who had extraordinary abilities due to a genetic connection with the gods.[10] Elsewhere, I have argued that since heroes' immortal ancestry was taken as an explanation for their athletic prowess, they provided an early link between athleticism and *aretē* (virtue, excellence).[11] It is likewise no surprise that prototypical Hellenic heroes such as Heracles and Achilles were renowned for their athletic ability, but it is important to note that these heroes were not made famous by their athletic feats. It is also important to recognize that these and all other Hellenic heroes are mortal; they die (usually gloriously) and are buried or cremated.[12]

Greek heroes have to be mortal because their heroism depends on struggle (*agōn*). The Greek heroes' *agōn* derives from the very specific cause of their being 'unseasonal,' displaced from their proper time and place by fate – something even the gods can't control. Because they are out of synch with the divine plan, they suffer and struggle. But it is precisely through this suffering and struggle that their virtues are revealed. Heracles is the paradigm example. On the day he was due to be born to the mortal Alcmene, Zeus decreed—at his wife, Hera's, behest—that the next-born descendant of Perseus should become king of the people around him. Zeus had Heracles in mind, but Hera delayed Heracles' birth and sped up the birth of Eurystheus, also of Perseus' line but not yet due to be born. Therefore, it was Eurystheus who became the king (and a perpetual thorn in Heracles' side) against the will of Zeus because Hera made sure that Heracles' birth was not "on time."

This story, told in *Iliad* XIX 76-138, can't help but remind us of the hard-luck backgrounds of so many modern sports heroes who

---

[10] Gregory Nagy, *The Ancient Greek Hero in 24 Hours* (Cambridge, MA: Harvard University Press, 2013), 0§4.

[11] Reid, *Athletics and Philosophy in the Ancient World*, ch. 1.

[12] Though Heracles eventually does become a god, his heroism derives from the part of his life when he was mortal.

grow up in adverse circumstances and overcome them through athleticism. The same passage describes Zeus' sorrow at seeing Heracles struggle with degrading labors because of Hera's trick. It is sometimes viewed as ironic that Heracles' name means 'glory of Hera' since she is the one who delayed his birth and caused most of his troubles. On the other hand, without her intervention, he would not have had the *athla* (labors) through which Heracles' heroic *aretē* was revealed.[13] In effect, Hera set up the challenging *agōnes* (struggles or contests) that ultimately made Heracles into a hero,[14] and after his apotheosis she performs a ritual which mimics giving birth to him.[15] Heracles, like all heroes, is made great though antagonism—often with a god. It is no coincidence that the Greek word for athletic contests is the same as the word for the heroes' struggles (*agōnes*), nor is it by accident that the term *athla* is connected to *athlete*, the one who performs a feat or competes for a prize. It is also no coincidence that the inspirational power of modern Olympic heroes depends as much on their personal stories of suffering as it does on their pure athletic achievements.

Heracles' immortalization was exceptional. Homer's Achilles consciously chooses to die gloriously and be remembered rather than to grow old back at home in Phthia (*Iliad* 9.497-505):

> Mother tells me,
> the immortal goddess Thetis with her glistening feet,
> that two fates bear me on to the day of death.

---

[13] It is even argued that the exclusion of females from the ancient Olympic Games derives their link to Heracles' cult and its repudiation of women based on the conflict with Hera. Mouratidis, "Herakles at Olympia,"41-45.

[14] The labors are extreme and so is the *aretē* needed to perform them (they include things like diverting rivers and killing lions with his bare hands). Nagy's second characteristic of heroes, likewise, is that they are extreme. Sometimes they are extreme in the positive sense of being superior, but they can also be extreme in the negative sense. Heracles is said to have murdered his own wife and children. It is through his labors that the hero expiates his sin.

[15] This story is told by Diodorus Siculus, 4.39.2.

I. Heroic Heritage

> If I hold out here and I lay siege to Troy,
> my journey home is gone, but my glory never dies.
> If I voyage back to the fatherland I love,
> my pride, my glory dies ...
> true, but the life that's left me will be long,
> the stroke of death will not come on me quickly.

At the highest moment of his or her glory, the hero becomes indistinguishable from a god—but that moment passes, just like the moment of victory passes for athletes—and the hero eventually dies. Indeed, ancient cults were often centered on the hero's *sēma* (tomb),[16] where worshippers would sacrifice animals, letting their blood run into the earth to activate the hero's spirit, which "evokes the idea of a vitality that animates the universe."[17] To get in touch with the hero's sprit was to get in touch with not only with one's glorious ancestry and the virtues it represented, it was to tap into the energy of life itself.

Could it be that the modern Olympics' social magnetism has something to do with a heroic context? It should be remembered that ancient Greek heroes, though athletic, were not primarily athletes, and ancient Greek athletes were not heroes. Still, there *was* a close connection between athletes and heroes that may shed light on the enduring link between athletics and heroism today. First, what ancient athletes did was to *re-enact* (*mimēsthai*) the struggles (*agōnes*) of ancient heroes as part of a religious ritual that allowed them to experience and display heroic virtues, or *aretai*. Second, these athletic contests brought the community together to celebrate their divine and heroic ancestry, and to bond emotionally with the athletes' struggles in a way that produced the kind of *catharsis* which Aristotle and Plato identified with learning. Third,

---

[16] There is broad cultural evidence suggesting that hero worship in ancient Greece was not created out of stories like that of the *Iliad* and *Odyssey*, but was in fact independent of them. The stories, on the other hand, were based on the religious practices, though not always directly. Nagy, *Ancient Greek Hero*, 0§12.

[17] Nagy, *Ancient Greek Hero*, 0§43.

the epinician poetry and art that celebrated the athletic victor reconnected him and his community with the heroic past, the epic poetry that recounted that past glory, and – more generally – with the divine. So athletes, athletics, and poetry combined to create a cultural aesthetic that celebrated Olympic *aretē* and inspired youth to strive for it. It is a model that immortalizes neither heroes nor athletes, but rather, virtue itself.

The Educational Role of Athletes

If we understand ancient Olympic athletics as part of an aesthetic celebration of heroic virtue, then athletes' role in that celebration is *mimesis*—the imitation, or better, re-enactment of the heroes' virtues. In the specific context, we might say that athletes are performing a religious ritual that re-enacts mythological struggles (*agōnes*).[18] But this is not to say that they are performing imagined fairy-tales or allegories; in Homeric terms a myth is considered genuine and true.[19] Nor is it to say that athletes are reenacting mythological athletic games—such as can be found in *Iliad* and *Odyssey*— remember that athletic feats within myth are rarely considered heroic.[20] What athletes do in the ritual of competition is re-enact the virtues (*aretai*) associated with mythological heroes as expressed through their labors (*athla*). This athletic *mimēsis* functions as experiential learning that leads to *catharsis*, a clarification of our understanding of what such virtues are and what it means to act from them.

---

[18] Nagy, *Ancient Greek Hero*, 0§13 says we should think of Greek religious practices as an interaction between myth and ritual. He defines ritual as "doing things and saying things in a way that is considered sacred" and myth as "saying things in a way that is also considered sacred."

[19] Nagy, *Ancient Greek Hero*, 1§8.

[20] According to Diodorus (4.14.1-2), Heracles' *athla* included founding the Olympic Games, and wining every event in their first edition. This is one of several myths about the founding of the Olympic Games, but as Nagy points out, it is a handy illustration of the perceived link between a hero's labors and an athlete's contests.

I. Heroic Heritage

Mimēsis is an educational tool recognized by both Plato and Aristotle. The latter clearly links it with the pleasure derived from learning in *Poetics* (1448b). Both philosophers, furthermore, understand education generally to be an intellectual movement from the particular toward the universal.[21] Aristotle suggests that artistic representations deepen our understanding of universal aspects of human life. He says, "The reason why we enjoy seeing likenesses is that, as we look, we learn and infer what each is" (*Poetics* 1448b). Plato worries that artistic representations, such as a painting of a tree, are twice removed from the original form or ideal we seek to understand.[22] Athletic *mimēsis* of heroic virtues would be endorsed by Plato, however, because such performances demand actual courage and self-control, thereby bringing us closer to the ideal by giving us experiential understanding of it.[23] Athletics, on this view, functions like a Socratic dialogue by constructing an experience that results in *catharsis*, understood in this educational context as an intellectual clarification, especially of universals.[24] Just as the dialogue *Euthyphro* clarifies our understanding of piety, the athletic *mimēsis* of Achilles may clarify our understanding of courage.

Likewise, analogous to the way Plato's dialogues bring Socratic values back to life, the ritual of athletics brings heroic virtues back to life so they can be experienced aesthetically both by the athletes performing and by the spectators witnessing the

---

[21] L. Golden, "*Mimēsis* and *Katharsis*," *Classical Philology* 64.3 (1969): 147.

[22] This metaphysical critique of *mimēsis* occurs in Book 10 of the *Republic*, the educational discussion is found in Books 2 and 3.

[23] Dramatic *mimēsis*, by contrast, asks me to inauthentically enact the flawed character and emotions of characters like Oedipus. Plato thought *mimēsis* of vicious actions harmful, but athletic *mimēsis* is not only authentic, it is positive. See H. Reid, "Performing Virtue: Athletic *Mimēsis* in Platonic Education," in H. Reid, D. Tanasi, S. Kimbell eds., *Politics and Performance in Western Greece* (Sioux City: Parnassos Press, 2017): 265-277.

[24] For a full argument of this interpretation of catharsis, see Golden, "*Mimēsis* and *Katharsis*."

performance. This idea of athletics as a ritual ordeal (*athlos* or *agōn*)[25] is quite consistent with modern conceptions of sport as an artificial challenge designed to evoke virtues or – in the resounding words of Bernard Suits, "a voluntary attempt to overcome unnecessary obstacles."[26] By creating challenges that demand such virtues as courage, self-control, respect, justice, and wisdom, we enable athletes and spectators alike to get a taste of what their ancestral heroes went through – not only the suffering, but also the sense of strength, achievement, and even joy that comes from great achievements. Although athletic activities lack the direct social benefit of traditional heroic labors, the virtues athletes cultivate and display in their performances can evoke those virtues and inspire others to strive for them. On this model, the athlete is not so much a role model as the (temporary) embodiment of a cultural ideal. Ritual, in fact, is designed to transform the people who perform it into something better – if only for a moment. Through the ritual of competition the athlete may morph temporarily into an ancient hero or even – like the hero himself does at the climax of achievement – into a god. At the end of the ritual, athletes

---

[25] According to Nagy, *Ancient Greek Hero* 8b§3, to endure such suffering, as an athlete, is to re-enact a prototypical ordeal of a hero. A more accurate way of understanding athletic contests in their archaic Greek historical contexts is to keep in mind the meanings of the ancient Greek words *athlos* (epic *aethlos*) 'ordeal, contest' and *athlon* (epic *aethlon*) "prize won in the course of participating in an *athlos*" and *athlētēs* athlete, "one who participates in an *athlos*." To restate the concept of athletics in ancient Greek terms: an *athlos* was the ritual 'ordeal' or 'contest' of an athlete engaging in athletic contests that were taking place in the historical present, but it was also the mythological 'ordeal' or 'contest' of a hero engaging in life-and-death contests that took place once upon a time in the heroic past; moreover, the ritual 'ordeals' or 'contests' of the historical present were viewed as *re-enactments* of the mythical 'ordeals' or 'contests' of the heroic past.

[26] Bernard Suits, *The Grasshopper: Games, Life, and Utopia*, 2nd ed. (Peterborough, ON: Broadview Press, 2005), 55.

morph back into their unheroic mortal selves – but both they and those who witnessed their feats are made a bit better by the aesthetic experience of heroic virtue and the illuminating *catharsis* that accompanies it.

It is worth noting, as well, that athletes' displays of heroic virtue are ephemeral – as symbolized by the quickly wilting crown of vegetation that serves as their prize. It is the virtue itself that is undying and eternally praised, like the gods. Indeed the mimetic chain between athlete, hero and god may be compared to the magnetic chain that Plato describes in *Ion* as briefly connecting audience, poet and muse (533de). The Greeks understood that heroes may resemble gods at the climax of their achievements, but they are by definition mortal and imperfect and very often capable of downright immoral actions. Achilles not only drags Hector's corpse on the ground, he expresses the most depraved desire to eat his enemy's flesh. Such actions are not condoned by the narrative,[27] rather they acknowledge the fallibility of even heroic human beings and lead us to focus on their achievements, or – as I have argued here – on the virtues evoked by those achievements in our celebration of them.

The distinction between persons, performances, and virtues may shed light on our modern worries about bad behavior among athletic role models. In ancient Greek culture, it was among the most grave of sins to commit hubris, that is, to confuse an imperfect mortal with a perfect god. If we take great athletic performances to be evidence of perfectly virtuous personhood, allowing them to generate the expectation of consistent virtuous behavior on-field and off, we commit a kind of hubris (and set ourselves up for almost guaranteed disappointment). Instead, what we should revere is the virtue itself, recognizing the performance as an ephemeral instantiation of it – a kind of epiphany, the brief appearance of something divine on earth. We may celebrate, be inspired by, and even ritually reenact Olympic heroes' moments of greatness, but we must acknowledge at the

---

[27] Nagy, *Ancient Greek Hero*, 1§52.

same time that athletes are imperfect mortals also capable of grave evils. The educational value of athletic *mimēsis* comes from the emulation of virtues, not persons.

The Social Role of Olympic Athletics

Modern sport philosophy often overlooks the educational value of sport for spectators and communities as opposed to individuals.[28] On the ancient Greek model, the community is expected to be educated and made better as a whole by the athletic ritual. Part and parcel of the Greek idea of contest (*agōn*) derives etymologically from the formation *syn-agein*, which means to bring together or assemble. Ancient athletic festivals, whether local or Panhellenic, had the explicit purpose of bringing communities together. In fact, the ancient hero worship that eventually gave rise to Olympic-style festivals was characteristically local – a derivative of ancestor worship centered on a specific location, most often the hero's tomb. The idea was that the hero, after death, becomes *olbios* (blessed), and worshippers may too become blessed by making spiritual contact with that hero—contact that was often achieved by physically touching the earth that contained the hero's corpse, or some other relic or sign of the hero.[29] In *Odyssey* (11.136-137), it is said that all the people who live in proximity to Odysseus' buried corpse will be blessed. Homer's description of the vicious battles for possession of a dead hero's body can be explained by

---

[28] An exception to this rule is Mumford, *Watching Sport* (Abingdon: Routledge, 2012) who discusses the moral potential of spectatorship at length. Much work on the topic of spectatorship emphasizes its degrading nature, i.e. C. Lasch, "The degradation of sport," in *The Ethics of Sports*, ed. Mike McNamee (Abingdon: Routledge, 1977) 369–381and W.J Morgan, *Why Sports Morally Matter* (Abingdon: Routledge, 2006) 26. McNamee, *Sports, Virtues and Vices* (Abingdon: Routledge, 2008), however, compares sports to medieval morality plays, and McFee, *Sports, Rules and Values* (Abingdon: Routledge, 2004) chapter 8, describes sport as a moral laboratory in which virtues and vices may be tested.

[29] Nagy, *Ancient Greek Hero*, 11§2.

beliefs about the corpse's spiritual power to evoke such goods as fertility and prosperity.[30]

That Olympic contests took place in a sacred space and attempted to revive the spirits of ancestral heroes no doubt derives from these characteristics of hero worship. Even today, certain athletic fields and stadiums hold a kind of sacred aura – though it is usually based on the feats of earlier athletes rather than the presence of hero's tomb. Such auras have a community-bonding effect, especially when the community is small and well-defined, as with a college campus, and when the history in question is especially long and venerable, as with historic stadiums like the Los Angeles Coliseum. In some cases, sports teams are named to evoke a community's 'heroic' past, for example, the San Francisco 49ers (named after the prospectors who came to the area during the Gold Rush of 1849), or Torino's Juventus, named after an Imperial Roman youth organization. In other cases, the connection is more dynamic, as when New Zealand athletes reenact ancient Maori war dances to intimidate opponents. Most often the spiritual presence evoked in modern sports is of past athletes, as when a statue of Jesse Owens is displayed near a running track, the names of deceased cyclists like Marco Pantani are painted on the mountain racecourses, or when teams wear throwback uniforms. Whatever the particular link with past 'heroes,' the effect is one of bonding over the virtues a community wishes to be identified with.

Likewise, what the audience of an athletic contest experiences when they witness an athlete's peak performance is an epiphany, a momentary reappearance of the hero (or sometimes a god) in the natural world and the temporary collapsing of time and distance between an idealized heroic age and their contemporary age.[31] I would go so far as to speculate that when an athlete, perhaps a

---

[30] Nagy, *Pindar's Homer*, (Washington DC: CHS, 1980), 32.
[31] According to Nagy, *Ancient Greek Hero*, 5§38, "An epiphany is a vision that is felt to be real, not unreal. It is the appearance of something divine, something understood to be absolutely real."

runner in the Olympic Games, experienced a moment of greatness in the stadium, he, for a moment became Achilles in the eyes of his audience.[32] Since history was generally viewed as a process of decline – a mentality symbolized by Hesiod's sequencing of gold, silver, bronze, heroic and iron ages, and reprised in Socrates' discussion of citizens' souls in *Republic*[33] – such a temporal collapse would have been just the kind of religious ecstasy the worshippers (and the athlete himself) were seeking. As with the case of *mimēsis*, I would argue that this kind of heroic epiphany derives its value from the virtues the athlete brings back to life to be experienced esthetically in a way that leads to catharsis – again understood as spiritual and intellectual clarification characterized by the pleasure of learning.

Catharsis, understood more traditionally as cleansing or purification, was another social outcome of athletic rituals in ancient Greece. When athletes were seen to display Achilles' "killer instinct," re-enacting his state of mind when dragging of Hector's corpse, they might be interpreted as purifying that mythological corruption.[34] Indeed it has been argued that athletic victors function as sacrificial victims, the purpose of which is to purify the community at large.[35] It may be the case that the dangerous excesses of modern athletic heroes – their violence, rage, all-consuming passion—also help communities to acknowledge and mitigate the darker side of their history and character. I have argued that gladiatorial contests, which put fearsome foreigners under the command of the emperor, helped

---

[32] Reid, "The Ecstasy of *Aretē*," in this volume, 8.

[33] The *Republic* passage is 415a-d. Hesiod's myth of the 'Five Generations of Humankind' is in *Works and Days* (V.106-201). This general view of moral and physical decline (which contrasts starkly with our contemporary idea of history as constant progress), created a moral urgency to reconnect through virtue with the nobler generations of the past.

[34] Nagy, *Ancient Greek Hero* 8a§14, says athletics is ritual compensation "for the pollution caused by the death of a hero in myth."

[35] Sansone, *Greek Athletics*, 82-4.

I. Heroic Heritage

ancient Rome deal with its increasing ethnic diversity.[36] Athletic ritual, helps communities to reaffirm valued virtues even as they struggle with their historical and actual failure to live up to those virtues. Athletics helps communities to reach beyond social barriers and choose heroes based on virtue.

The Cultural Role of Media

Athletes' function as role models depends ultimately on the media that interpret and communicate their character and achievements, integrating them into a larger cultural paradigm. The ancient Greek connection between athletes and heroes cannot be imagined without poetry – both the epic poetry that describes the feats of the heroes and the epinician poetry that assimilates the victorious athlete into that heroic paradigm. The epic poets Homer and Hesiod are identified by Herodotus (2.53.1-3) as the foundation of civilization. But without the actions of the heroes, the epic poets would have had nothing to sing about, and without the songs of the poets, athletes would have nothing to re-enact. Athletic and poetic performance should be seen as complementary – a kind of relay in which one inspires the other. There is a passage in *Iliad* where Achilles sings "of the glories of men" accompanying himself on the lyre, while Patroclus waits to do his turn. Not only does the scene suggest a relay performance between Achilles and Patroclus, it depicts Achilles singing about glory inside the poem that sings about *his* glory. This illustrates how the hero's actions are glorified and immortalized not simply in performance, but by becoming part of a larger cultural song that will continue to be sung long after the heroes have died. Likewise, what an athlete achieves through the contrived struggles of sport derives its social value from being absorbed into a larger cultural narrative about the meaningful struggles of life.

---

[36] Reid, "Was the Roman Gladiator an Athlete?" *Journal of the Philosophy of Sport* 33.1 (2006): 37–49. I apply the argument to college football in "Heroes of the Coliseum," in M. Austin, ed., *Football and Philosophy* (Lexington, KY: University Press of Kentucky, 2008): 128-140.

Again, it is not the hero himself who becomes immortal through song, rather it is heroic virtue that is perpetuated poetically. *Kleos* is glory, or a song that celebrates glory, but a more general definition is rumor, report, news.[37] In the context of Greek poetry, *kleos* is what poets hear from the muses who have seen and can remember everything.[38] But they don't sing about everything and it is only because Achilles chooses to die an untimely and glorious death that the muses sing a lament for him, which the poet hears and transcribes so that the story may live to be retold. It is through the performance of the song, like the performance of the athlete, that the hero's virtues are brought back to life and thereby perpetuated. In *Iliad* (23.326-331), we see that Nestor's storytelling about a chariot race links the contest taking place at Troy with the heroic past, and links Patroclus, in whose honor the games are held, with the heroes of the past (again, within the larger poem that will secure for him his *kleos*). Although we think of ancient games as being dedicated to gods, most, including the Olympic Games, were originally dedicated to heroes as a way of keeping the virtues alive. In modern sports, we not only keep the feats of past sports heroes alive by replaying videos of their achievements, we also embrace such traditions as retiring their numbers and naming events or awards after them. Awards in particular, fulfill the function of celebrating the virtues associated with an athletic hero and perpetuating them by regularly recognizing contemporary athletes who display the same virtues. Examples include the Marco Pantani Memorial in Cycling and the Terry Fox award in Olympic sports, which was created specifically to award "courage, humanitarianism, service and compassion."[39] In some cases, including that of Fox and Pantani, the award is partly inspired by the hero's untimely death. In others, it demands virtuous conduct beyond sports performance – as with the frequent criterion of community service. In all cases, such awards attempt to locate and

---

[37] Liddell and Scott, *A Greek-English Lexicon* (Oxford: Clarendon, 1940).
[38] Nagy *Ancient Greek Hero*, 2§15.
[39] *Terry Fox Humanitarian Award Program*. 2015.

celebrate the continued manifestation of the hero's virtues. Usually they do so in a way that is more focused than sports results and statistics, using committees of experts to make the relevant selections. The cultural celebration of athletes does not make them immortal, rather it is their virtue, as constructed and retold by the community, which lives on.

What ancient poetry – or in our case, the media – does is to merge the athlete and his or her deeds into a heroic paradigm that is the real object of celebration and the real source of inspiration. So, Homer's poems about Achilles and Odysseus are not so much biographies as celebrations of heroic virtues. This dynamic is especially clear in the victory odes of Pindar, Bacchylides, and others. These poems usually begin with a myth about gods and heroes like Heracles, they then associate the athletic victor, his family, and often his community with the noble and heroic traits those gods and heroes possessed. The aesthetic effect in the end is not so much to celebrate a particular individual, but rather to absorb that individual into the larger paradigm of *aretē* being celebrated by the culture through the means of epic poetry, athletic festivals, and victory odes. As I have argued elsewhere about ancient Greek athletic art,[40] these images are not so much portraits of individual persons as they are depictions of cultural ideals associated with athletic victory.

In a similar way, the modern media's construction (and sometimes destruction) of athletic 'heroes' is often an effort to place them in (or displace them from) a cultural ideal. In 2016, a film emerged about the African-American athlete Jesse Owens who competed at the 1936 Olympics in Berlin and has often been interpreted as a symbol of athletic virtue triumphing over racial bigotry. The film successfully absorbs Owens into a cultural paradigm of black excellence, which has a very different meaning in the Obama era than it did in the 1930s. Back then, Owens was the star of what was supposed to be a pro-Fascist documentary on the Games directed by Leni Riefenstahl. Later, his image was used

---

[40] Reid, "Athletic Beauty," 281.

to undermine Fascist ideals, and in 1984 his status as an "Uncle Tom" was explored in a television miniseries.[41] All of these accounts, whatever their particular ends, celebrated Owens' athletic virtues and tried to show their political importance. Modern media productions, just like ancient epinician poetry, have their own specific goals. But even the practice of idealistically celebrating athletic 'heroes' may have social value if it inspires others to strive for the virtues the athlete symbolizes. Jesse Owens, according to this view, is modeling not a role but rather virtues that our culture continues to value.

Conclusion

There is a reason that Plato combined *gymnastikē* and *mousikē* (athletic and poetic education) in the *Republic* (410bc). Ancient Greek song culture made effective use of athletic role models precisely because it allowed the real life experiences of athletes and spectators to be fused with the larger than life characters and values of epic poetry. When a normal athlete re-enacts the deed of a hero he does not *become* the hero, rather he (or she) re-presents the hero's action – or, more specifically, the hero's virtues as celebrated in poetry – within the realm of the here and now to be esthetically experienced by the community. The aesthetic angle is important from an educational point of view. We might say that athletics teaches us what it 'feels like' to struggle like the heroes did, and may even inspire us to achieve challenging goals beyond sport. In tandem with literature and other media, athletics can teach us about virtue through experience in a way that other media cannot do alone. This is true even for spectators who may bond emotionally with athletes and teams in a way that leads to a positive catharsis. Athletes on this model may be heroic, educational, and inspirational without needing to be actual heroes or even role models in that we can tap into their energy and re-enact their struggles without needing or wanting to re-enact the specifics of their circumstances. In Philostratus' famed essay *On*

---

[41] Tillet, "Jesse Owens, a Film hero once again," *New York Times*, 2/12/2016.

I. Heroic Heritage

Heroes, the beauty of a thriving garden indicated the presence of the hero's spirit. Let us cultivate modern sport to be a garden of virtue, populated by individual plants which may grow and wither, but which taken as a whole shall thrive and prosper eternally.

Section II
Ancient Olympic Philosophy

5. Racing toward Truth in Ancient Olympia[1]

Mother of gold-crowned games, Olympia, queen of truth,
where men who are seers interpret burnt offerings
and test the mind of Zeus of the flashing thunderbolt,
to see if he has any word for men who struggle in their hearts
to win rewards of excellence, and respite from their labours;
for men's prayers are fulfilled in accordance with their piety.
(Pindar, *Olympian* 8, Verity trans.)

Modern Olympic enthusiasts often propose idealized images of ancient Greek athletics as some kind of antidote to the debased culture of modern sports. Historians warn us, however, that ancient athletic practice fell far short of its ideals. If we want to recover the true "Olympic Spirit," we must look beyond idealizations of the past and try to understand how the Greeks themselves came to associate such notions as dedication, truth, and peace with athletics. This requires us to examine the religious dimension of ancient sport as well as its connection to the philosophy of the time. But first, we must set aside our modern distinctions among athletics, religion, philosophy, and science. For the ancient Greeks, divinity permeated nature, therefore its scientific study—what we now call natural philosophy—was neither a denial of nor a departure from religion. Rather, the work of the Pre-Socratic philosophers from Ionia: Thales, Anaximander, Xenophanes, and Anaximenes, should be seen as a more rational and universal approach to religion, one reflected in the same era by the incorporation of athletic events into religious festivals at Olympia, Delphi, Nemea, Isthmia, and elsewhere.

In what follows I attempt to uncover a conceptual connection between natural philosophy (nascent science), religion, and Olympic sport in the 7th and 6th c. BCE. It is a connection worth reflecting upon in our modern world where these practices persist

---

[1] Originally published as "Racing for truth: Sport, religion, and the scientific spirit in ancient Olympia." *Stadion: International Journal of the History of Sport*, 33 (2009): 211-20. Reprinted with Permission.

II. Ancient Olympic Philosophy

yet see themselves as entirely separate. Both Olympic sport and Ionian philosophy adopted a rational approach to religious questions. Philosophy's challenge to mythology and anthropomorphic conceptions of god resulted from a spirit of inquiry that embraced intellectual humility, impartial testing, adherence to reason, and observation of evidence: features already present in the structure of athletic contests. What this process rejected—or perhaps transcended—was knowledge based upon unquestioned authority, revelation, and faith. But this spirit of inquiry did not spring fully formed from Ionian soil, rather its roots reach out toward the various cultures with whom the Ionians had contact. Indeed, what is called "the birth of philosophy" may have resulted from the need for diverse peoples to interact. What philosophy sought was culturally independent truth acceptable to all—and in that sense it performed an intellectual function parallel to that political function of unification associated with ancient Olympic Games.

Olympia's Religious Heritage

To understand the Olympic spirit, we must return to its origins. The traditional start of the Olympic Games is 776 BCE, but Olympia itself is much older than that. Long before it witnessed athletic dedication and sacrifice, Olympia was a place of religious dedication and sacrifice, and this religious function remained primary even at the height of the Games' popularity. Archaeology finds evidence of sacrificial offerings on the site as early as the 10th c. BCE.[2] Mythology attributes the sanctuary's founding to the quintessential Greek hero Heracles who dedicated the site to his father Zeus after a bitter struggle with King Augeas of nearby Elis. After ridding the local community of this troublesome tyrant, Heracles sacrificed "the best portion" of his spoils there (Pindar, *Olympian* 10.27-77), initiating an Olympic tradition of toil and thanksgiving repeated by countless Olympic athletes—even

---

[2] A. Mallawitz, "Cult and Competition Locations at Olympia," in *The Archaeology of the Olympics*, ed. W. Raschke (Madison: University of Wisconsin Press, 1988), 89.

today. At some point, a footrace was added to the ritual at Olympia to decide who would light the sacrificial flame. As in Homer's games, the contest was probably motivated by competing claims to virtue and honor. But because the judge at Olympia was believed to be a god, the race was run open and fair. And so the Olympic blend of athletics and religion initiated a new attitude toward knowledge that presaged the birth of philosophy.

The central function of ancient Greek religious festivals, including the Olympic Games, was sacrifice: an offering of gifts in gratitude for benefits gained and also in the hope of benefits to come. Sacrifice seems to be the opposite of profit, the apparent aim of our modern sports economy. But in a context where gods are thought to control access to such benefits as food and health, the relationship between human and divine might be seen as one of investment and exchange.[3] Indeed, ritual sacrifice was serious business. It was an attempt to please an extremely powerful being whose preferences were difficult to know, but whose cooperation was essential for the survival and thriving of both individuals and communities. Understanding the preferences of gods was such an important and persistent question for ancient Hellenes that Plato devoted a dialogue to it. In *Euthyphro*, the tradition of imitating poetry and mythology in order to be pious is exposed as a miserable failure. Reliance upon oracles rarely fared much better. Oracular declarations may have been true, but they were hopelessly enigmatic. Aristotle (*Rhetoric*, 3.5) warns us to avoid the error of King Croeseus who went to war after being told by the oracle at Delphi that he would destroy a great kingdom; the kingdom he destroyed turned out to be his own (Herodotus, *Histories*, 1.53, 1.91). Socrates models a philosophical response to the Delphic oracle's declaration that no one is wiser than he. The Athenian treats the statement as a puzzle to be solved through a mission of rational inquiry that ends up serving both the philosopher and his community. Knowing the god's mind was

---

[3] Mikalson, *Ancient Greek Religion*, 25.

essential to Greek religion, but such knowledge was notoriously and frustratingly elusive.

As a Panhellenic sanctuary serving a diversity of tribes, the sacrificial stakes at Olympia were particularly high. In order to please the god, they knew that they had to sacrifice their very best, but it is easier to select the best bull than the best human beings. Each tribe brought its own social hierarchy and no doubt this created tension when it came time to select someone to light the sacred sacrificial flame. The addition of a simple footrace seems to have solved the problem. According to Philostratus (*Gymnasticus* 5), the first runners gathered one *stadion* (600 feet) from the altar, where the priest stood with the torch. The first runner to arrive was given the honor of lighting the sacrificial flame. One may interpret the addition of the footrace simply as entertainment for worshippers.[4] Given the historic association between virtue and athleticism as well as the importance of the ritual, however, a better explanation is that the race was used to select a human dedication most pleasing to the god.

It is unclear whether Olympia was the first sanctuary to use athletics to make such religious selections, but the Olympic Games were recognized as the oldest and most prestigious athletic festival in the ancient world. Furthermore, the immense collection of statues, armor, and other valuables left in the sanctuary as thanks for prayers answered stands as enduring evidence that Olympia's methods for pleasing the gods were considered reliable. Given the gods' involvement in the outcome of Homer's funeral games, one may even interpret the Olympic race as a chance for the god to select his own favorite victor. Or the race may be seen as a device to access the infallible mind of god, with humility, respect, and a public display of evidence.

Science vs. Theology

Olympia was already associated with truth when it began using athletics to search for knowledge; its original distinction

---

[4] Mikalson, *Ancient Greek Religion*, 28.

among ancient sanctuaries was the presence of an oracle. Pindar nicknames Olympia "queen of truth" and connects its oracle with people who are striving for virtue (*aretē*) and seeking respite from their toils (*Olympian* 8.1-7). What is most interesting about Olympia's use of athletics as a mode for discovering the mind of god, however, is that it reflects the principles that generated the birth of philosophy (and natural science) in the 7th and 6th c. BCE. What the first philosophers rejected (or perhaps transcended) was knowledge based upon unquestioned authority, revelation, and faith—the very kind of thinking reflected in the non-competitive pre-Olympic sport of early Egypt and Mesopotamia. Philosophy's challenge to mythopoeic thinking resulted from a spirit of inquiry that embraced the principles of Olympic style sport: intellectual humility, impartial testing, and demonstration of evidence.

The birth of western philosophy is traditionally located in the Ionian town of Miletus around 585 BCE when Thales predicted an eclipse of the sun. Many also consider this event the birth of science because Thales and his fellow Milesians were interested in observing the natural world and speculating about its character.[5] They sought to understand the origin of the universe (*archē*), which is to say that they sought to understand the divine, since they believed the *archē* to be both self-moving and omnipresent.[6] This integration of the divine into nature shows that when Aristotle distinguishes physiologists (i.e. natural philosophers) from theologists in *Metaphysics,* he is pointing out a difference of method

---

[5] On the Ionians as scientists see J. Barnes, *The Presocratic Philosophers*, (New York: Routledge) 1993, 52: "It is, I believe, perverse to deny that the Milesians were scientists- and great scientists at that. Their scientific shortcomings were not methodological: they approached their problems in an admirable fashion; and their failures were due not to lack of understanding but to lack of developed techniques of observation and theory construction."

[6] As Aristotle explains in *De Anima* 405a19-21, Thales considered the soul to be a thing that produces motion. Thales' association of movement, *kinēsis,* with souls and divinity provides an early clue to the reason for athletics' association with religion.

rather than subject. The *phusiologoi* are those who offer argument (*apodeixis*) to support their views, while the *theologoi* offer stories or speak "*muthikos*" (*Metaphysics*, 1000a9-20). His distinction reflects the contrast between claims to virtue based on songs and stories versus claims to virtue based on victory in a fair contest.[7]

The first principle shared by athletics and philosophy is humility. Some athletes may seem brave or even cocky in their approach to competition, but to enter a contest and stand naked on the starting line is a very humbling experience. If the contest is fair, we must admit our ignorance of the outcome and confront our limitations as fallible human beings. This humble admission of ignorance is not just Socrates' mantra,[8] it is the foundation of term 'philosophy.' Over a century before Socrates' birth, Pythagoras was said to have coined the term 'philosopher,' which means "lover of wisdom," in order to describe those thinkers who acknowledged their own ignorance (Diogenes Laertius 1.12). Says Aristotle "Whoever is puzzled and in a state of wonder believes he is ignorant" (*Metaphysics* 1.2 982b12). Underpinning this idea is religious recognition of the difference between humanity and divinity,[9] but what distinguishes athletes and philosophers from lovers of myth and tradition is that they seek to remedy their ignorance through rational testing and evidence rather than faith and storytelling.

The pre-Socratic philosopher Xenophanes is said to have laid the foundations of scientific humility with his explicit criticism of

---

[7] Says Barnes, *Presocratic Philosophers*, 95: "The decisive innovation of the *phusiologoi* was not that they abandoned the gods and eschewed theology, but that they replaced stories by arguments."

[8] Socrates is famous for saying that his wisdom lies precisely in the awareness of his ignorance. See Plato, *Apology*, 21d.

[9] Pindar, *Paean* 6, 51ff. G.S. Kirk, J.E. Raven, and M. Schofield, *The Presocratic Philosophers* (Cambridge, 1983), 179: "Yet this contrast is merely a special form of that between the capacity of the gods in general and the limitations of men, which is restated, after Xenophanes, by Heraclitus in fr. 78 and by Alcmaeon in fr. 1"

traditional approaches to religion and knowledge.[10] Questioning anthropomorphic conceptions of god ("horses would draw the shapes of gods to look like horses").[11] Xenophanes forces us to confront the fallibility of human judgment:

> No man has seen nor will anyone know the truth about the gods and all the things I speak of. For even if a person should in fact say what is absolutely the case, nevertheless he himself does not know, but belief is fashioned over all things.[12]

Olympia's footrace shows not only an admission of ignorance about divine preference, but also the philosophical resolve to discover an answer rationally. Said Xenophanes, "By no means did the gods reveal all things to mortals from the beginning, but in time, by searching, they discover better."[13] This was certainly a novel approach to religion; and maybe a distinctive Hellenic one.

The reliability of athletic as well as philosophical results derives largely from the rationality and impartiality of the process. As sports history shows, Egyptians and Mesopotamians used sport to affirm their existing religious beliefs. The Greeks, by contrast, adopted a questioning attitude toward divine wishes and attempted to understand them through reason.[14] When the Presocratic philosophers began theorizing about the origin of the universe, they took what had been "explained" by myth or religious doctrine and made it the object of rational investigation. It was not so much a rejection of religion as a novel approach to it. Likewise when Pythagoras based his religious philosophy upon

---

[10] Dodds, *The Greeks and The Irrational* (Berkeley: U. of California Press, 1951), 181: "[Xenophanes'] distinction between what is knowable and what is not . . . is the foundation of scientific humility."

[11] Xenophanes in Clement, *Miscellanies* 5.109, "God is one, greatest among gods and men, not at all like mortals in body or thought."

[12] Xenophanes as reported by Sextus Empiricus, *Against the Mathematician,s* 7.49.110, (tr. McKirahan).

[13] Xenophanes reported by Strobaeus, *Selections* 1.8.2, (tr. McKirahan).

[14] Frankfort & Frandfort, *Intellectual Adventure*, 366.

numbers, he sought a common and rational standard by which intangible things could be measured and understood.[15] In sport, the selection of winners is done logically and fairly, with care taken to ensure equal opportunity for each competitor and rewards according to merit. The Olympic Games avoided subjectively-judged contests and took measures to avoid corruption among athletes and officials.[16] Since the contests at Olympia were seeking to know the mind of god, they had to keep the contest free from human bias.

Another motivation at Olympia to promote fair and impartial contest was the presence of diverse tribes and, as was the case in Homer's *Iliad*, competing claims to virtue. Because the footrace provided publicly observed evidence for its results, it was presumably effective in convincing patriotic onlookers—even when the winner was not one of their own. It was Anaximines who insisted on evidence in philosophy. His theory that the origin of all things is air was significant because it accounted for the transformation of the material through the demonstrable evidence of condensation and rarefaction. As at Olympia, it is likely that the philosophical demand for evidence arose in response to the need for common ground between people from diverse religious and cultural backgrounds.[17] Observes Walter Burkert: "the complicated background of personal culture, the most beautiful and most sacred traditions, poetry, and religion mean nothing to

---

[15] A. Hermann, *To Think Like a God: Pythagoras and Parmenides The Origins of Philosophy* (Las Vegas: Parmenides, 2004), 106.

[16] S.G. Miller, *Ancient Greek Athletics*, 232-3.

[17] In fact the Ionian intellectual revolution was based upon political, social, and religious changes described by Kirk, Raven and Schofield, *Presocratic Philosophers*, p. 74-5, as a transition "away from the closed traditional society (which in its archetypal form is an oral society in which the telling of tales is an important instrument of stability and analysis) and toward an open society in which the values of the past become relatively unimportant and radically fresh opinions can be formed both of the community itself and of its expanding environment."

strangers."[18] By leaving the selection of victors (and therefore the honor of lighting the sacrificial flame) up to a publicly observed contest, Olympia's cult developed an approach to ritual that could accommodate the claims of competing social hierarchies. No matter the social class or geographical origin of the Olympic champion, the reasons and evidence for his selection were visible and (for the most part) acceptable to all.

From Sacrifice to Service

This revolutionary mix of philosophical inquiry and religious sacrifice explains the extraordinary symbolic worth of the Olympic victor's crown. The historical association between athleticism and virtue combined with the quasi-scientific reliability of the Olympic test resulted in victors who seemed genuinely god-favored and therefore capable of bringing benefits both tangible and intangible to their families, their communities, and the larger Hellenic nation. This explains why Olympic champions were showered with honors and gifts, including free meals at public expense and prime seats at community festivals.

Of course, the philosophical mindset inherent in athletic contest also questions such presumptions about the benefits of victory. As "punishment" for his philosophical service to the city of Athens, Socrates asks for the privileges accorded to Olympic victors, calling himself a more suitable recipient since "the Olympian victory makes you think yourself happy; I make you be happy" (Plato, *Apology*, 36de). His words echo the earlier declaration of that selfsame Xenophanes, whose social criticism didn't stop short of athletics:

> If a man wins a victory with swiftness of foot or in pentathlon where the precinct of Zeus lies beside the streams of Pisa in Olympia, or in wrestling or engaging even in painful boxing, or in the dread contest that they call pankration, and would be glorious for his townsmen to look upon and would win prominent pride of place in

---

[18] Burkert, *Greek Religion*, 306.

the contests, and would receive bread from the public larder of the city and a gift that would be a treasure for him, if even with horses he would obtain all these things, he would not be as worthy as I. Better than strength of men and horses is my wisdom. Those opinions are ill-considered. It is not right to prefer strength to my good wisdom. Even if a man good at boxing be among the people, even if a man good at pentathlon or wrestling, even if in swiftness of foot, which is held in pride of place in whatever deeds of men's strength belong to the contest, not for that reason would the city have better laws. Small joy would it be for the city if an athlete wins beside the banks of Pisa, for this does not fatten the storerooms of the city.[19]

Perhaps our modern skepticism about the value of modern sport also stems from a lack of demonstrable evidence that it benefits our communities. To be sure stereotypical modern sports professionals are self-interested and profit-oriented, no longer serious about representing their families, cities, or nations.

What's worse, the apparent absence of a higher purpose to our games has fostered relative indifference toward the accuracy of contest results. Athletes say that cheating isn't wrong as long as they don't get caught, and officials have been found to sell their influence on results to the highest bidder. At ancient Olympia cheating was perceived as an offence to the god and, by extension, the larger community, which would be denied the benefits of divine favor. Fines from cheaters (usually caught bribing their opponents) were used to erect statues of Zeus near the stadium entrance. These "*zanes*" bore inscriptions that reminded incoming athletes that "Olympic victory is to be won not by money but by swiftness of foot or strength of body."[20] In our modern sports culture, absent the religious context, one may wonder where the impetus for integrity will come.

---

[19] Xenophanes, qtd. in Athenaeus, *The Deipnosophists* 413F–414.
[20] Pausanias, 5.21.2-4.

On the other hand, Xenophanes' rejection of athletes for their failure to "fatten the storerooms of the city" ignores the important psychological benefits of witnessing athletes' struggles and success. Since ancient athletic victory was believed to come from combination of toil (*ponos*), sweat, and divine favor, it inspired onlookers to forge ahead with their day-to-day struggles, called *"agones"*, just like the Games themselves. Further, the gathering of diverse (and sometimes warring) peoples on neutral ground to worship a common deity seems to have had a bonding effect.[21] It unified and pacified the group, building real community ties as symbolized in the ritual of sharing a common meal at the conclusion of the festival. In modern times, the ritual of unifying diverse individuals through a common cause—even the sharing of common meals—is replicated at sports events around the world. The modern Olympic Games explicitly seek to unite the world, but scholastic sports of all kinds and even neighborhood softball games have a pacifying and unifying effect within diverse communities.

Conclusion

Of course the Hellenic unification fostered through games at Olympia and other Panhellenic sanctuaries is most often credited with their united defense against the Persians. Perhaps an even greater gift is the Olympic Games' enduring association with peace.[22] What I hope to have shown in this essay is that such Olympic ideals did not spring fully formed from the Alpheios river. Olympia began as a place of religious sacrifice and athletic contests arise there in response to a need to know the mind of god. By abdicating the selection of the victor to the rational parameters of the contest, the diverse Hellenes gathered at Olympia demonstrated awareness that their own social hierarchies and traditional beliefs were inadequate. By staging and open and fair competition, they pursued truth by means of an impartial test, and provided evidence for their conclusions, which served to negotiate

---

[21] Burkert, *Greek Religion*, p. 54.
[22] See "Olympic Sport and its Lessons for Peace" in this volume.

II. Ancient Olympic Philosophy

competing claims to supremacy among the diverse tribes gathered there.

This athletic solution to a problem of religious knowledge set the stage for the birth of philosophy and granted extraordinary prestige to athletic victors at the festival. And just as this more universal approach served to unite diverse worshippers at Olympia, the birth of science and philosophy might have united a diverse intellectual community. Today sport, religion, philosophy, and science seem to have little in common, but we should not neglect their historical connection because the need to find common ground among diverse peoples is as urgent as ever. Perhaps Pindar expressed this wisdom most eloquently; it is with these lines from *Nemean* 6 (1-9, trans. Lattimore) that I wish to conclude:

> There is one race of men, one race of gods;
> both have breath
> of life from a single mother.
> But sundered power
> holds us divided,
> so that the one is nothing,
> while for the other the brazen sky is established/their sure citadel forever.
> Yet we have some likeness in great/intelligence, or strength, to the immortals,
> though we know not what the day will bring, what course after nightfall
> destiny has written that we must run to the end.

6. From Aristocracy to Democracy at the Olympic Games[1]

Wreathed in myrtle, my sword I'll conceal
Like those champions devoted and brave,
When they plunged in the tyrant their steel
And to Athens deliverance gave.

-Edgar Allan Poe
Hymn to Harmodius and Aristogeiton

Introduction

"Do you believe in miracles? Yes!" These words marked one of the most storied upsets in Olympic history. In the midst of the Cold war, on the cold ice of Lake Placid, New York, just months before the boycott of Moscow's 1980 summer games, a motley collection of young United States hockey players defeated the heavily favored Soviet team. The event was hailed by some as a victory of democracy over tyranny. Politically, this conclusion is less than accurate; some might argue that the USSR was actually more democratic than the USA. But there is something about the athletic triumph of the underdog that calls forth the ancient spirit of democracy. The athletic contests staged at ancient Olympia and across Greece exhibited foundational ideas of democracy: freedom from tyranny, rule of law, human equality and public scrutiny. This conceptual connection between sport and democracy is insufficient to make claims about causation. But since the foundation of the Olympic Games predates democracy by more than 200 years, we may conjecture that sport helped to lay the foundations upon which democracy was eventually built.

Athleticism has been, since its earliest origins, associated with *aristeia*, being the best, and also with aristocracy, rule of the best. Egyptian and Mesopotamian athletes were almost always kings, and in Homer the games are for noble chieftains—the rank and file

---

[1] Originally published as "Boxing with Tyrants," in *Athletics and Philosophy in the Ancient World: Contests of Virtue* (Abingdon: Routledge, 2011) 32-42. Reprinted with permission.

are not included. Olympia, however, perhaps motivated by the religious mandate to find a legitimate *aristos*, seems to have cast a wider net in search of excellence. The first known Olympic victor (from 776 BCE) was said to be Koroibos of Elis; not a king but a cook, who nevertheless had the inaugural Olympiad named after him. An Olympiad is a four-year long block of time that was used by ancient historians and politicians to date particular events—it is not the sort of thing normally named after a commoner. Enduring doubts about the *aretē* of commoners has led even modern scholars to question whether Koroibos was in fact a noble priest who butchered and cooked sacrificial meat.[2]

There is no question that the ethos of ancient athletics was persistently aristocratic, even in democratic Athens. Referencing Aristotle's *Rhetoric* (2.1393b7), Mark Golden explains the Athenian mindset thus: "It might be appropriate to select magistrates by lot, but no one would pair athletes like that unless they had already established their ability."[3] Nevertheless, the Olympic and other Panhellenic games were open to any freeborn Greek. To be sure, the demands of training and travel made wealth a distinct advantage (as they do today); the mandatory 30-day training camp at Elis before the Olympic Games would be all but impossible for poor athletes. There is evidence, however, that financial obstacles were lowered by state and private sponsorship, and eventually a per-diem may have been paid to athletes during their stay at Elis. Given the immense value and prestige associated with Olympic victory, it should be no surprise to us that members of the lower classes sometimes entered the games and won. However, it probably was a surprise, at least at first, to cultures steeped in the tradition of hereditary aristocracy.

The great poet Pindar, author of numerous odes celebrating athletic victories, repeatedly attributes much of the glory to a

---

[2] On the social class of Olympic victors, see David Young, *The Olympic Myth of Greek Amateur Athletics* (New York: Ares, 1984), 89–176.

[3] Mark Golden, *Greek Sport and Social Status* (Austin: University of Texas Press, 2009), 26.

competitor's aristocratic and sometimes divine ancestry: "Natural talents are the best in every way," the poet sings in praise of the wrestling victor Epharmostos. "Many have taken lessons in prowess, / trying their utmost to achieve distinction; / but without a god's help every achievement / is best passed over in silence." (*Olympian* 9, 100–5). In all likelihood, Epharmostos' wrestling prowess was less a product of natural talent and divine favor, and more a result of dedicated training under the tutelage of a highly paid coach; something which wouldn't be mentioned in the ode precisely because it challenged the assumed effortlessness of aristocratic victory.[4] It is worth remembering, however, that Pindar wrote odes primarily for those who could afford to pay or at least lavishly entertain him, and those were the families most likely to have an aristocratic heritage. This explains why more odes for equestrian victories than gymnastic victories survive. But Pindar's association of athleticism with nobility, along with the notion that *aretē* passed through bloodlines, reflect widely held social beliefs rather than the poet's personal bias.

Philostratos claimed that it is simply 'human nature' to attribute more glory to an Olympic victor who repeats the feats of his ancestors, because people set a higher value on genetically inherited abilities (*Lives of the Sophists*, 611). It is probably because of such widespread beliefs that stories of apparently low-born champions stand out and endure in Olympic mythology—if not Pindaric poetry. One such tale concerns a boxer named Glaukos, the son of a common laborer, who was inspired to victory by his father's exhortation to 'remember the ploughshare' that he had supposedly repaired with his fist in the field.[5] Glaukos later

---

[4] As Nigel Nicholson, *Aristocracy and Athletics in Archaic and Classical Greece* (Cambridge: Cambridge University Press, 2005), 21, explains, "what motivated anxiety about professional trainers was that, by appearing to add new abilities such as skill to their pupils, they threatened the idea that the qualities on which victory depended were inherited."

[5] The story is told in Pausanias VI.10.1–3.

became the governor of his city,[6] but was he already a member of the landed nobility or did sport reveal a poor farm boy's potential for leadership? Answers to this question may vary according to a person's politics, but whether Glaukos was an aristocrat or not, his demonstration of *aretē* at Olympia seems inextricably linked to his later role as a leader. Stories like his reveal sport's ability to subvert established social hierarchies—an ability which likely contributed to the ideas that spawned democracy.

When contests designed to reveal *aristeia* select winners who are not among the aristocracy, it challenges presumptions about the link between social class and human excellence. Observers must conclude either that sport does not really demand *aretē*, or that *aristeia* can exist among members of the lower class. The reverence for and mythologizing about common-born Olympic victors suggests that many ancient Greeks chose the latter explanation—at least after the rise of democracy. Sports, especially boxing, remain an effective social ladder for the underprivileged today, even though modern athletes' skill is less often linked with virtue. Ancient boxing was associated with the noble god Apollo, but the pain tolerance, endurance and strength it demands simply are not qualities fostered by the pampered lifestyles of the privileged. Olympic boxers fought nude except for rawhide straps on their hands, there were no rounds or points, and the bout dragged on under the hot midday sun until someone signaled concession or was knocked out cold. The absence of weight classes favored bigger athletes, and for that reason it was counted among the so-called 'heavy' events. From a social perspective, however, boxing favors the 'little guy', and so it reflects the ideals of democracy.

Rule of Law

The natural enemy of democracy is not aristocracy, understood as the rule of the best, or even monarchy, understood as rule of the one, but rather the particular abuse of sovereign

---

[6] According to Kyle, *Sport and Spectacle,* 209.

power known as tyranny. Tyranny is characterized, above all, by lack of respect for law. Not only does the tyrant fancy himself to be above the law, he usually comes to power without the support of law, and lords over his subjects without respect for law.[7] As Euripides' Theseus says in *The Suppliants*, "There is nothing more hostile to a city than a tyrant. In the first place, there are no common laws in such a city, and one man, keeping the law in his own hands, holds sway. This is unjust" (428–535). Classical Athens lionized Harmodius and Aristogeiton, the "liberators" or "tyrannicides" who murdered the tyrant Hipparchus at the Panathenaic Games of 514 BCE.[8] Hipparchus had not so much broken the law as abused the privilege of his position in a way that offended Harmodius' family and disrespected the pair's freely-chosen partnership—a pairing which itself challenged social hierarchies since Harmodius was an aristocrat and Aristogeiton middle class. Their courageous act cost both of them their lives, but Aristogeiton's continued defiance of authority and refusal to reveal his co-conspirators, even under torture, seems to have cemented the pair's heroic stature in the eyes of democratic idealists. Hipparchus' brother Hippias was also overthrown, and the democratic reforms of Cleisthenes soon followed.

The later Athenian leader Pericles is famous for saying of his city, "we are called a democracy, for the administration is in the hands of the many and not of the few.'"[9] In a nutshell, democracy is government by the people, for the people and of the people. In ancient democracies that usually meant that all citizens were expected to participate in government, and administrative posts were frequently assigned by lot. More than the people, however, it is the law itself that acts as supreme 'ruler' in a democratic system,

---

[7] Paul Woodruff, *First Democracy*, (Oxford University Press, 2005), 64.
[8] The story is told, in slightly different versions, by Thucydides, *History of the Peloponnesian War* (VI.56–9), and Aristotle, *The Constitution of the Athenians*, XVIII.
[9] Pericles' Funeral Oration, in Thucydides, Peloponnesian War 2.2, Jowett translation.

since no individual or group can be held above it. Said Aeschines in praise of Athens: "In a democracy it is the laws that protect the individual and the *politeia*, whereas the tyrant and the oligarch are protected by mistrust and armed bodyguards." It is the general public's voluntary acceptance of and adherence to the laws of the state that makes democratic coexistence possible, and subjects each citizen equally to punishment under those laws. Aeschines continues: "Oligarchs, and those who run the unequal states, have to guard themselves against those who would overthrow the state by force; you who have an equal state based on the laws have to punish those who speak or have led their lives contrary to the laws."[10]

In sport, it is the rules that correspond to law, and without rules sport is not possible at all. Rules define the objective of the game as well as the acceptable means for achieving it. Even brutal combat sports such as boxing and *pankration* (an ancestor of today's ultimate fighting) are made up of rules. Philosophers of sport have repeatedly argued that it is logically incompatible to intentionally break rules and play a game at the same time. As in a democracy, the rules of sport should be publicly known and applied equally to all. It is the competitors' understanding of and voluntary subjection to contest rules that make a contest possible. In addition, the officials and ideally the spectators should be aware of the rules of the game. This common awareness creates a sense of collective responsibility for keeping everyone subject to the rules as the contest unfolds. If an umpire fails to call some transgression, he should expect the crowd to protest. Sport, like democracy, should produce a kind of collective authority.

Long before democracy emerged in ancient Greece, the Hellenes developed statute law, in which legal edicts were inscribed on wood or marble and displayed in public places so that

---

[10] Aeschines, *Against Timarchus* 1.4–5, quoted in Herman Mogens Hansen, *Polis: An Introduction to the Ancient Greek City State* (Oxford: Oxford University Press, 2006), 177.

every citizen might know his rights and obligations.[11] Likewise, the rules of ancient boxing were publicly established long before it became an Olympic sport in 688 BCE. We know, for example, that there was a ban on clinching, and vases show boxers who broke such rules being whipped on the spot by officials.[12] This kind of penalty carried psychological as well as physical pain, since flogging in public was something truly shameful, a punishment normally reserved for slaves. As Stephen Miller points out, the willingness of a free-born, possibly noble man to voluntarily subject himself to the rules of sport and risk being flogged in public if he transgressed them is a remarkable manifestation of the democratic spirit.[13] Today we often lament athletes' disrespect for the rules and scoff at the ineffectiveness of punishments meted out. The practice of fining multimillionaire sports stars for transgressions on the field and the acquittal on murder charges of American football player O.J. Simpson suggest that some athletes are above the rules and the law. But it is precisely the attention we pay to these phenomena that betrays our lingering democratic conviction that no one should be above the law, regardless of wealth, social class or athletic ability.

In democracy as in sport, the law is in essence the property of the citizens; something willingly accepted and communally imposed. To be sure, there are officials in charge of enforcing the rules or laws, but they are expected to serve the good of the whole and not the interests of a few. Democratic law is not a command from superiors, but rather it represents an agreement among citizens. The distinction can be seen in the evolution of Athenian dialect. The pre-democratic term for 'law' was *thesmos*, a word that implied something externally imposed by an agent occupying a position above and beyond the common man. The fifth-century term, *nomos*, by contrast, implied something "motivated less by the authority of the agent who imposed it than by the fact that it is

---

[11] Woodruff, *First Democracy*, 113.
[12] Poliakoff, *Combat Sports*, 80.
[13] Miller, *Ancient Greek Athletics*, 233.

II. Ancient Olympic Philosophy

regarded and accepted as valid by those who live under it."[14] This ideal of democratic law is ably illustrated by sport, where voluntary acceptance of the rules is essential for playing a game. Bernard Suits calls this the "lusory attitude" and marks it out as the principle that distinguishes the true player from a cheater, spoilsport or someone forced to perform some task by necessity.[15] This willing spirit is, in turn, essential to the sense of freedom associated with democracy and sport alike. Taking part in sport, like democracy, requires a community-based respect for the rules of the game. Breaking a rule or law, therefore, has the moral force of breaking a personal agreement.

This principle was illustrated in ancient sport by a boxing match at the Nemean Games that resulted in a posthumous victory.[16] Damoxenos of Syracuse and Kreugas of Epidamnos were still trading blows as evening drew near. In order to resolve the match, they agreed in front of witnesses to allow each other to land one undefended blow. Kreugas punched Damoxenos in the head, but did not knock him out. Then Damoxenos instructed Kreugas to lift his arm and expose his trunk, whereby the Syracusan held his fingers straight out and used his sharp nails to stab Kreugas under the ribs. He pulled out Kreugas' intestines and killed him on the spot. But the judges nevertheless awarded the victory to the dead man, arguing that Damoxenos' five-fingered blow constituted five punches instead of the agreed-upon one. Pausanias attributes the incident partly to the type of glove allowed at that time, but later Roman boxing gloves appear, if anything, more brutal.[17] The issue seems not to have been safety, or even the risk of death; the story of Damoxenos and Kreugas reinforces respect for the rule of law understood democratically as

---

[14] Ian Morris, "Equality and the origins of Greek Democracy," in *Ancient Greek Democracy*, ed. Eric W. Robinson (Malden, MA: Blackwell Publishing, 2004), 53.

[15] Suits, *Grasshopper*, 52–3.

[16] The story is recounted by Pausanias, *Description of Greece* 8.40.4–5

[17] Poliakoff, *Combat Sports*, 70–1.

an agreement among peers. The story seems to have enduring significance; larger-than-life Renaissance-era statues of Damoxenos and Kreugas still stand, among other Greek and Roman treasures, in the Vatican Museums today.

Equality

After liberty, which derives, as we have seen, from willing acceptance of the rule of law, democracy is most closely associated with the principle of human equality. Indeed Herodotus praises the rule of the many for having "the fairest of names," *isonomia*, which means equality before the law (*Histories*, 3.80–2). At first glance, the concept of equality may seem anathema to athletic contests, the purpose of which is to select one winner from many competitors. In neither democracy nor sport, however, does equality before the law preclude the recognition of excellence; rather it serves the principle of reward according to merit. As Pericles said of the Athenian democracy

> But while the law secures equal justice to all alike in their private disputes, the claim of excellence (*aretē*) is also recognized; and when a citizen is in any way distinguished he is preferred to the public service, not as a matter of privilege, but as the reward of merit. (Thucydides 2.37.1).

Democracy may entail a rejection of tyranny and a levelling-down of social classes, but it does not amount to the denial of individual excellence, virtue or *aristeia*. Hellenic democracy combined the principle of equality before the law (*isonomia*) with the principle of equal access or opportunity to participate (*isegoria*) to form a minimal idea of individual rights. Both *isonomia* and *isegoria* assume a theory of natural equality among human beings, which may seem familiar to us, but was quite unusual in the ancient world.

To be sure, this theoretical equality was both severely limited in scope and rarely reflected in reality. Almost always, in practice, the company of "equals" excluded women, slaves and foreigners. The Greeks' substantial innovation was simply levelling down the class distinction between rich and poor, noble and commoner.[18] Despite its limitations, this was a great achievement in its historical context; not least because it got people thinking about the possibilities of more widespread equality. Plato's trepidations about the equality of citizens and slaves (*Republic* 562e–563b) and Aristotle's vocal opposition to the idea of female leadership as "contrary to nature" (*Politics* 1254b) are significant not for the opinions they express, but rather because they reveal that such topics were considered worthy of discussion. The Olympic Games and other athletic festivals probably provided fodder for such discussions, despite their efforts to preserve an aristocratic aura. Sport seems inextricably linked with democratic ideals. It is worth noting that the frequency with which athletes are depicted in Attic vase painting rises and falls in synchronicity with the waxing and waning of democracy in Athens.[19]

More to the point, political and religious conditions at Olympia led to a logic of sport that favored egalitarianism. On the one hand, the religious context made differences among individual human beings insignificant in comparison with our collective inferiority to the gods. The gods were thought to respect piety—regardless of a person's wealth or social status—and they rewarded piety with favor, which could then lead to wealth and status.[20] On the other hand, using a foot race to select a single honored victor motivated rival communities to enter their best candidates regardless of social status. Some cities, such as Kroton, even seem to have recruited and trained athletes at public expense, obviating the need for personal wealth.[21] The real and perceived rewards of Olympic victory were simply too great for tribes

---

[18] Morris, "Equality," 63.
[19] Stephen G. Miller," Naked Democracy," in *Polis and Politics*, eds: P. Jensen, T. Nelson, and L. Rubenstein, (Copenhagen: Museum of Tusculanum Press, 2000), 284.
[20] Morris, "Equality," 61.
[21] Kroton's was apparently a successful strategy; their athletes won 11 of the 26 *stadion* crowns between 588 and 488 BCE, taking the top seven places at one Olympiad (Nicholson, *Aristocracy*, 128).

individually and Hellenes collectively to exclude any plausible winner. We might think of athletic contests as a kind of funnel that sorts through entrants at the wide end in order to spit out the best one at the narrow end. The funnel won't work if any potential best one is excluded from the wide end.

Even if we could put every human being into the wide end of our sporting funnel, however, accurate selection would still depend on a rational and fair process. The form of athletic selection used in ancient Greek boxing (and other heavy events) was the single elimination tournament. At the wide end of the funnel, entrants are paired by drawing lots. The two athletes who draw 'A' wrestle each other, B wrestles the other B and so on. Drawing lots was a process used to enforce impartial selections in ancient democracies, but at Olympia it was probably inspired by religious deference to divine preference; by using lots they were effectively letting the gods choose. After each round of matches, the victors advance, and are paired again until it comes down to two. The final victor will have defeated everyone either directly or by proxy. Judging controversies, so familiar in modern boxing, were avoided by granting victory only upon concession or knockout. In fact, none of the contests at Olympia was subjectively judged, again in deference to divine judgement and in esteem for the principle of equal opportunity. Even at the Panathenaia, where some competitions were adjudicated by a panel of ten judges, Stephen Miller notes that half of the ten votes were chosen by lot to reduce the potential influence of bribery or favoritism. He concludes: "This equality before absolute standards of distance and speed and strength—as measured by those of the other competitors present— that are subject to the interpretation of no man is basic *isonomia*."[22]

Advantages of Wealth

Pericles proudly claimed that poverty was no bar to achievement in Athenian democracy. "A man may benefit his country," he said, "whatever be the obscurity of his position"

---

[22] Miller "Naked Democracy," 279.

(Thucydides 2.37.2). Likewise, in the idealized logic of sport, poverty is no bar to achievement because contests are judged by impartial standards. The most visible manifestation of this ideal in ancient sport was athletic nudity, which stripped competitors of the sartorial symbols of their relative wealth and social status. Says Miller: "Once clothes are stripped off the human figure, it is difficult to distinguish the rich from the poor, the smart from the dumb, the aristocrat from the king or the democrat."[23] Of course physical health and stature were also taken as evidence of aristocracy; so athletic nudity didn't automatically challenge the aristocratic ethos of the games. In fact, the theory of athletic equality quickly clashed with the realities of wealth and privilege, as it does today. The religious and political realities of Olympic-style sport threatened to subvert the social hierarchy, but also gave the wealthy a means to defend their turf. As Nigel Nicholson explains, "Athletics offered the aristocrats an arena in which they could attempt to demonstrate that they possessed certain superior qualities by virtue of their birth (qualities that made them better rulers as well as better athletes) [which] were inherited and not freely available."[24]

Money can't buy *aretē*, but it can buy some things that help with athletic victory. The emergence of athletic trainers, equestrian events and eventually professional jockeys and charioteers reveal the aristocracy's attempt to justify their privilege through sport, even as sport simultaneously undermined it. The result of this internal class struggle was that athletics involved both rich and poor, reflecting the inclusivity of democracy itself. As we noted earlier, the particular virtues demanded by the heavy events of boxing, wrestling, and pankration are perhaps better cultivated in the harsher lives of the underprivileged. But nearly all of the *gymnic* (nude) events, running and pentathlon included, could be practiced without much money. Private coaches and pristine training facilities, as well as access to good nutrition and medicine,

---

[23] Miller "Naked Democracy," 283.
[24] Nicholson, *Aristocracy and Athletics*, 48.

were advantages that could be, and frequently were, bought.[25] It was not until the sixth century BCE that public gymnasia became widely available, and even then private gyms with highly-paid trainers provided a competitive edge.[26] Of course, the use of coaches and trainers challenged the aristocratic idea that athletic ability was inborn; they are therefore rarely mentioned in the odes and inscriptions that celebrate victory.[27]

Even more important than coaching and facilities was liberation from hard physical labor and the time off to train and travel to events. Competitors at the Olympic Games swore an oath that they had trained faithfully for at least ten months and were required to spend the month before the games at Elis training under the supervision of special judges. Few who worked daily for a living could make such a commitment to sport. Nevertheless, the religious and political value of victory was so great that efforts were made to overcome financial burdens, at least for promising athletes. Some cities, as we observed before, used public funds to sponsor and develop athletes. There is also evidence of private investment. Mark Golden relates the case from about 300 BCE of Athenodorus, a young resident of Ephesus in Asia Minor, who earned citizen status after winning the boxing event for boys at the Nemean Games. Afterwards his coach approached the council of Ephesus seeking the same privilege for two men who had supported the young boxer financially.[28] The process is reminiscent of modern agents and universities who recruit and support young athletes hoping to reap their own benefits down the road.

---

[25] Even today, wealthier and more technologically-advanced countries try to use those advantages in Olympic competition. See "Athlete Agency and the Spirit of Olympic Sport," in this volume.

[26] Golden, *Sport and Society in Ancient Greece*, 144.

[27] For a full account see Nicholson, *Aristocracy and Athletics*. The enduring effects of this belief are reflected in the stigma attached to coaching by the aristocratic culture surrounding the early modern Olympic Games, as shown in the movie *Chariots of Fire*.

[28] Golden, *Greek Sport and Social Status*, 25.

One thing that private sponsors and even public subsidies have a hard time buying, however, is a top-flight racehorse breeding program. Equestrian events, added to the program at Olympia in 680 BCE and featured prominently in many other ancient festivals, remained almost exclusively the province of the wealthy. In fact, they were probably added specifically to allow ageing aristocrats to compete.[29] The flamboyant Athenian Alcibiades brags about entering seven teams of horses, more than any other private citizen in history, at the Olympic Games of 416 BCE; they finished first, second, and fourth (Thucydides 6.16.2). His son recalled later that Alcibiades

> had thought these things through and, though in no way untalented nor weak of body, he held the gymnic games in contempt since he knew that some of the athletes were lowborn and from small city-states and poorly educated. Therefore he tried his hand at horse breeding, work of the uppermost crust and not possible for a poor man (Isocrates, *De Bigisi* 33).

It should not be concluded from this passage that Alcibiades was simply a snob; his efforts were part of a rivalry with Sicilian tyrants known for their lavish expenditure on horses.[30] And within the economy of religious sacrifice, his expenditure would have been seen as a generous dedication that also benefited the community.

Spending money to please the gods was an expression of the virtue Aristotle called magnificence (*megaloprepeia*) because it attracted divine favor not just for the individual, but also the common good (*Nicomachean Ethics* 1122b19–1123a). Aristocrats were motivated to sponsor race horses for reasons similar to those that motivate major corporations to sponsor charity events today: it allows them to play the role of generous patrons, building goodwill within a community even while they reinforce their elevated position within it. It is for these reasons that the victory

---

[29] Nicholson, *Aristocracy and Athletics*, 6
[30] Kyle, *Sport and Spectacle*, 214

crown in equestrian events was awarded not to the horse, rider or driver, but rather to the owner who had financed the display. If the owner had ridden or driven the horses himself, that fact was clearly noted on the memorial; if instead a professional horseman was used, his name was intentionally excluded, leaving the glory to the person who had paid the bills.[31]

Despite the religious and political explanations, it grates on our sense of athletic merit to think of owners rather than competitors receiving the victors' spoils. Indeed the only ever female victory at the ancient Olympic Games may have been a ploy to express the same skepticism. Probably because of Olympia's earlier association with Heracles, women were allowed neither to compete nor to attend the sacred Olympic festival,[32] but the Spartan princess Kyniska won as an absentee horse owner and erected a statue of herself in Olympia's Altis. Some see Kyniska as a symbol of women's liberation, but ancient commentators Xenophon and Plutarch interpreted her achievement rather as a statement that Olympic victory (at least in the horse races) was a matter of wealth rather than *aretē* or merit,[33] which females were presumed not to have. It is telling here how Kyniska's sex is set against her high birth in the effort to discredit the implications of the contest and perpetuate social presumptions. We have yet to see day when such presumptions are finally absent from sport.

As time went on, the advantages of wealth were mitigated in the ancient world by the rise of what can only be called a professional class of athletes. Lucrative prizes were offered at a variety of chrematic (money) games. Athens's Panathenaia awarded as prizes amphorae of olive oil valued in the hundreds of thousands of dollars, several examples of which still survive

---

[31] Nicholson, *Aristocracy and Athletics*, 40

[32] According to Mouratidis, "Herakles at Olympia," 55, women were not allowed to enter the sanctuaries of Heracles which explains their exclusion from Olympia. They did attend and eventually compete in other Panhellenic games.

[33] Xenophon, *Agesilaus* 9.6, Plutarch, *Ages* 20.1, both quoted in Kyle, *Sport and Spectacle* 191.

today.³⁴ Athens also offered free meals for life to any citizen victorious at Olympia. Socrates, as we know, deemed himself more worthy of that honor since his public service was more valuable than that of wealthy horse owners (Plato, *Apology* 36d). This allusion to public service should remind us, however, that the economy of ancient athletics was based on sacrifice and not ticket sales. Wealth was an advantage in ancient sport, as it is in modern sport, and in democratic societies. But then, as now, the democratic nature of sport logic opened up an avenue to glory and social advancement also accessible for the poor and working classes.

Public Scrutiny

Socrates' devaluation of Olympic sports appears not to extend to the gymnic events; after all he spent most of his days in Athens' public gymnasia—expecting to find *aretē* there. Indeed Socrates thought that all Greek-speaking persons, including slaves, were capable of finding answers for themselves, potentially achieving wisdom and therefore *aretē*.³⁵ In short, he recognized the universality of human reason, which is a foundation for democracy because it implies common people's ability to govern themselves.³⁶ From self-governance it is a small step to community government, and since every member of a democracy is bound by the group's decisions, it is only fitting that every citizen participates in the making of those decisions. "There is no exclusiveness," Pericles says of Athens' democracy; "in our private intercourse we are not suspicious of one another, nor angry with our neighbor if he does what he likes." This liberty characteristic of democracy, Pericles concludes, depends upon respect for

---

³⁴ Young, *Olympic Myth*, 99

³⁵ In Plato's *Meno* Socrates helps a slave boy find a geometric theorem.

³⁶ Unlike Socrates and Plato, most Greeks believed that women were irrational, and this is why they were excluded from government, which further proves the link between rationality and democracy. See M. Jameson, "Women and Democracy in Fourth-century Athens," in *Ancient Greek Democracy: Readings and Sources,* ed. E. Robinson (Malden, MA: Blackwell Publishing, 2004), 286.

authority and law, as well as fear of public reprobation (Thucydides 2.37.2). Paradoxically, democratic freedom depends on obedience to the laws and public scrutiny.

So too in sport, the rules of a game such as soccer do not dictate in detail how a goal is to be achieved, rather they set up a framework within which players have liberty to dribble, pass and shoot as they please. Ancient boxing styles, likewise, were notoriously diverse. Diagoras of Rhodes, winner of an Olympic crown among dozens of other championships, was known for his speed, agility and endurance; he allegedly won some bouts simply by exhausting his opponents with footwork, never once needing to land a blow. He was also known for his nobility and respect for the rules (Pindar, *Olympian* 7 90-3). Skill and intelligence were a prized way to box, but it was recognized that brute strength could also win the match. The mythical boxer Polydeukes was known for simply standing his ground and whaling away with both fists (Apollonius of Rhodes, *Argonautia* 2.90–2). Democratic debate, like sport, is open and adversarial: a public contest that assumes an audience informed enough to understand which idea deserves to win.

Democracy, like Olympic sport, cannot afford to exclude potential winners from its contests. In this way it should accommodate diversity and promote tolerance of differences as a precondition to finding the best answers. Paradoxically again, it promotes competitive conflict in order to achieve peace and harmony. Because everyone has access to the debate, either through participation or observation, everyone can scrutinize the process and the results. In contrast to secret proceedings, such as the mysterious Vatican process for selecting a new pope, democracy and sport make their decisions under the watchful eye of an interested public. As a matter of fact, the spectators of ancient boxing contests actually delineated the ring; in case the boxers refused to engage one another, referees kept them close by using poles or ladders to fence them in.[37] Partisanship is common in

---

[37] Poliakoff, *Combat Sports*, 79.

democracy just as it is in sport. In Olympic Games ancient and modern, the states of competing athletes might even be at war. But the rule-governed competition witnessed by all seems to promote peace rather than war. It was not just the truce that connected the Olympic Games with peace, it was the effects of publicly scrutinized competitive sport itself.[38]

Conclusion

The victory of an underdog is among the most cherished traditions in sport, one that hearkens back to Ancient Greece, birthplace of both democracy and the Olympic Games. The athletic contests staged at ancient Olympia and across archaic Greece exhibited the foundational ideas of democracy: freedom from tyranny, rule of law, human equality and public scrutiny of process. This conceptual connection between sport and democracy is insufficient to make historical claims about causation. But since the traditional foundation of the Olympic Games predates that of democracy by more than 200 years, we may conjecture that sport helped to lay the foundations upon which democracy was eventually built. Athletics remained largely the preserve of the aristocracy, but their dependence on professional trainers and horsemen revealed the precariousness of their privilege, even as they tried to use sport to defend it. Stories from the ancient games and ideas from ancient political philosophy reveal an important connection between sport and democracy in Ancient Greece. By appreciating that connection we may preserve and promote in our own time sport's ability to change ideas about the relationship between virtue and social class.

---

[38] See Reid, "Olympic Sport and its Lessons for Peace" in this volume.

7. Olympic Sacrifice:
A Modern Look at Ancient Tradition[1]

The inspiration for this paper came rather unexpectedly. In February 2006, I made the long trip from my home in Sioux City, Iowa, to Torino, Italy in order to witness the Olympic Winter Games. Barely a month later, I found myself in California at the newly-renovated Getty Villa, home to one of the world's great collections of Greco-Roman antiquities. At the Villa I attended a talk about a Roman mosaic depicting a boxing scene from Vergil's *Aeneid*. The tiny tiles showed not only two boxers, but a wobbly looking ox. 'What is wrong with this ox?' asked the docent. 'Why is he there at the match?' The answer, of course, is that he is the prize. And the reason he is wobbly is because the victor has just sacrificed this prize to the gods in thanksgiving, by punching him between the eyes. A light went on in my head; I turned to my husband and whispered, "Just like Joey Cheek in Torino." My husband smiled indulgently, but my mind was already racing. I realized that by donating his victory bonus to charity, Cheek had tapped into one of the oldest and most venerable traditions in sport: individual sacrifice for the benefit of the larger community. It is a tradition that derives from the religious function of the ancient Olympics and deserves to be revived today.

Introduction

Modern sport often evokes its ancient Hellenic heritage. The educational link between sport and character, the sociological link between sport and justice, and the political link between sport and peace all derive from the ideals and practice of athletics in ancient Greece. The modern Olympic festival conceives of itself as a revival of the ancient Olympic Games and it embraces their history and mythology insofar as they support its mission. One problematic and often overlooked aspect of the Hellenic legacy,

---

[1] Originally published in the *Philosophy: Royal Institute of Philosophy Supplement* 73 (2013) 1-13. © Cambridge University Press. Reprinted with permission. All rights reserved.

however, is the religious character of ancient sport. Whereas common religious belief was foundational to and instrumental in the millennium-long success of the ancient Olympic Games, the modern challenge of uniting a religiously diverse world community has pushed the religious legacy to the sidelines. Given the evidence that religious hegemony was responsible for the demolition of the ancient Olympic Games (they are believed to have been abolished as a pagan festival by the Christian emperor Theodosius), modern attempts to dissociate the Games from religion are certainly understandable. But in jettisoning the Olympics' religious heritage, have we thrown out the proverbial baby with its bathwater? I believe that we may have. The modern Olympic Movement is allowing a commercial paradigm to usurp its higher purpose. In order to ennoble itself, the Olympic Games should focus on humanitarian goals, thereby reclaiming the connection between Olympic sport and community service.

The Ancient Heritage

The connection may not be so distant as it first seems. Even in today's cynical and commercially-driven world of sport-entertainment, athletic champions are often lauded for their 'sacrifice.' Commonly, the word evokes the sweat and toil of training combined with the semi-monastic life supposedly led by athletes. In almost any other endeavor, the effort and lifestyle required would be termed 'professionalism,' or perhaps simply 'hard work.' Why in athletics do we call it 'sacrifice'? The obvious answer is an ancient one. Most sport in Greco-Roman antiquity was a form of religious sacrifice. Athletic performance at such festivals was considered an offering to the gods, offered as a service to the community. Extravagant rewards certainly *were* showered upon ancient Olympic athletes,[2] but the religious context of the Games reveals that such rewards were motivated by

---

[2] Young, *Olympic Myth*, debunks the idea that ancient athletes were amateurs. But even if financial rewards could athletics a lucrative career for some, we should not assume that the reasons they were paid are the same as the reasons athletes are compensated today.

perceived community benefits rather than commercial economy. The primary function of the ancient festival was not entertainment or advertising, but the collective garnering of divine favor in hope of concrete community benefits such as plentiful harvests, release from disease, or victory in war. Ancient athletes, in the religious context of the games, should be seen as community servants.

Let me illustrate my explanation with the example I mentioned earlier. Book five of Vergil's ancient Roman epic, *The Aeneid*, describes contests in rowing, running, archery, and boxing. Although the text was written in the last century before the Common Era and the games themselves are supposed to be set in the Bronze Age of Troy, modern sports fans would recognize something familiar in the boxing match. A cocky young Trojan named Dares taunts his would-be challengers by asking permission to take the prize without a contest. Reluctantly, a more experienced local Sicilian named Entellus deigns to fight the Trojan, despite misgivings about his advancing age. The match is a classic duel between the larger, slower, but wiser Entellus, and the younger, quicker, more eager Dares. The nimble Trojan dodges one of Entellus' mighty blows, and the heavier man falls to the ground under his own weight. He returns, however, with a vengeance and rains down such a fury of blows on his opponent that the fight must be stopped to save young Dares' life. Entellus is awarded the prize of an ox, and it is at this point that the narrative takes an unfamiliar turn for modern readers. The mighty boxer strikes the animal flush between the horns, 'bursting the brains out', and the ox falls lifelessly to the ground (V.480).

To make sense of Entellus' gesture, we must first understand the religious purpose of ancient Greek sport and, most specifically, the social function of sacrifice. The ancient Olympic Games are believed to have originated sometime around the 8th century BCE, not far from the time that Homer wrote about the Trojan War. Many scholars believe that the games depicted in Homer's *Iliad* depict the athletic contests of his own age, rather than those of the Bronze Age Mycenaeans. By the time Vergil writes his 'sequel' to Homer's epics (almost 700 years later), sport was major force in

II. Ancient Olympic Philosophy

Greco-Roman culture. Although both authors depict funeral or festival rather than Olympic Games, the religious association is undeniable. The gods Athena and Apollo actively involve themselves in Homer's games, and when Vergil's Entellus kills the ox, he follows it up with a prayer, describing the animal as payment for this victory and for his successful career.[3] The animal sacrifice is at once recompense to the gods and to the community that has supported him.

Greek athletics, perhaps in origin but certainly in their Olympic manifestation, were a form of religious sacrifice.[4] Long before 776 BCE, Olympia had been a holy place reserved for religious rites and gatherings. The purpose of such sanctuaries and festivals was to mark off a place dedicated to the god, and then to offer gifts to him or her, either in gratitude for fortune gained or in the hope of good fortune to come. Ancient Greeks believed that gods controlled things that they couldn't; things like health, fertility, weather, even love. The relationship between human and divine in this realm was seen as one of exchange.[5] I pray that my ships or army are successful, offering some portion of the benefits if they are. These items (usually a tithe of the booty collected) are left in the sanctuary as payment on my vow, and they become the property of the god.[6] During a typical animal sacrifice, one or more prize bulls or lambs is stunned, killed, and butchered on the spot. The thighbones are burnt on the altar along with some fat, the savory smoke a way of attracting the sky-dwelling god to the sanctuary to hear worshippers' prayers. The rest of the meat is roasted and fed to the worshippers in a public banquet.[7]

Somewhere along the line a footrace was added to sacrificial ritual at Olympia.[8] Part of its purpose may have been to entertain

---

[3] Vergil, *Aeneid*, note 3, V.482.
[4] Sansone, *Greek Athletics*, 40.
[5] Mikalson, *Ancient Greek Religion*, 25.
[6] Burkert, *Greek Religion*, 68.
[7] Burkert, *Greek Religion*, 56-7.
[8] It is clear from archaeological evidence that cult preceded athletic activities at Olympia. Mallawitz, "Cult and Competition," 79-109.

worshippers while the meat was butchered and cooked,[9] but it is easy to interpret the race itself as a kind of sacrifice—another way of attracting the god's attention and favor. The 'track' was originally located within the sacred area and the race was run in a straight line from the far end of the grounds toward the altar upon which the offerings would be made.[10] The Olympic winner (then, as now) did not receive a prize, but in a way, became himself a prize for the god. The tokens of victory: a palm branch, olive wreath, and ribbons tied around his head and limbs, are all associated with sacrificial animals and priests.[11] Given the gods' involvement in the outcome of Homer's funeral games, one may even interpret the Olympic race as a chance for the god to select the victor; to pick the symbolic sacrifice that pleases him most.

Accurate selection of a pleasing sacrifice was essential since so much was thought to be riding on the favor of the gods. This created a persistent epistemological problem in Greek religion; one important enough to be addressed directly in Plato's dialogue *Euthyphro*. It may be that Olympic-style sport, designed to select single winners from varied pools of contestants, was developed at least partly as a response to this problem.[12] In any case, the victor's status as a symbolic sacrificial offering is vividly evidenced by his being given the honor of lighting the sacrificial flame.[13] Remembering that the purpose of the smoke is to attract the attention of the god, we might speculate that the Games themselves did the same—not just by the skill and prowess displayed, but also by drawing large numbers of pilgrims to the festival. The better the show and the larger the crowd the more

---

[9] Mikalson, *Ancient Greek Religion*, 28.
[10] Valvanis, *Games and Sanctuaries*, 15, 50.
[11] Burkert, *Greek Religion*, 56.
[12] This is the thesis of Heather L Reid, 'Olympic Epistemology: The Athletic Roots of Philosophical Reasoning', *Skepsis* 17:1-2 (2007), 124-132. See also "Running toward Truth in Ancient Olympia," in this volume.
[13] Panos Valavanis, *Games and Sanctuaries in Ancient Greece,* translated by David Hardy (Los Angeles: Getty Publications, 2004), 15.

likely the deity was to turn his or her attention to the festival and therefore to the prayers of the worshipping community. The quantity and value of votive offerings housed at Olympia was renowned in the ancient world and stood as tangible evidence of the festival's practical success. Prayers made to Zeus in association with the Games were apparently being answered, so it makes sense that several other religious festivals followed Olympia's example and added contests of various kinds.

Interpreted in the context of ancient religious sacrifice, then, the athlete's Olympic success not only brings glory to himself and to his family, it also benefits the entire community by attracting the gods' attention to their prayers and bringing concrete goods such as successful harvests and release from disease. The most immediate and tangible example of practical community benefit from worship was, of course, the banquet of meat from the sacrificed animals. In a world without freezers such meat-based meals were rare, and much care was taken in the proper butchering and apportioning of the meat.[14] In addition there were important psychological benefits to witnessing the athlete's success. Since athletic victory was believed to come from a combination of toil (*ponos*), sweat, and divine favor, it inspired onlookers to forge ahead with their day-to-day struggles, called '*agōnes*' just like the Games themselves. Further, the gathering of diverse (and sometimes warring) peoples on neutral ground to worship a common deity had a bonding effect.[15] It unified and pacified the group, building community ties symbolized in the ritual of sharing a common meal at the conclusion of the festival.[16]

So Entellus' killing of the victory ox, in its socio-temporal context, is not a senseless act of violence. Instead, it should be viewed as a religious sacrifice that expresses a venerable athletic tradition. The victorious individual offers his earned glory back to

---

[14] H.W. Parke, *Festivals of the Athenians* (Ithaca: Cornell University. Press, 1977), 48.
[15] Burkert, *Greek Religion*, 54.
[16] See "Olympic Sport and its Lessons for Peace," in this volume.

his community, inspiring their hearts, filling their stomachs, and strengthening their bonds: he is an honored and honorable community servant.

A Modern Misunderstanding

The modern revivers of the Olympic festival were clearly aware of its religious heritage. As John MacAloon puts it, Pierre de Coubertin 'continuously and unambiguously regarded [Olympism] as a religious phenomenon'.[17] But Coubertin did not seek to revive the religious *function* of the Olympic Games—a function I characterize above as community service. Rather, he sought to make athletics themselves a kind of religion, a concept he called *religio athletae.* Coubertin described his vision thus:

> The primary, fundamental characteristic of ancient Olympism, and of modern Olympism as well, is that it is a *religion.* By chiseling his body through exercise as a sculptor does a statue, the ancient athlete 'honored the gods.' In doing likewise, the modern athlete honors his country, his race, and his flag. Therefore I believe I was right to restore, from the very beginning of modern Olympism, a religious sentiment transformed and expanded by the internationalism and democracy that are distinguishing features of our day. Yet this is the same religious sentiment that led the young Hellenes, eager for the victory of their muscles, to the foot of the altars of Zeus.[18]

Undeniably, Olympic symbols, rituals, and ceremonies give the modern Games a religious aura. But the ancient religious function of the games (i.e. to benefit the community) seems to have been

---

[17] J. MacAloon, "Religious Themes and Structures in the Olympic Movement and the Olympic Games," *Philosophy, Theology and History of Sport and Physical Activity,* eds. F. Landray and W. Orban (Quebec: Symposia Specialists, 1978), 161.

[18] Pierre de Coubertin, *Olympism: Selected Writings,* ed. Norbert Muller (Lausanne: International Olympic Committee, 2000), 580.

lost. In fact, the Olympic symbols have come to be regarded as the source of the Games' commercial rather than spiritual power. The Olympic rings are one of the most widely recognized brand logos in the world and the source of a large portion of the movement's revenue.[19] Has the sport's religious heritage been perverted into crass commercialism?

I think there is at minimum the risk that it has and I think that the culprit, paradoxically, may be 'amateurism.' It was Avery Brundage, a most zealous adherent of the amateur concept, who reluctantly presided over the influx of revenues from sponsorship and television into the Olympic movement. Brundage's commitment to amateurism supposedly derived from a desire to preserve the ancient 'purity' of sport – to keep 'sport for sport's sake' and prevent it from becoming a medium for personal promotion or commercial gain.[20] Twisted interpretations of the ancient Olympic Games (for example, as the exclusive province of wealthy elites) were trotted out to support this autotelic athletic illusion, but it was all for the benefit of the benefactors. Amateurism was, as Olympic scholar David Young puts it, 'the ideological means to justify an elitist athletic system that sought to bar the working class from competition.'[21] The early IOC culture was one of modern aristocrats—people who did not work day to day in order to earn their bread, and who often regarded with derision those who did.[22] The 'purity of sport' really meant the purity of the athletes in terms of breeding, class, and often race. Native American champion Jim Thorpe had his medals stripped,

---

[19] R. Barney, S. Wenn, and S. Martyn, *Selling the Five Rings: The International Olympic Committee and the Rise of Olympic Commercialism* (Salt Lake: University of Utah Press, 2004) xii.

[20] Avery Brundage, quoted in David C Young, "How the Amateurs Won the Olympics," in *The Archaeology of the Olympics*, ed. W. Raschke. (Madison: University of Wisconsin Press, 1988), 72. For more on Brundage's resistance to Olympic commercialism, see Barney et. al., *Selling the Five Rings*, especially chapter 4.

[21] Young, "How Amateurs Won," 56.

[22] See, for example, Young, "How Amateurs Won," 56-66.

ostensibly for having accepted money to play baseball, but many say he was singled out for punishment because of his race and class.[23] Most of us lucky enough to have jobs we love do not regard our salaries as a force of corruption. We might even do the work for free, if we were independently wealthy. It is part of who we are; our profession. Olympic amateurism amounted to exclusion based on nobility of class, not nobility of motivation.

Ancient athletes never were amateurs in the modern sense. Lucrative prizes were awarded at countless regional festivals, and Olympic victors were routinely granted immense public honors, including tax exemptions, choice seating at public events, and free meals for life in the municipal dining facilities. Evidence for such rewards can be found in no-less famous a text than Plato's *Apology of Socrates.* Unfortunately, pleasant fantasies about ancient aristocracies kept people like Brundage from asking the crucial question of why such rewards were offered to ancient athletes and what does it mean for modern Olympic sport? The answer to this question in the context of ancient religion is hardly a mystery, however. Athletic victors provided a valuable, community service by attracting the favor of the gods. In fact, it is precisely in this context that Socrates says he deserves the rewards given to Olympic victors for his own community service to Athens. He points out that the Olympian victor only makes the citizens think they are better off, whereas his philosophical questioning truly improves them (Plato, *Apology*, 36de). Socrates' skepticism about religious traditions (he was convicted of atheism) is the exception that proves the rule that Olympic victors were valued and rewarded as community servants.

Furthermore, Socrates did not advocate the abandonment of religion (he claimed his own service was motivated by the god), rather he sought a more functional and rational approach. Some say that Socrates' death was itself a sacrifice for the good of rational humanity. Unfortunately for the Olympics, when the IOC

---

[23] For example, Rodolfo Cremer, 'Professionalism and its Implications for the Olympic Movement', *Olympic Review* 26:14 (1997), 23-24.

II. Ancient Olympic Philosophy

abandoned the religious function of sport, it lost the venerable tradition of sacrifice. Prompted by their obsession with amateurism to view sport as an exclusive club, the Olympic Games ceased to look beyond sport for meaning. *Religio-athletae* made a religion of sport and when television money started flowing into the IOC, it was decided that those funds should be 'devoted to the future of amateur sport.'[24]

While there is no doubt that the modern Olympic Movement was and is justified in securing its own financial survival, I contend that it should, like Socrates, have adopted a rational and functional approach to its religious heritage by committing itself to a humanitarian cause. The ideals declared in the Fundamental Principles of the *Olympic Charter*, should be imagined and supported in concrete ways by the movement. Just as the ancients imagined that athletic victory would bring food, medicine, and conflict resolution to the Panhellenic community, we moderns should direct athletic profits toward providing food, medicine, and conflict resolution to our own world community.

Instead of this historically-sanctioned humanitarian turn, however, the movement experienced what Barney, Wenn, and Martyn call "a philosophical shift," and under Brundage's successors, the IOC was transformed into a corporate entity with a commercial identity. Critics decry the commercialism of the games, but is it anathema from an ancient point of view? As a religious festival, the ancient Games were not a "for-profit" operation. In fact, commercial activity—including the selling of food and drinks—was generally not allowed within ancient Hellenic religious sanctuaries or gymnasia. On the other hand, there were all kinds of vendors outside the *Altis* at Olympia selling all kinds of goods and services from the religious to the decidedly unreligious. It seems to me that the real concern about commercialism in the Olympics is not so much that they sell Coca Cola, but rather that their *purpose* should be reduced to selling

---

[24] David Lord Burghley, member of the IOC executive board, quoted in Barney et. al., *Selling the Five Rings*, 59.

Coca Cola.[25] There certainly is a cultural paradigm under which modern sport is seen as nothing more than a television commodity and athletes view themselves as professional entertainers—have the Olympic Games become absorbed into this paradigm?

For their own sake, I hope not. Anything more than a superficial understanding of the economics of the modern Olympic Games will reveal that the source of their fiscal viability just is the complex of heritage, ideals, and higher purpose that "over commercialization" seems to threaten. According to economist Holger Preuss, the Olympic aura, nourished by Olympic ideals, creates what he calls a "globally valid ideology." Preuss identifies this unique Olympic ideology as "the basis for the power, the financial resources and the lasting existence of the IOC."[26] In short, if the Olympics abandon their ideology and reduce themselves to a commercial entertainment product, they will no longer be viable as a commercial entertainment product.[27] By making a concrete commitment to humanitarian service, the Olympic movement, and sport more generally, can better embody its ideals, respect its ancient heritage, and ensure its long-term financial health. Some athletes have already taken the lead.

Reviving a Heritage of Service

The enduring and inspiring connection among Olympic sport, sacrifice, and service survives in a story that moves among Sicily,

---

[25] Supporters of the Olympic idea must recognize that the staging of the Games requires revenue that can either from public or from private sources. Of these, the private sources are certainly preferable since sponsorship is voluntary and taxation involuntary. What is to be resisted is not the financial support of corporate sponsors and the entertainment industry, but rather the *reduction* of the Games to a commercial entertainment product.

[26] Holger Preuss, *Economics of the Olympic Games* (Petersham, NSW: Walla Walla Press, 2000) 248.

[27] Many in the Olympic movement apparently recognize this fact; Preuss, *Economics of the Olympic Games,* 257, characterizes the IOC as "effectively fighting the issue" of over-commercialization.

II. Ancient Olympic Philosophy

Olympia, Athens, and Torino, between the 12th BCE and February, 2006. Let us return for a moment to the *Aeneid's* scene of Entellus sacrificing his prize bull. Strange as it may seem at first glance, this act might be taken to symbolize an enduring ideal for both the social role of athletes and the social value of sport. To discover how, we may compare Entellus' act to another athlete's post-victory gesture at the 2006 Winter Olympic Games in Torino, Italy. After winning the gold medal in the 500 meter sprint, American speed skater Joey Cheek announced in the inevitable post-race interviews that he would be donating his $25,000 United States Olympic Committee victory bonus to Right to Play, "an athlete-driven international humanitarian organization that uses sport and play as a tool for the development of children and youth in the most disadvantaged areas of the world."[28] Cheek's gesture not only highlighted his inspiring personal integrity, it presented a welcome image of American generosity and compassion at time when their international reputation was more commonly associated with military belligerence and blind economic self-interest. Furthermore, Cheek's action gave his bitterly divided country something to agree about; it was an image of American virtue that everyone could rally around.

Understood simply and within the relevant temporal and cultural contexts, the connection between Entellus' ritual sacrifice and Joey Cheek's Olympic gesture becomes clear. In the tradition of religious, athletic, and specifically Olympic sacrifice, Cheek's donation provided personal inspiration, practical benefit, and a unifying spirit to the wider community. Indeed a second medal brought another $15,000 bonus, which Cheek also donated, this time challenging other athletes and sponsors to follow suit. The result was over $300,000 US earmarked to help refugee children in Chad and the Darfur region of Sudan. Said Cheek, "I am thrilled that so many people watched my race and cheered for my teammates and me, but it means much more to be able to help

---

[28] Right to Play. "Right to Play at a Glance," *Right to Play.com*, 2006.

someone else."[29] Both Entellus and Cheek may be seen as heroes who put their athletic prowess in the service of their communities.

Joey Cheek is hardly the first modern athlete to sacrifice his spoils to a cause beyond himself. At Athens 2004, swimmer Otylia Jedrzejczak won Poland's first swimming gold then auctioned her medal to raise $80,000 for a children's hospital near her hometown. Jedrzejczak's story is quite explicitly one of religious-athletic sacrifice. After reading a book about a boy suffering from leukemia, she says she "made a promise to god" that if she won the gold medal in Athens it would be dedicated to help children suffering from leukemia. Just like an ancient athlete, she prayed for victory, won, and then paid her 'votive' as promised. It may even be the case that knowing their victories could help others gives some athletes that winning edge.[30] Professional athletes everywhere set up charitable foundations to support causes close to their hearts. America's National Football League has made a major public commitment to the United Way charity. Whether interpreted as divine intervention or simple motivation, the most sporting of all athletic advantages must be the athlete's awareness of his or her social responsibility.

Athletes who put sport in the service of their communities effect in our modern world the benefits of ancient athletic sacrifice. The first benefit is psychological: inspiration. Not only were Cheek, Jedrzejczak, and others inspired by the opportunity to do some good in the world, their athletic success in turn provides inspiration to people engaged in a variety of struggles. The second benefit of sacrifice is more tangible. Like the roasted meat from the sacrificial animal, the money raised by athletes provides for the basic needs of people everywhere. Food and medicine, as well as the space and facilities to play are of immediate benefit, especially to children in refugee camps. Finally, athletic sacrifice provides for

---

[29] Cheek quoted in ABC News, "Person of the Week: Joey Cheek." *ABC News.com*, February 24, 2006.

[30] Bud Greenspan, director, *Bud Greenspan's Athens 2004: Stories of Olympic Glory*, Showtime Network, January, 2006.

community bonding. Not only do the actions of philanthropic athletes unify their nations and communities, sport itself provides a public example of rule-governed, non-violent conflict resolution. By organizing soccer leagues in African refugee camps, organizations such as Right to Play have been able to cultivate peaceful tribal interaction among youths who had known nothing but sectarian violence.[31] Which brings us back to the most ancient founding principles of the Olympic Games: the pacification and unification of diverse peoples.

Conclusion

Modern sport has shed its ancient religious function, not least because it serves a world community, which contains a variety of [often conflicting] religions. Cynics might say that the religious function has been replaced with a commercial one. Sport is a branch of the entertainment industry, its potential for social utility surrendered to its immense profit potential. A closer look reveals, however, that some of sport's ancient religious heritage survives in modern times. The Olympic opening procession, oaths, torch, and flame still evoke the Games' higher purpose as a community-building ritual meant to reward and inspire. As in Ancient Greece, the athletic contests attract large and diverse audiences, drawing attention to the movement's goals of humanism, justice, and peace—goals, after all, that are as much within our own power as that of any god. In effect, the Games are now praying to us. Enlightened athletes, officials, and spectators have the ability to uncover the educational and inspirational potential of athletics and bring them back to the fore. Athletes should be regarded neither as entertainers nor as revenue-earners, but as community servants whose personal sacrifice can and should benefit the others.

The gestures of individual athletes and small organizations like Right to Play are not enough, however. Modern sport organizations, especially the Olympic Movement, need to publicly

---

[31] R. Briggs, H. McCarthy, and A. Zorbas, *16 Days: The Role of Olympic Truce in the Quest for Peace* (Athens: Demos, 2004), 61-2.

commit themselves and their sponsors to concrete humanitarian goals consistent with their stated ideals, partnering as appropriate with established service organizations. Anti-Olympic campaigners may argue plausibly that the most effective humanitarian act the Olympic movement could perform would be to eliminate the Games. Olympic supporters, however, can respond with the vision of the Games' immense public profile being turned toward beneficial projects—as has been done with limited results in the area of environmentalism. If the Olympic movement commits itself publicly to community service, not only will it revive an important aspect of its ancient heritage, but it may well change the culture of sports in general. It is time that athletes and sports self-consciously abandon the modern commercial paradigm and return to their ancient and venerated roles in honorable public service. Olympic champions Otylia Jedrzejczak and Joey Cheek have shown that this is still possible. The connection between sport, service, and sacrifice is as old as contest itself.

Section III
The Ethics of Excellence

8. The Soul of an Olympian[1]

What was it like to be an ancient Olympic athlete? A visit to the ancient stadium at Nemea, site of another Pan-Hellenic athletic festival, can help us to imagine the experience. You begin at the ruins of the *apodyterion,* literally the "un-dressing room," where athletes removed their clothes in preparation for their events—and a favorite setting for Socrates' spiritual undressing of Athenian youth. Like the otherworldly Greek sanctuaries themselves, the *apodyterion* was a place to shed your attachment to the mundane world of the everyday; to prepare to reveal and celebrate the higher dimensions of your humanity. Next, you walk down the long stone tunnel, where ancient athletes stood in cool and quiet darkness, waiting for their names to be called. Eyeing the bright light and shimmering heat of the track outside, hearing the muffled rumblings of the crowd, it must have been a moment of deep uncertainty, a delicate spot of aloneness. Finally, your name is called, and you burst out into the light, naked both literally and metaphorically, ready to face the challenge and be tested in front of everyone: family, friends, and enemies. Ready to submit your soul, under the brilliant Mediterranean sun, to be inspected by the gods themselves.[2]

In a society where shame and failure were unmercifully disdained, where there were no consolations for losers, or rewards for simply taking part, one has to ask: What drove a person to do this? What is that force that makes an athlete want to test himself in this way – to risk the humiliation of failure, to strive for unattainable heights? It was more than recreation, more than social custom, more than professional obligation. It was a burning drive for excellence that goes beyond the practical considerations of everyday life and strives to discover what is best in humanity. It is

---

[1] Originally published in *The Olympics and Philosophy,* eds H. Reid and M. Austin (Lexington KY: University Press of Kentucky, 2012) 86-98. Reprinted by permission, all rights reserved.

[2] Every four years the ancient Games of Nemea are reenacted by people from every walk of life. See www.nemeangames.org.

III. The Ethics of Excellence

a *philosophical* and humanistic force, something fundamental to human character and, though less pervasive than in ancient Greek culture, it is a force that I believe is still alive today. Indeed, I will show that the drive to achieve *aretē* is foundational to the origin and nature of sport itself—as well as the source of its value. My ambition is to unleash the power of that understanding among contemporary athletes and sports enthusiasts generally, providing us with a nobler alternative to the prevailing sports objectives of entertainment and revenue: the goal of developing an Olympian soul.

It is no secret that the ideals of Ancient Greece inspired the modern Olympics' founder, Baron Pierre de Coubertin. Neither is it a secret that his vision of ancient sport was romanticized and in some details inaccurate.[3] There is little doubt that professionalism, entertainment concerns, and even cheating were present in ancient sport. Not all ancient athletes and fans were consciously driven by the higher ideals in their society. The point here is not simply to revive the idealistic vision of antiquity that motivated the Games' founders, but to revisit the connections between ancient Greek philosophical texts and the metaphysical realities of sport itself—realities that were as apparent in the world of Homer as they are in today's high-tech stadiums. These connections will reveal that while money and entertainment may forever be a part of the popular conception of sport, they are not its true purpose; the true purpose of sport is the acquisition and celebration of human excellence . Because this is something intrinsic to the structure of sport itself, athletes who experience competition don't have to be pushed hard to understand that.

A bit of a nudge is necessary, however, to engender value for the ancient ideal of *aretē* in modern practitioners (and spectators) of sport. I propose to provide that nudge by interpreting the stated ideals of modern Olympism in terms of the ancient philosophical ideal of *aretē* in order to show how that ideal may be profitably cultivated though the practice of sport. I'll do this by interpreting

---

[3] See for example, Young, *Olympic Myth*.

the first article of the *Olympic Charter* in terms of the ancient Greek ideal of *aretē*. Second, I will explain the general connection between philosophy and sport. Finally I will connect the virtues traditionally associated with *aretē* to the metaphysical structure of sport. The hope is that these connections can reveal the philosophical pursuit of *aretē* as something possible within and even fundamental to the practice of sport.

Connecting Olympism and Aretē

Perhaps the first thing to remember when comparing modern Olympic sport with ancient Greek thought is that the term Olympian referred to gods, not athletes. However, ancient Greek gods symbolized and exemplified the perfection for which human beings strive. The ideal of *aretē* was envisioned as a god-like perfection of body, will, and mind. From this perspective, we can see how the connection between the modern ideals of Olympism and the ancient ideal of *aretē* is apparent in the first Fundamental Principle of Olympism, which reads:

> Olympism is a philosophy of life, exalting and combining in a balanced whole the qualities of body, will and mind. Blending sport with culture and education, Olympism seeks to create a way of life based on the joy of effort, the educational value of good example, social responsibility and respect for universal fundamental ethical principles.[4]

Combining this statement with other Olympic symbols and ideals, one can derive many concepts important to the ancient Greek ideal of *aretē*: general principles such as *kalokagathia*—the connection between beauty and goodness, and specific virtues such as *eusebeia* (reverence), *andreia* (courage), *sōphrosynē* (self-discipline), *dikiaosyne* (justice), and *sophia* (wisdom).

But understanding the connection between Olympism and *aretē* requires much more than a translation of the ancient words; it requires an appreciation of the concepts behind them and *that* requires a grasp of ancient Greek philosophy, especially the

---

[4] Olympic Charter (2015), 13.

III. The Ethics of Excellence

thought of Socrates, Plato, and Aristotle. Beyond the ideas of specific thinkers, however, we must become aware of the connection between philosophy, understood as the pursuit of wisdom, and athletics, understood as the pursuit of excellence. This connection is much tighter than it may first appear because for most classical Greek philosophers, *aretē* cannot be separated from wisdom.[5] In fact, *aretē* is often understood as the health of the *psychē* (mind or soul), but the soul is not just the source of thought, but also of *kinēsis*, physical movement.[6]

Plato, who was himself a competitive wrestler, makes extensive physical training part of his educational programs for *aretē* described the *Republic* and *Laws*, and states specifically that these gymnastics are for the *benefit of the soul* (*Republic* 410c). Although his explanation as to *how* gymnastics develops the soul is limited,[7] connections can be made between athletics and philosophy beyond their common goal of improving the soul. Indeed, Plato has Socrates compare as "counterparts" proper engagement in philosophic argument with proper participation in physical training at *Republic* 539d. His point here is that those who use argument for the "sport" of defeating others rather than the higher goal of finding truth and leading a virtuous life are akin to those who practice athletics for *philonikia*, the love of victory, rather than the pursuit of personal excellence or *aretē*. Plato feels that the former are not worthy of the name "philosopher" – are the latter worthy of the name Olympian?

---

[5] For the connection between wisdom and *aretē*, Plato's Socratic dialogues and Aristotle's comments at *Eudemian Ethics* 1216b and *Nicomachean Ethics* 1145b. There is an extensive secondary literature on this subject, for example, Terry Penner, "The Unity of Virtue," *The Philosophical Review* 82 (1973), 35-68.

[6] On *kinēsis* and *psychē*, see Plato *Phaedrus* 245c-246a; *Laws* X 894c; *Sophist* 254d; and Aristotle, *De Anima* 413a-b, 432a-433b.

[7] For a complete account see H. Reid, "Plato's Gymnasium," in *Athletics and Philosophy in the Ancient World*.

Looking at the Metaphysics of Sport

While it may be clear that using argumentation for anything less than the pursuit of truth is an abuse, the use of sport for the purpose of "winning a prize," or "beating the next guy" might seem entirely appropriate. Indeed, it may seem that sport is structured explicitly to declare one competitor superior to the others, and the Olympic Games organized for the purpose of declaring one nation superior to the others. No doubt sport can be—and frequently is—used for that. But in line with Plato's claims about argumentation, I contend that the metaphysics of sporting contests suggests a purpose much greater than "beating the next guy" or "showing national superiority," much less "providing entertainment" or "generating revenue." A look at the basic structures of sport, structures which haven't changed since ancient times, reveals that their fundamental goal is to cultivate and celebrate human excellences (i.e. *aretē*).

What do I mean by the "basic structures of sport"? If we look all the way back to Homer's *Iliad*, written around the 8th century BCE and set nearly half a millennium earlier, we find athletic contests that were sufficiently familiar to the practitioners to conclude that such games were already a longstanding tradition by the time of the Trojan war (23.256-24.6). The events include a footrace, chariot race, weight-throw, and contests in wrestling and boxing. Their formats resemble modern sport: competitors volunteer to participate, the criteria for victory and defeat are articulated, valuable prizes are offered, and there are extensive discussions about the justice of the races' outcomes. But what is most important about these and all sports events is that the challenges they create serve no practical purpose.[8] Even though the skills tested may be useful in war, the games are distinguished from combat precisely because there is no useful purpose to them: the runners, for example, end up where they started, having carried no message or cargo from point to point. Modern sports

---

[8] On the structure of sport, see H. Reid, *Introduction to the Philosophy of Sport*, (Lanham, MD: Rowman and Littlefield, 2012), 29-93.

like golf and figure-skating are even farther removed from practical concern. Bernard Suits' famous definition of games as "the voluntary attempt to overcome unnecessary obstacles" applies just as much to ancient sport as it does to modern.[9]

So if the contest activities themselves lack intrinsic purpose, we must ask where their obvious meaning comes from. I would submit that it comes from the human *excellences* or *aretai* demanded by these tasks. Sporting contests set-up challenges that act as a mechanism for cultivating and celebrating the same virtues that enable a person to excel in life's (meaningful) challenges. Achilles and his friends make it clear that they are celebrating the fallen Patroclus' excellences, excellences that served them well on the very serious field of battle. At the same time they are pushing each other to demand more of themselves, to test their *aretai* against that of their comrades as part of a *community* drive to achieve ever-higher levels of excellence. The prizes are rewards and incentives for the cultivation of such excellences, but they are not the reason for or goal of each contest.[10] Nor is the goal simply to "beat the other guy." If it were, then it wouldn't matter who the other guy was, but Achilles insists that his most-skilled men to take part in each contest. The purpose is not simply to set one man above the rest, but to test and to *celebrate* the excellences that the contests elicit and thereby to honor Patroclus and the gods themselves.

Sport and the parts of aretē

So sporting contests derive their meaning not from such acts as putting balls into nets, but from the human excellences that actions like putting balls into nets demand. And those excellences are themselves valuable because *aretē* is understood as a *dynamis*, a power in the soul that can be applied to such meaningful tasks as being a good citizen or achieving *eudaimonia* (happiness).[11] The

---

[9] Suits, *Grasshopper*, 55.

[10] On the role of prizes in ancient sport see Brown, "Homer, funeral contests and the origins of the Greek city," 123–62.

[11] For more on the nature of *dynamis* and its connection to *aretē*, see Plato, *Republic* 477bc and 430b.

list of specific virtues implied by *aretē* varied in ancient times (as it would across different cultures today), but generally it includes *eusebeia* (reverence), *andreia* (courage), *sōphrosynē* (self-control), *dikiaosyne* (justice), and *sophia* (wisdom). Furthermore, there is a strain of thought in Hellenic philosophy that these virtues are at least related, if not completely unified: to have one is to have them all, and to perfect one entails, in some sense, perfecting them all.

This last claim is sure to elicit a myriad of counterexamples involving athletes who excel in sports but display few, if any of the virtues on that list. Likewise there are many thinkers skilled in debate and argument who nevertheless fail to pursue knowledge or live a virtuous life. Both cases demonstrate the limitations of the activities (athletics and philosophical debate) to reliably elicit the excellences they are designed to reward. It is a failure of sport, noted by many including Plato, that it sometimes rewards skills in the absence of true *aretē*. But this doesn't diminish sport's potential to cultivate *aretē*, nor does it refute the observation that sporting contests are and should be intended to elicit those cardinal virtues. What follows is a brief account of these ancient Greek ideals accompanied by an explanation of how the practice of sport may help us to cultivate them.

Eusebeia, often translated piety, may best be understood as reverence for and duty to some ideal beyond oneself.[12] For the Ancient Hellenes, the commitment to excellence, including the practice of sport, was ultimately religious. Their stadia were within religious sanctuaries and the games were part of festivals to honor the gods. Olympia was a Pan-Hellenic religious sanctuary long before it hosted Games and indeed the first Olympic contest is said to have been run in order to select someone to light the sacrificial flame (Philostratus, *Gymnasticus*, 5). It has even been argued that ancient Greek athletics generally and even the athletes' sweat itself were items of ritual sacrifice.[13] While modern sport need not be

---

[14] For a detailed account see Paul Woodruff, *Reverence: Renewing a Forgotten Virtue*, (Oxford: Oxford University Press, 2002).

[13] See Sansone, *Greek Athletics*, 40 f.

III. The Ethics of Excellence

subsumed by any particular religion, the sense that athletic pursuits are aimed at ideals that transcend mundane existence remains. The Olympic prize of an olive wreath symbolically blends the idea of divine perfection with the short-lived nature of victory and human life; it was just as relevant at the Athens 2004 Games as it in ancient Olympia. Furthermore, the venerated tradition of *ekecheiria* (truce), adopted and endorsed by the modern United Nations, places sport above simple commerce and our quarrels among ourselves. It reaches for a higher standard of excellence reflected in the mystery of the divine realm. Both ancient and modern Olympic athletes compete not just for worldly goods but also to honor higher ideals by displaying the best and most noble in themselves.

Along with this appreciation for the divine ideal, *eusebeia* requires an awareness of our imperfection with respect to the ideal, and a wondering about our ability to live up to it. This combination then yields a desire to test oneself against the ideal or at least against others who may approximate it. I take Socrates' *eusebeia* to be a paradigm example. Famously, he appreciates the ideal of divine knowledge, acknowledges the fact that he doesn't have it, and sets about testing his ideas against the "wisest men" of Athens in order to try and achieve it. It's no coincidence that Socrates compares himself to an Olympic athlete in this effort and claims that he deserves the prizes routinely awarded to Olympic victors for the benefits he has provided to the city (*Apology* 36de).

Of course Socrates' fame lies not in his athleticism, but rather his humble and reverent admission of ignorance in comparison to the perfect knowledge of gods (*Apology* 23b). But this reflects the situation of athletes who, almost by definition, seek perfection while constantly facing up to their imperfections. Even the world's best athletes are often dissatisfied with their record-breaking performances, and all because they appreciate and are trying to approximate an excellence even higher. For many of us, sport provides our first experience with conceptualizing an ideal and measuring ourselves against it. Often the ideal begins as some champion athlete, but for most of us it evolves beyond a particular person to a more abstract idea such as "the perfect race." In both cases it is that tension between where we are and where we want to be that motivates us to train, compete, and strive for otherwise meaningless goals. Although our victories may bring prizes and popularity, those spoils are not the true objects of our striving. We are trying to find something out about ourselves, about ideals, and about the capacities of humanity itself. In short, we are showing respect and duty toward ideals greater than ourselves—we are exercising the virtue of reverence.

Andreia, translated bravery or courage, is grounded in the view of life as *agōn* or struggle.[14] The idea that life is *agōn* grows directly out of *eusebeia* since recognizing one's imperfection with respect to an ideal and then striving to attain it is by definition a struggle. *Andreia*, generally, it is that power that enables us to endure and even to excel in that struggle. Plato took pains to show in *Lachēs* (196d, 192e) that *andreia* is less an absence of fear than a kind of wisdom about what should and should not be feared. Socrates eventually describes it as wise endurance in the pursuit of noble goals. In *Republic* (430b, 442c), *andreia* is the quality of the spirited part of the soul that enables it to follow reason's lead. Plato's point is that it's not enough to be willing to take risks and face danger, because many risks and dangers are not worth taking. Nor is it *andreia* to fight one's way toward victory at any cost. Socrates' historic *retreat* in the battle of Delium saved many lives and so enabled the Athenians to fight another day.[15] Aristotle, likewise, defined courage as a midpoint between the excesses of cowardice and rashness (*Nicomachean Ethics* 2.8). What *andreia* demands is a willingness to follow through with what we discern to be right, one that includes the courage to risk one's wealth and reputation in order to pursue higher ideals.

To the ancient Hellenes, there could be no such thing as *aretē* without struggle since life itself *is* struggle. The problem is that

---

[14] The view that *agōn* characterized the Greek outlook on life is attributed to Jacob Burkhardt, *The Greeks and Greek civilization*..

[15] A historical event recounted in Plato, *Symposium* 221ab.

III. The Ethics of Excellence

life's meaningful struggles sometimes come along when we're least prepared for them. It makes sense, in that case, to prepare ourselves intentionally by establishing and engaging in "artificial" struggles that cultivate qualities like *andreia*. This is exactly what sporting contests, ancient and modern, do. They manufacture *agōn*, challenges that test our ability to follow rules and execute plans. When Plato designed competitive games for his ideal city (*kallipolis*) in the *Laws* (830e-831a), he specified that the fighting contests be real enough to incite fear and reveal bravery. The cultivation of *andreia* demands that not only physical risk, but more important, the psychological risk of trying and failing, of revealing embarrassing truths about ourselves in public. To take part in competitive sport is, by definition, to risk losing.[16] But not to take part is to lack the courage to strive beyond what's predictable and safe. Without the courage to face challenges, we cannot hope to achieve excellence in any endeavor.

Sōphrosynē, rendered 'temperance' or 'self-discipline', contains a sense of power and control that is not easily conveyed by those words. Nevertheless it's something easy for those who know sport to understand. *Sōphrosynē* applies the aesthetic qualities of harmony and balance to the metaphysical understanding of man as a limited combination of mind, body and spirit. It views *aretē* in terms of the harmonious balance and dynamic function of these three elements. In *Charmidēs* (159cd), Plato's Socrates rejects definitions of *sōphrosynē* as modesty or quietness by using counterexamples from sports such as boxing. Beauty, the central criterion for *sōphrosynē*, requires a dynamic and harmonious tension between power and control.

Power and control are precisely the qualities demanded by both the aesthetic ideal and practical objectives of most sports. In fact, much of Olympic sports' entertainment value may be traced to the aesthetic pleasure we take in athletes' displays of controlled power. The purpose of sport is not to market such beautiful

---

[16] For a detailed explanation see, H. Reid, *The Philosophical Athlete*, 2nd. ed. (Durham, NC: Carolina Academic Press, 2019), Chapter 5.

displays, but rather to elicit such human excellences as *sōphrosynē*, which reflect our human nature as powerful but inevitably limited beings. An important metaphysical characteristic of sport is that it quite consciously imposes limitations and boundaries on space, time, and action. Ironically, these boundaries carve out a space apart from the "mundane world" where we can "go all-out" and express unprecedented freedoms.[17] I can scream as loud as I want on the racquetball court, but not in my classroom, next door. What's fascinating about sports is the dynamic human power displayed within extreme limits—gymnasts do things on a 4-inch balance beam that defy imagination. Surely Plato had *sōphrosynē* in mind when he emphasized dignity and control in dancing and wrestling contests (*Laws* 814ef). While modern sport is often characterized by excesses and "winning ugly," the ideal remains a harmonious tension between power and control.

Dikaiosynē, or justice, is easy to translate but very hard to explain. There were many different ideas of justice in ancient times just as there are now. Fortunately, I think that Olympic sport's own concern with justice helps it to accommodate the variety of theories and to establish itself as something designed to celebrate and cultivate justice. The term *dikaiosynē* is roughly contemporary with the introduction of written laws and was meant initially to describe a man who obeyed these laws.[18] This ideal fits well with sport, since they are in some sense made up of rules, and very strictly, to break a rule is not to play the game at all.[19] But it is clear in both sport and philosophy that justice cannot simply be *reduced* to rule-obedience. What about the possibility of unjust rules or

---

[17] An observation made by Eleanor Metheny, "The Symbolic Power of Sport," in Elled Gerber, ed., *Sport and the Body: A Philosophical Symposium* (Philadelphia: Lea & Febiger, 1979), 231-236.

[18] F.E. Peters, *Greek Philosophical Terms: A Historical Lexicon*, (New York: New York University Press, 1967) 39.

[19] This "formalist" account of rules and games is a subject of hot debate among sports philosophers. For an overview, see H. Reid, *Introduction to the Philosophy of Sport*, 45-55.

III. The Ethics of Excellence

minor violations such as an unintentional handball in soccer that may nullify a justly-deserved victory?

In *Republic,* Plato characterizes justice in the individual and in the city as the proper ordering and harmonious function of the various parts of the soul or of the citizenry. For the soul, this means that the rational part must lead, with the spirited and appetitive parts following. Isn't this just the thing demanded of an athlete by sport? Think of a martial arts form, a complicated dance move, or even an offensive play in American football. One must rationally conceptualize the proper moves, then have the "heart" and "guts" to perform them. Justice in the city likewise depends on citizens suited to particular tasks performing them for the good of the community. This is the same distribution of labor demanded of athletic teams, which always perform best when roles are assigned according to talent and skill. While it may be difficult to isolate a single theory of justice in the ancient world, sport seems well suited as a mechanism for eliciting most of our conceptions of it; so much so that we often refer to sports to illustrate important aspects of justice, for example the concept of a "level playing field."

Sophia, wisdom, evolves in ancient thought from something like prudence to a philosophic understanding of good and evil. For Socrates at least, *sophia* seems to be that element of *aretē* that renders the individual virtues useful for the pursuit of happiness, which is the ultimate prize in the game of life. Just as a doctor's skills may be applied to help or harm the patient, athletic skills such as courage and self-discipline can be used in the pursuit of either base or noble ends. The ability to discern what's best, for oneself, one's community, and one's environment is the lynchpin of any athletic program aimed at personal excellence. And this ability is the goal of *philosophy,* the love of wisdom, as practiced by Socrates. Despite its intellectual nature, *sophia* can and should be pursued with the whole soul. Practiced thoughtfully, athletics can be understood as the pursuit of wisdom, i.e. *philosophy.*[20]

---

[20] This is the thesis of H. Reid "Sport, Philosophy, and the Quest for Knowledge." *Journal of the Philosophy of Sport* 36:1 (2009). 40-49.

The key here is the attitude and intellectual engagement of the athlete within the sports experience. Just as the philosopher recognizes truth (and not victory in argument) as her true goal, the Olympic athlete should focus on the ideals of excellence and perfection. The philosopher, like the scientist and the detective, tries to discover some truth about the world. The athlete tries to discover some truth about what he himself and humanity in general are capable of. In this sense, athletic contests resemble science experiments that must be conducted according to the rules and with a willingness to accept the truth of the results, even when the results are not what the scientist or her sponsor were hoping for. It also requires an effort to reflect upon and evaluate the meaning of those results in the context of ones greater goals.

Most of this process is already in place for successful athletes. They see their sport, say a 100 meter dash, as a "lived question"; a complex problem to be solved.[21] And they bring all their resources (physical, intellectual, and spiritual) to bear in their attempts to solve it. To progress, they must analyze and evaluate their results, searching for ways to inch closer to perfection within the limits imposed by their human nature. When things are going well, they experience states transcendence referred to as "flow" or "being in the zone." These are fleeting experiences of the truth they seek; akin to peak experiences of musicians and theorists.

Modern sport tends to fail in developing *sophia* among athletes when it *disengages* them from solving the "problem" of their performance and fails to place athletic pursuits in service of the larger projects of personal excellence and happiness. Many coaches and programs focus narrowly on the (intrinsically meaningless) objectives of the sport itself, viewing athletes as means to their own career or institutional goals. In some sports, tactics, strategies, and even specific moves are communicated by coaches via radios. Athletes follow prescribed training programs, without understanding the theories behind them or reflecting on their role in a balanced and happy life. Even student-athletes

---

[21] Reid, *The Philosophical Athlete,* section 1.1.

competing in institutions that claim to be driven by the mission of education are provided little or no opportunity to reflect on their sports experience in such a way as to decipher values and meanings that might be applied to other aspects of life. These and other shortsighted practices in modern sport help to explain why athletes so often fall short of the virtues I'm claiming sport is designed to develop. By recognizing the wisdom-seeking nature of sport, *sophia,* the virtue that renders all others valuable, might again become the recognized end for athletes and coaches alike.

The emphasis placed on sports in modern culture makes it easy to forget that they are intrinsically meaningless. That goal, touchdown, or world record that inspires and amazes us does not have the social value of a cancer treatment or peace agreement. Even its entertainment value seems to stem from something more than putting a ball into a net or riding a bike up a mountain. *We* invent sport and *we* attribute meaning to it. In ancient Greece, the motivation for doing this was spiritual—a religious attempt to approximate *aretē,* the perfection that gods represented; perhaps it was even a way to make their presence felt on earth. I would argue that the value of sport today—even its economic value—depends ultimately on that ancient spiritual connection. If we can see sport as spiritual striving, if we can revive its connection to *aretē* and such eternally valuable virtues such as *eusebeia, andreia, sōphrosynē, dikiaosynē,* and *sophia,* I think we can revive its social value. Many athletes strive to win an Olympic medal and very few will achieve it. But all of us can benefit from striving to achieve the greatest athletic prize of all: the soul of an Olympian.

9. Coaching for Virtue in Olympic Sport[1]

> The power to learn is present in everyone's soul [but] the instrument with which each learns is like an eye that cannot be turned around from darkness to light without turning the whole body. —Plato

Olympic philosophy suggests that sport builds character. Many social scientists contend that the opposite is true: sport actually degrades moral character. Purists shun the question entirely, believing that sport, as a form of play, requires no end beyond itself for justification. Olympism's assertion of the educational benefits of sport, however, deserves some sort of explanation. Recreation and health-promotion seem to be only part of the story; a part of the story out of proportion to the emphasis placed on competition. If sport can indeed function as a form of moral education, then the value of Olympic education is increased—not least because classroom presentation of ethical theories has very limited potential for improving moral behavior. Olympic sport, because it involves physical activity and interpersonal interaction in a rule-governed environment, may indeed be an excellent medium through which to habituate good moral character. Indeed this was the role of sport in Ancient Greek education: the cultivation of a kind of moral and personal excellence called *aretē*.

But as some modern social science data suggests, good moral character is not an automatic outcome of athletic participation.[2] Olympic education demands more than playing sports, and coaches who put character first, or at least near the top of their goals, need to be thoughtful and intentional about how they might

---

[1] Originally published as "Coaching for Virtue in Plato's Academy." *The Ethics of Coaching Sports.* Ed. Robert Simon. Boulder, CO: Westview Press, 2013, 27-40. Reprinted with permission.

[2] See Sharon K. Stoll and Jennifer M. Beller. "Do Sports Build Character?" in *Sports in School: The Future of an Institution*, edited by John Gerdy (New York: Columbia University Press, 2000) 18-30.

achieve it. They might even have to distance themselves from the conventions and reward systems common in sport today. Since moral education is such an important social task, however, coaches who strive to achieve it deserve to be called Olympic educators. I am part of a group of scholars who believe, in fact, that the cultivation of *aretē* is the highest social good that sport can bring and should therefore be the guiding principle of sports participation and promotion—an approach we call "aretism."[3] A better understanding of the relationship among *aretē*, athletics, and education in Ancient Greek thought may inspire the modern Olympic coach who puts character first to find creative ways to fight that good fight and to become a coach of virtue.

The History of Sport and Aretē

A link with *aretē* can be found at the very origins of sport. The earliest evidence comes from ancient Sumerian, Egyptian, and Minoan societies in which royal displays of athleticism were offered to the populace of evidence of their leaders' divine favor and worthiness to lead. Of course these were not open competitions, most often they were uncontested displays, or even unwitnessed feats that gained legendary status in their poetic retelling. Whether Gilgamesh actually out-wrestled Enkidu, or whether the Sumerian Shulgi in fact ran the 100+ mile length of his kingdom and back in a single day was immaterial.[4] The point was not so much to prove the leaders' worth to a skeptical public, but rather to provide comforting and inspiring tales of strength and virtue, not unlike the myths of Heracles or Theseus. What remains most interesting to us is that athleticism was taken to be a sign of virtue and civic worth so many millennia ago. Somehow the link between sport and moral character has endured, despite immense change in the nature of human life and society, up to this day. Although the nature of polities and conceptions of virtue vary with

---

[3] See M. Holowchak and H. Reid, *Aretism: An Ancient Sports Philosophy for the Modern Sports World* (Lanham: Lexington, 2011).
[4] See "Athletic Heroes" in this volume.

time and place, there seems to be a fundamental link between virtue and sport that transcends those differences.

We can see this variation even within ancient Greek literature. Originally the *aretē* associated with athleticism was understood to be something inborn: the product of divine ancestry or natural aristocracy. Heracles' strength comes from his divine father, Zeus, and is displayed immediately when he saves his brother by strangling two snakes as an infant in his crib—there are no ancient stories about him training. Homers' heroes Achilles and Odysseus seem naturally athletic as well. When Odysseus washes up on a foreign shore and a local makes the insulting insinuation that he is a tradesman rather than a nobleman, Odysseus puts the matter to rest by grabbing a discus and hurling it (without training or even a practice throw) farther than all the local athletes (*Odyssey* 8.130-233). Later, upon returning to his kingdom disguised as a beggar, he proves his *aretē* again through athletic feats, defeating even the superficially noble suitors of his wife. Athleticism and virtue were originally thought of in ancient Greece as gifts inherited through noble bloodlines rather than earned through training.

In real as opposed to mythical or literary athletic contests, of course, ancient Greek athletes hired coaches and trained regularly. But the lingering idea that the *aretē* associated with athleticism was inborn rather than acquired is evidenced by early efforts to hide the use of coaches and training. In early poetic and monumental celebrations, Olympic victory is attributed to divine favor and the glory of one's family—coaches' instruction and systematic training programs are almost never mentioned. But as the popularity of athletics and the prestige associated with victory grew (in no small part because of its association with *aretē*), the use of coaches and the success of athletes from humble origins became impossible to hide. The evidence that athletic success could be achieved through training, combined with the lingering link between athleticism and *aretē*, generated the revolutionary idea that virtue itself could be trained and was not just a matter of birth.

This belief that virtue is trainable underpins the whole concept of higher education, that is, education that goes beyond instruction

III. The Ethics of Excellence

in skills like writing and arithmetic and actually seeks to produce excellent human beings—a concept in the aretic context that implies good citizenship. This idea had special appeal in the Greek West (i.e. Southern Italy and Sicily) where émigrés seem to have used athletic festivals, especially the Olympic Games, to prove their *aretē* on the mainland. Indeed the 5th century BCE Sicilian Epicharmus of Syracuse was among the first to suggest that training or practice was more important to virtue than heredity.[5] He may have gotten the idea from Pythagoras, whose 6th century BCE school in southern Italy was among the first institutions to train virtue. It was not mere coincidence that Pythagoras recruited students in the gymnasium,[6] nor does it seem mere coincidence that Plato, after visiting the area in the 4th century BCE, opened his own school in an Athenian gymnasium called the Academy.

It is likely that Plato included athletic exercises in the Academy's program, partly because of tradition but more precisely because he embraced the idea they could contribute to moral education. In a letter describing his experiences in Italy, Plato laments his failure to transform Dionysios, the young tyrant of Syracuse, into "a man who was just and courageous and temperate and wisdom-loving [and therefore able to live] in subjection to justice combined with wisdom."[7] The educational program he outlined in the *Republic,* meanwhile, uses athletic games to select and train leaders with the very qualities that Dionysios lacked: the ability to strive for excellence while resisting temptation, to subject themselves to common laws, and to toil not

---

[5] DK 23 b33, Freeman translation.

[6] Iamblichus, *The Pythagorean Life,* 5, says that after watching the student play a complex ball game, Pythagoras concluded that he must also have the ability to learn complex ideas. This student eventually accompanied Pythagoras to the colony of Kroton in Southern Italy, where he again recruited students at the gymnasium and founded a community of scholars and athletes so renowned in the ancient world it gave birth to the proverb that "he who finishes last of the Krotonites is first among the rest of the Greeks" (Strabo 6.1.12).

[7] Plato, *Seventh Letter* 335d-336b, trans. Bury.

for individual glory but rather for the benefit of the larger community. Perhaps we can call Plato the first coach of Olympic virtue since he used sport to develop self-controlled, hard-working, law-abiding, team players—much like many modern coaches. The interesting question is: "How?"

Winners versus Wins

The first characteristic of true Olympic coaching is that its overarching goal is *aretē*. All other athletic goals, including victories, medals, and endorsements, must be subordinated to that. The objective is to produce winners—people with dispositional virtues such as respect, discipline, courage, justice, and wisdom—and not necessarily wins. Although a stable of medalists may provide some evidence of a coach's ability to cultivate *aretē*, it is hardly a reliable measure in and of itself. This is because Olympic victory is not a fail-safe indicator of virtue, and defeat is not always caused by the lack of virtue. Sometimes victory doesn't even indicate athletic superiority. Competitors who win by cheating, bribery, or other illicit means fail to be winners in both the moral and the athletic sense. But even in legitimate victories, virtue-irrelevant factors such as brute strength, superior equipment, good luck, or bad officiating can be the deciding factor.[8] Only in closely-fought contests where athletes are challenged to bring out their best can we say that victory indicates *aretē*; but in those cases the losers have demonstrated virtue as well. *Aretē* is not a zero-sum game and coaches aimed at virtue cannot judge their success strictly in terms of medals.

This is not to say that winning doesn't matter at all. Striving to win fairly in close competition is a manifestation of virtue in sport. It is victory without virtue that is worthless because it is *aretē* that gives winning its value in the first place. The athletic skills that lead to victory have little value beyond sport. It is not the ability to put a ball in a net or to overtake an adversary that is admirable in Olympic athletes—after all, we have machines and vehicles more

---

[8] See Nicholas Dixon, "On Winning and Athletic Superiority," *Journal of the Philosophy of Sport* 26:1 (1999): 10-26.

efficient even than athletes at completing such tasks. Rather, we value these skills and the medals that go along with them because of the virtues we perceive to be embedded therein. Courage is valuable not because it is needed to complete a marathon race, but because it is useful in more important human endeavors like battling disease or searching for the truth. In events such as the Susan G. Komen "Race for the Cure," which benefits cancer research, the efforts of all the runners, not just the winners, celebrate the kinds of virtues needed to fight disease. In this sense they resemble ancient funeral games, which celebrated the *aretē* of the deceased. The winner in such events becomes a symbol of those virtues. Without the association with *aretē*, however, he is just a guy who had the skills to make it across the finish line first—he hasn't done anything to benefit mankind.

Plato artfully illustrates the distinction between skill (*technē*) and virtue (*aretē*) with the example of telling falsehoods (*Hippias Minor*, 364c-370e). Being a good liar certainly does not equate with being a good person, but the skill of lying may be put to good use if the liar also has *aretē*. For example, a liar may use her skill to extort money from innocent victims, or she may use it to protect innocent victims from injustice—perhaps by lying to Nazi soldiers about the presence of Jews in her basement. The skill of lying is morally neutral, it is *aretē* that makes it valuable. Likewise, athletic skills may lead to victory, but virtue makes victory worthwhile.

Unfortunately, virtue is harder to measure than victory and reward systems for coaches and athletes alike are calibrated toward the latter. This is not a problem unique to Olympic sport. In society at large, both ancient and modern, the extrinsic rewards of fame and fortune draw people away from the intrinsic goods connected to happiness. Chastising the citizens of Athens in 399 BCE, Socrates said, "wealth does not bring about *aretē*, but *aretē* makes wealth and everything else good for men, both individually and collectively" (Plato, *Apology*, 30b). For some reason, legions of depressed millionaires and suicidal superstars are not evidence enough to deter young people from pursuing fame and fortune at a very high cost. Athletic paths to stardom are particularly risky—

any other college program with such a low professional placement rate would be considered a failure.[9] We may decry young athletes who are motivated by money, but we have to ask ourselves what values they are supposed to learn from coaching staffs preoccupied with salaries, and National Olympic Committees and sports federations who value medals primarily for the funding that they attract. Coaching for virtue means not only exhorting athletes to put *aretē* first, it also requires coaches and institutions to model this priority in their own choices and attitudes—despite an incentive and reward structure that often works against that.

In discussing the educational value of athletics, Plato's *Republic* never mentions wins or losses. Students are to be subjected to "labors [*ponous*], pains, and contests [*agōnas*]" so that they may be tested "more thoroughly than gold is tested by fire" (413cd). They are to be selected for advancement based on their performance in these contests, but not necessarily by whether they win, and certainly not by whether they have the physical size and strength to achieve Olympic victory. Socrates distinguishes these students from "all other athletes" on the grounds that their goal is psychic rather than muscular strength (410b). Platonic educators are therefore looking for spiritual qualities that can be developed into virtues: the willingness to confront imperfection, the desire to work hard without promise of immediate reward, the discipline to resist laziness and temptation, and the ability to subject oneself to rules as an equal with others. These, at least, are the kinds of traits that Plato describes in relation to the cardinal virtues in his ethical philosophy-- virtues still widely valued today, namely: respect (*eusebia*), courage (*andreia*), moderation (*sōphrosynē*), justice (*dikaiosynē*) and wisdom (*sophia*). Let us imagine how a coach in Plato's Academy might have used sport to help develop these virtues.

---

[9] According to the NCAA, the percentage of college athletes that go on to play professionally in the major sports of ranges from 1.0 to 1.7%. NCAA, "Estimated Probability of Competing in Athletics Beyond the High School Interscholastic Level," *NCAA.com*, 2011.

III. The Ethics of Excellence

Respect (Eusebia)

The foundation of education for *aretē* on the Platonic scheme is summed up in Socrates' famous declaration that his wisdom lays precisely in the awareness that he is not wise.[10] Not unlike a 12 step program, in which you must admit that you have a problem before you can begin to solve it, the Socratic admission of imperfection initiates and motivates the self-improvement process. Socrates explains his avowal of ignorance as a kind of religious humility. Having been declared by the oracle at Delphi (and therefore by the god Apollo) to be the wisest of men,[11] Socrates sets out to investigate the matter by questioning poets, politicians, and craftsmen who seem to him to be wise. What he discovers is that these men *think* themselves wiser than they really are, and so he concludes that the oracle has declared Socrates wisest because he, unlike these others, admits that he doesn't have knowledge. Furthermore he spends his days questioning others in search of the truth, as a kind of mission to the god. In other words, Socrates regards it as a kind of piety, first, to acknowledge his imperfection with respect to the gods' perfection, and second, to work tirelessly to bring himself and others around him closer to perfection through inquiry. In short, he is exercising the virtue of respect: respect for the excellence of the gods, respect for himself in striving for improvement, and respect for others in striving to help them improve.

Long before Socrates, Olympic sport was a milieu that symbolized this conception of respect. The gulf between perfection and imperfection was understood in terms of the contrast between gods and human beings. Respect demands that we humbly acknowledge the gods' superiority—failure to do so amounts to the vice of *hubris*, the characteristic source of dreadful consequences in Greek tragedy. Ancient Olympic athletes showed

---

[10] Plato, *Apology*, 21d. Socrates is sometimes quoted as saying that the only thing he knows is that he knows nothing, but this exact phrase does not occur in the Platonic dialogues.

[11] More precisely, the oracle said no one was wiser than Socrates

their humility partly by competing in the nude, stripped of the trappings of their worldly ties and status. Athletes were anointed with olive oil and victors were symbolically dedicated to the gods, wearing the same cloth fillets and crowns of olive used to adorn sacrificial animals.[12] In *Republic*, it is likewise said that a man must be "stripped" of his worldly reputation, honors, and rewards in order to be tested for the virtue of justice (424e). Even when we compete in clothes, athletic competition symbolically strips athletes of their social rank and demands that they respect not just the rules of the games they play, but also one another as imperfect equals under those rules. Just as Socratic questioning demonstrates respect by admitting imperfection and encouraging others to improve themselves, athletic competition demands that we admit our imperfection and encourage our competitors (by challenging them) also to improve themselves.

Coaching for respect means, first of all, admitting one's imperfection and helping others to come to terms with their own. Sport does a pretty good job by itself of making us aware of our limitations, but in cases of dominant athletes or lack of good competition, it may need a little help. When the goal is an ideal of excellence rather than mere superiority to others, there is room for criticism even in a runaway victory. Plato recognizes that flattery, which can come in the form of easy victory as well as verbal approbation, undermines the natural desire for improvement and replaces it with the desire for—and expectation of—constant praise (*Gorgias* 463b). Coaches talk about *being* respected, which is important, but *showing* respect for rules, officials, superiors, and especially inferiors, is the best way for a coach to teach respect.

As Socrates understood, our individual differences in excellence are negligible compared with our collective distance from the ideal of excellence, as symbolized by the gods. Olympic sports have their own "gods," namely the great athletes, coaches, and officials who have built the history of our sports, and these, too, deserve recognition and respect from athletes and coaches

---

[12] Burkert, *Greek Religion*, 56.

alike. Just because you can beat Jesse Owens' time in the 100 meters, does not mean you have achieved the same level of excellence or made the same social impact. Clearly not everyone deserves the same level of respect, but everyone deserves a basic level of respect—even people we neither like nor admire. As human beings, we all fall short of perfection, and our struggle for improvement should be shared. Opponents, officials, sponsors, and staff all benefit the athlete by making sport possible in the first place. Teaching respect means giving respect, and giving respect appropriately results in earning respect.

Courage (Andreia)

The respectful admission of imperfection provides a basis from which the passionate pursuit of Olympic excellence can be launched. The next thing Platonic educators look to be revealed through sport is an athlete's courage, as evidenced primarily by *philoponia*, literally the love of hard work (*Republic* 535bc). They are looking for souls that do not give up easily, even when there is little hope of immediate reward. It isn't hard to imagine how athletic competition might reveal such a quality; as the proverb says, you can learn a lot about a person by watching them play a game.[13] The reason Platonic educators are looking for courageous souls in sport has nothing to do with Olympic contests, however. What they want is to find students who will courageously pursue knowledge because, as Socrates says, people's souls give up much more easily in hard study than in physical training" (*Republic,* 535b). In short, they are looking for future philosopher-monarchs, people willing to "take the longer road and put as much effort into learning as into physical training, for otherwise, as we were just saying, he will never reach the goal of the most important subject and the most appropriate one for him to learn"(*Republic,* 504cd). In short, the courage a student shows in sport is expected to apply in academic studies, and eventually civic service.

---

[13] The similar proverb, "You can learn more about someone in an hour of play than a year of conversation," is sometimes attributed to Plato, but it does not appear in the extant written texts.

A plausible response to this idea of selecting leaders through sport is that Plato has no idea what he is talking about because in the real world (or at least the modern world), athletes who train and play with outstanding effort and courage, rarely employ those qualities beyond sport. As a matter of fact Plato does seem to have been aware of this problem. In *Republic*, Socrates says that athletes training and competing at the highest levels have little interest for anything else besides sleeping (537b). The period in which students are examined and selected on the basis of their athletic performance is accordingly limited to a two year period devoted strictly to physical training—the period devoted to study of difficult mathematical and philosophical subjects comes after that (*Republic*, 524d ff). It is never expected of individuals that they dedicate themselves simultaneously to the highest levels of sport and study. It is expected, however, that virtues like courage, which are revealed and rewarded by sport, will be applied to the more important tasks of learning and leadership. Plato's educational philosophy is not aimed at producing star athletes or even commercial titans (although both of these certainly existed in his day). The goal is to create excellent individuals who apply their virtues for the benefit of the larger community—something very similar to the stated aims of the Olympic Movement.

So what would it mean to coach for courage and other virtues that will be expressed beyond athletics? First, we should recognize that human beings cannot perform their very best at both athletics and academics simultaneously.[14] Second, incentives and accolades should be structured (within athletic and academic programs) to reward the cultivation of virtue and especially its application in activities that benefit the larger community. For most athletes, the level of excellence expected in their sports are much higher than

---

[14] The implications of this principle may include the decoupling of athletics and academics during specific time periods; lowering athletic expectations during intense study; or lowering of academic expectations during athletic striving. It does not imply that we must abandon one activity in order to pursue excellence another.

those expected in academics. Student-athletes are required to make only minimal academic progress toward graduation, while they must train and compete at a very high level to earn a place on a team. Community celebration and reward of top athletes, furthermore, usually outstrips that given to top students. Is it any wonder that individuals tend to "spend" their virtues on sport in this environment? As in the case of win-loss records, coaches need to swim upstream to encourage the application of virtues beyond the athletic field. They need to demand not that their charges always put sports first, but that they always put virtue first and never neglect their obligations to other worthwhile activities and relationships. Plato's *Lachēs* argues that courage requires not just endurance but also the wisdom to direct it toward good causes. Bravery shown exclusively in sport is not virtue at all; those who coach for virtue promote their expression beyond athletics as well.

Moderation (sōphrosynē)

Plato's Socrates explicitly rejects the idea that physical training is primarily for the benefit of the body, while the rest of education is designed to serve the soul (*psychē*). Rather, he argues that both physical and academic training are primarily for the benefit of the soul (*Republic,* 411e). To make sense of this, we must first understand that the Greek word *psychē* is more expansive than many modern ideas of soul. In Plato's philosophy, the soul encompasses three parts: the wisdom-loving intellect, the honor-loving spirit, and the appetitive part associated with desires for food and sex. *Aretē* in Plato is described as a harmony among these three parts of the soul, a harmony that is compared (but not equated) with physical health. Indeed, even physical health has its origin in the soul, for as Socrates says, a fit body does not produce *aretē*, but rather that the soul's virtue makes the body as good as possible (*Republic,* 403d). In fact, Socrates says that physical training alone risks squelching the soul's native love of learning, creating a person who "bulls his way through every situation by force and savagery like a wild animal" (*Republic,* 411e). A person pursuing *aretē*, even through of sport, explains Socrates, will not "assign first place to being strong, healthy, and beautiful, unless he happens to acquire moderation (*sōphrosynē*) as a result. Rather it's clear that he will always cultivate the harmony of his body for the sake of the consonance of his soul" (*Republic*, 591c).

This virtue of moderation (*sōphrosynē*) may be described in the context of Olympic sports as a kind of self-discipline. It combines the power to resist appetitive temptations ranging from laziness to greed, with the ability to discern and pursue noble goals with enthusiasm. In the dialogue *Phaedrus*, the virtuous soul is illustrated with the metaphor of a two horse chariot. The driver represents the intellectual part of the soul, one good and obedient horse represents the spirited or honor-loving part, and the other disobedient bad horse represents the appetitive part of the soul. In order for the chariot to perform well, the spirited and appetitive parts have to be trained to obey the rational part (*Phaedrus*, 247b). I don't think it is just by coincidence that Plato uses an athletic metaphor here. It is true even today that Olympic athletes must train themselves to resist destructive appetitive desires. The temptations to indulge in poor-quality food or alcohol, to stay out late or leave practice early, must be overcome to maximize athletic potential. Because the game tends to punish those who fail to control such appetites—sometimes in the humiliating form of a poor public performance—sports can help us to follow through in action with what the intellect discerns to be right. Socrates claims that athletic training helps to harmonize the three parts of the soul; to keep appetites in check and to pursue with enthusiasm the well-chosen goals of the intellect (*Republic*, 442a).

Coaching for moderation means letting that process take place. Athletes must develop not only the intellectual capacity to make wise choices, but also the moral capacity to follow through with those choices in action. On one level, this requires coaches to allow the space for athletes to make mistakes and suffer the consequences. For example, athletes should come to practice because they know it is the right thing to do and they are following through, as a matter of honor or pride, with what they know to be right. If they come to practice simply to avoid punishment, they

III. The Ethics of Excellence

will be learning to obey the appetitive fear of pain rather than the intellectual conviction of purpose. This is nothing more than doing what feels good, a habit that can lead to all kinds of troubling behaviors. If, on the other hand, the athlete learns to do what is right because she understands its importance, she will have acquired an important moral skill. As in the case of winning and losing, however, sport does not reliably reward the virtue of moderation and punish the vice of immoderation. For this reason, coaches might create rules and rewards designed to guide rather than force athletes toward virtuous behavior. For example, they might prohibit potentially dangerous supplements so that athletes may come to appreciate the joy of achieving goals without the "help" of shortcuts. Coaches might bench even top-performing players who behave immoderately as a public way of putting virtue first. But restrictions on athlete behavior should be aimed at the goal of self-regulation. Like training wheels on a bike, their purpose is to make themselves unnecessary.

Justice (dikaiosynē)

In using athletics to train and select the rulers of his ideal city, Plato was looking for outstanding individuals who, despite their personal excellence, could see themselves as equal with others before the law and ultimately understood their welfare to be inextricably connected with the good of the whole community. This social virtue was called justice (*dikaiosynē*) and it was learned through sports, on a foundational level, by the simple act of following rules. In the *Republic* it is stipulated that children's games be strictly governed by rules so they could develop habit of respecting and following laws (*Republic*, 424e). Ultimately, the model is of guardians and rulers completely devoted to the state; they are not allowed to have private property or even private families (*Republic*, 416d). Their decisions are expected to serve the greater good of the community, disregarding personal concerns or desires. Athletics formed part of the training and selection process through which "they must show themselves to be lovers of their city when tested by pleasure and pain and that they must hold on to their resolve through labors, fears, and all other adversities" (*Republic,* 502d–503a). To be a just person in Plato's Academy meant not only to have the three parts of your soul in harmony with one another, but also to be in harmony with your community, understanding your particular role within it, and regarding yourself as equal under the law.

Obviously the socio-political context of Plato's Academy is different from Olympic sport today. His understanding of the social virtue of justice, however, is as relevant as ever. In fact, the (relatively) modern invention of team sports seems to be a particularly good tool for promoting the understanding of even outstanding individuals' dependence on the larger group. Paradoxically, much of today's most selfish and immoderate behavior comes from athletes in high profile team sports. As with the ancient tyrants that plagued Greece in Plato's day, some superstar athletes are driven by their own appetites to regard themselves as above the rules and to disregard the deleterious effects of their selfish actions on their teams. Coaches, too, behave like tyrants when they use their teams as means to satisfy their own appetite for fame and fortune—and this is more dangerous than tyrannical players since coaches generally have more power. Fortunately, most team sports are structured to penalize selfish behavior. Individual superstars may command big salaries, but they can win only with the cooperation of their team. Meanwhile, players who put team harmony before personal desire tend to be rewarded by the game.

Again, however, sport does not reliably reward the virtue of justice and so Olympic coaches need to promote it separately. As Socrates says in *Republic,* "it isn't the law's concern to make any one class in the city outstandingly happy but to contrive to spread happiness throughout the city by bringing the citizens into harmony with each other" (*Republic,* 519e). The same could be said for the structure of a team. The basis of justice, it will be remembered, is equality before the law. Not only should players be treated equitably by their coaches, coaches should set an example of respect for rules, officials, opposing players, and

III. The Ethics of Excellence

coaches. Just as players should be smart enough to see the connection between their own success and that of the team, coaches should be smart enough to see the connection between their own success and that of the larger athletic and academic community. Coaches who bends rules or try to manipulate the system for the competitive benefit of the team may believe they are teaching loyalty and dedication to a purpose. But in fact, they are teaching their players to selfishly indulge their own desires at the expense of the larger community. Furthermore coaches should penalize players who fail to exercise the virtue of justice—even if it hurts the team competitively. These actions reinforce sport's ability to cultivate the virtue of justice and in some cases may spur the remaining players to work more closely together rather than relying on a selfish star. As Socrates says of the guardians, just people are even happier than Olympians because their victory is shared by the entire community (*Republic*, 465d).

Wisdom (Sophia)

The last of the key Platonic virtues is wisdom (*sophia*) though, unlike the other virtues discussed above, he dedicates none of his dialogues to it. I can think of two good reasons for this. First, wisdom is a kind of crowning virtue—the culmination of the harmonious acquisition of all the other virtues. Each virtue depends for its value on some level of wisdom: justice requires the understanding of one's relationship to the community, moderation demands the subjection of appetites and honor to a discerning intellect, courage entails not just the will to take risks, but the ability to understand which risks are worth taking, and respect is based on the wisdom of knowing that one doesn't know. This brings us to the second reason Plato never explicates wisdom, like Socrates he probably would deny that he has it. The Academy educates philosophers, lovers of wisdom who believe themselves to be in perpetual pursuit of it, rather than sophists, people who believe that they possess it.

To be sure, this wisdom and the virtues that Plato connects with it are strongly intellectual. But virtue and wisdom are relevant to sport because they derive their worth precisely from our ability to *act* in accordance with them. Human happiness, in fact, is defined by Aristotle as activity in accordance with virtue.[15] So athletics has its place in the academy because it is an activity, something that requires us to act. Olympic sport, insofar as it rewards virtuous action and penalizes the opposite is an important part of training for *aretē* and the wisdom that is essential to it. Coaches, insofar as they promote virtue and penalize its opposite, are accordingly Olympic educators and as such they have an important place not only in Plato's ancient Academy but in the modern Olympic Movement.

---

[15] Aristotle, *Nicomachean Ethics*, 1098a.

10. The Ecstasy of *Aretē*[1]

Modern athletes call it "the zone." Psychologists have defined it as "flow." The ancient Greek poet Pindar called it "a brilliant light" sent from Zeus (*Pythian* 8.97). Skilled performers of music, drama, and dance all report moments of ecstasy in which difficult tasks become effortless and a moment of harmony with the forces of life is inexplicably achieved. Audiences, too, get caught up in these moments, sensing the presence of transcendent beauty—even when the beautiful catch or goal is made by an athlete on the opposing team. There is something special about these moments that ties us together with one another, and even through time with heroes and events of the distant past. Indeed, I will argue that in ancient Greece, festivals like the Olympic Games were concocted to produce moments of ecstasy for the benefit of the community. It is not just an accident that ancient Greek games honoring gods and heroes included contests in music, drama, poetry and athletics. It is through the skilled performance of these arts—and the synergy between them—that gods and heroes were invoked and evoked. The catalyst was *aretē* (virtues) by re-enacting the feats and celebrating the virtues of gods and heroes, athletes and artists renewed and reaffirmed *aretē*'s cultural value. Moments of *aretic* ecstasy inspired, enlightened, and united entire communities—and they may still do so in the Olympic Games today.

To understand the link between a modern psychological concept like Flow and the ancient function of the religious festivals like the Olympic Games, we need to identify commonalities and acknowledge important differences. It will not be enough to compare the experiences of ancient and modern Olympic athletes—though there surely are important parallels—we need to consider the cultural context to understand how and why those ecstatic experiences were interpreted as they were. In particular, we need to consider the way that art, especially epic and lyric

---

[1] First published as "The Ecstasy of *Aretē*: Flow as Self-Transcendence in Ancient Athletics," *Studies in Sport Humanities* 15 (2014) 6-12.

poetry, framed the Olympic experience. And we need to consider how the presence of spectators and the proximity to natural and artificial beauty produced an awareness of oneself as part of something transcendent.

What I am arguing, in short, is that when an ancient Greek athlete competing in a festival—let's say a runner competing at the Olympic Games—experienced "Flow" during his race, he not only evoked the virtuous spirit of a god or hero like Achilles; at that moment he *became* Achilles, and the hero's spiritual presence was felt by nearly everyone present at the contest. Likewise a lyre-player at Delphi might have become Apollo, and a rhapsode at the Panathenaia could have become Homer (indeed this is what Plato's character Ion claims in the dialogue of the same name). The purpose of these events was precisely to effect the spiritual appearance of such gods and heroes through moments of *aretic* ecstasy and thereby to reaffirm the enduring presence and value of heroic *aretē* within the larger community.

The Elements of Flow

Psychologist Mihály Csíkszentmihályi defined Flow as a particular mental state in the late 1980s. He didn't take himself to be discovering something new, however. In fact, Eastern religions such as Buddhism, Daoism, and Hinduism had already described similar states thousands of years before. What Csíkszentmihályi[2] did was produce a list of six psychological factors which combine to create the state. These include "intense focus" and "merging of action and awareness," a loss of reflective self-consciousness, an altered experience of time, and an experience of the activity as intrinsically rewarding or *autotelic*. To this list I would add audience, physical environment, and cultural framing to produce my own list of conditions for *aretic* ecstasy in sport. In any case, Flow remains something better experienced than described. It is also difficult to depict, despite my claims that informed audiences sense it right away. One of the best attempts is in director Hugh

---

[2] Mihály Csíkszentmihályi and Susan Jackson, *Flow in Sports* (Champaign, IL: Human Kinetics, 1999), 16.

Hudson's 1981 film, *Chariots of Fire*. His depiction of Eric Liddell's victorious race at the 1924 Olympics takes place in a modern Christian context—but it effectively represents the runner's immersion in the race, his evocation of the divine, his awareness of the audience, as well as the altered sense of time and space.

Sacred Space

The first pre-condition I want to establish for *aretic* ecstasy is environmental. The space where the activity takes place needs to be sacred—or at least set apart from the ordinary workaday world. Now this is not a difficult thing to achieve for most sports, since the boundaries of the playing field, court, or race-course are clearly marked off. Aesthetically, this marking off creates a kind of frame within which the special activity is to take place.[3] Even today, athletic stadiums and gymnasiums are experienced as extraordinary spaces where special things are expected to happen—not unlike churches, sanctuaries, or graveyards.[4] In ancient Greece, the Olympic track was exactly such a sacred space: part of a religious sanctuary dedicated to Zeus and clearly marked off from the profane world by a wall called a *temenos*. When the athletic events at Olympia became too big and popular to stage within the religious sanctuary, the stadium built to house them was physically connected to the sanctuary with a tunnel. Statues lined the entrance to the stadium, reminding athletes of their special duties to the god. Olympia's sanctuary was itself full of altars, temples, and statues of victorious athletes from the past.[5] If visiting the ruins of Olympia's sanctuary is a spiritual experience today, the emotion for ancient athletes must have been a hundred times more powerful.

The sacred power of Olympic space derived not just from the amazing art and architecture that was housed within it, the natural

---

[3] Marjorie Fisher, "Sport as an Aesthetic Experience," *Sport and the Body: A Philosophical Symposium*, ed. E. Gerber (Philadelphia: Lea and Febiger, 1974), 318.

[4] Reid, *Introduction to the Philosophy of Sport*, 71-72.

[5] A. Mallawitz, "Cult and Competition," 79-90.

environment of Olympia is particularly beautiful—and beautiful in a particular way. Making one's way though the Hellenic countryside to Olympia in summertime, one cannot help but notice its verdant fecundity in contrast with its drier, rockier surroundings. In practical terms, this lushness is attributable to nearby water—Olympia is located at the intersection of the Kladeos and Alpheios rivers. Epinician poets mention such water sources as synonyms for the sanctuaries. In praising the wrestler Epharmostos of Opus, Pindar sings:

> For fate has allotted Opus to Themis and to her renowned daughter Eunomia [...]
> and it thrives on the strength of its people's deeds by your waters, Castalia,
> and by the streams of Alpheios.
> And so the finest crowns won in that place glorify the Locrians' mother-city,
> famed for its beautiful trees.[6]

In religious terms, this water and the land's fertility indicates the presence of a hero or other divine, life-giving force. In Philostratus' *On Heroes*, the deceased cult hero Protesilaos inhabits a sacred garden where the fragrance of blossoms and leaves is described as godlike (*theion*). Indeed, the fragrance is understood to be the breath of the hero, a physical manifestation of his presence.[7] According to Gregory Nagy, heroes like Protesilaos were thought to ensure the seasonality of nature—including the health and fertility of plants, animals, and humans.[8] This seasonality, called *hōra*, signaled more than natural order and health. As the modern Greek derivative *ōraia* suggests, seasonality was a kind of beauty.[9] Pindar personifies it:

---

[6] Pindar, *Olympian* 9.13-19.
[7] Philostratus, *On Heroes*, 3.3-5, and 11.3.
[8] Nagy, *Ancient Greek Hero*, 15§52.
[9] Nagy, *Ancient Greek Hero*, 15§43.

> To you, sons of Aletes, the many-flowered *hōrai* have often granted victory's glory. (*Olympian* 13, 13)

Indeed, the poets devote some of almost every victory ode to the natural beauty of the games' location and the athlete's home. Bacchylides sings of "Nemea's meadows dense with life" (*Nemean* 9), and of Olympia's "livid and envied olives," which grow where "Pelops' lawns slope pure" (*Pythian* 11). Pelops is the local hero of Olympia, but local heroes from the victor's hometown are also celebrated in the odes—their presence sometimes credited with the cultivation of such a virtuous young sapling as the victor himself. Sings Pindar (*Nemean* 8, 40-41):

> *Aretē* soars upward like a tree fed on fresh dews,
> lifted among the wise and just towards liquid heaven

In Philostratus' text, Protesilaos often does gymnastics when he makes a spiritual appearance in the garden (*On Heroes* §13.1-§13.2). Prominent among those who come to the garden to be inspired by him, moreover, are athletes (§14.4-§15.10). Heroes' spirits were thought to live in their tombs and athletic events, as well as other religious rituals, often took place beside and even on top of the tombs. The turning-point of the chariot race in Homer's *Iliad* turns out to be a hero's tomb. Chthonic sacrifices were made on the tomb of the hero Pelops at Olympia. Worshippers were even known to throw themselves upon a hero's tomb attempting to kiss and embrace the hero's spirit (Philostratus, *On Heroes* §22.3). In order for the hero's *aretic* life-force to benefit the individual or community, however, it needed to be activated through worship. I think ancient athletes understood this activation to be central to their task, and entering the space where heroes and gods were thought to be present would have put them into a special kind of mindset—one in which they were prepared to experience *aretic* ecstasy.

Sacred Responsibility

A key part of this mindset would have been caused by the presence of an audience—members of one's family and village at

III. The Ethics of Excellence

a local contest, distinguished members of one's city-state and of the larger Hellenic community at an Olympic festival. Tribes and cities took special interest in the performances of their athletes. Evidence in the form of coins excavated at Nemea suggests that spectators from different city-states sat in groups or "rooting sections" in the stadium.[10] There is also evidence that city funds were spent to train and send promising local athletes to the games.[11] These communities' interest in their athletes performing well wasn't just a matter of nationalistic pride, as it seems to be in the modern Olympic Games. Because the athlete's performance could to activate the spirit of the god or hero, the community he represented stood to benefit in very concrete ways—the natural fertility mentioned above, and perhaps the answering of prayers for peace or healing. Since Panhellenic festivals like Olympia were dedicated to Panhellenic gods like Zeus, the community in question would include everyone in attendance and all Hellenes in general. This must have created a great sense of responsibility and desire to perform for the athlete. The losing athlete, for his part, could be expected to feel shame. Pindar describes him as "slinking down alleyways, gnawed by failure" (*Pythian* 8.85).

The audience's expectations would have been formed by not just by shared religion, but more specifically by the shared heritage of epic poetry—especially that of Homer, whose descriptions of heroic glory simultaneously created that glory by immortalizing it in song.[12] I would argue that what Homer did, more precisely, was to immortalize the *aretē* of those heroes. Through the re-enactment of the heroes' *agōnes* or struggles in athletic contests, heroic *aretē* was revived and perpetuated—first by "appearing" through the athlete's performance, then by being re-celebrated in the poetic victory odes. The poet and athlete cannot be separated from one another. First the poet inspires the athlete to re-enact the ancient hero's *agōn* in the effort to evoke heroic *aretē*, then the poet himself

---

[10] Miller, *Ancient Greek Athletics*, 110.
[11] Nicholson, *Aristocracy and Athletics*, 127.
[12] Nagy, *Ancient Greek Hero*, 1§12.

re-enacts Homer's excellence by celebrating the athlete's *aretē* in a way that immortalizes it and inspires others to strive for it. Sings Baccylides (*Nemean* 13):

> Theirs perpetual glory
> Thanks to the eloquent Muses,
> Thanks to deathless song,
> *Aretē* flaming to all
> Does not black out,
> Not even dim,
> Under night's folding drifts,
> But alive with esteem
> Irrepressibly wings the earth
> And trackless sea.

Cultural Conspiracy

The process might be seen as a cultural conspiracy. Since the common denominator of ancient Hellenic culture just *is* the *aretē* of heroes described in Homer's epics and traditional mythology, the entire community of spectators knows what they are looking for as they wait for the god or hero to appear within the athlete's performance. They come to Olympia not just to see Astylos of Kroton win another running event, they come to Olympia hoping to see Achilles appear in the form of his virtues as expressed in athletic performance—and to reap the benefits of his spiritual power. And when a statue or poem is created to celebrate the athlete's victory, it celebrates *aretē* as a cultural value. Indeed, epinician poems were performed at public gatherings by choruses of citizens in a ritual designed to "communalize" athletic victory,[13] thereby making the evoked heroic *aretē* the property not just of the athlete, but of the larger community.

An athlete must have felt this sense of sacred responsibility; he knows that the audience's hopes for *aretic* ecstasy depend on his *aretic* ecstasy, which depends on his heroic performance. So he trains. A lot. All that poetry and art that celebrates heroic *aretē*

---

[13] Nagy, *Pindar's Homer*, 5§11.

III. The Ethics of Excellence

conspires to inspire the young athlete to try and achieve it. "Take wings by means of my art," sings Pindar to the wrestler Aristomenes.[14] There is beauty in *aretic* ecstasy, which means that there is truth and goodness in it. It was something worth dedicating a young life to. Even Plato philosopher monarchs in *Republic* dedicated some years to all-out athletic training (524d).

Most modern athletes practice sport instrumentally—as a means to some further end such as a trophy, college scholarship, or professional career. Some may practice for educational reasons—to learn the virtues of self-discipline and endurance; to learn how to deal with failure. But even the modern athlete who dedicates herself to *aretē* would not be performing the kind of community service that ancient athletes conceived themselves to be performing. Her cultivation of *aretē* is primarily self-serving; the ancient athlete, by contrast, is attempting to evoke and perpetuate a divine and heroic spirit of *aretē* upon which his community depends.[15] The ancient athlete is more monk than entrepreneur, and he would have been expected to approach his training with complete dedication and focus.

Focus on and immersion in the activity is foundational in Csíkszentmihályi's account of flow. To some degree, this can be trained like other athletic skills. Professional basketball coach Phil Jackson is famous for using Daoist and Native American techniques to teach his athletes to completely clear their minds—to *stop* thinking about anything but the athletic task at hand.[16] Martial artists call this state *mu-shin* (no-mind) and they associate it with the kind of peak performance linked to Flow, as well as the *wu-wei* (effortlessness) that comes from being in harmony with the Way.[17] For the ancient Greek athlete, this focus would also be based on the ideal of *autotelicity*—the experience of an activity as

---

[14] Pindar, *Pythian* 74.

[15] Reid, *Athletics and Philosophy in the Ancient World*, 28-29

[16] Phil Jackson, *Sacred Hoops* (New York: Hyperion, 1995) 115.

[17] Winston King, *Zen and the Way of the Sword* (New York: Oxford University Press, 1993) 177.

intrinsically rewarding and meaningful. For Aristotle, the idea of something being an end in itself is what characterizes the highest form of *aretē*, the form associated with goodness and beauty known as *kalokagathia* (*Eudemian Ethics* 1120a24). I don't think the athlete can *try* to invoke the hero's spirit directly—the way a priest or medium might. The ecstasy of Flow is not something that happens at will. Rather it happens spontaneously—or with the grace of the gods—when a very skilled performer is deeply engaged in a very challenging activity that she finds intrinsically rewarding.

Reenactment and Reproduction

The performer's immersion in the activity, in turn, leads to a loss of self-consciousness. Musicians describe being one with their music. Poets claim to be possessed and guided by the Muse. Athletes report the sensation that they are watching themselves from the stands or the heavens as someone else occupies their bodies. In the cultural context of ancient Greece, I believe that athletes would have interpreted this sensation as being possessed by or even temporarily becoming the god or hero whose exploits they are re-enacting and whose virtues they are trying to reproduce. "It is only through a god's agency that a man's poetic skill grows to fruition," says Pindar (*Olympian* 11.8-9). So too athletes achieve glory "with god's help" (*Olympian* 10.21) for "it is the god who provides" glory (*Pythian* 8.75). Athletics are re-enactments of the *agōnes* (struggles, ordeals) of heroes as recounted in the poetry and mythology central to ancient Greek culture.[18] Events like running, wrestling, javelin-throwing, and chariot racing are often interpreted as practical military training, but I think they represent, rather, the *athla* (exploits) of heroes like Heracles, Antilochus, and Achilles. It should not be forgotten that Homer's *Iliad* Book 23 includes nearly all the events of the early Olympic Games as part of the funeral games for Patroclus. These funeral games, furthermore, are representations and celebrations

---

[18] Nagy, *Ancient Greek Hero* 8§53.

III. The Ethics of Excellence

of the deceased hero's virtues.[19] As ancient Greek athletics evolved from its earliest form in funeral games to games honoring local heroes, then finally to Panhellenic games, they remained, in an important sense, re-enactments of heroic *agōnes* designed to evoke *aretē*.

Athletics in this sense should be seen as kind of *mimēsis*—directly related to the *mimēsis* characteristic of art and drama so passionately debated by Plato and Aristotle. Aristotle praises *mimēsis* as a natural way of learning (*Poetics* 1448b). We learn language through imitation and good character through exposure to good role-models. *Aretē*, for Aristotle, is the product of *ethos*, habituation or training (*Nicomachean Ethics* 1103a). Keeping in mind Aristotle's tendency to classify and describe contemporary practices rather than invent novel methods, we may infer that athletics was a kind of education for character that combined both aspects of *mimēsis*—the imitation of role models and the training of virtues. Athletic events re-create the *agōnes* or struggles of gods and heroes, while holding their mythical performances up as ideals to be striven for. Wrestling matches, for example, recreated the mythological wrestling feats of Zeus, Heracles and Theseus. The god Apollo was linked with boxing. Hermes, Achilles, and Atalanta were great runners. Eventually, great athletes such as Theagenes were themselves worshipped as heroes, and young athletes would have been very interested in recreating their feats and evoking their virtues as well. Thus epinician poetry links not only gods and heroes, but also athletic ancestors with the victorious performance.

Because the athlete is imitating the *agōn* with real virtue, this understanding of athletics bypasses Plato's main concern about *mimēsis*—namely that the audience may confuse authentic *aretē* with the mere representation of it (*Republic* 605b). It is the *agōn* that is imitated, and it is imitated in such a way that real virtues are demanded by it. When a pair of athletes wrestle, their match is presumably not quite as monumental as, say, the mythological

---

[19] Reid, *Athletics and Philosophy in the Ancient World*, 16-17.

wrestling match between Heracles and Antaios, or even the Olympic wrestling matches between Milo and his challengers. But the same sorts of virtues are demanded by it—courage, strength, *sōphrosynē,* and the rest. If the wrestling match were to be staged as part of a drama, it would be the kind of *mimēsis* Plato worried about precisely because authentic virtues would not be demanded by it—the wrestlers wouldn't struggle the way they do in a real contest. But athletic *agōnes* do demand virtues. When Plato himself prescribed war-games for his ideal society in *Laws* (830e), he specified that the missiles thrown be dangerous enough to incite real fear—and presumably thereby to evoke real virtues. Again, the *aretē* demanded by sport may be a step down from the *aretē* of the heroes, but when the challenge is at its highest and the best of athletes performs his best—just for a moment that heroic virtue may appear within the athlete's performance. For a moment he may enter a state of Flow. At that moment of *aretic* ecstasy, I claim, the athlete "loses himself" and becomes the hero, or perhaps even the god whose *agōn* he is reenacting.

Alteration of Time

These moments of *aretic* ecstasy also involve an alteration of time. Modern accounts of Flow usually describe a slowing down of time—not unlike cinematic slow motion—or a speeding up of time, especially in events like the marathon where the virtues of patience and endurance are central to success.[20] Ancient athletes no doubt had similar experiences at the moment of *aretic* ecstasy, but there would also be another alteration of time more specific to the context. At the moment when the athlete "becomes" the hero or god, the present time is collapsed or flattened in such a way as to bring us into direct contact with an idealized past. The significance of this derives from the general view of history as decline, as symbolized by Hesiod's myth of the "Five Generations of Humankind" in *Works and Days* (V.106-201). The myth tells of our descent from a Golden Age when gods and humans

---

[20] Reid, *The Philosophical Athlete,* 64-65.

intermingled as near-equals, through silver and bronze ages (yes, that's where the modern Olympic medals come from) to the heroic age of Achilles and Odysseus, and finally to the Iron Age occupied by Hesiod himself. This general view of moral and physical decline (which contrasts starkly with contemporary ideas of history as constant progress), created a moral urgency to reconnect through virtue with the nobler generations of the past.[21]

Athletes were able to evoke this idealized past with their size, strength, and most important, their public displays of *aretē*. The great Krotonite wrestler Milo was so closely associated with Heracles, he was said to have entered battle bearing the club and lion skin characteristic of the hero. It is logical that an audience witnessing the ancient Olympic Games, aware of and even looking for a point of contact with the Hellenes' golden past, would understand great athletes to be incarnations of ancient gods or heroes. It is worth noting in this connection that athletes in the so-called heavy events of boxing, wrestling, and *pankration*, which lacked weight classes, would have been extraordinarily big and therefore resembled ancient races, which were imagined to be larger. American football and basketball players dwarf "mere mortals" in the same way today, but we no longer understand them to be relics of an idealized past. Now we attribute their size and strength to technological "advances," including steroids and synthetic human growth hormone (which, by the way, diminish the role of *aretē* in sport). The ancient Greek interpretation of athletic heroism was more in line with the wistful Simon and Garfunkel lyric dedicated to a baseball player, "Where have you gone, Joe Dimaggio, a nation turns its lonely eyes to you."

But even beyond the inspirational nature of athletic heroes, I suspect that a moment of *aretic* ecstasy would have been understood as a moment of temporal transcendence in which the moral distance between the heroic and contemporary ages

---

[21] Charles Stocking, "Ages of Athletes: Generational Decline in Philostratus' Gymnasticus and Archaic Greek Poetry," *CHS Research Bulletin* 1.2 (2013): §15.

temporarily disappears. Pindar seems to suggest as much in *Nemean* 9 (38-49) when he compares a victorious athlete to the Trojan hero, Hector:

> It is said that Hector's glory burst into flower beside Scamader's stream
> But beside the steep, rocky banks of Heloros,
> At the place which men call Areia's Crossing,
> The same brightness shone on Hagisedamos' son in his early prime.

There is a theme in ancient Greek thought of events repeating in history and of stories being temporally manipulated by the techniques of compression and expansion. In Homer's *Iliad*, for example, we see micro-narratives, which tell compressed stories about heroes (from an even more distant past) that reflect the macro-narrative about Achilles.[22] Likewise Achilles himself is described strumming a lyre and singing of the glories of men, there within the very song which sings of *his* glory. "Not even in death did the songs desert him," sings Pindar of Achilles. "The maidens of Helicon stood by his pyre and poured over him a many-voiced dirge, and the gods too resolved that noble men should become a theme for the hymns of these goddesses even after their death" (*Isthmian* 8.55-60). In other words, heroic *agōnes* and the *aretē* they demand—like the songs that celebrate them— are recurring and repeated throughout history. Despite the general decline of humanity depicted in the myth of the "Five Generations" there are occasions on which these heroic virtues re-appear in the world— occasions of *aretic* ecstasy, which serve as a thread that connects Hellenes with their living and glorious past.

Conclusion

Of course the real question may be what thread can connect us today with our glorious Hellenic past (I say "our" because Hellenic culture is humanistic rather than ethnic and it rightly stands at the root of so much of our globalized culture today). I

---

[22] Nagy, *Ancient Greek Hero* §17.

III. The Ethics of Excellence

would argue that moments of *aretic* ecstasy experienced within sport, as well as other performances including music, poetry, and drama, can play an important part. To do this, however, we need to heal the breach between art and athletics, as well as between ethics and aesthetics more generally. *Aretē* again needs to be central to our culture and that means that instrumentalism needs to give way to autotelicity. In short we need to strive again to realize what Pindar (*Pythian* 8.95-7) said about humankind.

> Creatures of a day!
> What is man?
> What is he not?
> He is the dream of a shadow;
> yet when Zeus-sent brightness comes
> A brilliant light shines upon mankind
> and their life is serene.

Section IV:
Beautiful Goodness

11. Athletic Beauty in Ancient Greece: A Philosophical View[1]

Introduction

Among the most memorable experiences of my life was the night in Beijing's Bird's Nest Stadium when Usain Bolt sprinted to Olympic glory in the 100 meter dash. The whole place was engulfed in euphoria and every spectator present seemed connected to Bolt's achievement—not least when he paused in front of us and the cameras to strike his famous victory pose. The stance resembles an archer drawing a giant bow, ready to shoot an arrow up into the heavens. It has been called the lightning pose, which reflects Bolt's nickname, but it also recalls those ancient Greek statues of Zeus hurling lightning bolts with naked athletic grace. It would not be surprising if Bolt imagines himself as an ancient athletic statue when he strikes this pose for the crowd. After all, there is a palpable link between the athletic aesthetic of Classical Greece and his own sprinting prowess and sculpted physique. What is more, the crowd's and cameras' adoring gaze completes the dynamic within which athlete and spectator combine to produce a mutually inspiring experience of beauty that reaches beyond mere sport into the moral and semi-divine dimension captured by the ancient philosophical ideal of beautiful goodness called *kalokagathia*.[2]

Or maybe he's just exploiting his physique in order to sell a product. Bolt's main sponsor markets a line of clothing and accessories emblazoned with his signature pose. In all likelihood they have trademarked it and employed a legal team to protect their investment. Perhaps Bolt's contract requires him to adopt the pose when cameras are present. Such a shallow understanding of

---

[1] Originally published in *Journal of the Philosophy of Sport,* 39:1 (2012), 1-17. Reprinted with permission. All rights reserved.
[2] For an overview, see I. Martinkova, "*Kalokagathia:* How to understand harmony of a human being," *Nikephoros* 14 (2001): 21–8.

IV. Beautiful Goodness

the "value" of athletes and their particular brand of beauty is perhaps more plausible, and certainly more common today. Modern athletes, females in particular, are sometimes better known (and better paid) for their sex appeal than their results. Beach volleyball promoters have been particularly adept at using the bikini-clad physiques of players to market their sport.[3] Male athletic bodies may be less explicitly sexualized, but their aesthetic and erotic appeal is undeniable. Even the completely covered American football player strikes an unmistakably masculine silhouette, his shoulders and thighs broadened by pads, his waist left thin and often exposed as he stretches up to catch the ball.

The modern aesthetic of athletic bodies can seem irrevocably commercialized, objectified and sexualized.[4] Although they appear almost constantly in the media, rarely are athletes the subject of high art these days—much less the imagined embodiment of divine ideals. But does this imply that we are no longer capable of associating them with the aesthetic ideals of Classical Greece? Is athletic beauty now completely removed from the moral and educational ideal of *kalokagathia*? To answer those questions we must first strive to understand athletic beauty in the context of Classical Greek philosophy. We need to ask ourselves what the Greeks saw then they looked at an athlete sculpted from bronze, marble, or flesh and blood. And we need to inquire after what they took this image to mean. We must recognize the eroticism inherent in athletic beauty, but we should distinguish it from the sexualization of modern athletes. We must also wonder

---

[3] Although more lenient clothing rules have been adopted since the London Olympics, women's bodies will continue to be showcased in the event. See C. Weaving, "*The Burning Flame Within*: The Sexualization of Women Athletes in Beach Volleyball," in *The Olympics and Philosophy*, eds. Mike Austin and Heather L. Reid (Lexington: University of Kentucky Press, 2012), 228-41.

[4] For an explanation of what it means for athletes to be "sexualized," see Paul Davis, "Sexuality and sexualization in sport," in *Ethics and Sport*, eds. W. Morgan, K. Meier, and A. Schneider (Champaign IL: Human Kinetics. 2001), 285–92.

about the social and civic dimension of athletic beauty, addressing the question of female athletes and whether they were thought to have the same kind of beauty. Exploration of these questions will lead us to a basic understanding of *kalokagathia*, and allow us to reflect upon its relevance to athletics today.

What Did the Greeks See?

Standing in a museum and gazing at a Classical Greek athletic statue, we might believe that we are having an experience similar to that of the ancients who originally viewed the work in a sanctuary like the one at Olympia, where victors in the famous games had the right to dedicate images of themselves. We might even imagine ourselves walking through the sanctuary to the adjacent stadium to watch live athletes struggle and sweat, their oiled skin glistening under the sun. However, even if we were to witness similar images in modern athletic stadiums (not to mention in photography and film), and even if we were to look at the exact same statue that stood in ancient Greece, it would be presumptuous to say that we are *seeing* the same thing that the ancients did. Aesthetic experience is not merely a matter of sense data. It engages a set of beliefs and attitudes, personal, cultural, and historical, which condition the way we experience that data. What "shows up" when we look at a given image, and how we make sense of it are part and parcel of an aesthetic experience. So to understand the Classical Greek ideal of athletic beauty, we must ask what "showed up" for them when they looked at a typical athletic nude like Myron's *Discus-thrower*, or Polykleitos' *Spear-bearer*. Of course, it is impossible to answer the question with any precision, but there are some cultural and philosophical clues that might help us to make an informed guess.

Clearly one of the first things they saw was muscle—in this they hardly differ from us. The rounded deltoids, the sculpted pectorals, the "six-pack" abdomen, the pronounced quadriceps, the protruding buttocks. The physical structure of an athletic male has not changed significantly in 3000 years—even though the amount of muscularity deemed aesthetically pleasing wavers. The

IV. Beautiful Goodness

smooth and understated lines of Praxiteles' *Hermes* contrast markedly with Lysippos' *Hercules*, whose bulging muscles almost resemble that modern bodybuilder's. Of course the ancient Greeks were aware that different athletic events favor different physiques; the distinction between "light events" like running or jumping, and "heavy events" such as boxing or pankration, derives from the size of the athletes (weight classes were not used in ancient sports). Heavyweight boxers and wrestlers appear occasionally in vase paintings, but rarely were subject of life-size sculpture (or the object of the erotic gaze).

The most popular subject of athletic sculpture was rather the pentathlete, praised even by Aristotle for possessing the prized characteristics of balance and harmony:

> Beauty varies with each age. In a young man, it consists in possessing a body capable of enduring all efforts, either of the racecourse or of bodily strength, while he himself is pleasant to look upon and a sheer delight. This is why the athletes in the pentathlon are most beautiful, because they are naturally adapted for bodily exertion and for swiftness of foot. (*Rhetoric* 1361b11)

Much of ancient athletic art depicts the pentathlete's distinctive disciplines: discus, javelin, and long-jumping (the other events, running and wrestling, were also stand-alone contests). Aristotle is not speaking merely as a sports fan here. Balance is essential to his ethical doctrine of the mean, which requires the agent to seek virtue at the midpoint between excess and deficiency – courage, for example, is the midpoint between cowardice and rashness (*Nicomachean Ethics*, 1106a). Ethical action, furthermore, is described by Aristotle as something both beautiful and done for the sake of beauty (*to kalon*) (*NE* 1120a and 1116b).[5] The

---

[5] For a fuller account of Aristotle's philosophy applied to sport see Reid, "Aristotle's Pentathlete" *Athletics and Philosophy in the Ancient World*, 69–80, and "Athletic Virtue and Aesthetic Values in Aristotle's Ethics," *Journal of the Philosophy of Sport* 47:1 (2020).

pentathlete's beauty symbolizes the values of Aristotelian ethics. Balance and harmony were also expressed through Polykleitos' famous *Kanon*—a text and corresponding statue (both now lost) said to demonstrate the mathematical basis for the symmetry and proportion essential to depicting a beautiful nude. Attempts to reproduce Polykleitos' formula by measuring Roman copies of his work such as the *Doryphoros* or *Diadumenos* have met with varying success; some suspect he may not have had a hard and fast formula at all.[6] Others claim the formula applied equally to male and female bodies, children as well as adults.[7] What cannot be claimed is that every flesh and blood Greek athlete was built to conform to Polykleitos' *Kanon*. Athletes can sculpt their muscles with careful training, but they cannot change the lengths and proportions of their limbs. In any case, they should be training to optimize performance in their sport and not simply to resemble a statue. The point is not just to look the part of the athlete from the outside, but rather to have athletic virtues within.

The balance and harmony we see in artistic images of ancient athletes reflects not so much how the athletes really looked but was rather an expression of the desired state of their souls. It is for this reason that I talk about the beauty of athletes, rather than the beauty of athletic bodies. The soul (*psychē*), after all, is the principle of movement in ancient Greek thought, and athletic beauty, even in sculpture, cannot be separated from movement. Psychic harmony was also expressed artistically through facial expression and body language. Classical statues of victorious athletes look nothing like images of modern winners smiling broadly or celebrating wildly, their arms thrust euphorically into the air. The statues instead exhibit modesty and serenity, their gaze cast slightly down and to the side, even as they reach up to touch the winner's crown (*stephanos*) or ribbon (*tainia*) tied around their

---

[6] N. Spivey, "Meditations on a Greek Torso," *Cambridge Archaeological Journal*, 7:2 (1997): 312.

[7] N. Spivey, *The Ancient Olympics: A History* (Oxford : Oxford University Press, 2004), 58.

heads. I don't think we should conclude from this that ancient Greek athletes were indifferent about winning, or that they typically reacted to victory with the serenity and decorum depicted in athletic art. Rather the statues depict a philosophical reaction to victory in a religious context.

It is important to remember, in contrast to modern sports, that ancient athletic festivals were a form of religious worship and that athletic competition served a communitarian function.[8] Many of the athletic images we see in museums today were commissioned to be dedicated to the relevant god in appropriate sanctuaries as a memorial of victory, or to be part of a funerary monument recalling a deceased athlete's glorious past. These environments call for an attitude of decorum, or even sadness. It is also an appropriate milieu for recalling an athlete's mortality in contrast to the gods. Even ancient images depicting athletes at the height of effort show none of the intense focus, strain, and pain familiar in photographs of modern athletes. I have never seen a human discus thrower with the peaceful face of Myron's *Discus Thrower*, but we shouldn't conclude that ancient athletes didn't strain or grimace when they competed. Rather the artistic image portrays a desired state of soul.

Indeed, this expression of a harmonious and serene athletic soul is meant to resemble the soul of a god. Many athletic statues and paintings actually depict ancient gods, who would have no reason grimace or strain—even when performing the most difficult athletic feat. The relief in Ancient Olympia's museum of Athena helping Heracles to shoulder the sky with an effortless touch of her fingertips illustrates this principle well. Even "portraits" of human athletes set up in religious sanctuaries were probably aimed less at representing the victor's real appearance than they were an attempt to merge that individual into a culturally-valued paradigm of *kalokagathia* derived from ideas about the nature of gods. In other words, the image we see in Classical art is not an image of the athlete as he is or even was, but

---

[8] For an explanation see "Olympic Sacrifice," in this volume.

rather of the athlete as a kind of god, elevated, like the mythical Heracles, to divine status through his achievements. The Greek athlete at the moment of victory resembles a god, but like the leafy crown that graces his head, his glory is passing and ephemeral. When ancient Hellenes observed athletic beauty, they saw a fit bodies but also a balance and harmony expressing an ideal state of the soul, which ultimately reflected their gods.

What Did it Mean to Them?

What was the philosophical basis for this understanding of athletic beauty? What, in short, did it mean? If I had to answer that question with one word, the word would be *aretē*. But that is not a simple solution, because *aretē* itself is a deep and complex idea that does not even have a good English translation. "Virtue," the most common rendering, too quickly evokes examples like Mother Teresa. "Excellence" may be better, but people can be excellent at things like lying without having any share of *aretē*. "Virtuosity" captures the sense of being excellent in a worthwhile endeavor and provides an aesthetic angle, but its modern usage is confined almost exclusively to the music world, whereas *aretē* was associated more readily with the gymnasium. *Aretē* is not merely an athletic value, however, it is the central concept in Classical Greek ethics. The goal of Aristotle's ethics is identified as activity in accordance with *aretē* (*NE* 1120a) and Plato describes *aretē* as the health of the soul (i.e. *Republic* 444de, *Charmides* 156e–157a). Interpreting athletic beauty philosophically, then, means interpreting it in terms of *aretē*.6

Athletic muscles evoke *aretē* first and foremost as evidence of voluntary hard work. The Greek word *ponos*, so common in Pindar's athletic victory poetry, signifies not just pain but more importantly toil. In the context of the gymnasium, *ponos* is the toil necessary to achieve not only muscular development but military usefulness, athletic excellence, and ultimately *aretē*. Aristotle praised the pentathlete's beauty in part because it resulted from hard work (*NE* 1114a), something also essential to good ethics (*NE* 1109a25). In ancient Greek *euandreia* (masculine beauty) contests,

IV. Beautiful Goodness

there was a kind of consolation prize for being *philoponos*—a lover of hard training.[9] Presumably the winner of the prize was decided not by counting the hours spent in training, but rather according the aesthetic evidence of a contestant's efforts in the gym, namely, his muscular development. The existence of a *philoponos* prize suggests, furthermore, that gymnastic toil was recognized and valued even if it did not result in the highest level of beauty (which would have entailed winning the contest outright). The athletic aesthetic, then, places special value on voluntary effort.

The voluntary nature of the effort also distinguished the athletic muscularity achieved through gymnastic *ponos* from the servile muscularity that results from intensive manual labor. In the cultural context of Classical Greece, that kind of work would have been mostly done by slaves, who were not fed and cared for in such a way that would lead to athletic excellence—much less a symmetrical and harmonious physique. The disassociation of athletic muscularity from slaves and low-class laborers is illustrated by Homer's description of the athletic thighs, arms, and chest of noble Odysseus in sharp contrast to the large but unbalanced physique of his low-class boxing opponent, Iros (*Odyssey* 18.96f). It is also illustrated by the enduring connection between liberty and gymnasia. Not only were slaves generally barred from public gymnasia, free men went there and trained of their own accord—not least to fulfill their responsibility to stay fit for military service, which was understood as the primary means for protecting the community's liberty. The aesthetic appeal of athletic muscularity derives not only from its mathematically measurable balance and harmony, but also from its association with the noble voluntary effort to achieve a state of *aretē* capable of preserving the community's liberty.

Embedded in the notion of balance and harmony is also an understanding of *aretē* itself as a kind of balance or harmony—for Plato, a harmony of the soul. In *Republic* (435e–44e) and through the metaphor of a chariot in *Phaedrus* (246a–247b), Plato describes

---

[9] Spivey, "Meditations on a Greek Torso," 312.

the human soul as consisting of three parts: a rational part, a spirited part, and an appetitive part. The appetitive part is strong but hard to control, representing as it does our desires for food, drink, sex, and other appetites we share with the animals. The rational part represents the divine part of our nature, and is depicted in the *Phaedrus* metaphor as the driver of the chariot, while the spirited part is depicted as an obedient horse alongside the unruly appetitive horse. Education for *aretē*, including gymnastics and athletics, is aimed at order and harmony among these three parts of the soul – with reason leading and the other two parts following. In fact, Socrates says that the virtuous person "harmonizes the three parts of himself like three limiting notes in a musical scale—high, low and middle" (*Republic* 443d). The result of this internal harmony will be not only a symmetrical physique, but also the expression of serenity seen upon the faces of ancient Greek athletic statues.

The same understanding of *aretē* can explain athletic beauty's association with the divine. After all, on Plato's tripartite model for *aretē* in the soul, it is the divine part which leads and essentially tames our animalistic—or some might say bodily—urges. It is in this way that the image of an athletic body paradoxically exalts the non-physical aspects of the human being. Athletic beauty symbolizes the triumph of our divine, spiritual nature over our animalistic, physical nature. Just as the beauty of a sleek and well-trained race horse was thought to represent its owner's excellence rather than its own (in ancient equestrian sports, the crown of victory always went to the owner), the well-trained body's beauty reflects excellence of the soul. Furthermore, since athleticism was associated with divine ancestry, even before the emergence of sport, athletic beauty also reflected the noble effort to "become like a god."[10] Heracles is a role-model for athletes here, since he achieved apotheosis through his *athla* (labors) in service of the

---

[10] This is another of Plato's metaphors for *aretē*, for a discussion, see J. Armstrong, "After the ascent: Plato on becoming like God," *Oxford Studies in Ancient Philosophy* 26.1 (2010): 171–83.

community. Indeed, the divine Heracles, whose labors had the effect of defending communities from a variety of threats and menaces, was one of three gods commonly worshipped at the gymnasium.[11] The athletic aesthetic, as we have seen, means striving to resemble a god in terms of *aretē*, which includes service to the community cause of liberty.

How Was it Erotic?

My claim that the beauty of the athletic body is paradoxical testament to the primacy and potential divinity of the soul may suggest to some that I have overlooked the explicit eroticism of athletic beauty. Eros, after all, was another god worshipped at the gymnasium. The erotic appeal of a fit athletic body, especially a naked one, certainly was part of the ancient Greek athletic aesthetic. As I cautioned earlier, however, we should be careful about assuming that our own idea of eroticism reflects that of the Classical Greeks. Heterosexual eroticism is one thing, and the question of female athletic beauty will be discussed below. But in the case of Classical athletic beauty I think we are dealing primarily with homoeroticism, which cannot be sexual in the biological sense because it does not lead to reproduction, and is not the same as sexualization in the modern sense—at least not in its philosophical expression. Erotic relationships between youths and older men were accepted and even institutionalized as a form of education in Classical Greece, one explicitly associated with the civic values of the gymnasium. So to fully understand the erotic appeal of athletic beauty, we must first move beyond a biological notion of sexuality aimed at reproduction.

Of course something can still be sexual without having anything to do with reproduction. Many heterosexual couples have enduring relationships and fulfilling sex lives that never result and are never intended to result in offspring. Clearly, the basis of these relationships is something other than reproduction, and in most cases it is something more than sex. It has to do with

---

[11] T. Scanlon, *Eros and Greek Athletics*, (Oxford: Oxford University Press, 2002), 329.

partnership, emotional bonds, common values, mutual support. Likewise, the ancient Greek partnership between a more mature *erastēs* (lover) and a younger *erōmenos* (beloved) was expected to satisfy more noble desires than the animalistic urge to reproduce, or even the physical urge for sexual satisfaction. In its ideal Platonic form, it was supposed to exclude sexual activity. In Plato's *Symposium* (219c), the beautiful Alcibiades describes being stunned by Socrates' refusal to have sex with him, despite the philosopher's obvious affection for him. Socrates charges that Alcibiades' offer of his youthful body is an attempt to exchange bronze for gold—to trade Socrates' real beauty for Alcibiades' mere appearance of it—so he refuses. Socrates does have deep affection for Alcibiades and no-doubt is tempted by the youth's athletic beauty, but he is able to defeat those physical urges and focus his erotic attention on Alcibiades' soul.

The Greek word for this ability to control one's appetites is *sophrosynē*. It is another part of *aretē* expressed through athletic art, not just on athletes' faces but also by the size of their genitals. Unlike modern images of sexually alluring males, ancient Greek athletic statues de-emphasize the genitals, depicting them smaller than they would be in real-life. This is symbolic of the *sophrosynē* achieved through athletic training. Aristophanes' *Clouds* (1009–23) describes the student of the gymnasium as having broad soldiers and large hips, but a small tongue and penis. Ancient athletic art also depicts infibulation, the tying off of the foreskin to conceal the glans; as another symbol of gymnastic chastity and *sophrosynē* (12: 131).[12] Large and erect phalluses do show up in Greek art, but they are considered ugly and shameful symbols of a lack of self-control or of man's animalistic nature as depicted by the satyr, a creature that is half man and half goat. Socrates resembles a satyr more than an athlete, but his *sophrosynē* is extolled by Alcibiades, who reports

---

[12] Scanlon, *Eros and Greek Athletics*, 234–5, notes that the Greek term for the practice, *kunodesmē*, literally means "dog-leash." Since "dog" was often used as slang for the penis, the use of a "dog leash" had the implication of controlling one's sexual desires.

IV. Beautiful Goodness

that the philosopher is impervious to hunger, cold, and the effects of heavy drinking—not just the sexual allure of a beautiful youth (*Symposium* 219c).

So what was this Greek athletic eroticism, if it was not about sex? Again, the one-word answer is *aretē*. Eros is a god who embodies desire generally—not just sexual desire, but the desire for wisdom at the heart of philosophy and the desire for *kalokagathia* associated with athletics. In Plato's *Symposium*, Eros is described as the child of poverty and resource: we erotically desire what we lack, and it is only by recognizing this lack that we may come to desire it. "What's especially difficult about being ignorant is that you are content with yourself, even though you're neither beautiful and good (*kalon kagathōn*) nor intelligent," explains Socrates. "If you don't think you need anything, of course you won't want what you don't think you need" (*Symposium* 204a). Hence Socrates' mission to make people aware of their ignorance is designed to initiate the erotic pursuit of wisdom. Ultimately, such erotic pursuits—athletic, philosophic, or otherwise—are by nature aimed at beauty, which is identified with the good (*Symposium* 202de, *Hippias Major* 297bc).

This is the kind of eroticism that both Plato and Xenophon take to be the proper foundation of *erastēs-erōmenos* partnerships associated with the gymnasium. Socrates' role in both authors' work consists in directing those relationships' erotic energy toward their ideal aim. In Xenophon's *Symposium*, the athletic youth Autolycos has attracted the attention of a wealthy suitor named Kallias with a victory in the pankration at the Panathenaic Games. But Socrates subtly discourages the youth (and his father, who is present) from accepting Kallias' advances because the philosopher suspects they are misdirected. Part of the concern is about sex, something Socrates thinks should have no part in these relationships because the youthful *erōmenos* does not share in the pleasure of such encounters (Xenophon, *Symposium*, 8.19–23). In effect, the lover is selfishly using the youth as a means to physical satisfaction rather than guiding and supporting him in the shared pursuit of *aretē*. Socrates also seems suspicious that Kallias is more interested in impressing his friends than educating the boy (Xenophon, *Symposium*, 8.42f).[13] There was much social prestige to be gained through public pairing with a promising youth such as an athletic victor. But again, this motivation is selfish and hollow unless the aura of *aretē* that such partnerships conferred on both *erastēs* and *erōmenos* really is the object of their love.

In Plato's *Lysis*, Socrates chastises the *erastēs* Hippothales for flattering his *erōmenos* and making a fool of himself with gushing poetry and tongue-tied awe (206a). The problem here is not that the *erastēs* is selfish, but rather that he is so drunk on love that he neglects the youth's development. Flattery undermines the natural desire for improvement and replaces it with the desire for—and expectation of—constant praise.[14] We have already noted the importance of modesty in artistic depictions of athletic beauty as an expression of the victor's awareness that he is not a god right at the moment when he most resembles one. Pindar, likewise, praises athletes' modesty even as he extols their divine ancestry and demonstrated *aretē* (*Olympian* 13.115). Indeed, the dynamic between athletes and artists like Pindar provides a model for the kind of *aretic* eroticism that Socrates has in mind. Because the artist is able to recognize *aretē*, the athlete tries to demonstrate it in his performance—to live up to the ideal inside the artist's mind. This spectacle in turn inspires the artist to create a beautiful song or statue to honor the athlete's demonstrated *aretē*. Likewise the *aretē* an *erastēs* has achieved inspires the *erōmenos* to strive for excellence, and this, in turn, inspires the *erastēs* to responsibly demonstrate the *aretē* appropriate to his age and position as a military officer, politician, philosopher, or artist.

These erotic partnerships are expected to endure a lifetime, not least because the goal of *aretē* and therefore the good and beautiful, demands a lifelong pursuit. Merely physical beauty

---

[13] For a full discussion of this, see C. Evangeliou, "Socrates on Aretic Athletics," *Phronimon* 11.1 (2010): 45–63.

[14] In Plato's *Gorgias*, 463b, Socrates calls rhetoric a form of flattery (*kolakeia*) which makes the soul seem healthy when in fact it is not.

IV. Beautiful Goodness

fades with the passing bloom of youth (Xenophon, *Symposium* 8.14). Maturity, meanwhile, reduces the distractions of the body and makes it easier to focus on the perfection of the soul, although regular exercise in the gymnasium persists throughout the span of these relationships. Socrates seems forever to be hanging out in the gymnasium,[15] and exercise is mentioned in both Plato's and Xenophon's *Symposium*. In some ways Socrates' presence stands in paradoxical contradiction to the athletic beauty associated with gymnasia since he is by all conventional standards rather ugly. In Xenophon's *Symposium*, his bulging eyes, snub nose, and thick lips are lampooned in a lighthearted beauty contest (5.3–8). Even Alcibiades admits that Socrates resembles Silenos, a fat, bald, drunken figure, on the surface. But he explains that inside, the philosopher possesses amazing, godlike beauty (*Symposium* 216e–217a). The story of Socrates and Alcibiades makes for a paradoxical reversal of the dirty old man chasing the beautiful young athlete: here the deficient young soul chases the embodiment of spiritual beauty.[16] The paradox of athletic eroticism, like the paradox of

---

[15] In Plato's *Euthyphro* (2a) Socrates' "usual haunt" is identified as the Lyceum gymnasium. *Charmides*, *Euthydemus*, *Theaetetus*, and probably *Sophist* and *Politicus* are set in gymnasia. At *Lysis* 203–4a Socrates is going from one gymnasium (the Academy) to another (the Lyceum) when he is pulled aside into new wrestling school.

[16] One cannot help but feel sad that the erotic bond between Socrates and Alcibiades never achieved its purpose. It was unfortunate not just for Alcibiades, but also for Athens, since these partnerships played an important civic function of educating values and creating strong community bonds outside of the family. In the end, Alcibiades led Athens into the disastrous Peloponnesian war, then switched sides and contributed even further to his native city's undoing. Socrates, to some degree, was probably blamed for Alcibiades' vices, which shows the civic importance of these relationships. In writing Alcibiades' speech for the Symposium, Plato seems to some degree to be apologizing for Socrates, but he is also suggesting the political importance of erotic relationships based in the gymnasium

Athletic Beauty in Classical Greece

athletic beauty, is that it isn't about sport, sex, or even bodies—it is ultimately about the soul.

What about Female Athletes?

What are we to say, then, about females and their apparent exclusion from the athletic aesthetic and its erotic appeal? There were female athletes in ancient Greece, although they were excluded from the Olympic Games and are very rarely discussed in literature or depicted in the arts.[17] To my knowledge, neither Pindar, Bacchylides, nor Simonides ever wrote a victory hymn for a female, and the Classical period, at least, seems bereft of statues depicting female athletes. The Spartan Princess Kyniska, who won an olive crown in the Olympic Games by virtue of owning a victorious horse, is said to have erected a statue of herself in Olympia's sanctuary, but it does not survive and I cannot believe that it resembled even remotely the images of naked males that must have surrounded it. Small bronze statuettes of running females do survive, their muscular calves and thighs evidence of a serious training program. These are clothed in short tunics, in some cases leaving one breast exposed, as was customary at the Heraia, games for maidens in Olympia held in honor of Hera. Girls running in races at the sanctuary of Artemis in Brauron seem to have shed similar outfits as they got older, perhaps in the final race before their transition to adulthood and marriage.[18] Occasionally the mythological female athlete Atalanta is depicted (nearly) nude, but otherwise athletic females are almost always clothed.

The fact that athletic females, including goddesses like Artemis and Athena, were generally depicted as clothed suggests their exclusion from the Classical athletic aesthetic. Nude female statues from this period exist, but they usually depict Aphrodite and rarely show signs of athletic training. One practical reason for

---

[17] Events for female athletes included the Heraia, in which girls raced on Olympia's track, and sprints at the other Panhellenic games. For an overview, see Scanlon, *Eros and Greek Athletics*, ch. 4–7.

[18] S. Blundell, *Women in Ancient Greece* (Cambridge, MA: Harvard University Press, 1995), 133.

IV. Beautiful Goodness

this may be artists' relative ignorance of the athletic female form. In stark contrast to the case with males, there was little to no opportunity for artists to observe female athletes naked. There were not that many of them to begin with, most of the time they seem to have competed in clothes, and their athletic days ended with marriage. Another possible reason for depicting female athletes clothed could be that their erotic appeal was focused on their souls rather than their bodies – but we have already learned that the costume of male nudity just was a statement about the soul's *aretē*. The reluctance to portray females nude may rather suggest a belief that their souls' were incapable or inappropriate locations for athletic *aretē*. I will return to this question below.

We should not conclude from their relative absence in the arts, however, that ancient athletic females lacked erotic appeal. The mythological athlete Atalanta accumulates so many suitors that according to Hyginus (*Fabulae* 185), their severed heads lined the stadium where she outran them in order to avoid marriage. Amazon warriors, too, seem to have had erotic appeal despite (or maybe because of) their wholesale rejection of men. Achilles is said to have fallen in love with the Amazon queen Penthesilia at the moment that he slays her during the Trojan War (Apollodorus *Library* 5.1). We must remember, however, that athletic females — Atalanta, Amazons, and girls in general — were associated with the goddess Artemis, whose followers were expected to remain virginal and shun the company of men.[19] The footraces for girls in the Heraria and at Artemis' sanctuary of Brauron were probably part of the rite of passage from girlhood into marriage — from Artemis to Aphrodite. To the Classical Greek mind, females were "wild" until they became civilized through marriage. At Brauron, the girls were accordingly thought of as 'little bears' that one day

---

[19] Athletic women may have been erotically attractive to other women. There exist several examples of bronze mirror handles in the shape of naked athletic females. It has been suggested that the handle had erotic value for woman who grasped it. See Scanlon, *Eros and Greek Athletics*, 137–8.

would be tamed. Some have speculated that prospective husbands actually viewed the girls' races in order to shop for prospective brides. Even if this was not the case, in contrast to the case with males, the eroticism surrounding athletic females had everything to do with marriage and reproduction.

I will stop short, however, of claiming that athletic females were sexualized in ancient Greece the way many of them are in modern sports iconography. There is nothing in ancient athletic art that remotely resembles the favored beach volleyball photograph of a bent-over woman's behind—a pose that closely resembles explicitly pornographic images. Even ancient statues of the naked Aphrodite, the goddess of sex, conceal her genitalia as they depict her innocently emerging from a bath or perhaps changing her clothes. To be sure, erotic dancing and other forms of sexually explicit entertainment took place in Classical Greece, but such sexualization would be considered appropriate only for prostitutes and other women specialized in these skills—not for goddesses or unmarried girls, and certainly not for athletes. Even though reproduction is cited as the motivation for Spartan girls exercising in the nude in front of the boys, this is something different than sexualization or titillating entertainment.[20] Spartan education for girls closely resembled that given to boys; perhaps the Spartans reckoned that female souls were as worthy of training as those of the males.

Plato was one admirer of Spartan education who thought female souls were capable of *aretē*.[21] In the *Republic*, he even has Socrates propose that females strip and train naked in the ideal city's gymnasium with the males. The proposal is not expected to earn quick approval or even prurient curiosity—what is expected is laughter and ridicule. But Socrates presses his point, explaining that the mockery would quickly pass because the women would be "clad in their virtue" (457ab). Since the same text describes

---

[20] Scanlon, *Eros and Greek Athletics* 121–38.
[21] In contrast with Aristotle, who thought women's souls were distinct. See Reid, *Athletics and Philosophy in the Ancient World*, 77–8.

IV. Beautiful Goodness

gymnastics primarily as aretic training for the soul, we can infer that Plato thinks females' souls capable of *aretē*. By the time he wrote *Laws*, Plato had reconsidered athletic nudity for females, but not the educational value of athletic activity. Females still take part in gymnastic training and athletic games "suitably clothed for modesty" (*Laws* 804d, 833d). When Plato imagines Atalanta's soul choosing a male body for its next life (*Republic* 620b), it confirms that he believes athleticism to be a property of the soul, though it may also suggest that he thinks the male body is the better vessel for that kind of soul.

The *Republic* makes a serious argument for including females equally—not only in education and athletics, but also in the military, government, and every other facet of public life. The suggestion that male bodies are better vessels for athletic souls is therefore troubling, especially since Plato makes these arguments precisely because he reckons sex to be a property of the body but *aretē* to be property of the soul. Female bodies are said to be physically weaker in most cases (*Republic* 451e), but failing to include women in the pursuit of *aretē* amounts to a civically irresponsible waste of perfectly good souls (*Republic* 454cd). I think Atalanta's choice reflects the limitations of her society rather than any belief that all athletes should be male. In fact Plato says that she is unable to resist the prizes and honors accorded to male athletes (620b)—a motivation based on the lower parts of the soul and one he would reject—but also an acknowledgement of society's resistance to the idea of females' access to athletics as well as *aretē*. The lesson is reinforced by the love story between Atalanta and the hero Meleager, who is pilloried for his decision to include her in the Calydonian Boar Hunt, and then to award her the skin after she ended up striking first blood. Theirs might even be said to be an erotic partnership based on *aretē*, in line with the ideal of *erastēs-erōmenos* relationships, but it was never accepted this way by their society. The Greek athletic aesthetic is clearly tied to male bodies and gender roles, but the commitment to *aretē* it represents is available, a least on Plato's account, to the souls of both sexes.

Conclusion

The story I have told about Greek athletic beauty and its connection to *aretē*, education, and civic duty is essentially the story of *kalokagathia*. Kalokagathia is an educational ideal that connects ethics, aesthetics, and athletics, setting out to elevate the erotic impulse inherent in human life toward the higher ideal of beauty and the good. I say that *kalokagathia* is—and not simply was—an educational ideal because I believe that it remains relevant in our time. The commercialization, objectification, and sexualization of athletic bodies today can and should be replaced by the nobler idea of *kalokagathia*, which, in fact, reflects many of our contemporary athletic values. *Kalokagathia* tells us, first of all, that athletic beauty is a property of persons and not merely of bodies. The beauty that an athletic body reflects through its muscularity, balance, harmony, and serenity are expressions of a soul which has tamed and trained its animalistic nature to serve the more noble commands of reason. Such moderation may be at odds with the highest levels of athletic success, but we can admire athletes for reasons other than victory; indeed the most admired Olympic athletes are praised precisely for their ability achieve excellence off the field as well as on. As in ancient Greece, we should interpret the ideal of athletic beauty as an expression of internal beauty, conceptually connected to the good and the true.

The erotic appeal of athletic beauty, likewise, should transcend biology and even sexuality. It calls for mutually supportive spiritual partnerships based on the shared pursuit of *aretē*, which serve not only to inspire individual excellence but also to unite and protect the community. Though in ancient Greece these relationships were conventional, the problems that cause us to condemn pederasty today were already recognized. It is absolutely imperative that children be protected from sexual predators in sport and every other activity. There is no reason, however, that the bonds of friendship valued in ancient Greece cannot be achieved by adults of any age, gender, or number; perhaps as part of a team. Furthermore, although females were rare in the athletic art and public life of ancient Greece, there is no philosophical reason to detach them from the ideal of *kalokagathia* today, especially in light of their changed social roles. The erotic appeal of the female athlete should be based on her *aretē* and personal worth, as opposed sexual appeal.

Kalokagathia is a political value and athletes are expected to put their virtues into the service of their communities.[22] By connecting athletics with aesthetics and ethics, understood in terms of *aretē*, the ancient Greek ideals of *kalokagathia* and athletic beauty provide a framework for putting sport in the service of the greater good. Usain Bolt may not have all this in mind when he strikes his victorious "lightning" pose, but by reflecting the beauty of the ancient Greek aesthetic he rightly points upward to a higher athletic ideal.

---

[22] For more on the idea of athletes as community servants in ancient Greece see "Olympic Sacrifice," in this volume.

12. Virtuous Viewing of Olympic Athletes[1]

The *Terme Boxer*—a life-size, naked bronze athlete, complete with bleeding cuts, a broken nose, and cauliflower ears—is by any account, a striking piece of sculpture. The statue, found in a Roman bath, and now on display in the *Museo Nazionale Palazzo Massimo*, provokes varied responses. Is he an example of athletic beauty, or an indictment of a sport which has lost all its dignity? Walter Hyde, writing in the 1920s, occupies the latter camp:

> If we like to think of victors as having noble forms, we are rudely startled on looking at this brutal prize-fighter. If we compare it with works of the 5th and 4th century, we see in it, as in no other example of Greek sculpture, the great change which professionalism had later wrought in the Greek ideal of athletics. Here are massive proportions, bulging muscles, arms and legs hard and muscled […]. Such realism and delight in the hideous, show that the work belongs to the Hellenistic age.[2]

But where Hyde sees "delight in the hideous," others see the beauty of virtue—the toil, the endurance, the ability to deal with pain. Unlike a victory statue, it isn't clear if this boxer has won or lost—or even whether the contest is over. But the philosophy of the Greek gymnasium is not about victory, it is about virtue. Were Imperial Romans interested only in blood and violence, or could they discern the Olympic beauty of athletic virtue?

It is hard to know what Imperial Romans saw when they looked at Olympic athletes. But we do know that the Roman experience of Greek athletics was more about viewing and less about doing, and that there were several writers concerned that

---

[1] Originally published as "Athletic Beauty as a *Mimēsis* of Virtue," in *Looking at Beauty: το καλόν in Western Greece*, eds. H. Reid & T. Leyh (Sioux City: Parnassos Press, 2019): 77-91. Reprinted with permission. All rights reserved.

[2] Walter Woodburn Hyde, *Olympic Victor Monuments and Greek Athletic Art*, (Washington DC: Carnegie Institution, 1921), 146-7.

spectators saw the right thing. In the Imperial period, and especially in the city of Rome, Hellenic *paideia* became a mark of the elite, and there was great social pressure to understand and appreciate it—if not to actually participate in it. Writers, in what has come to be called the Second Sophistic, not only promoted this resurgence of classical Greek culture, they competed among themselves, like ancient philosophers and sophists once had in Hellenic gymnasia, to renegotiate and reinterpret this idealized past. And they instructed their readers—often indirectly through parable and metaphor—in what it meant to be properly educated in Hellenic culture; to be a *pepaideumenos.* At least three of them, Dio Chrysostom (40-115 CE), Lucian (125-180 CE) and Philostratus (170-250 CE), took up the specific subject of athletics, with the latter writing a full-length treatise called *On Gymnastics* (*Peri Gymnastikē*). All of these essays, including Philostratus', ostensible handbook for coaches, focus not on the practice, but rather the visual appreciation, of Greek athletics.

At the same time contemporary philosophies of Roman Stoicism and Epicureanism also focused on achieving a particular point of view—a way of looking at things that tames desires and aversions, aiming at a concept of virtue characterized by inner peace (*ataraxia*). The Imperial-era philosopher Epictetus (55-135 CE) describes the process of achieving this state of perspective in explicitly athletic terms, as analogous to training for the Olympic Games. In Book I of his *Discourses,* he says that "God, like a trainer in the gymnasium, has matched you against a tough young opponent…so that you may become an Olympic victor; and that is something that can't be achieved without sweat" (1.24.1-3). Although Stoicism rejects the social hierarchies affirmed by the Second Sophistic, it shares the technique of applying athletic values to a new *agōn*: the struggle to achieve a virtuous vision—a way of recognizing beauty outside in order to achieve beauty inside. Becoming *kaloskagathos* in this context is not about how you look, but rather what you see. And what a Roman saw when he looked at Olympic athletes said a lot about who he was. It revealed whether he was a virtuous spectator or a classless barbarian.

The Virtuous Spectator

When a Hellenically-educated person witnessed an Olympic athlete, he was supposed to see a special kind of beauty. Judging by Dio Chrysostom's oration *On Beauty*, however, few Imperial-age observers were able to do that:

> A handsome (*kalos*) man is not only getting to be a rare sight nowadays, but when there is one, the majority fail to notice his beauty, much more than muleteers fail to observe beautiful horses. And if people do by any chance take an interest in handsome men, it is in a wanton way and for no good purpose. (21.2)

This contrast between an idealized Hellenic past and a degenerated Roman present is common in Second Sophistic literature. Indeed, the oration begins with Dio commenting on the beauty of an ancient athletic statue "like those set up at Olympia," he says, "the very old ones." He muses that more recent statues are less beautiful, not because the sculptors are now less skilled, but because the people portrayed are no longer so handsome (*On Beauty* 21.1). The cause of this lack of beauty, it turns out, is not a lack of gymnasia or a degeneration of humanity generally. The cause is a lack of *appreciation* for beauty. "For it is not only virtue that is increased by commendation, but so beauty is likewise by those who honor and revere it," Dio explains. "But when it is disregarded and esteemed by no one, or when wicked men esteem it, it fades away like reflections in a mirror" (*On Beauty*, 21.2). The virtuous appreciation of athletic beauty, it seems, is even more important than cultivating it in the gymnasium. At stake is nothing less than the survival of beauty itself.

It is no surprise, therefore, that Imperial literature offers instruction, or at least fodder for debate, about what a *kaloskagathos-pepaideumenos* should be seeing when he watches the Capitoline or Olympic Games. First of all, he should exhibit a more sophisticated vision than his Republican-era predecessors had, even though their anti-athletic views were still being expressed. According to Tacitus (*Annals* 14.20), the Olympic-style *Neronia*

IV. Beautiful Goodness

Games were greeted with hand-wringing by conservative Romans, who insisted that no citizen be required to compete, lest:

> The national morality, which had gradually fallen to oblivion, was shaken to its foundations by this imported [Greek] licentiousness... and our youth, under the influence of foreign tastes, should degenerate into the followers of gymnasia, of luxury and laziness—and this at the encouragement of the emperor and the senate.

Noting that Roman nobles were already disgracing themselves on the stage under the pretense of being poets and orators, they asked, "what remained but to strip to the skin as well, put on the gloves and practice that [Hellenic] mode of conflict instead of the profession of arms?" A letter recorded by Pliny suggests that abolition of the *Capitolia* was considered for similar reasons.[3]

The main concern here seems to be nudity, which was thought to promote homosexuality of a kind incompatible with ideas of Roman manhood. The gaze in ancient thought was imbued with such power that being looked at erotically was analogous to being penetrated sexually. Looking at others erotically was only slightly less degrading, and equally troubling, for a Roman keen to avoid even the suggestion of homosexuality.[4] As Cicero recognized, however, being moved by masculine beauty was the first step in a Platonic ladder that leads to the good itself. He says that homoeroticism "seems to have begun in the gymnasia of the Greeks, in which those kinds of love are free and allowed," adding that "we philosophers have risen up (with Plato as our authority...) to assign authority to love." Still, Cicero balks at the ladder's lower rungs, preferring the Stoic idea of love as "an attempt to create friendship out of the form of the beautiful."[5]

---

[3] Christian Mann, "Greek Sport and Roman Identity: The Certamina Athletarum at Rome," in *Sport in The Greek and Roman Worlds*, vol. 2, ed. T. Scanlon (Oxford: Oxford University Press, 2014), 169.

[4] S. Bartsch, *The Mirror of the Self: Sexuality, Self-Knowledge, and the Gaze in the Early Roman Empire* (University of Chicago Press, 2006) 67 ff.

[5] Cicero, *Tusc.* 33.70-71, translated by Bartsch in *Mirror of the Self,* 101.

Nearly all Roman thinkers, despite their enthusiasm for classical Greek philosophy, explicitly reject its homoeroticism.[6] Epicurus condemns love in general, and recommends specifically that we avoid looking at those who might spark it (*Vaticane Sententiae*, 18).

How, then, was the *pepaideumenos* supposed to view naked athletes? How was he to appreciate their beauty, and begin his Platonic climb up the "ladder of love" toward the good, while avoiding the charge (or at least appearance) of homoeroticism? The literature of the Second Sophistic provides instruction in this, largely by leaving out homoerotic references recognizable to any but the most Hellenically sophisticated. Dio Chrysostom's discourses on masculine athletic beauty, for example, are careful to denigrate effeminacy. Lucian's *Anacharsis* offers a "barbarian" view of Greek athletics that is humorous, even ridiculous, but homoeroticism is not among the very serious moral concerns that it discusses. Philostratus, too, conspicuously omits discussion or even suggestion of homoeroticism in the *Gymnasticus*, despite a long and detailed discussion of athletes' bodies. When he does mention sex, he uses varieties of the verb '*aphrodisiazo*' (to have sex), and denigrates it as a corrupting form of luxury inappropriate for and harmful to athletes. "In what sense are they men?" he asks of those who would "exchange crowns and victory announcements for disgraceful pleasures" (*Gymnasticus* 52). The Second Sophistic vision of Greek athletics, it appears, has been scrubbed clean to suit Roman tastes.

It is nevertheless the case, however, that these authors promote classical Greek eroticism in other texts, and in subtle ways. Dio imitates the language of Xenophon's *Symposium*, the topic of which is athletic beauty in the context of pederastic love.[7] Lucian alludes to the setting of Plato's *Phaedrus*, a dialogue

---

[6] Bartsch, *Mirror of the Self*, 103.

[7] Dio compares beauty to light at *On Beauty* 12.51 and 71.14, recalling Xenophon's description of the athlete Autylocos's at *Symposium* 1.9. Meanwhile comments on the agelessness of Melancomas's beauty in *Melancomas I* 29.5, reprise Xenophon's *Symposium* 4.17.

devoted to the connection between beauty and homoerotic love.[8] Philostratus's other writings, especially the *Love Letters* and *Imagines*, show a great appreciation for youthful male beauty and the erotic power of the gaze. "It is not loving but loving not that is a disease," says letter 52. "For if 'loving' is derived from 'seeing,' the blind ones are those who do not love."[9] To the trained Hellenic eye, the erotic appeal of athletic beauty is based on *sophrōsynē* (self-control), which is characterized not by open sexuality, but by modesty and chastity. This ideal is reflected in gymnastic imagery and practices, such as infibulation. Like a sculptor who deliberately downsizes the genitalia of an athlete to represent his chastity, Second Sophistic writers deliberately sublimate eroticism in their portrayal of Greek athletics, in an effort to simultaneously demonstrate and depict a proper appreciation of athletic beauty.

Dio Chrysostom's Beautiful Boxer

The goal of the virtuous Roman spectator, then, is to appreciate athletic beauty as a *mimēsis* of virtue and manifestation of the good, rather than an incitement to forbidden lust. Dio Chrysostom promotes this cause not just by explaining how such appreciation comes about in *On Beauty*, he also demonstrates his own appreciation of it in his orations on the boxer Melancomas. *On Beauty* proceeds from its lament about the lack of viewers who appreciate masculine beauty to a clarification that such beauty is characteristically Hellenic, and devoid of the effeminacy that earlier Roman writers had associated with the gymnasium. This comment has been prompted by a Greek athletic statue, and he elaborates it by setting up a contrast between the classical Greeks, who almost never praised effeminacy, and their arch-rivals, the Persians, whose preference for effeminacy was so strong that they often made eunuchs of their beautiful males. The fact that Persian boys do not exercise naked with their peers in the palaestra and

---

[8] See König, *Athletics and Literature*, 88, who follows Simon Goldhill, *Being Greek under Rome* (Cambridge University Press, 2001) 2-3.

[9] Philostratus, *Letters*, 52: Letters 4, 33, and 59 degrade as *anerastos*, anyone insensitive to love.

gymnasium is offered as a further cause of their effeminacy (*On Beauty* 71.5. The unstated conclusion is not just that males should see one another naked in the gym, but that this experience will enable them to appreciate masculine beauty in the noble way that actually *begets* such beauty in art, as well as in flesh and blood.

After a brief digression, Dio's interlocutor, as if on cue, demonstrates that he, at least, can appreciate athletic beauty—whether or not he has trained naked with other men—perhaps as a result of Dio's earlier instruction. He declares that he has never been so "struck with admiration" for anyone as he is for the statue. He says the statue's "modesty" (*aidōs*) is such that it makes anyone approaching feel abashed (*aideisthai*) at once." Only someone "made of stone" (like the statue?) could actually stand his ground while looking at him face to face. "And this effect surprises me very much," the interlocutor says, "that beauty when combined with modesty makes even brazen-faced men turn away and forces them to feel abashed" (*On Beauty* 71.13). Dio responds by comparing the youth's modesty to sunlight, the reflection of which makes beholders feel ashamed. Here, he samples the classical writer Xenophon, who uses a similar metaphor to make a similar point about the beauty of an athletic youth (*Symposium* 1.8-1). The scene comes dangerously close, for Imperial Roman tastes, to promotion of homosexuality. But the overriding message is about the erotic power of *aretē* (the youth is just a statue, after all). To love the athlete's beauty is to love his *aretē*—especially his modesty and self-control (*aidōs kai sophrōsunē*)—and to feel abashed at one's own lack of *aretē*. Not only does the viewer's appreciation of the athlete's beauty inspire him to become more beautiful, it also inspires him to become, more virtuous, more of a *kaloskagathos*.

Dio's plea for renewed appreciation of traditional athletic beauty is partly answered by his own orations in praise of a boxer named Melancomas. Here we have a flesh-and blood example of "perfect and true beauty" (*olokleron de kai alethinon kallos*). But again, the beauty of this athlete's body derives directly from the virtue of his soul. His beauty is described as a kind of eternal light that infuses his whole body, no matter the physical changes it might go through. The eulogist declares that, although he died young, "he would never have lived long enough, even if he had reached an extreme old age, to have dimmed his beauty" (*Melancomas I* 29.5). Here again, Dio is emulating Xenophon's *Symposium* (4.17), but ultimately his account is more spectatorial and less intimate. Melancomas's beauty is always portrayed from a distance, from the perspective of a trainer or fan.

In the earlier account, anachronistically entitled *Melancomas II*, Dio *is* a spectator who has just arrived at the harbor in Naples to see the games. He stretches and strains from behind a crowd to view the boxer Iatrocles, who is working out. "He was a very tall and beautiful (*kalos*) young man;" Dio observes, "and besides, the exercises he was taking made his body seem, quite naturally, still taller and more beautiful." Dio describes the boxer's performance as "brilliant" (*lampros*) and "spirited" (*phronēmatos*), and compares his figure to "one of the most carefully-wrought statues." (*Melancomas II*, 28.2-3). But when a trainer informs Dio that Iatrocles had been defeated by Melancomas, who is now dead, we realize that this boxer's beauty corresponds to the faint worldly copy of the ideal found at the bottom of Plato's ladder.

The more perfect, more theoretical beauty represented by Melancomas himself is discussed in his absence—seen through reflection, as it were, since it might, like Plato's metaphorical sun, be too bright to look at directly. It is the trainer who makes this speech, which dwells on the boxer's beauty almost independently of his accomplishments, and devoid of homoerotic overtones. He says Melancomas would have been renowned for his beauty even if he was an athlete, and that he dressed inconspicuously as if to hide it from view: "but when he was stripped, no one would want to look at anyone else" (*Melancomas II*, 28.6). The story points up the boxer's modesty, suggesting again that beauty comes from virtue and not athletic training. The part of his beauty attributed to opponents failing to land a blow is likewise explained in terms of virtue. "For he did not consider it courage to strike his opponent or to receive an injury himself, but thought this indicated a lack of stamina and desire to have done with the contest"(*Melancomas II*

28.7). In the spirit of Roman Stoicism, furthermore, he seems to have triumphed not just over external misfortunes, but also over internal desires:

> What indeed the most surprising thing about a man, is to have remained undefeated not only by his opponents but also by toil (*ponos*) and heat and gluttony and sensuality (*aphrodisiōn*); for the man who is going to prove inferior to none of his opponents must first be undefeated by these things."(*Melancomas II* 28.12)

Dio, as narrator, interjects here, as if to prove the stoic point, since the trainer has collapsed into tears from his grief.[10]

Beauty Beyond Body

The later oration, *Melancomas I*, takes the form of a funeral oration delivered in an otherwise unidentified voice that claims to be the athlete's personal friend. Beauty, again, is the focus of the speech; the eulogist explains that when a person is known to possess a particular quality, we only need to praise its nature (*phusin*). "For the eulogy of this will be at the same time also a eulogy of its possessor" (29.8). This eulogy of beauty immediately becomes a eulogy of *aretē* (i.e. beauty of the soul), however, as the point is made that Melancomas' beauty of figure was surpassed by his courage. "Indeed, it seems to me," the eulogist continues, "that his soul vied (*philonikesai*) with his body and strove to make herself the means of his winning a greater renown" "(29.9). This personification of the athlete's soul reinforces its status as the source of his beauty, as does the comment that "he held that it was the truest victory when he forced his opponent, although uninjured, to give up; for then the man was overcome, not by his injury, but by himself" (29.12). Since the soul is the origin of choice—and in stoic philosophy, freedom of choice is basically the only freedom we have—the choice to compete without injuring an opponent, forcing him to choose defeat, is clearly the triumph of

---

[10] Epictetus, *Discourses*, 1.24.1-3ff. identifies these things as our real opponents.

IV. Beautiful Goodness

the more beautiful soul. Even Melancomas's choice to dedicate himself to athletics is driven by *aretē*. "Recognizing that, of all the activities conducive to courage, athletics is at once the most honorable and the most laborious," says the eulogist, he "chose that" (29.9).

Melancomas's choice reprises Heracles's famous choice between the paths of virtue and vice, which again, comes from Xenophon (*Memorabilia* 2.1.21-34). Melancomas not only follows Heracles on the harder path of Virtue, his decision to dress simply, hiding his physical beauty and refusing to adorn himself (*Melancomas II* 28.6), explicitly rejects the habits represented by Pleasure in the story. This this is an important corrective to the Imperial tendency to equate external appearance, if not with virtue, then with social class.[11] Xenophon's *Symposium* (2.4) had also made this point, pointing out that the athletic smell of olive oil was more attractive than even the fanciest perfume.

In a world where men had their armpit and leg hairs painfully plucked in the baths, external appearance was often confused with internal beauty. In a discourse entitled "On Personal Adornment" (*peri kallōpismou*), the Stoic philosopher Epictetus questions a particularly well-groomed student about the nature of beauty. He argues that dogs, horses, and every other creature—including human beings—are beautiful or ugly according to their particular nature (*Discourses*, 3.1.1-3). He illustrates with an athletic example: "For what makes someone a fine pancratiast, I fancy, doesn't make someone a good wrestler, and would be absurdly out of place in a runner; and the same man who appears fine for the pentathlon would appear quite the opposite for the wrestling?" (3.1.5). He concludes that human virtue depends upon human *aretē* (3.1.7), and warns the youth that if he neglects the virtues, "you're bound to be ugly, whatever techniques you adopt to make yourself appear beautiful" (3.1.9). This argument is followed by a veritable diatribe against grooming, especially the aforementioned plucking, which is cited no less than six times! Epictetus concludes

---

[11] Mann, "Greek Sport," 176.

by asking the youth what Socrates meant when he told Alcibiades to make himself beautiful. "Curl your hair and pluck the hair from your legs? Heaven forbid. But rather, beautify your moral choice, and eradicate your bad judgments"(3.1.42).

Epictetus understood the authentic process of self-beautification to be tantamount to athletic training, especially for the Olympic Games. Not only does he use the nouns *askēsis* (training) and *agōn* (contest, struggle), he uses the verb *gumnazō* (to train, especially naked in the gymnasium) nearly 50 times in the *Discourses*. In most cases, the term is used metaphorically to describe a process for achieving a certain perspective that tames our desires and aversions—including in resistance to visual impressions. "Here is the true athlete," Epictetus declares, "one who trains himself to confront such [tempting] impressions" (2.18.27). He says the training may include "all the practices that are applied to the body by those who are giving it exercise," but only "if they're directed in some way towards desire and aversion" (3.12.16). He means that philosophers, like athletes, become stronger by willingly subjecting ourselves to challenges: temptations, annoyances, and so on.

> What advantage does a wrestler gain from his training partner? The greatest. And that man, too, who insults me becomes my training partner; he trains me in patience, in abstaining from anger, in remaining gentle. (3.20.9)

Kalokagathia, for Epictetus, resides in the soul:

> Young man, you're seeking the beautiful, and rightly so. Know, then, that it grows up in that part of you where you have your reason...your poor body is by nature nothing more than clay. (4.11.25-27)

Conclusion

Dio Chrysostom's encomium of Melancomas sets the boxer up as an example to be emulated, not just for his beauty, but for his virtue, which is the source of the beauty that infuses his entire being while eschewing both adornment and luxury. It is as if the

IV. Beautiful Goodness

boxer incarnates Socrates's ideally educated citizen in the *Republic* (402d-403a): "If someone's soul has a fine and beautiful character and his body matches its beauty and is thus in harmony with it...wouldn't that be the most beautiful sight for anyone who has eyes to see?" Crucially, though, having "eyes to see" depends precisely on having a proper education, one that enables a person to love the beautiful youth without touching him, because his real love is for the "fine and beautiful." In Imperial Rome, being properly educated meant being a *pepaideumenos*. Melancomas's eulogy ends with an exhortation:

> Come then, train zealously and toil hard, the younger men in the belief that this man's place has been left to them, the older in a way that befits their own achievements; yes, and take all the pride in these things that men should who live for praise and glory and are devotees of virtue.(*Melancomas I* 29.21)

If we have understood these Imperial authors correctly, however, devotion to virtue is as much about discernment of Olympic beauty as it is about sweat and toil. The *kaloskagathos* has become a *pepaideumenos*—a virtuous spectator capable of appreciating and even loving athletic beauty—perhaps even the battered athletic beauty of a statue like the *Terme Boxer*.

13. Olympic Ethics as *Kalokagathia*[1]

The International Olympic Committee requires that every International Federation, Local Organizing Committee, National Olympic Committee, Olympic athlete and official adopt in writing their official Code of Ethics in order to "restate their commitment" to the Fundamental Principles of the Olympic Charter and "affirm their loyalty to the Olympic ideal."[2] It would be a mistake to believe, however, that Olympic ethics might amount to such written declarations, or even to strict abidance by the Code's rules and principles. After all, the Olympic Charter's Fundamental Principles say nothing about rules. Rather, they describe a "philosophy of life" which "exalts and combines in a balanced whole, the qualities of body, will and mind."[3] They identify the values of "good example, social responsibility, and respect for universal fundamental ethical principles." They ban all forms of discrimination, and they demand the adoption of an "Olympic Spirit," characterized as "mutual understanding with a spirit of friendship, solidarity and fair play."[4]

In short, Olympic ethics requires us to be certain kinds of persons—persons who play by the rules, to be sure, but more important, persons who strive to exemplify an ideal set of personal, social, and aesthetic values. Rules, after all, merely express some higher conception of moral goodness and try to direct us toward it. To understand the Olympic conception of moral goodness, I think it is very helpful—as in so many Olympic matters—to return to the ideas of ancient Greece which originally inspired the Games. The ideal I have in mind for Olympic ethics is *kalokagathia*, a quality that unites the concepts of beauty and goodness. *Kalokagathia* appears frequently in ancient literature but is discussed most fully in Aristotle, where it emerges as the

---

[1] Originally presented at the International Olympic Academy session for NOAs and NOCs in May, 2014.

[2] IOC, Code of Ethics (2012), 127.

[3] IOC, Olympic Charter (2013), 11.

[4] IOC, Olympic Charter (2013), 11.

distinctive disposition of the *kalos k'agathos*—the morally good and beautiful person. It is closely related to the concept of *aretē* (virtue or excellence) much discussed in Olympic ethics, but *kalokagathia* is something more than virtue, something beyond social responsibility, something further than knowledge of and abidance by ethical codes. To understand *kalokagathia* as an Olympic value today, we must examine its personal, social, and aesthetic aspects, observe their connection to Olympic sport, and identify obstacles. Olympic ethics requires more than codes, it requires moral understanding that is able to engage the beautiful.

Autotelicity versus Instrumentalism

At the opening of *Eudemian Ethics* 8.15, Aristotle describes *kalokagathia* as "the excellence that arises from a combination of [excellences]" (*Eudemian Ethics* 1248b9-10). At the end of the brief discussion, he concludes that *kalokagathia* is "perfect excellence" (*EE* 1249a16-17). This implies that the *kalos k'agathos* not only has *aretē*, she has something more—a certain kind of disposition,[5] a particular *way* of exercising her goodness, a kind of moral beauty.[6] But where does this beauty come from? Aristotle describes virtuous actions as not only beautiful (*kalai*) in themselves, but also done for the sake of beauty (*to kalon*).[7] In short, *to kalon* is both the beginning and the end of moral excellence.[8] On the face of it, this seems circular, and indeed a good way to describe *kalokagathia* is as something autotelic—intrinsically rewarding; an end in itself. Autotelicity is important because it differentiates moral excellence

---

[5] Says Aristotle: "it does not suffice that [actions] themselves have the right qualities. Rather, the agent must also be in the right state when he does them." *Nicomachean Ethics* 1105a29.

[6] As Aristotle puts it, the *kalos k'agathos* not only acts beautifully, he "practices the beautiful (*kalon*)." *Eudemian Ethics* 1248b35

[7] *Nicomachean Ethics* 1120a24. *Eudemian Ethics* 3.1230a27-34, "goodness makes a man choose everything for the sake of [*kalon*]".

[8] In *Metaphysics* 5.1013a22, Aristotle declares that "the good and the beautiful are the origin both of knowledge and of the movement of many things."

from instrumentalism, or what Aristotle calls expedience, i.e. using virtues as means to acquire benefits such as wealth, health, honor, or power.[9] Says Aristotle, "the man who thinks he ought to have excellences for the sake of external goods does deeds that are beautiful only by accident" (*EE* 1249b14-15). The *kalos k'agathos*, by contrast, holds beautiful things "for themselves" and practices the beautiful "for its own sake" (*EE* 1248b34-35).

The connection to Olympic ideals should be fairly obvious here. The first Fundamental Principle of Olympism celebrates "joy of effort" as a foundational Olympic value. The Olympic Creed declares that "The most important thing in the Olympic Games is not to win but to take part, just as the most important thing in life is not the triumph but the struggle. The essential thing is not to have conquered but to have fought well."[10] Ontologically speaking, autotelicity is characteristic of sport, art, and their common ancestor, play. Athletic competition may entail an effort to win, but it is only by adopting a *lusory* attitude—i.e. by seeing the game as an end in itself, that we are able to meaningfully participate in sports at all. Historically, autotelicity characterizes the realm of the divine—gods who have no needs are naturally playful and when humans act autotelically, we more closely resemble the divine. The ancient Olympic Games were staged to please the gods and the crowns of wild olive they awarded were regarded as more valuable than the lucrative prizes of the so-called money games precisely because they lacked practical worth. The Modern Olympics continue this legacy of merely symbolic prizes, while the participation of otherwise highly-paid professional athletes like Lionel Messi and Rafael Nadal only reinforces the idea that sport

---

[9] Although *kalokagathia* must be cultivated for its own sake and not for any further end—including pleasure and even happiness—such rewards were thought to accompany on its achievement. Says Aristotle, "the absolutely pleasant is also beautiful and the absolutely good is pleasant." *Eudemian Ethics* 1249a18-21.

[10] The Fundamental Principles of Olympism appear on page 11 of the 2013 *Olympic Charter*. The Olympic Creed appears in a variety of historical documents related to the Olympic Games.

IV. Beautiful Goodness

at its best is engaged in autotelically. The IOC's banning of commercial signs in the arena and continued focus on volunteerism are further evidence that autotelicity persists as an Olympic value.

There is also evidence, however, that instrumentalism may be taking over. The Olympic motto, *citius, altius, fortius* (faster, higher, stronger) is widely interpreted as opposing the creed by putting an emphasis on winning—which is inevitably associated with the kind of extrinsic rewards that Aristotle warned against: wealth, honor, and power. Meanwhile the benefit of health is often left behind as athletes and nations pursue victory at all costs. The IOC itself is widely seen as a money-grubbing organization interested in marketing a sports-entertainment product in cooperation with amoral multi-national corporations. Insofar as organizations teach moral values through their actions rather than their words,[11] all members of the Olympic Movement must strive to exhibit Olympic values though their actions. In this, they must oppose the pervasive instrumentalism of society and the expected instrumentalism of their corporate partners. The media's depiction of the Games and ceremonies plays a very important role here, as does discourse *within* the Olympic community. Attempts to legislate the Olympic spirit, however, are bound to fail. Aristotle was clear that *aretē* requires us to be "moved by *to kalon* and not compulsion" (*NE* 1116b4–5). As the sad history of Olympic amateurism shows—attempts to ban instrumentalism with rules only exacerbate the problem. What must be promoted is a moral disposition that values goodness intrinsically; a disposition of moral beauty or *kalokagathia*.

Community Responsibility vs. Liberal Individualism

The social dimension of *kalokagathia* was obvious to the ancients but may be overlooked today. In contrast to modern western moral ideas based on liberal individualism, in ancient Greek thought there is no distinguishing the morally excellent

---

[11] D. Bok, "Can Higher Education Foster Higher Morals?" in *Social and Personal Ethics*, ed. W. H. Shaw (Belmont: Wadsworth, 1996), 494.

individual from his community. *Kalos k'agathos* is often translated as 'nobleman' or 'gentleman' in modern texts—a rendering which suggests that the quality is inherited rather than earned. But ancient Greek athletics and moral philosophy both emphasize demonstrated excellence over and against social hierarchy. Aristotle says that social goods like wealth, high birth, and power are "fitting" for the *kalos k'agathos*, not because he has them by reason of birth or social status—and certainly not because these privileges cause him to be *kalos k'agathos*—but rather because he *uses* such goods to benefit the community (*EE* 1249a9-10). The benefit may be direct and material, as when a wealthy man spends his money to build a public fountain (like the one Herodes Atticus financed at Olympia). Just as often it was indirect and spiritual, as when an Olympic athlete unifies and inspires his community with a beautifully excellent performance. Ancient Greek athletes saw themselves as community servants; it is for this reason that Socrates asks at his trial to be rewarded as Olympic athletes are for his service to Athens (Plato, *Apology* 36d). When Aristotle describes the *kalos kagathos* as one who "practices the beautiful," he is thinking of someone who serves his community (*EE* 1248b35).

This idea of social responsibility is very much a part of the Olympic ideal as well. In fact, "social responsibility" was recently enshrined alongside "the educational value of good example" and "respect for universal fundamental ethical principles" in the first Fundamental Principle of Olympism.[12] It is further attested by the goal of "placing sport at the service of the harmonious development of humankind [and] promoting a peaceful society concerned with the preservation of human dignity."[13] It is even part and parcel of the Olympic spirit, defined in terms of mutual understanding, friendship, solidarity and fair play.[14] I have argued elsewhere that the Olympics' peace-promoting heritage derives from certain aspects of sport itself: dedicated time and space,

---

[12] As far as I can tell, it first appears in the 2011 version of the Charter.
[13] Olympic Charter (2013), 11.
[14] Olympic Charter (2013), 11

equality of opportunity, and respect for difference.[15] Those aspects of sport persist and thrive in the modern Games, as does their product, friendship, understood by Aristotle to be the virtue that binds communities together (*NE* 1155a20-25). Modern Olympic athletes serve their own communities as well as the world community when they demonstrate not only athletic excellence, but teamwork, understanding, and friendship that transcends national boundaries and individual interests. I daresay the most beautiful moments in the Olympic Games today are not just displays of athletic excellence, but also displays of social excellence: shared joy, sympathetic understanding, even selfless gestures of aid to competitors. It is instructive that we call these things good sportsmanship; even today we can recognize moral beauty in sport that transcends rules and obligation.

Unfortunately, the community-building lessons of sport are regularly ignored and sometimes counteracted by competitive paradigms focused only on results. Individualism among athletes is one thing, but often it derives from the more insidious phenomenon of nationalism found within teams and NOCs, in what is supposed to be an international community. It may *seem* like nationalism (including sacrificing one's personal interests for the good of the team or nation) just is a form of community service, but more often it is simply a collectivizing of morally repugnant individualism—the attempt to gain an advantage unavailable to competitors. Take, for example, the controversy surrounding bobsled design at the recent Winter Games in Sochi. The super high-tech American sled was financed, researched and designed by the German company BMW to gain a competitive advantage over other countries' sleds; including team Germany, with whom BMW did not share the technology. Some may say that a country's technological advancement is a legitimate part of Olympic competition (I disagree), but even this justification doesn't apply here. Likewise, the rhetoric surrounding defense-contractor Lockheed Martin's development of a high-tech suit for American

---

[15] Reid, "Olympic Sport and its Lessons for Peace," in this volume.

speed skaters not only suggested a warlike view of sport, it backfired by distracting athletes who performed below their potential. The social responsibility expected of athletes must also be demonstrated by officials, teams, federations, committees, and even sponsors. The beauty of the Olympic Games depends on the *kalokagathia* of everyone in the Olympic community.

Fair Play

The aesthetic dimension of *kalokagathia*, specifically its linking of morality and beauty, may seem the most foreign to us. In modern thought, morality and beauty are usually seen as independent concepts; ethics and aesthetics are considered separate sciences. This is because we now associate morality with pure rationality. Kant's moral theory begins in and aims for unadulterated reason, while major utilitarian theories are based on rational interests and calculations. The *kalos k'agathos*, by contrast, exercises a kind of moral aesthetic which enables him to recognize the beauty inherent in good actions and to perform them as an expression of the beauty he has cultivated within.[16] In this way, the morally good person functions more like an artist than a lawyer, but that is not to say that she abandons reason. According to Aristotle, it is through *logos* (conventionally translated as reason) that we discern moral beauty, and that discernment then moves us—perhaps effortlessly—to right action (*EE* 3.1229a14). "Our aim is not to know what courage is but to be courageous," says Aristotle (*EE* 1.1216b19-25), explaining later that an apparently courageous act is actually shameful if done out of ignorance or in pursuit of pleasure rather than beauty (*EE* 3.1230a27-34). It is the

---

[16] The comparison of moral understanding with aesthetic taste need not suggest relativism or solipsism. The ancients believed that truth was intimately connected to beauty. It is possible, even common, to make mistakes about a thing's beauty. Expedient things like health, wealth, and honor appear beautiful to the merely good man, whereas the *kalos k'agathos* finds beauty in what is intrinsically good. *Eudemian Ethics* 1249a4-5.

IV. Beautiful Goodness

performance of an act autotelically—out of beauty and for the sake of beauty—that makes it morally beautiful and good.

If this concept of moral beauty seems foreign to Olympic ideals, it is because we have forgotten the aesthetic dimension of fairness. Fair play is not only a key component of the Olympic spirit, its prevalence is item number one on the Olympic Charter's description of the Mission and Role of the IOC.[17] Respect for the spirit of fair play is also listed as a key criterion for eligibility to participate in the Olympic Games.[18] Too often we understand fairness analytically in terms of adherence to written to rules. This neglects not only the aesthetic dimension of the English word (fair is synonym for beautiful), but also the metaphysical reality that rules require a theoretical basis to be written and interpreted in the first place. Olympic officials in particular must appeal to an aesthetic sense of justice to do their job well. This seems to be what happened at the London 2012 Games when badminton officials disqualified eight players for "not using their best efforts" in preliminary matches in order to gain advantageous matches in the finals.[19] The Olympic Charter consistently describes fair play as a "spirit" and the IOC Code of Ethics goes so far to describe it as "the spirit of sport."[20] The apparently circular idea that sport both begins and ends with fairness should remind us of the autotelicity of *to kalon*—and of sport's very deep kinship with it.

Despite the beauty of the Olympic Festival, ugliness is never completely absent. Not only do athletes sometimes display acts of violence or hatred, they can be quite adept at hiding morally repugnant acts like doping, bribery, and fraud. Meanwhile,

---

[17] Olympic Charter (2013), 16: "to encourage and support the promotion of ethics and good governance in sport as well as education of youth through sport and to dedicate its efforts to ensuring that, in sport, the spirit of fair play prevails and violence is banned."

[18] Olympic Charter (2013), 77.

[19] British Broadcasting Corporation,"Olympics badminton: Eight women disqualified from doubles," *BBC Sport*, 2012.

[20] Code of Ethics (2012), 194. (To be fair, the Code of Ethics also describes fair play as a principle, p. 198).

affiliated corporations, organizing committees, and even national governments often engage in unfair, unjust, and sometimes belligerent acts before, after, and during the games. These also are frequently ignored or covered up. I remember at the 2008 Beijing Games watching a destitute man emerge from a doorway hidden within a brightly-colored Olympic billboard. The billboard had been placed there to cover up the squalor of his neighborhood. Similar attempts to whitewash abuses are found at many other Games. The media has a responsibility to reveal such moral ugliness, but they also can manufacture it by fomenting fears of terror attacks or exaggerating political scandals. Even something so apparently innocuous as the Olympic medal count violates the principles of fair play by inventing a competition in which teams do not enter willingly, have different numbers of contestants, and compete in different disciplines. It may seem insignificant, but how often are immoral tactics motivated by the desire to improve a country's ranking in the rigged-game of the medal count? Why not return to the poetic and artistic celebrations of Olympic excellence in ancient times? The spirit of fair play, like *kalokagathia*, demands that we celebrate beauty.

Conclusion

Aristotle imagined virtuous competition aimed at beauty as part and parcel of his ethics. In fact, he said that that the virtuous man will give up all his worldly goods, including wealth, power, and even his life to secure beauty for himself; since "he would prefer an hour of rapture to a long period of mild enjoyment, a year of beautiful life to many years of ordinary existence, one great and glorious exploit to many small successes" (*NE* 1169a). Something similar may be said about modern Olympic athletes—they give up a lot to try and achieve the rapture of glory. But for everyone involved, the value of Olympic glory depends on its beauty, and the beauty of Olympic glory depends on ethics—on morally beautiful activity. Olympic ethics is not just a matter of abiding by rules or codes, it is a matter of striving for moral beauty—for the Olympic ideal of *kalokagathia*.

Section V
Modern Olympism

14. The Philosophy of Olympic Revival[1]

The award winning movie *Chariots of Fire* offers a glimpse of Olympic sport shortly after its late 19th century revival in Europe. The story involves two British sprinters, a Jew named Harold Abrahams and a Christian named Eric Liddell, both of whom face challenges derived from issues of class and diversity. Abrahams, a Cambridge University student, employs a professional coach to improve his technique. This is considered unethical by the college dons since it runs contrary to the ethos of the gentleman amateur who should rely on natural athletic gifts and not take sport too seriously. Eric Liddell, meanwhile, finds himself torn between a strong commitment to his faith and the practical demands of his sport. When the Olympic final for his best event falls on the Sabbath, he chooses not to run, despite a personal appeal to his patriotism by the Prince of Wales. In the end, Abrahams wins his event, foreshadowing the demise of amateurism. And Liddell, buoyed partly by a note of support from competitor Jackson Scholz, gains unexpected victory in his weaker event, the 400 meters—sweet reward for his unwavering dedication to his faith.

On the one hand, these scenes seem far removed from the Olympic Games of Ancient Greece. On the other, we recognize familiar issues such as aristocratic entitlement, transcendence of social class, competitive respect, and religious dedication. But what of Olympic sport's link to philosophy? What of its role in education? Sport did find its way into schools and universities in the modern era. Philosophy had its place as well, but it was now kept separate from sport. College athletics were detached from academics, and philosophers generally shunned sport as a subject unworthy of serious inquiry.

I think it is fair to claim, nevertheless, that the ancient link between philosophy and sport born in ancient Greece was revived

---

[1] Originally published as "The Modern Olympic Revival" in *Introduction to the Philosophy of Sport,* Lanham, MD: Rowman and Littlefield, 2012. Reprinted with permission, all rights reserved

V. Modern Olympism

with the founding of the modern Olympic Games in 1896. Indeed the modern Olympic Games may represent the first time in history that a sporting event was self-consciously driven by philosophy.

The Games' primary founder, Pierre de Coubertin and his colleagues were interested not only in promoting a sporting event, but also in promulgating a set of philosophical ideals that they thought would improve the world. Drawing on ideas from ancient Greece as well as the European Enlightenment and British pedagogical thought, Coubertin coined the term "Olympism" to describe this philosophy. Coubertin was not a professional philosopher and Olympism, arguably, is not a philosophical system, but it does present definite philosophical guidelines for the practice of sport. What is more, these guidelines have endured despite the more than 100 year history of the modern festival and its unprecedented global reach. Modern Olympism's continued appeal is testament, I believe, to the profound link between sport and philosophy discovered in ancient Greece.

The interesting question that arises from studying the Olympic Games as a manifestation of philosophy is just what it means in practice to adopt a philosophy of sport, and, more specifically, how a movement spanning so many different epochs and cultures can be guided by a single philosophy? Philosophies, like sports, are generally thought to be products of particular cultures, epochs, even particular lives. We speak of Confucianism or Kantianism, referring to specific people. Even philosophies with more general names, such as Daoism or Utilitarianism, are easily linked with a particular time, place, and thinker or group of thinkers. Olympism, in a way, is linked with the time and place of the ancient Olympic Games—but it is not an effort to impose ancient Greek culture and values on the modern world. Rather it is an attempt at a universal philosophy based upon values common to everyone in the world. In the same way that people all over the world can play the game of soccer, people all over the world are supposed to be able to embrace Olympism. Is such a thing even possible?

Olympism as a Philosophy

First we must ask whether *philosophy* itself can be universal, and before we can answer that question we have to ask what is meant by the term. The idea of Olympism, which can be traced to Pierre de Coubertin, clearly presents itself in philosophical terms:

> Olympism is a philosophy of life, exalting and combining in a balanced whole the qualities of body, will and mind. Blending sport with culture and education, Olympism seeks to create a way of life based on the joy of effort, the educational value of good example and respect for universal fundamental ethical principles.[2]

Self-declaration does not make something a philosophy in the strict sense, and Olympism is criticized for its lack of systematic propositions.[3] Philosophy—at least in the context of the European Enlightenment familiar to the Olympic founders—must be based on clear propositions established through reason and knowledge.

Coubertin's countryman René Descartes is a good example of this idea of philosophy. Descartes developed a philosophical method based on rejecting all previous traditions or opinions and then reconstructing knowledge by solely rational means from the cornerstone of a logically irrefutable truth.[4] This understanding of philosophy would have appealed to the Olympic founders' interest in internationalism because it took itself to be culturally transcendent. Descartes regarded himself as a "citizen of the world" and believed the power of reason to be "naturally equal in all men."[5] According to this way of thinking, philosophical propositions based on reason demonstrated through logic are

---

[2] Olympic Charter (2010), 11.

[3] Lamartine DaCosta, "A Never-Ending Story: The Philosophical Controversy over Olympism," *Journal of the Philosophy of Sport* 33:2 (2006): 157-73.

[4] Rene Descartes, "Discourse on Method", in J. Cottingham, R. Stoothoff, D. Murdoch, eds., *The Philosophical Writings of Descartes*, vol. I (Cambridge, UK: Cambridge University Press, 1985), 111-51.

[5] Descartes, *Philosophical Writings*, 2 n.1; and 111.

V. Modern Olympism

universally valid and applicable across cultures. The problem, however, is that not all cultures regard clear propositions to be philosophy's goal. The Chinese classic *Daodejing*, for example, seeks to understand the "Way" (*Dao*), but asserts at the beginning that this understanding cannot be explained or even "named."

It seems fair to say that the modern Olympic founders did not have Daoism in mind when they drafted the Fundamental Principles of Olympism, but it would not be fair to deny that Daoism is indeed a philosophy. After all, Olympism defines its goal as creating a certain "way of life" right after it declares itself to be a philosophy. Indeed if we define philosophy according to its ancient Greek meaning as the love (*philia*) of wisdom (*sophia*), or characterize it as a disposition for learning and contemplation following Pythagoras (who is said to have coined the word),[6] our understanding becomes compatible not only with European rationalism, but also with Chinese Daoism, and most important with a flexible interpretation of Olympism itself.[7] Olympism may be criticized for changing over time, but philosophies (i.e. process philosophy) just are continual negotiations.[8] Olympism may be eclectic, but eclecticism is itself a 19th c. European philosophy that consolidates and conciliates diverse systems. Olympism need not be the same kind of philosophy that Rationalism or Empiricism are in order to be a philosophy.

In fact, the qualities that make Olympism seem weak when tested against some strict definitions of philosophy, may explain the strength and endurance of the Games on a global scale. One of these paradoxical strengths come from the lack of a detailed and definitive text— there is no book in any language that spells out Olympic philosophy at length. If Olympism can be said to have a text, it would be the Olympic Charter, or more specifically, the page in the Olympic Charter which lists the "Fundamental Principles of Olympism," only the first of which (quoted above) is

---

[6] According to Cicero, *Tusculan Disputations*, 5.8.
[7] For the full argument, see H. Reid, "East to Olympia" in this volume.
[8] DaCosta, "Never-Ending Story," 166.

explicitly philosophical. Olympism's principles are sometimes vague and always open to multiple interpretations. Nevertheless, one can discern within Olympism elements of philosophy's traditional branches: metaphysics, ethics, and politics. Each of these branches is discussed more fully in subsequent sections of this book, but a brief discussion of Olympism in terms of them will help us to see the relationship between philosophy and sport.

Olympism and Metaphysics

Metaphysics is the branch of philosophy that examines the fundamental nature of things. What are Olympism's metaphysics? Within the description of Olympism as a philosophy that exalts and combines "in a balanced whole, the qualities of body, will and mind," we recognize a humanistic viewpoint that posits an idealized metaphysics of mankind. It is this aspect that motivated professional philosopher and Olympic medalist Hans Lenk to interpret Olympism as a philosophical anthropology— that is, a philosophy concerned with the nature and status of humanity.[9] The lack of any clear definition of just what this ideal Olympic human being would be, however, might seem to keep the philosophical anthropology of Olympism from having much normative force—that is, the ability to bind a person morally to that ideal. How can we use the ideal Olympian as an ethical guide when it is unclear what the ideal Olympian is?

Coubertin, no doubt, was inspired by the Hellenic idea of *aretē* and the images of heroism to be found in ancient Greek poetry and mythology—images like that of Heracles, Achilles, and Odysseus. But any attempt to draw a portrait or even point to an example of the ideal Olympian would run up against the immense diversity of individuals who have exemplified the Olympic ideal over the history of the modern Games. Coubertin's ideal was probably a strapping European male, but tiny female gymnasts and lanky African marathoners have come to exemplify the ideal, as have

---

[9] Hans Lenk, "Towards a Philosophical Anthropology of the Olympic Athletes and the Achieving Being" *International Olympic Academy Report*, (Ancient Olympia, Greece: 1982): 163-177.

lithe male figure skaters and husky female shot-putters. The point here is that the *lack* of a strict definition has allowed for a variety of interpretations of the ideal, without leaving it devoid of meaning. In a similar way the simple definition of a goal in soccer can accommodate a variety of playing styles without sacrificing the notion of excellence.

The language of a balanced "body, will, and mind", on the other hand, seems to evoke a specifically Western metaphysics of mankind derived from medieval Christian philosophy and the Muscular Christianity of Victorian England. In fact, the "ancient Greek" adage of a "sound mind in sound body," only makes sense as a tenet of Olympism when reinterpreted through the eyes of modern British pedagogical thought— where it appears as the slogan on a gymnasium in Henry Fielding's popular novel, The *History of Tom Jones*. The Latin saying, *mens sana in corpore sano*, came from the Roman satirist Juvenal who was talking about prayer—it originally had nothing to do with sports or even exercise.[10] Olympism's ability to reinterpret Juvenal's words into a motto for a physically- as well as mentally-active lifestyle, however, is further evidence for the importance of philosophical flexibility. We can clearly affirm that Olympism is a philosophy that values humanity generally— after all, it identifies as a goal "the harmonious development of mankind"[11]—without definitively articulating the exact image of humanity it promotes.

Indeed Olympism's failure to define its vision for humankind may have inspired its commitment to non-discrimination. Among the current Fundamental Principles of Olympism is the statement: "Any form of discrimination with regard to a country or a person on grounds of race, religion, politics, gender or otherwise is incompatible with belonging to the Olympic Movement."[12] This declaration flies in the face of modern Olympic Games history. Coubertin himself wished to bar females from the Games, and

---

[10] Young, "Mens Sana in Corpore Sano?"60-61.
[11] Olympic Charter (2010), 11.
[12] Olympic Charter (2010), 11.

discrimination and exclusions of all kinds mar Olympic history. But philosophical ideals should not be derived from the practices of flawed human beings, rather they should serve as a guide and inspiration to improve those practices over time. The ever-increasing diversity of athletes participating in the Olympic Games today reveals the power of a vague and sketchy philosophical ideal not only to accommodate a variety of interpretations, but also to expand our collective conception of an ideal human being. If Olympism is to be a globally-relevant philosophy, the ideal image of humanity it presents is best left vague enough to accommodate a variety of interpretations across cultures and over time.

Olympism and Ethics

The next question to ask of Olympism as a philosophy is whether its soft metaphysics can support any kind of meaningful ethics. Ethics—the branch of philosophy concerned with right and wrong action—traditionally depends for its normative force on a clear metaphysics. For example, Immanuel Kant's metaphysical understanding of human beings as essentially ends in themselves leads him to assert that it is a moral imperative to always treat humanity, others as well as oneself, as ends and never merely as means to some end.[13] It may be charged that Olympism fails to present a philosophical anthropology or that the image of the ideal human it does present is too vague to have ethical force. But Kant's characterization of human beings as ends in themselves is likewise vague and open to interpretation. Olympism's promotion of an inclusive and holistic ideal of mankind that values harmony and balance as well as excellence is sufficient to support the kinds of ethical principles inscribed in the logic of sport—principles like equality and fairness.

The first Fundamental Principle of Olympism demands "respect for universal fundamental ethical principles" without ever articulating what these principles are. Some would say that

---

[13] Immanuel Kant, *Grounding for the Metaphysics of Morals*, translated by James W. Ellington (Indianapolis: Hackett, 1981), 96.

ethical principles are always the product of a particular culture, so there can no more be universal ethical principles than there can be a universal culture. Even very general moral guidelines like the Golden Rule or Kant's categorical imperative cannot capture the moral beliefs of every culture under the Olympic umbrella. There is something common to all members of the Olympic Movement, however—a sincere value for sport. Sport-related moral principles, such as equality of opportunity and reward according to merit, may therefore be considered universal within the Olympic Community. These principles are manifest in the rules of sport. In the 100 meter dash, for example, runners must start from the same line at the same time (equality of opportunity), and the gold medal is awarded to the first athlete across the finish-line in the final heat (reward according to merit).

It can be dangerous, however, for Olympism to try and codify these general moral principles into rules and regulations beyond sport. As the sad history of Olympic amateurism shows, some noble ideals quickly lose their moral force once they become written regulations. The ideal of the amateur is an athlete who competes for the love of the sport rather than any external reward—especially money. By defining amateurs in terms of income sources rather than motivation, however, the Olympic Movement promoted a culture of greedily "gaming the system" rather than valuing sport as something to be appreciated as an end in itself. Individual athletes and entire nations responded to amateur regulations by finding clever ways to pay athletes—for example, by giving them special government jobs. Athletes for whom sport was strictly an avocation found it difficult to compete in this environment. And soon the rule designed to *remove* the influence of money on Olympics put money at the center of athletes' and coaches' concerns.

Eastern philosophy could have predicted amateurism's demise. The *Daodejing* of Laozi warns that increasing prohibitions and rules only increases the commission of crimes, and Confucius observes that most people respond to legislation by thinking only about exemptions.[14] Although sports depend for their existence upon rules, Olympism's "universal ethical principles" are better left as general ideas than codified into specific set of rules. This allows for universal agreement about the importance of ethics, and even about the value of general principles like equality and fairness, without privileging the specific interpretation of any particular culture. The enduring debate about female participation from conservative Muslim countries illustrates the complexity of such issues. Olympism declares sport to be a human right and demands that it be practiced "without discrimination of any kind and in the Olympic spirit, which requires mutual understanding with a spirit of friendship, solidarity and fair play."[15] But does forcing a country like Saudi Arabia to send a certain number of female participants to the Games show friendship and understanding?

Since the Postmodern turn in 20th century philosophy, there has been a return to the ancient tradition of virtue ethics—a form of moral thought that focuses on persons rather than principles (as in Kantianism) or consequences (as in Utilitarianism). A key benefit of virtue ethics for Olympism is that it has roots in both the ancient Greek tradition of Socrates, Plato, and Aristotle and the ancient Chinese tradition of Laozi and Confucius. It even plays an important role in contemporary feminist ethics of care. Perhaps more important, an ethical emphasis on virtue rather than legislation better reflects Olympic values, not least because it looks inward toward personal perfection, rather than outward toward the correction and control of others.[16] Virtue is understood as a kind of "moral force" that is contrasted favorably with physical (and especially violent) force. Virtue is conceived not as a social construction, but as an innate disposition which is cultivated, like

---

[14] Laozi, *Daodejing*, 57. Confucius, *Analects*, trans. E. Slingerland (Indianapolis: Hackett, 2003), 4.11. All *Analects* quotations are from this translation unless otherwise indicated.
[15] Olympic Charter (2010), 11.
[16] See "Athletic Virtue: between East and West," in this volume.

athletic talent, through intentional training and inspiring examples—a model that well reflects Olympism's professed promotion of the "educational value of good example."

Of course specific conceptions and lists of virtues vary inevitably across history and cultures. Even though specific virtues typically demanded by Olympic sports—e.g., courage and self-control—are universally valued, how these values are expressed might vary from culture to culture. Thus, there is more room for cross-cultural consensus on the question of virtue than may first appear.[17] Olympism may affirm that certain virtues are universal, while allowing for different expressions of them within different activities. A judo player's courage in facing an opponent's charge is different, for example, from a gymnast's courage in facing the parallel bars—but they are both forms of courage, and they are valued in Eastern and Western sports alike. Virtue ethic can help Olympism to accommodate Western demands for philosophical rigor, while respecting Eastern philosophy's (as well as Postmodern philosophy's) skepticism about hard and fast rules.

Olympism and Politics

Finally, we must acknowledge Olympism's explicitly political dimension in addition to its metaphysics and ethics—despite the Olympic Movement's frequent attempts to disassociate itself from politics. IOC members swear an oath to keep themselves free of any political influence.[18] National Olympic Committees are instructed to resist political pressure.[19] Political demonstrations are barred from Olympic sites or venues.[20] And part of the mission "Mission and Role of the IOC" is "to oppose any political or commercial abuse of sport and athletes."[21] Another part, however, is "to place sport at the service of humanity and thereby to

---

[17] Mike McNamee, "Olympism, Eurocentricity, and Transcultural Virtues." *Journal of the Philosophy of Sport* 33:2 (2006), 174-87.
[18] Olympic Charter (2010), 31.
[19] Olympic Charter (2010), 62.
[20] Olympic Charter (2007), 98.
[21] Olympic Charter (2010), 15.

promote peace."²² Because it promotes a particular vision of community, this is an explicitly political goal—one that reflects the IOC's stated goal of "promoting a peaceful society concerned with the preservation of human dignity."²³ What is distinctive about Olympism's politics, not unlike its ethics, is its connection to sport. The IOC wants to use sport rather than conventional governmental means to achieve the political goal of peace.

This approach may be unique, but I would not call it innovative. Indeed I think it derives from the ancient Olympic Games, whose own association with peace does not seem to have originated as a political decree but rather grew out of the unifying and pacifying effects of multicultural competition— specifically the ability to set aside differences, treat others as equals, and tolerate differences.²⁴ Of course the ancient Olympic Games—in stark contrast to the modern festival—were initially open only to Greeks, more specifically free male Greeks with enough wealth and leisure time to train and travel to competitions. But there were real cultural differences between the loosely organized collection of Greek tribes and city-states—the frequently cited contrast between Athens and Sparta is just one example. What is more these tribes were constantly competing for resources and very often at war with one another.

What the Olympic festival did was give them a religious reason to set their differences aside, declare a temporary truce and come together upon neutral ground to worship a common deity. The first footrace was staged at Olympia to select an honoree to light the sacrificial flame.²⁵ Obviously each tribe would have its own best candidate for the honor, I believe that the footrace

---

[22] Olympic Charter (2010), 14.
[23] Olympic Charter (2010), 11.
[24] See "Olympic Sport and Its Lessons for Peace" in this volume.
[25] Philostratos, "Gymnasticus" in S. Miller, *Arete: Greek sports from ancient sources* (Berkeley and Los Angeles, CA: University of California Press, 1991), 38. For an analysis, see Panos Valavanis, "Thoughts on the historical origins of the Olympic Games and the cult of Pelops in Olympia," *Nikephoros* 19 (2006): 137–52, 141.

functioned as a mutually acceptable way to make this selection without resorting to established social hierarchies or to violence. In order for the selection made by the footrace to be valid (and therefore pleasing to the all-knowing deity), each contestant needed to be given a fair chance—they needed to be treated as equals for the purpose of the race, no matter how much they hated each other outside the sanctuary. In addition, they had to tolerate their differences long enough to live and dine together for the duration of the festival. No doubt there was friendly sharing of songs, stories, food, and wine brought from back home, and it is likely that some of them actually came to value their differences. In this way the Olympic Games taught ancient Hellenes a political lesson about peace, even though their original purpose was religious.

Because engaging in sport requires us to set aside conflict, treat others as equals under a common set of rules, and at least tolerate if not appreciate our differences, it lays the groundwork for peaceful coexistence. And because the modern Olympic Games do this on a global scale with the whole world looking on, they too can place sport in the service of peace—as the Fundamental Principles of Olympism declare. This political philosophy conflicts somewhat with tradition since it relies not on the authority of a civilizing force, but rather on the need for cooperative decision making in the *absence* of a single authority. Western philosophers like Thomas Hobbes understand law as something imposed by an authority to overcome our uncivilized and violent natural state. Eastern thought, meanwhile, tends to associate violence with law and authority and seeks peace by "going back" either to Confucianism's remote and idealized past, or to Daoism's uncorrupted natural state.[26] What is important for Olympism is not to promote peace through the force of authority, even IOC's own authority, but rather to focus on staging the Games and promoting

---

[26] Obviously, these are very general observations and there are exceptions on both the Western and Eastern side. The point is that Olympism needs to account for divergent understandings.

sport for all, because sport functions a vehicle for promoting peace precisely by gathering diverse groups together and treating them all as equals in an open, publicly observed forum.

Sport's metaphysical structure provides a better model for Olympism's political goals than does the Games' troubled history. Nationalistic abuse of the Olympic Festival by host governments, competing nations, and even terrorist groups has interfered with the Movement's larger political goal. The practice of boycotting the Olympic Games—which reached its peak in the 1980s with the Moscow and Los Angeles protests—hampers the Olympics' peace-promoting potential by preventing diverse athletes from interacting. The current practice of housing athletes outside the Olympic Village to avoid distractions that may harm performance has an analogous effect. Other political uses of the Games, such as Tommie Smith and John Carlos' 1968 protest against civil rights abuses in the USA—captured in the famous image of the barefoot athletes raising gloved fists on the Olympic medals stand—may be interpreted as part and parcel of the Olympic promotion of peace. The United Nations now declares a modern Olympic Truce, but its principles are widely violated, as when the USA hosted the Salt Lake Games while fomenting war in Iraq, or when Russia invaded Georgia nearly simultaneously with the opening ceremony of Beijing's Games.

Despite such frustrations, what Olympism demands is a nonviolent and non-authoritarian philosophy of peace that rejects hegemony and embraces diverse interpretations. It demands Coubertin's notion of a sincere internationalism, which embraces cultural differences while seeking common ground, rather than the paradigm of hegemonic cosmopolitanism which seeks to impose a single "superior" culture upon all.[27] The ideal is neatly captured in the contemporary concept of multiculturalism, but the

---

[27] This distinction is explained by W. J. Morgan, "Cosmopolitanism, Olympism, and Nationalism: A Critical Interpretation of Coubertin's Ideal of International Sporting Life." *Olympika* 4 (1995): 79-91, 88.

political dimension of Olympism should perhaps allow even more interpretations than those limited to the discourse of nations. Recently the IOC committed itself to the principle of global environmental sustainability—a commitment easily interpreted as an outgrowth of Olympism's peace-promoting philosophy.

The political philosophy of the Olympic Games depends on the "Olympic spirit" which The Fundamental Principles of Olympism define in terms of mutual understanding, friendship, solidarity, and fair play.[28] These terms, like the rest of the Olympism's language, must be open to translation in hundreds of languages and to interpretation across history and culture. Such flexibility and vagueness may disqualify Olympism from the status of a legitimate philosophy in the academic sense, but it turns out that an enduring international phenomenon like the Olympic Movement needs philosophical principles flexible enough to expresses common values that can be interpreted in different ways without losing their meaning. Just as Olympic athletes from diverse cultural backgrounds compete in a common arena, diverse understandings of Olympism can find common ground. Understanding Olympism as a philosophy both derived from and expressed through sport, demands a multicultural approach. In this sense it can teach us something about the problem of philosophy—and its relation to sport— in the age of globalization.

---

[28] Olympic Charter (2010), 14.

15. Olympism: a Philosophy of Sport[1]

The philosophy that underpins the Olympic Movement is generally referred to as 'Olympism,' but it is far from clear exactly what Olympism is, where it comes from, and where it is going. The purpose of this chapter is to explore those questions, beginning with a discussion of whether Olympism can legitimately be called a philosophy at all. The second question addressed is whether Olympism constitutes a philosophy of sport, or rather is a philosophy informed by sport—specifically values intrinsic to sport which support the larger goals of the Olympic Movement. One of these values is that of human excellence, but it can be hard to discern exactly what Olympism's idea of human excellence is. Olympism also touts the value of education through sport—specifically the educational value of good example, but it needs to be made clear what these examples are and how they are expected to educate. The values of justice and athletic fair play are also affirmed but they face the challenge of diverse ethical views within international communities. This leads to the political ideal of a world community and the question of how the Olympics might promote it without falling into the traps of hegemony or homogenization. Given the Movement's grand social and political goals, Olympism can appear inadequate as a philosophy. This inadequacy, paradoxically, may be the secret to Olympism's success.

Is Olympism a Philosophy?

Before we can discuss Olympism as a philosophy, we must first address the question of whether it *is* a philosophy of sport—or even a philosophy at all. If we think of Olympism expansively as a philosophy emerging from the ancient Olympic Games and the rich philosophical heritage of Greece, we may conclude that it

---

[1] Originally published as "Olympism: A Philosophy of Sport?" In *Routledge Handbook of the Philosophy of Sport*, eds. Mike McNamee and William J. Morgan (Abingdon: Routledge, 2015), 368-382. Reprinted with permission, all rights reserved.

is one of the most important philosophies of sport in history.[2] If we think of Olympism more historically as the eclectic and often-contradictory ideas of the French pedagogue, Baron Pierre de Coubertin,[3] we may conclude that it is not a philosophy at all but at best an ideology that served the needs of the 19th century revival which has since become outdated and irrelevant.[4] And if we think of Olympism in practical terms, as a philosophy that must unite and guide the modern Olympic Movement with its massive global reach and ambitious social goals, we may conclude that it is hopelessly thin and vague—incapable of articulating clear principles or setting rigid guidelines, and therefore impotent to face such challenges as multiculturalism, globalization and environmental degradation.[5] It turns out, paradoxically, that Olympism's weakness as a philosophy may be its strength as an international philosophy of sport.

In his detailed examination of Olympism from the perspective of the history of ideas, Sigmund Loland considers Olympism to be an ideology rather than a philosophy—that is, a set of beliefs designed to bring about a particular social order.[6] That analysis is certainly consistent with the aims of Pierre de Coubertin, who was neither a professional philosopher nor a great intellectual—but rather an idealistic pedagogue seeking to organize an ambitious

---

[2] This is the view of Nissiotis, "The Philosophy of Olympism," *Olympic Review* 13.6 (1979): 82-85, as well as my own work.

[3] Sigmund Loland, "Coubertin's Olympism from the Perspective of the History of Ideas," *Olympika* 4 (1995): 49-78; Dikaia Chatziefstathiou, "Olympic education and beyond: Olympism and value legacies from the Olympic and Paralympic Games," *Educational Review*, 64.3 (2012): 385-400.

[4] J. Bale and M. K. Christensen, Post Olympism? Questioning Sport in the Twenty-first Century (London: Berg, 2004).

[5] J. Segrave, "Toward a Definition of Olympism," in *The Olympic Games in Transition*, eds. J. Segrave and D. Chu, (Champaign, IL: Human Kinetics, 1988), 149-161.

[6] S. Loland "Coubertin's Olympism from the Perspective of the History of Ideas," *Olympika* 4 (1995): 49.

event for the tangible benefit of his French compatriots and, ultimately, all of mankind. Coubertin apparently coined the term 'Olympism' in 1894 during the run-up to the first modern Games of 1896, but he never seems to have completed his articulation of the philosophy. In 1936, the year before his death, he regretfully concluded that he had failed to define Olympism in an accessible way.[7] This "failure" may be due to the fact that Coubertin's idea of Olympism changed throughout his lifetime; the writings and speeches he left behind paint an eclectic and sometimes contradictory picture of his philosophical vision.[8] But Olympism's "failure" to be rigidly defined would turn out to be the secret of its success. In an overview of the philosophical controversy surrounding Olympism, Lamartine DaCosta concludes that it should be considered a process philosophy—an ongoing philosophical conversation merely started by Coubertin and open to the contributions of subsequent philosophers.[9] As a matter of practice, that is exactly what Olympism has turned out to be—a philosophical conversation about the value of sport for promulgating a particular vision of humanity and for achieving international social goals.

The foundational text of Olympism can be found in the Olympic Charter, specifically the section that articulates six "Fundamental Principles of Olympism." Of these, only the first two are obviously philosophical. In fact, it is the first fundamental principle that declares Olympism to be a philosophy:

> Olympism is a philosophy of life, exalting and combining in a balanced whole the qualities of body, will and mind. Blending sport with culture and education, Olympism seeks to create a way of life based on the joy of effort, the

---

[7] Pierre de Coubertin, "Les sources et les limites du progrès sportif," *Revue Olimpique* 5 (1939): 1.
[8] As evidenced by the volume Coubertin, *Olympism: Selected Writings*.
[9] DaCosta, "Never Ending Story," 169-170.

educational value of a good example, and respect for universal fundamental ethical principles.[10]

Embedded in this statement are metaphysical and ethical claims about the nature of human beings and the kinds of lives they ought to live, as well as an assertion that there are (or at least should be) universal ethical principles of some sort. The second fundamental principle lays out Olympism's political vision:

> The goal of Olympism is to place sport at the service of the harmonious development of man, with a view to promoting a peaceful society concerned with the preservation of human dignity.[11]

This goal is political in the Aristotelian sense of being concerned with community, in this case world community. The very assumption that the world should be a community is itself a political statement. More specifically, the Olympic Movement here is declaring its political goal to be peace—something confirmed by the fourth item under the "Mission and Role of the IOC," which is to "...endeavor to place sport at the service of humanity and thereby to promote peace".[12]

To understand Olympism as a philosophy, however, we must go beyond its published "Fundamental Principles." We must examine its philosophical heritage from ancient Greece as well as the enlightenment ideas that influenced the articulation of those ideals. We should also consider the symbols and sayings of the Olympic movement, such as the five interlocking rings, the Olympic motto: *citius, altius, fortius* (faster, higher, stronger), and the Olympic creed: "The most important thing in the Olympic Games is not to win but to take part..." Finally, we must look at Olympic history, at the way the Movement has behaved in light of its stated ideals. Olympism is, if nothing else, a living philosophy that has served and must continue to serve the practical needs of

---

[10] Olympic Charter (2011) 10
[11] Olympic Charter (2011), 10.
[12] Olympic Charter (2011), 14.

the Olympic Movement for vision and guidance. And even if we successfully discern (or perhaps construct) a coherent philosophy from all of these elements, it is still unclear whether we will have a philosophy of sport.

A Theory of Sport?

What could we mean by a "philosophy of sport" in this context? Does the philosophy of Olympism offer, for example, a metaphysical account of sport? The IOC sets out criteria for inclusion of sports in the Olympic program, so there is some meaningful debate about what an *Olympic* sport should be.[13] But this is not a discussion of what *sport is*, it is rather an eligibility discussion concerning which sports are appropriate for the Games, which is to say which sports are conducive to the goals of the Olympic Movement—including such practical concerns as media-friendliness, commercial potential and so on. What this shows is that Olympism is primarily a social and political philosophy of sport, one that considers how to use sport or what can be accomplished through sport, rather than a philosophy that seeks to define what sport is.

Even though Olympism does not define or even discuss the metaphysical nature of sport *per se*, its social goals dictate to a certain extent what sport *should be*. Indeed, if we take the expansive view of Olympism as a philosophy arising from the ancient Olympic Games, we may observe that practical social problems during that era gave shape to the configuration of sport as we know it. The initial problem for the ancient Greeks was how to select among competing claims to a social honor—a problem still common today and very often resolved through a competition in

---

[13] As Jim Parry,. "Sport and Olympism: Universals and Multiculturalism," *Journal of the Philosophy of Sport* 33 (2006): 21, explains, the criteria for inclusion of a sport in the Olympic program are based on popularity and universality, but Coubertin also wanted the Movement to contribute to the development of all sport. The debate about which sports should be included and why is accordingly complex.

V. Modern Olympism

which each candidate is given an equal opportunity and the reward is allotted according to merit. Places in college, contracts for work, even architectural designs, are frequently decided this way.

Since its origins, ancient Olympia had been a religious sanctuary where diverse tribes would gather to sacrifice to common gods. The honor of lighting the sacrificial flame would conventionally go to the highest ranking member of a given society—the king or primary ruler. But Olympia was a Panhellenic sanctuary—one dedicated to all the Hellenes rather than any single tribe—and so there must have been multiple sovereigns making claims to this particular honor. What is more, from a religious point of view, it was important to choose an honoree who would be pleasing to the god in question—a god who was understood to transcend the social rivalries and hierarchies of mere mortals. This social problem seems to have been solved by running a race from the edge of the sanctuary to the sacrificial altar.[14] Equal opportunity, reward according to merit, public observation of the process—this set of foundational qualities endures in Olympic and non-Olympic sports alike.

Looking at the challenges faced by the modern Olympic movement—especially with regard to their selection of sports to be included in their program—these qualities remain central and they go beyond sport. Equality of opportunity may be enshrined in the rules of individual events, but it is difficult to achieve when observed from a global perspective. Not only do most Olympic sports have a western heritage (Judo and Taekwondo are the only non-western sports on the current program), global economic disparities exclude large numbers of people from expensive sports such as sailing and equestrian. Sports like figure skating, track cycling, luge, and gymnastics require facilities that are not available publically in much of the world. Other sports, such as

---

[14] This is the story told by Philostratus (*Gymnasticus* 5), for a fuller discussion, see Reid, "Sport, Philosophy, and the Quest for Knowledge," 40-49.

skiing, cycling, and bobsled are influenced by expensive technologies available to only a select few. Accordingly, Olympic participants from poor countries and families are underrepresented in these sports, whereas sports requiring minimal facilities and equipment such as running, soccer, and wrestling boast a more geographically diverse slate of participants. This diversity is important to the Games' political goal of "a peaceful society concerned with the preservation of human dignity."[15]

Olympic sport cannot uphold the ideals of equal opportunity if social and economic disparities impede large numbers of athletes from participation in the first place. This lesson had been learned already in the ancient Olympic Games where aristocrats had hoped that athletic excellence would justify their social privilege, but the success of lower class athletes undermined this hope. So they attempted to gain competitive advantage with their wealth, first by hiring coaches and trainers and eventually by adding equestrian events in which the victory crowns were awarded to the owner rather than the rider or chariot driver.[16] Stephen Miller argues with much support that there is a connection between the equal opportunity inherent in sport and the birth of democracy in ancient Greece.[17] Although wealthy countries and individuals still try to buy competitive advantages in the modern Games, Olympism demands that sport be kept as free as possible from economic disparities. In fact, since 1981 the International Olympic Committee has promoted a program called Olympic Solidarity, which distributes a proportion of Olympic television revenues to athletes and organizations in need, to live up to the ideal of equal opportunity and reward according to (athletic) merit—as opposed to wealth or social position.

---

[15] Olympic Charter (2011), 10.
[16] H. Reid, *Athletics and Philosophy in the Ancient World* (Abingdon: Routledge, 2011), 37-39.
[17] S.G. Miller, *Ancient Greek Athletics*, 233.

V. Modern Olympism

So even if Olympism does not offer a metaphysical account of sport, the goals and ideals of the Olympic movement seem to dictate that Olympic sports must exhibit the principles of equal opportunity and reward according to athletic merit. These principles may seem to be guaranteed internally by the rules of sport, but in an international context they demand an effort to compensate for external social inequities, and to regulate or exclude sports which emphasize technology and financing at the expense of the human element. The Olympics may include sailing on the program, but the boats are identical and relatively inexpensive—in stark contrast with the Americas' Cup yacht race, which is as much a contest of wealth and technology as it is one of sailing. It is only by applying the foundational sports value of equal opportunity—as symbolized by the common starting line—beyond the contests themselves and in the larger global community, that Olympism can meet the contemporary challenges of the Games. Olympism does not proffer a theory about what sport is, but what sport is—in terms of its internal values and principles—shapes the contours of Olympism.

A Theory of Human Excellence through Sport

Another way to look at Olympism as a philosophy is as a theory of human excellence through sport, or as Hans Lenk and Jim Parry describe it, a philosophical anthropology.[18] To be sure Olympism is a humanistic philosophy. Its first fundamental principle says that Olympism "exalts" humanity as a "balanced whole" of the qualities of "body, will, and mind."[19] This particular language reflects the modern European metaphysical idea of persons as combinations of body, will, and mind, but it also emphasizes—contrary to the received opinion of the day—that these qualities should be balanced and that the emphasis should be placed on the whole. Ever since Rene Descartes' radical

---

[18] Lenk "Towards a Philosophical Anthropology," and J. Parry, "Olympism at the Beginning and End of the Twentieth Century," *Proceedings of the International Olympic Academy* (1998): 81-94.
[19] Olympic Charter (2011), 10.

separation of body and mind in the 17th Century, the emphasis had been put on mind rather than body. Descartes' famous statement, *"Cogito ergo sum"* (I think, therefore I am) promulgated an interpretation of humanity that not only took our minds to be more important than our bodies, but declared us to be *essentially* thinking (rather than playing, dancing, or even moving) things.[20] Unsurprisingly, under this intellectual hegemony sport and physical education—as well as general health and fitness—were significantly undervalued. Coubertin was one of several pedagogues trying to fight this devaluation by re-emphasizing the physical dimension of our being.

"Mens sana in corpore sano" (sound mind in sound body) was among the favorite slogans of the pedagogical movement called Muscular Christianity. Its origins suggested a connection with the ancient Greco-Roman world, which was in fashion at the time due to new archeological excavations and academic discoveries. Tapping into that sentiment was a great way to increase Olympism's appeal. In practical terms, however, the Roman writer Juvenal's coining of the phrase *"mens sana in corpore sano"* had nothing to do with the Olympic Games, sports, or even exercise. He was simply recommending a prayer.[21] It was absolutely correct, however, to associate a holistic view of human excellence with the ancient world. Whether he knew it or not, Coubertin was tapping into a very rich philosophical tradition when he placed human excellence at the center of Olympism.

The Greek word for human (and other kinds of) excellence is *aretē*, and it is at the center of the most venerated ethical traditions of the ancient world. Starting no later than Socrates, and moving through Plato, Aristotle, and even the Roman Stoics, the cultivation of *aretē* is the central focus of a good life. Socrates

---

[20] The Latin formulation of this saying comes from *Principles of Philosophy* 1644, 1.7. The more popular text that makes the "cogito" argument is *Meditations on First Philosophy* 1.16-17.

[21] D. Young, *The Modern Olympics: A Struggle for Revival* (Baltimore: John Hopkins University Press, 1996), 189.

chastises the Athenians at his trial for caring too much for wealth and not enough for *aretē* (Plato, *Apology,* 29de); Aristotle defines human happiness (*eudaimonia*) as activity in accordance with *aretē* (*Nicomachean Ethics*,1098a); and the Stoics were said to believe that "nothing is good except for virtue."[22] Pythagoras, before all of them, had gone to the gymnasium in search of good students for philosophy, not least because athleticism been long interpreted as a sign of *aretē*.[23] What the 8th century BCE advent of the Olympic Games did was to generate the idea that *aretē* was not just a matter of noble birth, but could be acquired through training like athleticism. This training for virtue became the task of moral philosophy and indeed the ancient Greek philosophers' methods of dialogue and dialectic are not far removed from athletic competition. Both sport and philosophy in the ancient world were understood as means of cultivating excellence.

What is more, this ancient Greek and Roman notion of excellence was understood holistically as a quality that engaged body and mind. Although most ancient philosophers conceptually divided body (*sōma*) and mind/soul (*psychē*), they understood the *psychē* to be the origin not only of intellect and thinking, but also of locomotion and of life itself. *Aretē* was therefore an excellence of both body and mind, the source of the strong and beautiful movements associated with athletes. In Plato's famous political treatise, *Republic,* sport and exercise are prescribed explicitly for the health of the *psychē* (411e). Even famous Greek athletic statues like Myron's *Discus Thrower* are to be interpreted not as portraits of great physical specimens, but rather as the expression of *aretē through* the body.[24] *Kalokagathia*, a concept combining beauty and

---

[22] According to some scholars this comment may be misleading, see Nicholas White's introduction to the *Handbook of Epictetus* (Indianapolis: Hackett, 1983), 7-8.

[23] Iamblichus, The Pythagorean Life, 5.

[24] H. Reid, "Athletic Beauty in Classical Greece: A Philosophical View," *Journal of the Philosophy of Sport* 39 (2012): 1-17. Reprinted in this volume.

goodness, is practically synonymous with *aretē* and specifically associated with youthful athleticism.[25]

So Olympism's exaltation of humanity as a "balanced whole," like the 19th century slogan of *"mens sana in corpore sano,"* taps into a very rich and very relevant philosophy of human excellence even if they do so inadvertently. In addition, this ancient tradition of virtue ethics meshes well with the Eastern philosophical traditions of Daoism and Confucianism, thereby shielding Olympism somewhat from the criticism that it is an irretrievably Eurocentric philosophy.[26] Likewise, by failing to spell out in much detail exactly what this ideal of humanity looks like—by failing even to list the particular excellences prized in human beings—Olympism also manages to transcend the limitations of a specifically historical philosophy.[27]

By exalting human excellence but keeping our minds open about the various ways it may be instantiated, the Olympic Games have managed to put a very diverse set of faces on the conception of an excellent human being. Athletes admired for their excellence include tiny females like Nadia Comaneci and imposing males like Usain Bolt. They come from every human race, every socioeconomic class, and a variety of religious backgrounds. But they all have a common athletic excellence which, in the language of the Fundamental Principles of Olympism "exalt(s) and combine(s) in a balanced whole the qualities of body, will and

---

[25] I. Martinkova, *"Kalokagathia:* How to understand harmony of a human being," *Nikephoros* 14 (2001): 21–8; see also "Olympic Ethics as *Kalokagathia"* in this volume.

[26] A. Inoue, "Critique of Modern Olympism: A Voice from the East," in *Sports – The East and the West,* eds. G. Pfister and L. Yueye (Sant Agustin: Academia Verlag, 1999) 163-7.

[27] As is well known, the ancient Olympic Games excluded females, slaves, and non-Hellenes. The first modern Olympic Games also excluded females and discrimination based on race, religion, class, politics, and disability continue to be issues in the modern Games. The point is that Olympism should be based on ideals rather than historical practice.

mind."[28] These few words and the Olympic Games' long history result in a theory of human excellence robust enough to carry philosophical weight, but not so clearly defined as to exclude the possibility of human excellence through sport coming from an unexpected place, perhaps even from a disabled athlete. Olympism's ideal of human excellence should tap in deeply to its ancient roots in order to find philosophical structure, but it should also look to the future with an open mind and heart.

A Theory of Education through Sport

A third way to interpret Olympism is as a theory of education through sport. I say education through sport rather than sports education or even physical education to emphasize that the goal of Olympism is not primarily the acquisition of athletic skills or physical strength and fitness. Even from Pierre de Coubertin's perspective, physical education was a means to larger social and political goals.[29] The humanistic vision of Olympism aims at cultivating excellence and, as the first Fundamental Principle of Olympism states, it expects to do this at least partially through "the educational value of a good example." The Olympic motto and creed, meanwhile, suggest a pursuit of excellence (higher, faster, stronger) through participation (the important thing is not to win, but to take part). Superficially, these three things may seem contradictory. Is Olympism promoting education through spectatorship, pursuit of victory, or participation? Is the example to be followed a champion, a gracious loser, or perhaps not a person at all but a particular kind of spirit exhibited through gestures of fair play?

The obvious interpretation of what Olympism means by a "good example" would be the Olympic athlete and specifically his or her display of excellence, which inspires others to strive for excellence, too. The stories of kids taking to sport after watching the Olympics on television are legion and the idea is hardly new; in fact ancient Greek athletes performed the same educational

---

[28] Olympic Charter, (2011), 10.
[29] Chatziefstathiou, "Olympic Education," 385.

function. Winners at the ancient Olympic Games earned the right to erect statues of themselves at Olympia, sometimes they also commissioned poets like Pindar to compose victory odes that celebrated their glory. The odes and the statues intentionally idealized the beauty of the athletes and their feats because their social function was to celebrate the community's shared value of *aretē*—a quality which was understood to bring humans closer to divine perfection. Like the prize of the olive crown, which dries up and disintegrates quickly, human excellence is ephemeral and merely reflective of that of the gods—as Pindar put it famously, "a dream of a shadow is man" (*Pythain* 8, 97). Even today Olympic victors represent—at least symbolically—such globally admired virtues as courage, self-discipline, and respect.

There is a danger, however, with the educational use of athletes as role models—one recognized even by Socrates when he said Athens should reward him for his educational services rather than rewarding Olympic athletes for their victories because their victories only made them think themselves better while his questioning actually made them better (Plato, *Apology* 36de). The modern Olympic Games have had to deal with the problem of athletes whose virtues in the contest are not always reflected in their behavior outside of competition—Oscar Pistorius facing trial for murder immediately comes to mind—as well as athletes who turn out to have gained their medals through dubious or illicit means, such as doping.[30] Marion Jones and Lance Armstrong are prime examples of this problem. The danger is not only that individuals sometimes succeed in sport without actually having the virtues the victor is supposed to symbolize, but also the larger educational message that what *matters* is victory by any means and not the virtues associated with it.

---

[30] A. Schneider and R. Butcher, "Why Olympic Athletes Should Avoid the Use and Seek the Elimination of Performance-Enhancing Substances and Practices From the Olympic Games," *Journal of the Philosophy of Sport* 20-21 (1994): 64-81, explain how doping conflicts with Olympism.

Unfortunately the ethos in many Olympic sports and even some National Olympic Committees is focused squarely on results or private rewards and only tangentially on the human excellences that give the medals their symbolic value.[31] This focus on results may be thought to represent the Olympic motto "*citius, altius, fortius*" described in the *Olympic Charter* as expressing "the aspirations of the Olympic Movement."[32] It is also a phrase, as Loland points out, that seems to reflect the fascination with records of progress common in Coubertin's era.[33] But the Olympic motto need not be interpreted exclusively as a focus on results, or even more generally as the overcoming or outdoing of others. That latter interpretation would, as several philosophers have noticed, be at odds with the Olympic creed, which states "The most important thing in the Olympic Games is not to win but to take part, just as the most important thing in life is not the triumph but the struggle. The essential thing is not to have conquered but to have fought well."

As sport philosopher Cesar Torres observes, an enlightened understanding of Olympism—and athletic competition itself—requires that we see the Olympic motto and creed as compatible, even complementary.[34] Meaningful participation in athletic competition implies a concern with performance and results insofar as these represent the goals of the contest itself. But it is the *process* of engagement in competition—the taking part, the

---

[31] National Olympic Committees pay particular attention to the so-called medal count, not even considering the fact that this constitutes an unofficial and unfair competition which clearly favors the larger and richer countries. For an interesting account, see Bernard and Busse, "Who Wins the Olympic Games: Economic Resources and Medal Totals," *The Review of Economics and Statistics* 86 (2004): 413-417.

[32] Olympic Charter (2011), 21.

[33] S. Loland, "Record Sports: An Ecological Critique and a Reconstruction," *Journal of the Philosophy of Sport* 28 (2001): 127-39.

[34] C. Torres, "Results or Participation? Reconsidering Olympism's Approach to Competition," *Quest* 58, (2006): 243.

struggle—that makes sport and even victory itself valuable. You can buy an Olympic medal on eBay but its purchase value is nothing compared with the value of actually winning it through good competition. Likewise a competition may be won without struggle, through lack of good competition, or maybe just luck— as when Steven Bradbury won a gold medal in short track speed skating at the 2002 Olympics because all the competitors ahead of him crashed into each other in the final turn.[35] But this kind of victory lacks value—indeed it lacks the spirit of *citius, altius, fortius*—the athletic ethos of constantly improving and performing as well as one can, whatever the result.

So Olympism's educationally valuable good examples are not limited to winners or even individuals. The entire spectacle of striving for excellence through fair competition itself, taking into account particular obstacles overcome and challenges met, qualifies as an educationally valuable example. It is characteristic of the Olympic Games to celebrate athletes who overcome particular social and economic barriers. Even athletes who perform well below international standards such as Eric "The Eel" Moussambani, a swimmer from Equatorial Guinea, or Wojdan Shahrkhani, the first female Olympian from Saudi Arabia, are cheered by the crowds and feted in the media. Unlike world championships and most other competitions, the Olympic Games leave some room for athletes to participate who would not otherwise qualify based on performance. This practice entails, however, that some potential medalists will be left at home (as when one country has the top three athletes in a given discipline, but is only allowed to send one or two of them to the Games), and it provides strong evidence to counter the charge that Olympism cares only about performance. The IOC's emphasis on diversity and inclusion is itself an important educational example.

---

[35] R. Baka and R. Hess, "Doing a 'Bradbury'!: An analysis of recent Australian success at the winter Olympic Games," in *The global nexus engaged*, eds. K. Wamsley, R. Barney and S. Marty (London, ON: University of Western Ontario Press, 2002): 177-184.

Furthermore, encouraging and facilitating diverse participation produces a wide variety of role models. By failing to define its educational examples—even in terms of athletic success—Olympism allows for a conception of excellence valid around the world.

A Theory of Justice through Sport

If Olympism is characterized, as may philosophers claim, by an effort to promote moral values through sport, its most important educational examples will not be athletes but actions—especially its own institutional behavior.[36] Although the first Fundamental Principle cites "respect for universal fundamental ethical principles," it does not specify what those principles are or how they are to be understood. Those who consider ethics to be culturally relative would deny the existence of universal principles, and indeed Olympism risks a kind of ethical imperialism if it understands Anglo-European principles to be universal.[37] Doing ethics in a multicultural environment requires some form of common ground and in the Olympic Games, sport provides the common ground. The primary ethical principle of sport is fair play, which the fourth Fundamental Principle of Olympism identifies, along with mutual understanding, friendship, and solidarity, as essential to the "Olympic spirit." If fair play is understood as the ethical principle of justice applied to sport, Olympism may be interpreted as a theory of justice through sport.

In ancient Greek philosophy, justice is understood generally as the excellence appropriate to communities. It is the subject of

---

[36] As Bok, "Can Higher Education," 494–503, has shown, moral behavior (good and bad) is learned more by observing an institution's behavior than from teaching of theory.

[37] Indeed European Rationalism, a movement that includes such philosophers as Rene Descartes and Immanuel Kant, took its philosophy to be universal since human reason is universal. But other ethical traditions, such as Daoism and Confucianism, believe that ethical truths transcend rational expression.

Plato's utopian dialogue *Republic,* and it is discussed extensively by Aristotle in the *Nicomachean Ethics* and *Politics*. Although the concept of fair play seems specific to or at least derived from sport, it is relevant to justice understood as the excellence of communities because—as Alisdair MacIntyre's work has shown—sport *is* a kind of community. For one thing, sports are governed by rules similar to the way communities are governed by laws, and it is important both to sport and to communities that these regulations are well-formed, generally respected, and properly enforced. Democratic communities consider themselves to be ruled by law. In all communities, rules and laws should be constructed in such a way that excellence may be cultivated, expressed, and appropriately awarded. One of Olympism's primary ethical demands, we may conclude, is for the proper administration of the rules and regulations of sport. It is no mistake that Olympic athletes and officials take oaths in which they swear "to respect and abide by the rules" governing the Games.[38]

It would be wrong, however, to reduce Olympism's conception of justice or fair play merely to rule adherence. After all, the fourth Fundamental Principle characterizes fair play as a "spirit" rather than a principle. In this it resembles ancient Greek ideas about justice. Aristotle, in particular, took the concept of beauty (*to kalon*) to be essential to ethical social action. In the *Eudemian Ethics*, he describes justice as something beautiful and says that the good and beautiful person (*kaloskagathos*) does just actions in the community not because they provide any personal benefit, but simply because they are beautiful.[39] The English word 'fair' retains this aesthetic link between beauty and justice, although it often is forgotten in discussions of fair play, which tend toward the technical and legalistic. For example, the advantage

---

[38] Coaches and IOC Members also take similar oaths. The text of the IOC member's oath can be found on p. 30 of the *Olympic Charter*. The athletes, officials, and coaches' oaths can be found in IOC, *Factsheet on the Opening Ceremony of the Games of the Olympiad* (2013), 3.

[39] Aristotle, *Eudemian Ethics*, 1249a

gained by hydrodynamic swimsuits in the 2008 Beijing games was largely accepted because it violated no rules. It took a larger sense of justice for the International Swimming Federation to finally ban the suits in 2009, under pressure in part from Michael Phelps, who had arguably been the biggest beneficiary of the suits, winning eight gold medals in Beijing. Phelps' opposition to the suits was aimed to benefit his sports community,[40] something Aristotle might have recognized as beautifully just.

If it is to be a universal ethical principle, justice in the Olympic community cannot depend on the legalistic authority of a single body—even an international body like the IOC. It needs to transcend individual and national interests to serve the common interests of the international sports community. This lesson was learned in ancient Olympia, which was a Pan-Hellenic sanctuary, by definition the property of all Hellenes and therefore lacking a sovereign ruling authority—other than the god Zeus, whom all officials, athletes, and spectators were there to worship. The race to select an honoree to light the sacrificial flame was a fair solution to the problem of competing claims to that honor, not least because everyone present could witness the contest and attest to its impartiality and the validity of its results. The open and transparent process seems to have had a unifying and pacifying effect on rival tribes who, in most other contexts, would address their differences through violence. One might even say the ancient contest had been conducted with "a spirit of friendship, solidarity, and fair play," that is to say, in the Olympic spirit, which cannot be dissociated from the aesthetics of justice.

The transparency required by this Olympic aesthetic of justice explains why "invisible" problems like doping and corruption are such a big threat to the Olympic Games. Unlike fouls committed in the contest, doping is a form of injustice that cannot be seen by the audience or even the officials without the aid of sophisticated

---

[40] This is, at least, suggested by Phelps' comments at the time. See The Associated Press, "FINA moves up bodysuit ban," *ESPN Olympic Sports*, July 31, 2009.

scientific testing. Since those responsible for policing doping in sport often had a financial interest in preserving the illusion of justice, they usually acted not like Aristotle's *kaloskagathos* to preserve the intrinsic good of the community, but rather on the basis of lower motivations such as avoidance of shame and accumulation of wealth. When doping cases were exposed—like Ben Johnson's after his victory in the 100 meter sprint at the 1988 Seoul Olympic Games—it was usually due to a courageous and sometimes insubordinate act by a single individual. It was not until 1999, when the doping problem was perceived to threaten the entire Olympic movement, that the independent World Anti-Doping Agency (WADA) was founded. About the same time, the text of the Olympic athletes' oath was changed to include the phrase, "committing ourselves to a sport without doping and without drugs." Only in recent years has this massive anti-doping effort begun to restore public confidence in the fairness of Olympic competition. Maintaining transparency may be seen as central to the goal of promoting Olympic justice.

Philosopher Claudia Pawlenka argues that fairness as a moral concept actually derives from sport.[41] Given that sport is the common denominator for the multicultural Olympic community, it makes sense that a sport-inspired concept of justice should be its primary ethical principle. Furthermore, since the Olympic community must operate in the absence of a single authority, the democratic idea of rule of law, exemplified by sport's close association with rules, is very promising. However, the Olympic understanding of justice must not be reduced, as noted, to rule-adherence. In fact Olympism, as also noted, characterizes fair play as a "spirit" or attitude that includes community based concepts of mutual understanding, solidarity, and friendship. This characterization harkens back to the aesthetic aspect of justice touted by ancient Greek philosophy, which demands transparency

---

[41] C. Pawlenka, "The Idea of Fairness: A General Ethical Concept or One Particular to Sports Ethics," *Journal of the Philosophy of Sport* 32 (2005): 49-64.

and group observation. In the London 2012 Games, this aesthetic conception of Olympic justice as a kind of spirit seems to have been employed by badminton officials who disqualified eight players for "not using their best efforts" in preliminary matches in order to gain advantageous matches in the finals.[42] Olympism's theory of justice may indeed be derived from the principle of fair play that informs sport itself, but the concept turns out to be ethically robust while accommodating diverse cultural beliefs.

A Theory of World Community through Sport

The attempt to create an international or indeed universal philosophy may be Olympism's most distinctive characteristic. The Olympic ideal of a world community is expressed in its symbol of five interlocking rings, which "represents the union of the five continents and the meeting of athletes from throughout the world at the Olympic Games."[43] The fourth Fundamental Principle of Olympism demands universal access to this world sporting community: "The practice of sport is a human right. Every individual must have the possibility of practicing sport without discrimination of any kind." The sixth principle reinforces the point, "Any form of discrimination with regard to a country or a person on grounds of race, religion, politics, gender or otherwise is incompatible with belonging to the Olympic Movement." These very strong statements are at odds with Olympic history—which is riddled with exclusions based on race, creed, politics, and gender. Olympism's effort to provide some kind of coherent philosophy for an extremely diverse community—without capitulating either to hegemony or homogenization—is daunting. It should not be seen as trivial or quixotic, however, because this reflects the challenge posed by the phenomenon of globalization.

Globalization is the 21st century version of a phenomenon that has appeared in the world before. It refers to advances in travel and communication technology which increase contact between

---

[42] British Broadcasting Corporation, "Olympics badminton: Eight women disqualified from doubles," *BBC Sport*, 2012.
[43] Olympic Charter (2011), 21.

people and cultures that were formerly more isolated from one another. In our current times internet technology and air-travel characterize the phenomenon, but developments in telegraph and train technology can be correlated with the inauguration of the Modern Olympic Games in 1896, and even the 8th century BCE founding of the Ancient Olympic Games can be linked with expansion of shipping and trade in the Mediterranean. The link between the Olympic Games and such "world-shrinking" phenomena is that both bring diverse people together and challenge them to get along despite their differences. First of all this requires at least a temporary change of attitude—an effort to see oneself as part of a world community, what the ancients called 'cosmopolitanism.'[44]

Unlike cosmopolitanism, globalization is not an ideal. It is a phenomenon that brings with it the twin dangers of hegemony and homogenization, both of which challenge the Olympic Movement's goals.[45] Hegemony is imposition of the dominant group's values upon all others and in the case of the modern Olympic Movement, the dominant group has historically been

---

[44] At the ancient Olympic Games, that larger community was that of all Hellenes as opposed to particular tribes and its purpose was to worship a common deity. The concept of a world community appropriate to the Modern Olympic Games also emerged in ancient Greece with Diogenes, the 5th century BCE Cynic philosopher who is said to have coined the Greek term *cosmopolis*, which means world community. The idea was later embraced by the Roman Stoic school, especially Marcus Aurelius who envisioned the well-being of all mankind to be intertwined and advocated cosmopolitanism, an attitude of world citizenship. For a full account of Stoic cosmopolitanism in relation to Roman sport see Reid, *Athletics and Philosophy*, ch. 9.

[45] Nationalism and "insincere internationalism" are also threats. See H. Iowerth, C. Jones and A. Hardman, "Nationalism and Olympism towards a Normative Theory of International Sporting Representation," *Olympika* 14 (2010): 81-110, and W. Morgan, "Cosmopolitanism, Olympism, and Nationalism," *Olympika* IV (1995): 79-91.

European and North American. Globalization, furthermore, tends to favor the wealthy and powerful. As Parry points out, this combination portends a perfect storm in which Olympism's world community risks becoming a giant Europe or USA rather than a multicultural society.[46] Charges of Eurocentrism or American dominance are accordingly common in the Olympic Movement, but as Mike McNamee notes, the social practice of sport furnishes Olympism with a notion of universal human virtues that transcend distinctively Western values.[47] A similar conclusion is reached by Nanayakkara.[48] Even if charges of Eurocentrism are overblown, however, Olympism demands that the Movement fight against the risk of Western hegemony by striving for diversity in terms of its official sports, host cities, and organizations—not least the IOC itself.

Diversity is also essential to resist globalization's tendency toward homogenization—the elimination of differing styles and approaches not just in sport but in all kinds of social practices. Often this happens in the name of efficiency—a particular approach to a sport increases the chances of success and pretty soon everyone is using it. Complex sports like soccer can and do accommodate a variety of playing styles and approaches—indeed the great success of FIFA's world cup is the diversity of styles employed by the various national teams. As Sigmund Loland observes, however, less-complex, record-type sports like the 100 meter dash do not allow for much diversity because the standards for performance are so strictly defined.[49] These sports have the tendency to become homogenized to the point that the athletes,

---

[46] Parry, "Globalization, Multiculturalism, and Olympism," *Proceedings of the International Olympic Academy* (2000): 86-97.

[47] McNamee, "Olympism, Eurocentricity," 185.

[48] S. Nanayakkara, "Olympism: A Western Liberal Idea That Ought Not to Be Imposed on other Cultures?" in *Pathways: Critiques and Discourse in Olympic Research*, ed. K. Wamsley (London, Ontario: University of Western Ontario, 2008), 351-358.

[49] S. Loland, 2006, "Olympic Sport and the Ideal of Sustainable Development," *Journal Of The Philosophy Of Sport,* 33:2 (2006) 147.

their preparation, and even their styles all start to resemble one another. Very often they train together in one place under one or a few coaches, no matter the country they actually compete for at the Olympics. As we noted earlier, the emphasis on records and performance has its place in Olympism, but diversity is an equally important value and sports should be chosen and regulated in such a way as to promote it.

A special case of diversity very important to Olympism is that of women. Despite the exclusion of women from the ancient Olympic Games[50] and Pierre de Coubertin's initial opposition to their participation in the modern Games, women have competed in every Olympics since 1900 and in at Rio 2012, they competed in every sport on the program, making up 45% of all athletes.[51] The Olympic Charter, furthermore, defines one of the roles of the IOC as follows: "to encourage and support the promotion of women in sport at all levels and in all structures, with a view to implementing the principle of equality of men and women."[52] This commitment to female participation engages the issue of diversity in a special way because it can be just as easily interpreted as a case of cultural hegemony as prevention of sex-discrimination. In some countries females are not considered equal to males under the law and their participation in sport is discouraged. When the IOC pressures these countries to include females on their Olympic teams, are they demonstrating "mutual understanding with a spirit of friendship,

---

[50] Women were excluded from the Olympic Games, but not all of ancient Greek sport. There is evidence they competed in other Panhellenic games, including Delphi, Isthmia, and Nemea. For female exclusion at Olympia, see Mouratidis, "Heracles at Olympia," 41-55. For women in Greek sport, see Scanlon, *Eros and Greek Athletics*, chapters 4-7. For the philosophical debate between Plato and Aristotle on the females and sport, see Reid, *Athletics and Philosophy*, 64-68 and 77-78.

[51] IOC *Factsheet on Women in the Olympic Movement*, 1. They are expected to reach 48.8% at Tokyo 2020.

[52] Olympic Charter, (2011), 14.

solidarity, and fair play" or arrogantly forcing their own views on a minority?

The participation of women from conservative Muslim countries has been a particular concern for the Olympic movement. As William Morgan's essay on Algerian runner Hassiba Boulmerka shows, this issue engages issues of religion, culture, politics, and economics.[53] Not only does the IOC's declaration of equality between males and females contradict traditional Muslim beliefs and laws, the uniforms required by many sports along with the public display more generally is seen by many—male and female—to flout appropriate standards of female modesty.[54] What is more, the honor and reputation of a woman's entire family is often thought to depend on perceptions of her morality.[55] For the London 2012 Olympics, the IOC pressured the Saudi Arabians to include female athletes in their team. The Saudis complied by entering a judoka but then threatened to withdraw when the International Judo Federation declared that she could not wear a headscarf in competition for safety reasons. Eventually the athlete was allowed to wear a modified scarf that addressed the safety concerns. The episode illustrates the complexity of Olympism's commitment to non-discrimination and the challenge of building a world community through sport that does not amount to an empire. Olympism must provide a philosophical foundation from which to negotiate

---

[53] Morgan, "Multinational Sport and Literary Practices and Their Communities," in *Ethics and Sport*, eds. M. McNamee and J. Parry (London: E & FN Spon, 1998), 184-204.

[54] This is true not only for Islam, but for conservative communities within most major religions including Judaism and Christianity. For more female bodies at the Olympic Games see Weaving, "Smoke and Mirrors: A Critique of Women Olympians' Nude Reflections," in *Olympic Ethics and Philosophy*, eds. M. McNamee and J. Parry (Abingdon: Routledge, 2013), 130-148.

[55] Pfister, "Outsiders: Muslim Women and Olympic Games," *The International Journal of the History of Sport* 27.16-18 (2010): 2946.

particular issues, without becoming so rigid as to work against the goals of the Movement.

Conclusion

Olympism's goal of a "peaceful society concerned with the preservation of human dignity" incorporates all of the interpretations we have surveyed in this essay. Though Olympism does not offer a metaphysics of sport, the principles implied by the structure of sport—such as equal opportunity and reward according to merit—provide common ground and common values around which a flexible and adaptable philosophy can be constructed. Part of this philosophy is a theory of human excellence, which is tied closely to sport but not necessarily to victory or to any particular type of human being. Like ancient Greek virtue ethics, Olympism promotes an ideal that is harmonious, holistic, and based on activity rather than status. Olympism also offers a theory of education through sport, both through participation and through the observance of good examples. Olympism's theory of justice derives from the sporting idea of fair play—incorporating both rule-based and aesthetic understandings of fairness. Finally Olympism promulgates an ideal of world community, characterized by non-discrimination and a commitment to mutual understanding, but also conditioned by the claim that sport is a human right. The Olympic Movement must remain aware of the twin dangers of globalization: hegemony and homogenization, if is aim is to create a peaceful international community.

As the philosophical beacon for the modern Olympic Games, Olympism is right to make sport its common denominator and to remain flexible enough to adapt to a constantly changing world. We might wish for a more clear and robust Olympic philosophy, but such an articulation may in practice be less conducive to the Movement's goals. Olympism is a philosophy of what can be achieved through sport, rather than a philosophy of sport *per se*. But the question of what can be achieved through sport just is the central concern of the philosophy of sport—an improved critical

V. Modern Olympism

understanding of sport is valuable insofar as it enables us to improve our lives as human beings and perhaps even to promote "a peaceful society concerned with the preservation of human dignity."

16. What counts as an Olympic Sport?[1]

On the face of it, defining 'Olympic sport' may seem simple: it is a sport practiced in the Olympic Games. But this superficially acceptable definition raises important philosophical questions, including what we mean by 'sport' in the first place. Since that topic is discussed extensively elsewhere, I will focus instead on what distinguishes Olympic sport from the greater class of sporting activities of which it is, presumably, some kind of a subset. I will also refrain from the method of listing the activities already practiced in the Olympic Games and trying to find common features among them because I don't want to beg the question that every sport ever included in the Olympic Games is automatically, much less equally, "Olympic." The Roman Emperor Nero once "moved" the Olympic Games from its traditional time to coincide with his excursion in Greece and introduced novel events, such as a ten-horse chariot race, which he conveniently proceeded to win. Hardly anyone, ancient or modern, considers that to be an authentic Olympic sport, though it would satisfy our superficial definition. How can we tell? The problem is not that chariot racing isn't a sport. The problem is that Nero's contest violates a higher ideal—the Olympic spirit.

Defining Olympic Sport in terms of the "Olympic spirit" is dangerous, however. As any historian of the modern Olympic Games can tell you—trying to define a spirit can destroy it. In the early 20th century, the International Olympic Committee attempted to codify the spirit of amateurism—doing something out of love—into a set of eligibility rules. By trying to remove financial interest from the Games, however, they inadvertently placed it at the center. Every effort to define an amateur in terms of not making money ended up promoting efforts to make money without breaking the letter of the rules. As the Chinese

---

[1] Originally published as "Defining Olympic Sport," in *Defining Sport: Conceptions and Boundaries*, ed. Shawn E. Klein (Lanham, MD: Lexington Books, 2017), 65-77. Reprinted with permission.

philosopher Confucius wisely warned thousands of years earlier, most people respond to rules by looking for exemptions.[2] Defining Olympic sport in terms of the Olympic spirit need not be an exercise in trying to codify and legislate a particular set of ideals, however. For one thing, the Olympic spirit, or more precisely, the philosophical ideals that underpin the Olympic Movement, are already articulated in the Olympic Charter, especially the "Fundamental Principles of Olympism."[3] The International Olympic Committee also stipulates specific criteria for the selection and evaluation of Olympic sports.[4] Though useful, these criteria are too complex and pragmatic to pinpoint what makes a sport truly 'Olympic.' What we need is a succinct definition of Olympic sport that distinguishes it from other forms of sport by invoking the values of Olympism.

In this essay I propose a definition of Olympic sport that reflects the enduring values of the Olympic Games as revealed by their ancient history and as articulated in the Fundamental Principles of Olympism. This will be a *prescriptive* rather than a merely *descriptive* definition in that it will seek through its usage to promote a particular set of values and behaviors worthy of Olympic ideals. It will not, however, be a *stipulative* definition seeking to attach a new meaning to particular word. Rather, I am proposing a *theoretical* definition of 'Olympic sport' – one that seeks to attach the term to a wider intellectual framework already established in Olympic history and literature. The criteria that render a sport 'Olympic' under this definition, may also be applied to athletes, coaches, and even behaviors. If we can change what people think about when they use the term 'Olympic', we may promote a positive ethos within the community of language users. The values and goals of the Olympic Movement are clearly stated, let the definition and subsequent usage of the term 'Olympic sport' faithfully reflect them.

---

[2] Confucius, *Analects* 4.11
[3] Olympic Charter (2014), 11.
[4] IOC, *Evaluation Criteria for Sports and Disciplines* (2012).

Sport vs. Olympic Sport

In order to modify the way people think about and use the term 'Olympic,' it may be useful to begin by observing the way people already use the term to distinguish among different forms of sport. One thing the modifier 'Olympic' seems to imply immediately is a certain level of excellence. If I ride my bike around with friends or enter a local race, we may say that I am participating in the sport of cycling. We may also acknowledge that cycling is an Olympic sport. But the term isn't necessarily transitive. It doesn't seem quite right to say as I ride around the block with other enthusiasts that I am participating in an Olympic sport, and it is certainly incorrect to say that I am an Olympic cyclist or even an Olympic-level cyclist. On the other hand, people may use the term 'Olympic' to describe something that is not a sport but is done seriously at a high level of excellence, as in "Olympic lawn mowing." The association between excellence and the term 'Olympic' derives primarily from the Olympic Games being the most prestigious and competitive athletic event in antiquity. It also reflects a philosophy focused on human excellence, an effort to perfect oneself and better resemble the gods of Mount Olympus, especially Zeus, to whom the ancient Games were dedicated. The ancient Greek concept of excellence, *aretē*, was closely linked with sport and had a big influence on the Olympic revival and the ethos of modern sport, more generally.

Another thing that seems to distinguish Olympic from non-Olympic sport in common usage is a commitment to ideals beyond sport itself and especially beyond commercialism. In part, this is reflected in the opening and closing ceremonies which are distinctive of the Olympic Games and other events specifically designed to imitate them. Again, these ceremonies derive from the religious rituals that surrounded the ancient Olympic festival, but in the modern Games they are intended to promote Olympic ideals. The Olympic flame and torch relay were not part of the ancient Games, yet they symbolize the modern Games' connection to Ancient Olympia and to the quasi-religious ideals that underpinned the contests there. It is also significant, though seldom noticed, that advertising is not allowed in and around Olympic venues, and that Olympic symbols may not be used for commercial purposes, except as authorized by the IOC for the benefit of the Games and their ideals.[5] People often complain about commercialism in the Olympic Games, but this is not because non-Olympic sports are not commercialized. Rather, it is because there is a public expectation that Olympic sports should differ from other sports by rejecting commercialism and focusing on higher ideals such as fair play. We can see, when comparing the Olympic and non-Olympic iterations of a sport like beach-volleyball, that the ubiquitous advertising and antagonistic rhetoric from courtside announcers are replaced by more conservative uniforms and special emphasis on friendship and fairness in the Olympic version.

There is also an expectation in common usage that Olympic sport is international. American football is certainly a sport, but too regional to be Olympic. Indeed the exclusion of baseball and softball from the Olympic Games in 2005 had partly to do with its lack of international appeal.[6] It seems disingenuous to call Major League Baseball's championship the "World Series" when all of the eligible teams are based in North America. Baseball's Olympic internationalism is closely linked with the Movement's emphasis on peace, which is not as widely recognized as it should be. Ancient Olympic history suggests that by coming together as equals under the rules of sport, rival tribes were able to interact peacefully and even work together for a common cause. The Modern Games were founded with a similar goal in mind and even when people have used the Games to trump up nationalism or exercise political rivalries, a sense that peace may at least be possible usually prevails. It has been argued that national teams should be eliminated from the Games, but even if athletes represented only themselves, the expectation of bringing together

---

[5] *Olympic Charter* (2014) Rule 7.
[6] Associated Press, "Secret Ballot Eliminates Baseball, Softball" *ESPN online*, July 8, 2005.

people who are culturally, linguistically, and religiously diverse seems central to the concept of Olympic sport.

Based on these observations about the contemporary use of the term 'Olympic sport', along with a forthcoming analysis of Olympic history and philosophy, I would like to argue that what makes a sport Olympic are its values, goals, and philosophy. I therefore propose the following definition:

> An Olympic sport is one that focuses on human excellence, commits itself to justice, and promotes peace.

To argue for this definition, I will examine the philosophy of Olympism as stated in the Olympic Charter, the technical criteria used by the International Olympic Committee to evaluate Olympic sport, and events from Olympic history which have come to exemplify a distinctive Olympic spirit.

Focus on Human Excellence

The Olympic emphasis on human excellence is evident in the first fundamental principle of Olympism, which has changed little over the century-plus history of the modern Games. It states,

> Olympism is a philosophy of life, exalting and combining in a balanced whole the qualities of body, will and mind. Blending sport with culture and education, Olympism seeks to create a way of life based on the joy of effort, the educational value of good example, social responsibility and respect for universal fundamental ethical principles.[7]

The claim that Olympism is a philosophy designed to engage all aspects of the human being hearkens back to the classical philosophers of ancient Greece whose ethical theories focused on *aretē*—virtue or excellence. In his famous *Apology*, Socrates admonished Athenians to care for *aretē* rather than fame or wealth (Plato, *Apology*, 29de) and Aristotle went so far as to define human happiness (*eudaimonia*) as activity in accordance with *aretē* (*Nicomachean Ethics*, 1098a). In fact, *aretē* had been associated with

---

[7] Olympic Charter (2014), 11.

athletics long before the philosophers started promoting it. It is though athletic feats that Homer's Odysseus demonstrates his nobility and worthiness to lead. The rising phenomenon of the Olympic Games, however, taught ancient Hellenes that *aretē* was not just a matter of birth, but something trainable and within the grasp of even low-born people.[8] Achieving excellence in ancient Greece meant becoming like a god—not just in body but in will and mind. *Aretē* is the excellence of the whole human being, and it is expressed not just in athletics but in intellectual and political endeavors as well.

Olympism's vision of a holistic balanced human excellence derived from blending sport, culture, and education may seem to be at odds with the purely athletic and results-oriented excellence suggested by the Olympic motto: *citius, altius, fortius* (faster, higher, stronger).[9] However, the aspiration for human excellence is neither incompatible nor identical with athletic achievement. Ideally, athletic performance is an expression of balanced *aretē*. This means that distinctively Olympic sports should challenge the mind as well as the body and that they should reward the effort and discipline of training while penalizing techniques that improve performance without increasing *aretē*. What kind of educational example is set by an athlete who gains a winning advantage through performance-enhancing equipment or drugs? The need for Olympic sports to focus on human excellence motivates the requirement that all Olympic sport federations adopt the WADA (World Anti-Doping Agency) code,[10] and control the technological evolution of their sport.[11] They are also expected to assist athletes with studies, development of life-skills, and post-athletic career transitions.[12] The Olympic creed, which emphasizes participation over victory and struggle over triumph, is not

---

[8] For the full argument, see Reid, *Athletics and Philosophy*, ch. 10.

[9] Olympic Charter (2014), 23.

[10] Olympic Charter (2014), 84.

[11] *Evaluation Criteria for Sports and Disciplines*, #30.

[12] *Evaluation Criteria for Sports and Disciplines*, #26.

opposed to the Olympic motto. Together the creed and motto show that the struggle to improve is what produces human excellence.[13] Distinctively Olympic sports should link results with human excellence as much as possible.

Memorable moments in Olympic history reveal the importance of human excellence to the Olympic ideal. It is not just a matter of winning and triumph, but paradoxically the emphasis on excellence comes from the distinctively Olympic practice of staying to cheer on the final finishers of a long race. In 1968, an injured John Stephen Akhwari of Tanzania finished the marathon more than an hour after the winner—to a huge ovation from the crowd and the glowing praises of journalists, one of whom said he "symbolizes the finest in the human spirit" and "gives true meaning to sport."[14] When 2014 gold medalist cross-country skier Dario Cologna waited nearly half an hour at the finish line to greet the last athlete in the race, he exemplified the Olympic idea of human excellence, which exalts not just the virtues of victory but also those of participation and struggle. Likewise marathoner Abebe Bikila made a much bigger Olympic impression by winning the 1960 race barefoot, than cyclist Chris Boardman made by setting a world record in the 1992 Games with a super high-tech proprietary bicycle. Among the lowlights of Olympic history are contests falsified by drugs; notoriously the disqualification of sprinter Ben Johnson from the 1988 Games. It is not just victory that counts in Olympic sport, it is virtue.

Some people claim that the amount of money involved in the Games is what causes the privileging of victory over virtue, the sacrifice of human excellence for the sake of efficiency. Such concerns are only heightened by the IOC practice of evaluating sports according to "popularity" criteria, including public and especially youth appeal,[15] the number of tickets sold to spectators,

---

[13] See Torres, "Results or Participation," 243.

[14] Bud Greenspan, *The 100 Greatest Moments in Olympic History* (Los Angeles: General Publishing Group, 1995), 180.

[15] *Evaluation Criteria for Sports and Disciplines*, #14 and #15.

the number of media accreditations granted, and the amount of coverage in the television, print, and social media—including YouTube, Facebook, and Twitter.[16] Sponsorship is also a criterion.[17] It will be remembered, however, that the Olympics' association with human excellence is precisely what draws sponsors and fans to the Games in the first place. Performance-enhancing technologies that diminish the role of human excellence run contrary to sponsors' interests as well. It was, in fact, Olympic sponsors such as John Hancock Mutual Life Insurance who pressured the IOC to get control of the doping situation in sports and found the World Anti-Doping Agency.[18] The popularity and economic viability of Olympic sport depends on its continued emphasis on human excellence.

Committed to Fair Play

The fourth fundamental principle of Olympism says that fair play is essential to the "Olympic spirit" in which sport should be practiced.[19] As is clear from our previous discussion, an atmosphere of fair play is needed to cultivate human excellence. Although fair play is a modern concept, it may be profitably understood as the sporting manifestation of justice, which was conceived by ancient Greeks to be an excellence (*aretē*) of communities. If, we understand sports to be practice communities, as MacIntyre argues,[20] then a commitment to fair play is an essential characteristic of Olympic sport. Since sports are governed by rules and nations are governed by laws, fair play, like justice, demands the proper administration of a sport's rules and regulations. Fairness should not be reduced to rule-adherence, however. As the adjective 'fair' suggests, there is an aesthetic element that can be sensed and judged by spectators. Fair play

---

[16] *Evaluation Criteria for Sports and Disciplines*, #s 17-22.

[17] *Evaluation Criteria for Sports and Disciplines*, #23.

[18] J. O'Leary, *Drugs and Doping in Sport* (London: Routledge, 2013), 140.

[19] Olympic Charter (2014), 11.

[20] MacIntyre, *After Virtue*, (Notre Dame, IN: University of Notre Dame Press, 1981) 175.

demands equal opportunity and reward according to merit, but it should also celebrate athletes who go beyond rule adherence with gestures that indicate the other elements of the Olympic spirit: friendship, solidarity, and mutual understanding.

Unsurprisingly, ethical governance is prominent among the evaluation criteria for Olympic sport. International federations must have a code of ethics that aligns with the IOC's code, procedures to fight against competition fixing, rules to sanction members of an athlete's entourage involved in doping or sexual harassment, and efforts to promote transparency and fairness on the field of play.[21] In fact, the first item listed under "The Mission and Role of the IOC" in the Olympic Charter is "to encourage and support the promotion of ethics and good governance in sport [and] to ensuring that, in sport, the spirit of fair play prevails and violence is banned."[22] Anti-discrimination is central to Olympism's concept of fair play. Principle #4 declares that "the practice of sport is a human right" and #6 specifically bans discrimination based on race, color, sex, sexual orientation, language, religion, political or other opinion, national or social origin, property, or birth.[23] Olympic sports are evaluated according to criteria of gender equity and "sport for all"—an effort to encourage wide participation rather than focusing on the elite.[24] If fair play demands equal opportunity as well as reward according to merit, Olympic sports should be structurally resistant to discrimination, allowing a variety of body- and character types to flourish, and they should challenge the status quo of socioeconomic privilege, rather than reinforcing it.

Many of Olympic history's most cherished moments involve the breaking down of racial and gender stereotypes. African-American Jesse Owens' friendship with German Luz Long in the face of Nazi propaganda at the 1936 Games in Berlin is a favorite

---

[21] *Evaluation Criteria for Sports and Disciplines*, #s 2, 5, 27, 33.
[22] Olympic Charter (2014), 6.
[23] Olympic Charter (2014), 11-12.
[24] *Evaluation Criteria for Sports and Disciplines*, #s 31 and 32

example of the Olympics' ability to transcend injustice. More recently, the IOC has made huge strides toward gender equity in sport, achieving 46% women's events and 44% female participation at the 2012 London Games, and 50% women's events with 40% female athletes at the 2014 Winter Games in Sochi.[25] A more formidable challenge to fair play in Olympic sport is economic advantage in sports such as equestrian, sailing, skiing, and cycling, where participation is costly and a technological edge can be bought by wealthier athletes and countries. The problem is only exacerbated by the evaluation criterion that quantifies a sport's sponsors.[26] Sponsors value expensive sports such as equestrian and sailing because they attract a wealthy following, but the Olympic movement has larger concerns. Olympic sports must demonstrate their commitment to fair play by adopting rules that ban discrimination and diminish economic advantage, and by administering those rules ethically and transparently.

Promotes Peace

After excellence and fairness, the third defining characteristic of Olympic sport is its promotion of peace. The second fundamental principle states that the goal of Olympism is "to place sport at the service of the harmonious development of humankind, with a view to promoting a peaceful society concerned with the preservation of human dignity."[27] That this peaceful society is global is made clear by principle three, which points out the Movement covers all five continents, the unity of which is symbolized by the interlaced Olympic rings.[28] The modern Olympics' internationalism contrasts with the ancient Olympics' ethnic homogeneity, but only in scope. The Hellenic tribes that came together on neutral ground for common worship in Olympia were diverse and often warring; indeed their safe travel had to be

---

[25] *Factsheet on Women in the Olympic Movement*, 4-5.
[26] *Evaluation Criteria for Sports and Disciplines*, #23.
[27] Olympic Charter (2014), 11.
[28] Olympic Charter (2014),. 11.

protected by a sacred truce called the *ekecheiria*.[29] The Games were credited with helping the Hellenes to overcome their enmities, to share ideas, and eventually to unite against their common enemy, the Persians.[30] The revival of the Games in the 19th century was partly inspired by this legacy of peace-promotion through sport. Playing sports together seems to humanize "the other," by overcoming cultural and linguistic barriers and demanding mutual respect. Sometimes it even fosters unlikely friendships. To make it work, though, Olympic sport needs to bring together people culturally and politically diverse enough that they might otherwise be fighting.

It is difficult to quantify the contribution that the Olympic Games makes to peace in the modern world, but there have been important symbolic achievements, such North and South Korea's decision to march together under one flag in the opening ceremony of the Sydney Games. It was neither an athlete nor an Olympic official, but a young spectator named John Ian Wing who suggested in 1956 that athletes break national ranks for the closing ceremony and enter the stadium mixed together as one nation.[31] At those same Games in Melbourne, an ongoing political conflict between Russia and Hungary seemed to tarnish the water polo competition with violence and vitriol that was patently un-Olympic and required police intervention to prevent a riot.[32] However the 2006 documentary called *Freedom's Fury* on the match and its aftermath reveals that the politicized hype surrounding the match contrasted with the athletes' own experience. It also staged a 50 year reunion of athletes on both teams which showed that the Olympic spirit prevailed even in what may seem like the nadir of Olympic efforts at peace.[33] Since 1994, the United Nations has been urging its members to observe an Olympic Truce, and an Olympic

---

[29] Finley and Plecket, *Olympic Games*, 98.

[30] Crowther, *Athletika*, 21.

[31] Greenspan, *100 Olympic Moments*, 206.

[32] Greenspan, *100 Olympic Moments*, 90.

[33] Colin Keith Gray, director. *Freedom's Fury*, 2006.

Truce Resolution has officially been adopted for every Games since 2004.[34]

It is for the sake of peace promotion that Olympic sports are expected not only to have national federations and participants all over the world, but also to award Olympic and world-championship medals to athletes from a variety of continents.[35] Working against such "universality" criteria, however, are the "history and tradition" criteria, which consider how long a sport has been part of the Olympic Games and other multi-sport events, such as the Pan-American or Commonwealth Games.[36] The problem here is that the sports in the modern Olympic Games reflect the Movement's European origins. These sports are more likely to meet the universality requirements precisely because they have already been exported globally as part of the Olympic Games. Judo and Taekwondo, the only non-western sports on the Olympic program, were not added until 1964 and 2000, respectively.[37] If the Olympic Movement wants to place sport at the service of all humankind and thereby promote peace, it cannot define history and tradition in terms of its own biased past. It needs to choose sports that reflect the cultural diversity of the Movement rather than reinforcing the traditional domination of the west.

Implications

Defining Olympic sport in terms of excellence, fairness, and peace not only reflects the history and philosophy of the Olympic Movement, it implies that athletic practices should be critically evaluated and progressively improved according to this standard. Under this definition, a sport, an athlete, even a coach, official, or administrator can become more 'Olympic' by better exemplifying these ideals. I would argue, for example, that the fledgling Youth Olympic Games are in many ways more 'Olympic' than the

---

[34] *International Olympic Truce Foundation*, www.olympictruce.org.

[35] *Evaluation Criteria for Sports and Disciplines*, #s 10-14.

[36] *Evaluation Criteria for Sports and Disciplines*, #s 7 and 8.

[37] Karate debuted at Rio 2016, with golf and rugby sevens, but the martial art of Wushu was again left out of the program

regular Olympic Games. The balanced ideal of human excellence is expressed by the requirement that athletes stay for the duration of the festival and participate in "Learn and Share" activities with such themes as Olympism, skills development, well-being and healthy lifestyle, social responsibility, and expression. Exemplary Olympians also are invited to share their experiences and act as role-models for the younger athletes.[38] In support of fairness and peace promotion, the Youth Olympic Games have been experimenting with mixed gender and international teams in archery, athletics, cycling, equestrian, fencing, judo, modern pentathlon, swimming, table tennis, tennis and triathlon, biathlon, curling, luge, ice skating, and skiing.[39] These events allow athletes from different cultures and even different genders to work together for common goals—an intentional promotion of Olympic ideals through sport.

The innovations achieved in the Youth Olympic Games show how sports can become more 'Olympic' when they are consciously guided by the principles of Olympism. It also illustrates how some of the events in the Games may be more 'Olympic' than others. A vision of excellence that engages body, will, and mind, for example, favors complex and strategic sports over simpler tests of strength and skill. A weightlifting event like the clean and jerk, which emphasizes speed, technique, and planning over sheer strength, is more 'Olympic' than power-lifting events such as the bench press or squat. Likewise, the emphasis on "joy of effort" seems to point toward sports like running or cycling more than technical sports like shooting or popular activities such as computer gaming. Expensive sports like equestrian and sailing might be dropped in favor of less expensive activities such as ultimate Frisbee or tug-of-war. Meanwhile, disciplines that require less expensive facilities within a given sport might be favored, such as mountain biking over velodrome cycling. The Youth Olympic Games prohibits the construction of new venues for the

---

[38] *The Youth Olympic Games Vision and Principles*, (Lausanne: IOC, 2014).
[39] *The YOG – Sports Programme*, (Lausanne: IOC, 2014).

Games[40]—a requirement that respects the environment and keeps financial demands under control, thereby promoting diversity.

Given the demands of promoting peace through diversity in a globalizing world, the Olympic Movement might even reconsider what counts as a sport, or more specifically, an event. In Rule 45, the Olympic Charter distinguishes sports (i.e. cycling) from disciplines (i.e. road racing) and events (i.e. the 1984 women's Olympic road race). It says an event is "a specific competition in a sport resulting in a ranking giving rise to the awarding of medals and diplomas"[41] Many athletic activities that may promote Olympic ideals are not set up to generate rankings and award material prizes. Many purists objected to the traditional Chinese martial art called *wushu* becoming part of the Olympic Games because its goal is the cultivation of an internal energy called *qi*, which cannot be easily quantified by judges and should not be reduced to a point system. Some say, likewise, that the established Olympic sport of figure skating has been ruined by judging scandals that gave rise to a rigid point system that upsets the balance between the sport's technical and artistic aspects. Defining Olympic sport in terms of values rather than structures invites debate about the nature of sport itself.

From Prescription to Description

Defining Olympic sport prescriptively in terms of focus on excellence, commitment to justice, and promotion of peace may seem like little more than an exercise in idealism. But ethics, like language, is learned and exercised within a community. If we are able to imbue our use of the term 'Olympic' with normative force, we may well inspire more normatively Olympic behavior within that community. It must not be forgotten that sport is not a natural phenomenon, like lightning or childbirth. Sport is defined and interpreted by human beings, and *how* we define and interpret sport impacts the ethics of its performance. Indeed the British

---

[40] *Youth Olympic Games Vision and Principles*

[41] Olympic Charter (2014), rule 45.2.2, 84.

already do this with their use of the term 'sporting'. The first definition of that term in the Oxford English Dictionary is simply, "Connected with or interested in sport." The second definition, however, is "Fair and generous in one's behavior or treatment of others, especially in a contest."[42] More prescriptive is the use of the expression "It's not cricket" to describe morally questionable conduct, even outside sport. Both expressions may hearken back to a gentlemanly ethos which raises its own moral questions, but they are good examples of how a sport-specific term can have normative force in usage that transcends sport.

The process of imbuing the term 'Olympic' with a moral force derived from the enduring values of Olympism can begin with academics—especially those of us who write about ethical issues in the Olympic Games. Just because certain sports, athletes, and actions are part of the Olympic Games, we do not have to describe them as 'Olympic'. We should save that term to describe the sports, athletes, and actions that best exemplify the ideals of Olympism. Furthermore, we should use the term as a standard of evaluation. We might say, for example, that swimming is a more Olympic sport than shooting, that Jesse Owens was a more Olympic athlete than Ben Johnson, or that the cross-country ski coach who handed a spare pole to competitor who had broken his behaved more Olympically than one who tries to motivate an athlete by denigrating her competitor. We might say that FIFA behaved Olympically when they adapted the safety rules to allow Muslim women to wear head coverings when they play, or that National Olympic Committees behave Olympically when they help athletes pursue their educations and not simply medals. Those who understand the values of Olympism must be the first to use the term 'Olympic' in a way that reflects them.

Normative use of terms like 'Olympic' has the potential to spread, especially if adopted by the media, which facilitates most people's experience of the Olympic Games. Like sponsors, members of the media generally understand that it is the

---

[42] The Oxford Dictionaries Online

distinctive Olympic values that make the Games so much more important than their non-Olympic cousins. Indeed it is the media's depiction of athletes' individual stories and their coverage of Olympic gestures— such as crowds cheering on a late finisher, or athletes helping competitors to their feet—that teach most people what Olympism is all about. Sponsors in "The Olympic Program" also devote part of their advertising to promotion of Olympic values. Sports officials can help as well, as in the London Games of 2012 where athletes were disqualified for "not using their best efforts" in preliminary matches in order to gain advantageous matches in the finals.[43] Such penalties may grate against our analytical sense of justice since those athletes broke none of their sport's rules, but our aesthetic sense of fair play makes such disqualifications appropriate, even 'Olympic.'

Conclusion

From the point of view of Olympism, the first and vaguest criterion for the selection and evaluation of Olympic sport is the most important. It is called the "value added" criterion—meaning the value that the sport adds to the Olympic Games and the value that the Olympic Games add to the sport. Value here should not be construed in terms of money or even exposure, but rather in terms of values—the values of Olympism. To be truly Olympic, a sport must embody and reflect the values of Olympism. Succinctly put, Olympic sport should focus on human excellence, make a commitment to fair play, and promote peace.

---

[43] British Broadcasting Company, "Badminton."

Section VI
Justice as Fair Play

17. The Ideal of Justice and Olympic Reality[1]

At a famous moment in Book I of Plato's *Republic,* the rambunctious sophist Thrasymachus, exasperated with the philosophical ramblings of Socrates and his companions, boldly defines justice as "the advantage of the stronger" and promptly asks for applause (338c). What he gets instead is a very long discussion designed to disabuse him and anyone else who will listen of this popular and practical view. And so begins the philosophical elevation of justice from the worldly reality of "might makes right" to a lofty ideal that promises the peaceful thriving of human communities. The Ancient Greeks' philosophical interest in justice is well known. What is often overlooked, however, is the way that their ideas about justice were reflected in the concurrent cultural phenomenon of competitive athletics, in particular the Olympic Games. Indeed, throughout its historical development, the philosophical ideal of justice has been paralleled in sport by the conception we call fair play. Perhaps it was this ancient connection between justice and fair play that inspired the founders of the Modern Olympic Movement to use sport as a means of modeling global justice and fomenting world peace. But is such a plan defensible, much less effective?

In what follows, I argue that the ideal of justice manifest in Olympic sport can and does have the potential to inspire social justice, even in our modern world. I begin by surveying the development of the philosophical ideal of justice from Plato to Aristotle and on through such moderns as Immanuel Kant and John Rawls. From this survey, I distill three common principles of justice: equality, impartiality, and moral reciprocity. Next, I show how these principles manifest themselves in sport as the fair-play principles of equal opportunity, reward according to merit, and an attitude of moral respect. I then focus in on Olympic sport,

---

[1] This paper was originally presented at the annual conference of the International Association for Philosophy of Sport, in Dallas, Texas, 2004.

VI. Justice as Fair Play

identifying justice as an essential part of the Olympic Ideal, with reference to the modern *Olympic Charter* as well as examples from ancient and Olympic Games. Finally, I examine the question of whether fair play in Olympic sport has and can continue to inspire justice beyond the Games.

Far from claiming that Olympic sport can somehow save the world, I do believe that the Games have the potential to cultivate and present a model of justice in which diverse individuals with competing interests are able to pursue competing goals in an atmosphere of peace and mutual respect. In fact, the promotion of ideals such as justice, humanism, and peace was a key part of the Olympic Games' purpose even in ancient times. Just as modern philosophers must carry on Plato's project of understanding the ideal of justice, so to the modern Olympic Games have a responsibility to model that ideal by sticking to just principles, both in the Movement's own conduct and its administration of sporting events.

The Ideal of Justice vs. The Reality of Power

To the Ancient Hellenes, justice was as much an excellence of the individual person as it was an excellence of some community. In fact, Plato's *Republic* should be read as a plan for personal harmony as much as social harmony. Even the personal virtue of justice, however, concerns an individual's role in his or her community. So it's fair to say that justice has always been a philosophical concept concerned with the health and well-being of communities. At the same time, this concept cannot be separated from individual human interests and reduced to a simple mechanism such as law-adherence or productivity. Justice is the excellence (*aretē*) of a community: its ability to accommodate and facilitate the needs and interests of its members. In *Republic* the character Thrasymachus looks at the world and declares, quite accurately, that justice is whatever benefits the stronger — that is the way things worked in the ancient world and it is the way things often work in our modern world. "Might makes right" is undeniably a common reality, but it is the *ideal* of justice that philosophers seek, and our understanding of that ideal insists that a distinction between power and justice is made.

Consider, the story of the ancient boxer Damoxenos who was competing at the Nemean games against an opponent named Kreugas. According to Pausanias, Damoxenos "overpowered" Kreugas by stabbing his fingers under Kreugas' ribs and pulling out a handful of intestines. Kreugas died on the spot, but the judges of the bout did not award the victory to Damoxenos, instead they crowned Kreugas posthumously (Pausanias, 8.40.3-5). Although it was arguable whether Damoxenos had violated any rule (Pausanias reports that the official reason for disqualification was that he illegally used more than one punch since each of his fingers constituted a separate blow), it was clear that he had violated some ideal of justice or fair play with his actions. If instead, the contest had been a war, Damoxenos would have won; but sport seeks to emulate a higher ideal and few would argue that Damoxenos was denied the victory unjustly.

So justice needs to be understood as an ideal above and apart from the practical reality of power. But what is this philosophical ideal of justice? Are there any commonalities among the theories propounded by the Ancient Greek philosophers and moderns such as Immanuel Kant and John Rawls? The short answer is yes. All agree that just societies and organizations should contribute to general human flourishing. Plato suggests in the *Republic* that this is accomplished largely by everyone performing their proper work, that is, according to their native excellences (433ab). Aristotle concludes in the *Nicomachean Ethics* that "Justice is treating equals equally and unequals unequally in proportion to their relevant differences" (1131a10-25). Meanwhile, Kant's 19th c. CE "Categorical Imperative" states that we should "Act in such a way that you treat humanity, whether in your own person or in the person of another, always at the same time as an end and never simply a means,"[2] a reflection of the Bible's venerable "Golden Rule." More recently, John Rawls' *A Theory of Justice* claims that

---

[2] Kant, *Grounding for the Metaphysics of Morals*, 429.

rational egoists will adopt fair principles from equal standing under what he calls a "veil of ignorance" about our particular social situations.³

By distilling common ideas from among these theories of justice, I have derived three common principles of philosophical justice: equality, impartiality, and moral reciprocity. Since justice in the contexts we are discussing is first and foremost an excellence of some human community, we may characterize these three characteristics according to three aspects of just communities. First, they involve an agreement or shared understanding among participants that is usually codified in a set of laws, rules, or guidelines—and justice demands that these treat individuals as equals. Second, just communities demand the fair and even-handed application of such rules, which means that justice requires impartiality in the administration of the community. Finally, justice requires that community members regard each other as having a particular moral standing—it requires an *attitude* of moral reciprocity. So, very loosely, the ideal of equality refers primarily to the nature of the *laws or rules* governing a community, impartiality to the *administration* of those laws or rules, and moral reciprocity to the *attitudes* of the community members.

In the Olympic Games, this philosophical ideal of justice is manifest in a corresponding ideal that has come to be called "fair play." More specifically, equality is manifest as the principle of equal opportunity for contestants (sometimes referred to as the common starting line), impartiality is manifest in the principle of reward according to merit (sometimes expressed as the level playing field), and moral reciprocity is demonstrated in an attitude of mutual respect (sometimes simply called good sportsmanship). Again, these are recognized as sporting *ideals,* which are not always realized in reality. But they can serve as criteria by which to evaluate sporting contests and practices. Furthermore, since sport in general and the Olympic games in particular act as a kind

---

³ John Rawls, *A Theory of Justice* (Cambridge, MA: Harvard University Press, 1971) 136-42.

of laboratory for social interaction purposely isolated from many of our "real-world" concerns, their attempts to approximate and model social ideals are extremely important. Even in ancient times, athletic games manifested these social ideals well before they became social realities. It has been argued that Greek democracy was actually developed at Olympia and through other athletic games.[4] In any case, the Olympic Games were and remain a sincere attempt to promote the ideals of social justice. Let us examine these connections more closely.

Equality

A foundational idea of justice is that it is based on an agreement (i.e. a social contract) that treats equals equally. Of course there is much historical and cultural controversy about who may be included or excluded from a community of equals. Even Thomas Jefferson, who declared the principle that "All men are created equal" to be a self-evident truth was himself an owner of slaves. Nevertheless this principle rose above the social realities of its author and was instrumental in the eradication of slavery in America. Despite the massive inequalities existing in all of their societies, philosophers generally agree that justice is a right and duty for every member of a community, not a matter of charity or benevolence granted by the most powerful. In fact, Rawls argues that rational self-interested agents, veiled from knowledge about their particular skills and virtues, would only agree to enter communities where everyone is treated equally.[5] Although people are never truly equal in terms of situation or ability, justice demands that community laws or rules treat them as equals in order to best manage those inherent inequalities for the overall benefit of the group. This legislative equality is both liberating and restrictive: it grants community members certain rights and opportunities but also obligates them to respect the corresponding rights of others. If we understand sport as a kind of community governed by rules, then athletes are clearly its primary citizens.

---

[4] Miller, *Ancient Greek Athletics*, 233.
[5] Rawls, *A Theory of Justice*, 19.

And if we examine the basic principles of fair play, we will see that game rules treat athletes equally—even though the contest seeks to determine their athletic inequalities.

The principle of equality was foundational in ancient Greek athletic competition. An athlete's strength may win him victory in the wrestling match, but his military rank, social class, and worldly wealth provided no advantage under the rules. Reflecting his awareness of such principles, Alexander the Great said he would run in the Olympic Games only if his opponents were limited to kings.[6] According to the principles of fair play, an accurate determination of contest-relevant inequalities, such as running speed, *depends* on the elimination of irrelevant inequalities, such as noble birth.[7] Contest rules strive to provide equal opportunity for all competitors, going beyond the basic principle of a common starting line to the extreme of drawing lots for particular lanes on the track or switching sides of the basketball court or playing field. At Olympia boxing matches were held close to noon to be sure that neither competitor would have the sun in his eyes.[8] Most symbolic of all, ancient athletes were literally stripped of their worldly differences: they competed in the nude.

In ancient Greece, the equality before the rules characteristic of athletic games was very rarely reflected in society. Although the distinction between a free Greek and a barbarian slave had huge legal consequences in Greek society, a free man who competed as an athlete at the Olympic Games had to be willing to accept the punishment of a public flogging. Stephen Miller takes this fact to be a paradigm example for his argument that Greek athletics actually created the concept of *isonomia* or equality before the law—the foundational principle of democracy.[9] For the Greeks, the

---

[6] Plutarch, "Life of Alexander" in *Plutarch's Lives* (Cambridge, MA. Harvard University Press, 1919), 4.5.

[7] Loland, *Fair Play in Sport*, 46.

[8] Judith Swaddling, *The Ancient Olympic Games* (London: British Museum Publications, 1980) 79.

[9] Miller, *Ancient Greek Athletics*, 233

need to provide equal opportunity in athletics was directly connected to the obligation to select the most worthy victor. In the earliest days of Hellenic sport, the victor was symbolically sacrificed to the gods so the need to authentically select "the best" had religious overtones. But Hellenes also saw athletics as a means of education and the experience of competing on equal terms with ones peers was certainly good preparation for the challenges of democracy.

Likewise modern sport and the modern Olympic Games seek to preserve the educational benefit of equality before the law among diverse peoples. Indeed the emergence of international sports governing bodies, which codify and enforce a uniform set of rules for their sports were largely an outgrowth of the Olympic Games' 19th century revival.[10] When we watch an event such as the Olympic 1500 meter final, we witness a group of people who speak different languages, have vastly different personal incomes, live under different legal systems, and are subject to governments who may be concurrently at war with one another—we witness these people competing for a common prize under a single set of rules that treats them all as equals and demands that they treat each other accordingly. At the Olympic Games we witness a kind of world community guided by a universal ideal of justice. Of course it's only a temporary glimpse of the ideal, but it portends well for the future. The Greeks, too, invented sporting *isonomia* before they created democracy.

Impartiality

Of course, it is not enough that the rules of Olympic sport exhibit equality and justice—the rules must also be administered fairly. Hence we arrive at the second commonality among philosophical theories of justice: the ideal of impartiality. In effect impartiality applies the equality principle to the administration of the community. In short, impartiality demands that everyone is judged according to objective standards (as opposed to personal

---

[10] Guttmann, *Ritual to Record*, 46.

or social preferences). Justice demands not only that rules or laws are inherently fair, but also that such codes be applied to individuals equitably. It is the basic idea of "rule of law" over tyranny—or more philosophically—the attempt to let us be guided by our common ideals rather than our competing worldly concerns.

Philosophers tend to justify the principle of impartiality in terms of pure reason. Rawls shows that agents must get beyond their vested personal interests in order to arrive at a purely rational social contract—a condition he calls the original position. "Impartiality," says Rawls, "prevents distortions of bias and self-interest; knowledge and the capacity for identification guarantee that the aspirations of others will be accurately appreciated.[11] Kant believes that human rationality makes us automatically subject to what he calls the "Universal Law," an concept codified in the maxim that one should never treat others as a means to any personal end.[12] In short Kant thinks that we need to be *impartial* and not make exceptions for ourselves. Aristotle adds that communities which evaluate individuals according to objective standards stand the best chance of producing or conserving their happiness (*Nicomachean Ethics*, 1129b). In short, the rationality which demands that equal treatment be inherent in just laws, also demands that such laws be applied impartially—objections could only be based on personal interests or biases.

Whereas in social communities impartiality is demanded of the government and/or justice system, athletic communities depend on federations, promoters, referees and judges. A primary responsibility of such officials is to ensure that competitive conditions are equal—not just that the playing field is level, but also that runners cover the same distance, that javelins are of legal weight, that timing equipment is accurate, etc. In short, it is the officials' responsibility to weed out in practice the irrelevant inequalities excluded by the rules. In this sense officials become

---

[11] Rawls, *A Theory of Justice*, 187.
[12] Kant, *Grounding for the Metaphysics of Morals*, 429

the embodiment of the rules and must put aside their own real-world interests in order to reflect in their judgment the objectivity inherent in the rules themselves. Accordingly, Olympic officials swear an oath alongside the athletes to respect and abide by the rules, officiating with "complete impartiality"—a challenge that demands of them the transcendence of personal interests, whether financial, patriotic, or convenience.[13]

The Ancient Olympic games were administered by the agrarian district of Elis, a place so dedicated to impartiality that it avoided military conflict and remained as neutral as possible in the conflicts of others.[14] It regarded its central responsibility to be honoring the gods, and the Olympic festival was the foremost expression of that. Elis' pacifism and neutrality was such that it even disdained the protection of city walls.[15] The Games officials were called *hellanodikai* (literally "judges of the Greeks"), and they were chosen by lot among eligible citizens after a pre-selection procedure, probably a popular vote.[16] Not only were the judges unpaid, they were probably expected to bear some of the organizational expenses.[17] Still, since selection as a judge implied duties both to the city of Elis and to the god in whose honor the games were celebrated, the motivation to judge as fairly as possible must have been great. Incidents of corrupt judging are accordingly rare. Most accounts of bribery involve athletes bribing their competitors, not the judges in charge.[18] The *Hellanodikai* seem to have taken impartiality seriously.

Indeed gestures toward impartiality are found throughout ancient Olympic sports. Elaborate starting mechanisms were devised to assist judges in assuring fair starts in the races.[19] Judges were not allowed to enter their own horses in the chariot races and

---

[13] IOC, *Factsheet on the Opening Ceremony of the Games of the Olympiad*, 2.
[14] Finley & Plecket, *Olympic Games*, 23.
[15] Drees, *Olympia*, 37.
[16] Finley & Plecket, *Olympic Games*, 59.
[17] Finley & Plecket, *Olympic Games*, 60.
[18] Finley & Plecket, *Olympic Games*, 65.
[19] Miller, *Ancient Greek Athletics*, 38-46.

VI. Justice as Fair Play

there was even discussion of excluding all Elean athletes from the games to assure absolute impartiality.[20] Furthermore, the Olympic Games resolutely avoided subjectively-judged contests, such as those in music, poetry, drama, and beauty, which were common throughout the ancient world. Miller takes this insistence on objectivity to be another instantiation of democratic *isonomia*, as well as an explanation for Olympia's unsurpassed prestige and longevity among ancient athletic contests.[21] He even takes this objective spirit to be central to the revival of the Olympic idea in modernity.[22]

Unfortunately, the modern Games are not administered by a militarily neutral district with a religious obligation to preserve their integrity, although the International Olympic Committee and their administrative seat in Switzerland come close. Olympic officials are now selected by the international sporting federations according to whatever formula they see fit. This situation has led to some high-profile judging scandals, perhaps the most famous being in the pairs figure skating competition at the Salt Lake Games in 2002. Judges from France and Russia had apparently colluded to exchange favorable marks for their respective countries in different events, but the result was so obviously unfair that a second set of gold medals was awarded to the Canadian pair. According to IOC official Dick Pound, this was just one of numerous judging scandals in ice-skating and other sports.[23] Subsequent changes in scoring systems for various events have not eliminated the judging problems.

Much of the problem could be alleviated by following the example of ancient Olympia and eliminating subjectively judged sports. These would include not only technique sports such as gymnastics, diving, synchronized swimming, and dressage, but also combat sports such as boxing, taekwondo, and judo—just to

---

[20] Drees, *Olympia*, 42.
[21] Miller, *Ancient Greek Athletics*, 233.
[22] Miller, *Ancient Greek Athletics*, 19.
[23] D. Pound, *Inside the Olympics* (New York: Wiley & Sons, 2004) 19-48.

mention the summer Games. In the absence of such a drastic measure, the Games should take great steps to encourage and enforce the impartiality of the judging process, such as the elimination of high and low scores and the random selection of scores to be used. Also the process for selecting and rewarding judges should be taken as seriously as it was in ancient times. Sports judges, like legal judges, should be selected according to their ability to uphold the spirit of the rules. Furthermore steps should be taken to ensure that judges are not burdened by conflicts of interest, professional, patriotic, or personal. In Plato's *Republic,* the guardians were not allowed to own property or even to have families of their own (415d-417b). Such drastic measures are of course impractical, but the importance of impartiality and the just administration of communities cannot be discounted.

Moral Reciprocity vs. Competitive Advantage

Beyond the legal principle of equality and the administrative principle of impartiality, justice requires an attitude of moral reciprocity among the agents in any community—a willingness to place one's own interests on the same *moral* footing as others. The spirit of moral reciprocity is perhaps best expressed in the Golden Rule's demand that we treat others as we would like to be treated. As a manifestation of social justice, however, it might be better understood in terms of the social contract, specifically in the understanding that our entrance into a community demands that we exit any "state of nature" in which dominance carries the day. Implicit in this is the acknowledgement of what might be called a natural tendency to exploit others and a conscious commitment to override that tendency through the use of reason. Kant expresses it in the second formulation of his Categorical Imperative, which demands that we treat others always as ends in themselves and never as means to some other end.[24] As members of a just community, two people may have competing personal interests in becoming the head of a hospital, but they temper that ambition

---

[24] Kant, *Grounding of the Metaphysics of Morals*, 429.

with a recognition of their stake in the communal good of selecting the best person for the job. Therefore they reject the law of the jungle in favor of a fair and just competition. Justice demands that they acquire their proper share, as Aristotle would say (*Nicomachean Ethics*, 1131a), and therefore it demands an attitude of moral reciprocity.

In sport, the justice principle of moral reciprocity is expressed in the fair play principle of mutual respect. Loland describes such attitudes as informal fair play, in contrast to such formal fair play standards as adherence to the rules, but he does not downplay their importance.[25] The modern *Olympic Charter* stipulates this attitude as central to the Olympic spirit, which it defines as "mutual understanding with a spirit of friendship, solidarity, and fair play."[26] Since the Olympic movement takes international peace to be among its central goals, and since the cultivation of such attitudes is its main vehicle for promoting such peace, it must take the attitude of mutual respect very seriously. Fortunately, the attitude derives from the principles of equality and impartiality already inherent in the structure and proper administration of sporting activities. An athlete who really understands the connection between equal opportunity and meritocracy cannot help but respect her opponent—after all, the opponent's goal is identical to her own. Tonya Harding's infamous plot to injure her opponent led to the total destruction of her career. Other competitors thought it illogical: eliminating a good opponent means never knowing if you could have beaten her fair and square.

In practice, participation in properly administered athletic competitions *does* lead to a spirit of mutual respect and even friendship among opponents. Displays of respect and affection are common at the Olympic games, sometimes to the puzzlement of journalists and spectators. While we lack detailed accounts of such gestures at the ancient Games, we might conclude that friendships were cultivated both at Olympia and during the month-long

---

[25] Loland, *Fair Play in Sport*, xiv.
[26] Olympic Charter, (2004) Fundamental Principle of Olympism #4

communal training period leading up to the festival. We might also notice that King Iphitos was said to have re-established the games, on the advice of the Delphic oracle, as an antidote to warring and enmity among the Hellenes.[27] The most telling fact is that athletic competitions, Olympic and otherwise, ancient and modern, are not possible unless people are willing to put aside their worldly conflicts and accord each other at least the modicum of respect demanded by the rules. In the 2004 Games in Athens, an Iranian *judoka* withdrew from the competition rather than meet an Israeli athlete under the rules.[28] It is unclear to what extent his decision was forced by his government, but this failure of mutual respect is best noted as an exception that proves the rule. Italian players shook hands and exchanged jerseys with Iraqi opponents after the bronze-medal soccer game—their jerseys bore a black band in memory of an Italian journalist killed by Iraqi captors just days before.[29] The game provided a place to treat each other with respect in an atmosphere of justice at a time when the world beyond was failing that ideal.

So the three principles of philosophical justice—equality, impartiality, and moral reciprocity—are all interconnected. They differ primarily in that equality is a principle of community structure, impartiality is a mode of administration, and moral reciprocity is an attitude to be found among the agents. Although these principles are manifest differently (and with differing success) in real-world communities, they serve as enduring ideals of well-functioning communities, including sports communities. Whether or not they actually invented sport, the ancient Greeks were first to use it as a mode of education. Not only did it prepare young citizens for the physical challenges of battle, it provided them with a foundation for the obligations of democratic

---

[27] Drees, *Olympia*, 34.
[28] Associated Press, "Iranian judo competitor rewarded after failing to compete against Israeli," *USA Today*, September 8, 2004.
[29] British Broadcasting Corporation, "Italy-Iraq match marred by death," *BBC News*, August 27, 2004.

VI. Justice as Fair Play

citizenship. Furthermore the ancient Olympic games promoted an ideal of social interaction that was meant to improve the lives of all Hellenes. The modern games have the potential to make that project international, but only if they take that project as seriously as the Greeks did.

18. Performance-enhancing Technology and Olympic Fair Play[1]

An Ethical Understanding of 'Olympic'

When Speedo developed the special hydrodynamic swimsuit that Michael Phelps wore *enroute* to his record-breaking medal haul in Beijing, it was a triumph of technology, a marketing masterpiece, and an apotheosis for American swimming. But was it Olympic? I ask that question believing that the adjective 'Olympic' indicates not just an athletic level, historical category, or commercial trademark. I ask that question believing that the adjective 'Olympic' indicates an ethical ideal—one driven by the social and political goals of Olympism as well as the intrinsic values of sport.[2] What makes something Olympic in an ethical sense is its congruence with the values, principles, and goals proclaimed in the *Olympic Charter* and implied by the metaphysics of sport itself. When deciding whether, when, and to what extent performance-enhancing technologies[3] belong in the Olympic and Paralympic Games, we must appeal to ideals that transcend the interests of individual athletes, their sponsors, even national Olympic committees. Technology is not itself an Olympic value.

---

[1] Originally published as "The Ethics of Efficiency: Performance-Enhancing Technologies and Olympic Fair Play," *Intersections and Intersectionalities in Olympic and Paralympic Studies*, eds. J. Forsyth, C. O'Bonsawin, and M. Heine (London, ON: ICOS, 2015), 11-17.

[2] Certain events, such as Jesse Owens' gesture of friendship to Luz Long at the Berlin Games, Abebe Bikila's marathon victory in Rome, or Nadia Comaneci's parallel bar performance in Montreal, seem prototypically "Olympic." Phelps' performance in Beijing is often counted alongside these, but I would argue that the performance-enhancing technology he used made it *less Olympic*.

[3] These technologies include equipment, techniques, and substances that improve an athlete's competitive results. In this paper, I focus equipment technologies, although the arguments are meant to apply to other PETs including doping and genetic modification.

Instead it needs to be made an instrument of and not an obstacle to Olympic values.

Respect for the Game

To evaluate the role of performance-enhancing technologies in sport, we should begin with a metaphysical theory of sport, such as Bernard Suits' characterization of games (of which sport is a subset) as "the voluntary attempt to overcome unnecessary obstacles."[4] What sports do is to contrive challenges by stipulating the object of the game (i.e. putting a ball into a goal) and then restricting means used to achieve that end to those permitted by the rules, where in Suits' words, "the rules prohibit use of more efficient in favor of less efficient means."[5] In soccer, for example, we are not allowed to handle the ball and we must battle defensive players in order to score goals. Such inefficiency is, for Suits, what separates sport from work, making it a species of play. Furthermore we accept the rules prescribing the inefficiencies because, in Suits' words, "they make possible such activity."[6] In other words, inefficiency is part and parcel of the nature of sport, and our acceptance inefficiencies is what makes the game possible in the first place. Formalists claim that intentionally breaking rules amounts to failure to play the game.[7] The attempt to circumvent a sport's inefficiencies likewise seems like a failure to play the game—or at least a lack of respect for the game, whether one takes a formalist view of sport, or not.

Angela Schneider and Robert Butcher's more conventionalist understanding of fair play as respect for the game holds that thoughtful athletes recognize that the joy and value of sporting achievement depends on a "fair and challenging process."[8]

---

[4] Suits, *Grasshopper: Games*, 55. On Suits' definition in relation to sports technology, see Reid, *Introduction to the Philosophy of Sport*, 110-12.
[5] Suits, *Grasshopper: Games*, 54.
[6] Suits, *Grasshopper: Games*, 55.
[7] For a discussion of formalism and its limits see Reid, *Introduction to the Philosophy of Sport*, 50-55.
[8] Schneider & Butcher, "Why Olympic Athletes," 71.

Respecting the game, furthermore, means giving one's opponent every opportunity to provide a worthy challenge.[9] Seeking to gain a technological advantage not available to one's opponent—even if it is permitted by the rules—denies the opponent that opportunity and reduces the athletic challenge that the game is designed to produce. Unlike robot-building contests, sporting contests produce challenges to be addressed athletically, not technologically. As Cesar Torres has shown, challenges created by the constitutive rules of a game are meant to be addressed through athletic skills. Deciding a soccer match through penalty kicks may be efficient, but it is notoriously dissatisfying because it avoids some of the most central skills of the game.[10]

Insofar as performance-enhancing technologies circumvent inefficiencies or diminish the role of athletic skill in deciding a contest, they harm the sport. Even the adjective "performance-enhancing" may be misleading. Imagine a Paralympian who has the goal of running a certain 400 time to qualify for the Olympics. She has been training for several years with this goal, but still finds herself a couple of seconds short. Then one day, she is given a new set of higher tech prostheses, and she instantly makes the qualifying time. Has her performance improved, or just her result? Manufacturers are constantly producing golf clubs, tennis rackets, bicycles, and baseball bats that promise to yield better results from a given level of athletic skill. But most sports are designed to test athletes rather than equipment engineers (or pocketbooks), and that purpose should be preserved by regulating the use of technology.

The Olympic Value of Human Excellence

Olympic sports have special reasons to limit technology. First among them is the Movement's philosophical emphasis on virtue or human excellence. This value goes back to the ancient Greek

---

[9] Schneider & Butcher "Fair Play as Respect for the Game," *Journal of the Philosophy of Sport* 25:1(1998), 15.

[10] Cesar Torres, "What Counts as Part of a Game? A Look at Skills," *Journal of the Philosophy of Sport* 27.1 (2000), 89.

origin of the Olympic Games (and of athletics and moral philosophy more generally). For Hellenes, athletics was an expression of *aretē*, and the moral philosophies of Socrates, Plato, and Aristotle were also based on virtue. The modern philosophy of Olympism embraces that tradition, declaring itself to be "a philosophy of life, exalting and combining in a balanced whole the qualities of body, will and mind."[11] The goal of Olympism, furthermore, is "to place sport at the service of the harmonious development of humankind."[12] The very idea that sport could serve the cause of human development belies an assumed connection between athletics and virtue—one that links the development of athletic skill with virtue.

As beautiful, inspiring, entertaining, and marketable as they may be, athletic skills are generally useless beyond sport. Their acquisition, however, comes from training and practice, which in turn demands such virtuous dispositions as courage, patience, and persistence. These dispositions are extremely useful in social endeavors and for human flourishing in general. The ancient Greeks understood this and embraced sport as part of their education.[13] Athletic skills like hitting homeruns don't cure cancer or grow food. People cure cancer and grow food. But by striving to gain the skills necessary to hit homeruns, people can develop the kind of virtues needed for those endeavors. When the Olympic Movement talks about placing sport in the service of human development, they have to be talking about cultivating virtues through sport.

---

[11] Olympic Charter (2013), 11.

[12] Olympic Charter (2013), 11.

[13] Some believe that Greeks viewed athletics as practical military training, but as far back as Homer, its practical usefulness was questioned. The militaristic "look" of athletics is better explained by its religious function of re-enacting the feats of mythological heroes from the Trojan War. See Nagy, Ancient Greek Hero 1§41. In *Republic*, Plato uses athletics in general for training the soul, see Reid, "Sport as Moral Education in Plato's *Republic*," 160-175.

Sports technologies, insofar as they diminish the importance of virtue for gaining particular results, interfere with sport's ability to cultivate virtues, and therefore its Olympic service to the "harmonious development of humankind." This may not be true of all technologies. W. Miller Brown argues that performance-enhancing technologies are compatible with the cultivation of virtues through sport when they allow someone to participate who otherwise would not be able.[14] This is certainly true for many Paralympians, who depend on specialized equipment just to perform the requisite actions. It may also be true of technologies like the fiberglass vaulting pole, which opened the sport to a much wider variety of body types—including females. Some technologies give athletes the opportunity to cultivate virtue through sports. But technologies like steroids or genetic engineering that give athletes only better results or a higher level of competition than would otherwise be possible cannot be justified in terms of virtue, because virtue is also cultivated (perhaps more easily) at lower levels of competition. Technology serves the Olympic ideal of human excellence when it facilitates participation, not when it circumvents the virtuous development of athletic skills.

The Olympic Principle of Fair Play

In addition to the virtue-ethical commitment to human excellence, the Fundamental Principles of Olympism pledge "respect for universal fundamental ethical principles."[15] This suggests a vaguely Kantian (i.e. universalizing) deontological approach, without specifying any particular principle. The most plausible candidate, however, would be the principle of fair play. Fair play is identified as part of the Olympic spirit in Fundamental Principle #4,[16] and its prevalence is listed in item #1 under the

---

[14] W. Miller Brown, "Practices and Prudence," *Journal of the Philosophy of Sport* 17:1 (1990), 77.
[15] Olympic Charter (2013), 11.
[16] Olympic Charter (2013), 11.

"Mission and Role of the IOC.[17] Respecting the spirit of fair play is also required for Olympic eligibility.[18] The IOC's *Code of Ethics* declares that, "Fairness and fair play are central elements of the competition," and "Fair play is the spirit of sport."[19] It also describes fair play as a principle.[20] I understand fair play to be based on the ideas of equal opportunity and reward according to merit. On the face of it, these principles are embedded in contest rules—the common starting line, the level playing field, etc. Olympic fair play, however, extends beyond the contest.

Because the Olympic Movement strives to put sport in the service of social ideals, its idea of equal opportunity and reward according to merit must consider factors beyond an athlete's natural ability and personal effort, including access to quality nutrition, coaching, and equipment. Loland and Hoeppler justify the ban on performance-enhancing drugs based on the idea that sports should minimize the influence of sporting inequalities that athletes "cannot influence or control in any significant way."[21] Quality nutrition, coaching, and equipment need not be banned on this argument, however, since they facilitate rather than replace the athlete's virtuous development of skill. Indeed, the Olympic Solidarity program attempts to equalize access to the kinds of knowledge and facilities that allow athletes to make the most of their potential. Efforts in this area should be increased in demonstration of the Movement's commitment to fair play.

Might equipment and substance-based technologies also be a way of equalizing opportunity and facilitating the display of merit? They might. More often, however, athletes adopt performance-enhancing technologies (legal and illegal) either to gain an advantage over competitors or to match the advantage

---

[17] Olympic Charter (2013), 16.
[18] Olympic Charter (2013), 77.
[19] IOC, *Code of Ethics* (2012), 194.
[20] IOC, *Code of Ethics* (2012), 198.
[21] S. Loland and H. Hoeppler, "Justifying Anti-doping," *European Journal of Sport Science* 12:4, (2012), 347.

they perceive competitors already using the technology to have. Even the use of legal performance-enhancers at the Games, such as blood transfusions or xenon gas (both now banned), is tellingly concealed from competitors and media, which suggests the attempt to gain a non-meritocratic competitive advantage.[22] After the use of such technologies is revealed, athletes routinely defend it as necessary to equalize their opportunity against competitors using the same technology. This only strengthens the argument for a ban, though, since the greater role that non-meritocratic factors play in deciding Olympic contests, the less the contest serves the values, principles, and goals of the Movement.[23]

One apparent solution to the problem of Olympic fair play is to make equipment identical—as in Olympic sailing. This may help to isolate athletic skill in that sport, but it may not be the best solution for other sports' equipment, much less Paralympic prostheses. In cycling, for example, the diversity equipment options allows a variety of athletes to compete. A minimum weight, meanwhile, addresses safety and cost concerns. Equality need not be identity. Nor should performance-enhancing technology be used to compensate for the natural inequalities.[24]

---

[22] Both of these now-banned techniques have been used at the Olympics to improve performance in aerobic sports. The USA Cycling team used blood transfusions in 1984 and the Russian cross-country ski team was accused of using xenon gas in 2014.

[23] FINA's ban of the hydrodynamic body suits seems to have been at least partially motivated by the desire to return attention to the basic skills of swimming. Michael Phelps, an apparent beneficiary of the suits in Beijing, commented that he was looking forward to talking about "swimming and not suits again" once the ban was in place. Phelps quoted in Associated Press, "FINA Moves Up Bodysuit Ban," *ESPN Olympic Sports*, July 31, 2009.

[24] John Gleaves, Matthew Llewellyn, and Tim Lehrbach suggest in response to Loland/Hoeppler that blood transfusions might compensate for unfair genetic differences. "Before the Rules are Written: Navigating Moral Ambiguity in Performance Enhancement," *Sport, Ethics, and Philosophy* 8:1 (2014): 95.

Genetic differences are part of one's starting place in the contest, just like the hand a poker player is dealt. The purpose of the game is to test one's skill in playing that hand. Artificially compensating for poor hands, or dealing each player an identical hand would fundamentally change the test. An expectation of diverse genetic potential is built into the structure of sport. Again, the task of Olympic fair play is to equalize opportunity in such a way that it maximizes the contribution of merit-based factors to contest results.

The Olympic Goal of Peace

A third way of looking at the Olympic ethics of performance enhancement is in terms of the desired political consequence of peace. Again, this consideration need not apply to all sports, but the Olympic Charter declares that the goal of the Olympic Movement is "building a peaceful and better world,"[25] that Olympism's goal is "promoting a peaceful society concerned with the preservation of human dignity,"[26] and that the promotion of peace is part of the Mission and Role of the IOC.[27] I have argued elsewhere[28] that the Olympic Games' ability to promote peace derives from three aspects of sport: the creation of a time and space where people set aside conflict, equal treatment under the rules, and respect for differences. Although athletes represent nations during the Games, a truce is declared and the expectation is that national rivalries and political enmities will be set aside. Unfortunately, nations often exploit the Games for ideological, economic, and technological warfare, which is not conducive to peace.

National teams sometimes prescribe the use of performance-enhancing substances or techniques. More perspicuous and less controversial, however, is the equipment technology arms race that exists in sports such as cycling and bobsleigh. Results in these

---

[25] Olympic Charter (2013), 15.
[26] Olympic Charter (2013), 11.
[27] Olympic Charter (2013),15.
[28] Reid, "Olympic Sport and Its Lessons for Peace," in this volume.

(and several other) sports cannot be completely separated from equipment technologies, but their role in deciding contest results should be minimized. Technological arms races among nations do not contribute consequentially to the goal of peace because they advantage those already advantaged rather than setting aside differences of wealth and power for the purpose of the Games.[29] It's no surprise that bobsleigh's most "Olympic" moments are not triumphs of technology, but Eugenio Monti's 1964 lending of equipment to a rival, and the Jamaican team's limited success—which was based primarily on the athletic elements of pushing and driving.

As with individual athletes, treating national teams as equals under the rules is necessary to promote the ideal of peace through sport. This means minimizing the role of non-meritocratic factors like wealth and resources—something any nation in a Rawlsian "original position" would do.[30] It is no coincidence that sports such as soccer, running, and wrestling, where these factors are minimized provide the greatest diversity of participants and medalists. Again, any attempt to equalize opportunity for poorer countries by providing them with high-tech equipment misses the point. You can give a hydrodynamic suit to an African swimmer who can't afford one, but allowing the suits in the first place unnecessarily increases the cost of competing for all. The

---

[29] Even of the German company BMW's development of technology for the American team and the German sledder Machata's leasing of his sled to Russian who won gold in Sochi only serve to reinforce the dominance of a few already dominant nations in this event. For a discussion, see Mike McNamee, "Whither Olympism," *Sport, Ethics, and Philosophy* 8:1 (2014): 1-2.

[30] In *A Theory of Justice*, 12, John Rawls argues that rational free agents, from an "original position" in which their social positions were unknown to them, would assign basic rights and duties equally. Applied to sport, this means that we would not construct games in such a way as to privilege social positions of wealth or power. For a discussion of Rawls' principle applied to equality in sport, see Reid, *The Philosophical Athlete* (2002) 251-255.

opportunity to improve results through technology, furthermore, draws national team resources away from athlete development and grass-roots programs, which better serve the Movement's goals.[31] The ability to gain results with technology is a flaw in Olympic sport that impedes the Movement's goals.

Conclusion

Ethical theories are usually grouped into three basic categories: virtue, deontological, and consequentialist. The ethical considerations that make something truly "Olympic" should encompass all three. In this paper I have tried to show that Olympic sport should limit the use of performance enhancing technologies first, because the structure of sport privileges inefficiency; second, because sport's capacity to produce human excellence or virtue depends on the minimization of technologies in the acquisition of skills; third because the principle of fair play demands the maximization of merit in results; and finally because the goal of peace requires the Olympic Movement to discourage technological arms races among nations. Although I have focused primarily on equipment technologies, the same arguments apply to Paralympic prostheses and doping products. In order to effectively regulate the use of performance-enhancing technologies, the Olympic movement needs to engage its values, principles, and goals. The sport of swimming has not been destroyed by the banning of full-body suits—in fact it has become more Olympic than it was before.

---

[31] It is a flaw in the system that was artfully illustrated by the recent example of United States defense contractor Lockheed Martin's patriotic development of a high-tech suit for American speed skaters at Sochi. The hoopla surrounding the suits seemed to distract the athletes, who eventually performed much worse than expected. What may seem like poetic justice was in fact an injustice to the athletes who seemed unable to perform to their potential and be rewarded according to their true merit.

19. Athlete Agency and the Spirit of Olympic Sport[1]

Imagine a common college student who hasn't done his homework facing the following pop-quiz:

Why is doping banned from Olympic sport?
A. Because it improves sport performance
B. Because it poses a risk to the athlete's health
C. Because it violates the spirit of sport
D. All of the above
E. None of the above [write in the correct reason]

Working on process of elimination, the student immediately crosses out option A because almost everything an athlete does is dedicated to improving their performance; improved performance clearly is what sport is all about. He recalls from an earlier lesson that the Olympic motto is "Faster, Higher, Stronger," so he crosses out option C, since it is hard to imagine what the spirit of sport could mean if it rules out improving performance. Next, "All of the above" can be eliminated just by logic since A and C are false. That leaves B or E. It makes sense to protect athlete safety, but many sports are already risky and some banned substances actually contribute to an athlete's health or healing. The answer, our imaginary student concludes, must be "None of the above," and the reason must be marketing or tradition or just because the IOC are naïve idealists who don't understand modern sport.

After more than twenty years of teaching undergraduates, I find this scenario completely plausible. I also know the correct answer is D, "all of the above." As a scholar of Olympic Studies and philosophy of sport, however, I realize that this hypothetical student's reasoning is not far off from that of my colleagues. It is for this reason that I entered the doping debate in an invited response to an excellent article by Sigmund Loland which

---

[1] Originally published in the *Journal of Olympic Studies* 1:1 (Spring 2020). Reprinted with permission. All rights reserved.

distinguishes between morally acceptable and unacceptable means of performance enhancement by appeal to a biological difference between training and doping.[2] I agreed in principle with Loland's argument, but still contended that such distinctions carry little moral weight in a community driven by what I call the "Efficiency Ethos," a set of values that privileges a quantitative understanding of athletic performance.[3] "If, under the Efficiency Ethos, the spirit of sport just is perfecting performance through any legal means necessary," I wrote, "talk about substances like EPO violating this spirit begs the question."[4] It seems to me that since inefficiency is inherent to the nature of sport, no special justification is needed to add performance enhancers to the list of efficiencies banned.[5] From the viewpoint of the Efficiency Ethos (and our hypothetical student) however, this argument also begs the question of what the "spirit of sport" truly is. I argue that the World Anti-Doping Association's spirit of sport criterion can be clarified in such a way that it not only appeals to moral intuitions and Olympic ideals, it also offers criteria capable of commanding moral authority in a community dominated by the Efficiency Ethos. The concept I propose for doing this is athlete agency.

The Perils of Precision

The only people who disagree that WADA's "spirit of sport" criterion needs clarification are those who believe that it should be eliminated altogether, leaving enhancement and health risk as the only criteria for whether the use of a substance or technique should be prohibited. This the opinion of Henne, Koh, and McDermott,[6] and they are far from alone. Kornbeck argues that the spirit of

---

[2] "Performance-enhancing drugs, sport, and the ideal of natural athletic performance," *The American Journal of Bioethics*, 18.6 (2018): 8–15.
[3] See "Why Olympic Philosophy Matters," in this volume.
[4] Heather Reid, "Responsibility, Inefficiency, and the Spirit of Sport," *American Journal of Bioethics*, 18.6 (2018): 22-23.
[5] Reid, *Introduction to the Philosophy of Sport*, 110-12.
[6] "Coherence of drug policy in sports: illicit inclusions and illegal inconsistencies," *Performance Enhancement and Health* (2013), 48–55.

sport is irretrievably subjective.[7] Waddington et. al. complain that the criterion is vague, "as is apparent from the fact that almost all of [the criterion's] eleven descriptors are compatible with doping. And those that are not, are not compatible with elite sport either."[8] That last comment paints a rather jarring picture of sport, given the eleven descriptors in question:

1. Ethics, fair play and honesty
2. Health
3. Excellence in performance
4. Character and education
5. Fun and joy
6. Teamwork
7. Dedication and commitment
8. Respect for rules and laws
9. Respect for self and other participants
10. Courage
11. Community and solidarity

The point here is not that ethics, honesty, and respect for the rules don't matter, however, but rather that using certain substances (and Henne et. al. have in mind recreational drugs like marijuana) is only unethical in the first place because it is against the rules. Geeraets, meanwhile, contends that "values like courage make no sense as criteria" for what constitutes doping in the first place.[9] As McNamee pointed out in 2013, however, "values characterize an ideal, they do not provide a definition or description."[10]

---

[7] J. Kornbeck, "The Naked Spirit of Sport: A Framework for Revisiting the System of Bans and Justifications in the World Anti-Doping Code," *Sport, Ethics and Philosophy* 7.3 (2013): 313-330.

[8] Ivan Waddington, A.V. Christiansen, J. Gleaves, J. Hoberman, and V. Moller, "Recreational drug use and sport: Time for a WADA rethink?," *Performance Enhancement & Health* 2.2 (2013): 43, n3.

[9] Vincent Geeraets, "Ideology, Doping and the Spirit of Sport," *Sport, Ethics and Philosophy* 12.3 (2018): 258.

[10] Mike McNamee, "The spirit of sport and anti-doping policy: an ideal worth fighting for," *Play True* 1:1 (2013): 14-16.

In seeking clarification of "the spirit of sport," furthermore, we must be careful what we wish for. As the sad history of Olympic "amateurism" reveals, the attempt to codify an Olympic ideal can easily backfire. The very clear rules designed to keep Olympic sport from being about money, arguably had the effect of doing the exact opposite of what they were supposed to. Amateur codes were also used to slip social biases into rules supposed to be about sport, and to preserve the athletic advantages enjoyed by the upper classes.[11] Keeping in mind the danger that comes with leaving room for interpretation, however, I believe that a certain amount of vagueness is needed to avoid legalism and allow for effective judgment. Indeed, it is circular to use "respect for rules" as a reason why for something should be against the rules, and Geeraets is right to ask for a criterion that can be "properly applied."[12] Recently, McNamee and Loland have proposed a solution that eliminates the eleven descriptors, agreeing with others that they do not enhance the selective power of the criteria.[13] I agree that the task should be to achieve a coherent understanding of the spirit of sport that reliably guides judgment—not to eliminate the criterion or reduce it to a formula.

I suggest that we begin that process not by nitpicking the list of descriptors of the spirit of sport, but rather by examining the preamble to that list in the "Fundamental Rationale for the World Anti-Doping Code":

> Anti-doping programs seek to preserve what is intrinsically valuable about sport. This intrinsic value is

---

[11] See Heather L. Reid, "Amateurism is Dead: Long Live Amateurism," in *The Olympic Idea Nowadays*, eds. D. Chatziefstathiou, X. Ramon and A. Miragaya (Barcelona: Centre d'Estudis Olímpics, 2016), 61-63. Also, M.P. Llewellyn and J. Gleaves, *The Rise and Fall of Olympic Amateurism* (Urbana: University of Illinois Press, 2016).

[12] Geeraets "Ideology," 259.

[13] S. Loland and M. J. McNamee, "The 'spirit of sport', WADAs code review, and the search for an overlapping consensus," *International Journal of Sport Policy and Politics*, (2019): 9.

> often referred to as "the spirit of sport." It is the essence of Olympism, the pursuit of human excellence through the dedicated perfection of each person's natural talents. It is how we play true. The spirit of sport is the celebration of the human spirit, body and mind, and is reflected in values we find in and through sport.[14]

I think there are three key ideas worth analyzing here. First, the idea of *intrinsic value*; second, the emphasis on *humanism* (human excellence, human spirit); third and most important, the statement that the "spirit of sport" is "the essence of Olympism." To better understand what the intrinsic values of sports are, we should examine their metaphysics. To honor the emphasis on humanism, we should focus on sport's most human element, which I will describe as 'agency.' And to unpack the *essence of Olympism*, we should turn to the Fundamental Principles of Olympism as stated in the Olympic Charter. By examining these three notions in reverse order, I will demonstrate that the 'spirit of sport' may be better applied as a criterion by maximizing the proportion of sport performance attributable to athlete agency and minimizing extrinsic factors, including wealth and access to technology.

The Essence of Olympism

The first Fundamental Principle of Olympism has changed little over the years. In the 2018 Olympic Charter (11), it reads

> Olympism is a philosophy of life, exalting and combining in a balanced whole the qualities of body, will and mind. Blending sport with culture and education, Olympism seeks to create a way of life based on the joy of effort, the educational value of good example, social responsibility and respect for universal fundamental ethical principles.

In my 2015 analysis of Olympism as a philosophy, I concluded that "Olympism is a philosophy of what can be achieved through sport,

---

[14] World Anti-Doping Agency, *World Anti-Doping Code: 2015 with 2018 Amendments* (Montreal: WADA, 2018), 14.

VI. Justice as Fair Play

rather than a philosophy of sport *per se*,"[15] and, as the second Fundamental Principle of Olympism makes clear, what it wants to achieve is irreducibly humanistic:

> The goal of Olympism is to place sport at the service of the harmonious development of humankind, with a view to promoting a peaceful society concerned with the preservation of human dignity.[16]

It is not stated precisely what this human development entails, but that is appropriate since the concept has to be flexible enough to serve a global movement that takes itself to be multicultural rather than hegemonic. I think it is very clear, however, that 'human development' in the context of Olympism is *not* to be equated with 'human performance' understood in terms of quantified athletic achievement, such as running a four-minute mile or setting a world record. Such feats, in and of themselves, have little social value. As stated in the first fundamental principle, the human development sought by Olympism is characterized by "a balanced whole [of] body, will and mind," and it is to be achieved through "a way of life based on the joy of effort."[17] Furthermore, it has a distinctly social dimension that entails respect for ethics, responsibility, and human dignity.

It is also very clear that we are not just talking about sport here, and worth noting that these human ideals apply not just to

---

[15] Heather Reid, "Olympism: A Philosophy of Sport?" In *Routledge Handbook of the Philosophy of Sport*, eds. M. McNamee and W. J. Morgan (Abingdon: Routledge, 2015), 379.

[16] Olympic Charter (2018), 11.

[17] Francisco Javier Lopez Frias, "Unnatural Technology in a "Natural" Practice?: Human Nature and Performance-Enhancing Technology in Sport," *Philosophies* (2019): 4-35.; argues that 'effort' is a code-word for a philosophy of sport based on a Protestant ethic that may be incompatible with other conceptions of sport. In this paper, I am analyzing a specifically Olympic conception of sport and I believe its emphasis on effort and excellence are actually traceable to ancient Greek ideals.

athletes, but to "all individuals and entities" in the Olympic Movement, as stated in the third fundamental principle.[18] Every athlete, coach, administrator, official, bureaucrat, and sponsor is expected to keep the global humanistic goals of Olympism in mind as they make their daily choices – as they chose their "way of life." And they are expected to be aware of "the educational value of good example," a concept which implies the educational danger of a bad example. This idea reflects Jean-Paul Sartre's ethical insight that in choosing for myself, I chose for all humankind.[19] The way we live our lives makes a statement about how we think human life should be lived. The social impact of our ethical choices is so unavoidable, thought Sartre, awareness of it causes nausea – the kind of nausea an Olympic athlete may experience in sport. The crucial point, however, is that Olympism *is not* primarily concerned with athletes or sport; it is concerned with humanity and with international community.

So how can the "spirit of sport" be the essence of Olympism if Olympism is not primarily about sport? As I concluded in my 2015 analysis, Olympism is less a philosophy of sport than a philosophy of what *can be achieved through* sport.[20] Sport is the *means* by which the Olympic movement tries to realize its humanistic goals, and, as we shall see, the metaphysics of sport provides the clues for how Olympism's humanitarian goals may be achieved. To those, such as McNamee and Loland, who say that Olympism should be removed from the WADA code because it does not represent a

---

[18] Olympic Charter (2018), 11.
[19] Paraphrased from Jean-Paul Sartre, "The Humanism of Existentialism" in *Existentialism from Dostoevsky to Sartre*, ed. Walter Kaufman (New York: Meridian Books, 1975) 292. Sartre's responsibility point is also quoted by David Cruise Malloy, Robert Kell, and Rod Kelln, "The spirit of sport, morality, and hypoxic tents: logic and authenticity," *Applied Physiology, Nutrition and Metabolism* 32 (2007): 293. For a fuller discussion of Sartre's ethics in relation to sport, see Reid, *The Philosophical Athlete*, 132-34.
[20] Reid, "Olympism," 379.

universal view and not all sports are Olympic sports,[21] I reply that Olympism's articulation of the social purpose of sport underpins the moral authority of the code.[22] The crucial thing we learn from understanding WADA's "spirit of sport" criterion as a distilled form of Olympism is that it is about human beings and not athletic performance; about global community and not just sport.

Spirit of Sport and Athlete Agency

It makes sense to describe Olympism as the "spirit of sport" even if every sport is not part of the Olympic Games because the metaphysical structure of sport itself supports Olympism's emphasis on humanity and community. In his 2002 book, *Fair Play: A Moral Norm System*, Loland develops a whole list of moral norms that can be derived from the structure of sport. Fundamental among these is "Equality of Opportunity," which is conveniently symbolized by such ubiquitous features of sport structures as a common starting line, changing sides of a court halfway through the contest, or requiring contestants to use comparable equipment. The purpose of these is to compensate for what Loland calls "irrelevant inequalities," that give one competitor an advantage

---

[21] McNamee & Loland, "Spirit of Sport," 9 :"Olympism has been the object of considerable critical scholarship. It is not a timeless essence of certain sports forms, nor is it a publically shared view, but rather a socially and historically conditioned ideal that finds its specificity in several different conceptions. The WADC, with the aim of being a global and harmonised anti-doping tool, seems an inappropriate instrument in which to articulate a singular vision of ethical sport."

[22] Olympism does admit of multiple conceptions, but I argue that this flexibility is important for its multicultural goals and that sport itself provides sufficient common ground for making ethical distinctions, such as the ban on doping, see Reid, "Olympism," 378. Those, such as Julian Savulescu, who argue that doping is compatible with an ethical approach to sport, generally overlook Olympism and its social goals. See, for example, J. Savulescu; B. Foddy; M. Clayton, "Why we should allow performance enhancing drugs in sport," *British Journal of Sports Medicine* 38 (2004), 666–670.

over the other.[23] If, for example, a football field runs slightly uphill, the advantage of attacking the downhill goal can be equalized by switching sides at the half. In cases where it is impractical for all competitors to use identical equipment, for example because it is adapted for different biological characteristics like height and weight, that equipment is regulated to prevent a competitive advantage. Even in the case of biological differences, such as sex or body size, different classes of competition are organized to compensate.

It should be observed that the inequalities Loland calls "non-relevant" are quite relevant to athletic performance. Height and mass may provide an advantage in many sports, as do biological sex characteristics, so measures, usually classifications, are made to compensate for them. High performance sports equipment, meanwhile, is marketed and coveted for the athletic advantage it provides, even as the rules try to minimize such advantages. I often hear of cycling equipment that will "save watts" in competition. The claim here, of course, is not that the athlete will actually produce more watts when they use that equipment, but rather that their quantitatively-measured performance will be equal to someone who produces more watts but lacks the advantage provided by the gizmo being marketed. Most sports' rules regulate or compensate for such advantages because, despite the marketing rhetoric, they are irrelevant to sport in the same way certain biological differences are.

I believe that what is behind the moral intuition that these inequalities should be regulated or banned is the fact that they account for a portion of the athlete's "performance" that is not a product of her own agency, and as such they do not contribute to the *human* development sought through sport by Olympism. In my 2018 response to Loland, I illustrated this idea as follows. Imagine everything that goes into an athletic performance depicted on a pie chart. Some things, such as strength and endurance acquired through training, are a product of the athlete's personal agency.

---

[23] Loland, *Fair Play in Sport*, 46 ff.

Others, including what Loland calls "biological background conditions and constraints" (such as an athlete's genetic profile) are not a product of her agency.[24] Applying that model to Michael Phelps' performance at the Beijing Olympics, we might say that factors such as strategy and stroke efficiency, which were a product of training and experience, made a legitimate contribution to his victory, whereas the efficiency provided by his hydrodynamic bodysuit (since banned) did not because it *actually reduced the proportion of the performance attributable to the athlete's agency*. I argued that Phelps' victories gained their value from the proportion of the performance that was, in Loland's words, "the unique expression of an individual," and not his access to external resources like the suit.[25]

The distinction between the proportion of the performance derived from athlete agency and the proportion derived from extrinsic factors is important because we *praise* Olympic victors for their athletic performance. In moral theory, praise and blame are appropriate only to the extent that a person is *morally responsible* for the act in question. In the words of ethicist Andrew Eshleman, "to be morally responsible for something, say an action, is to be worthy of a particular kind of reaction—praise, blame, or something akin to these—for having performed it."[26] In Olympic sport, we single out athletic victors for ceremonial honors, lavish them with rhetorical praise, and interview them about their accomplishments. In short, we exhibit the three characteristic behaviors that indicate an assumption of moral responsibility: applying ethical predicates such as "good," or "courageous;" displaying "reactive attitudes" such as gratitude, respect, and indignation; and expecting agents to explain their achievements.[27]

---

[24] Loland, "Performance-enhancing drugs," 8.
[25] Reid, "Responsibility," 22.
[26] Andrew Eshleman, "Moral Responsibility," *The Stanford Encyclopedia of Philosophy* (Winter 2016 Edition), Edward N. Zalta (ed.).
[27] John Martin Fischer, "Free Will and Moral Responsibility," in *The Oxford Handbook of Ethical Theory,* edited by David Copp, (Oxford: Oxford University Press, 2007).

Those who would separate virtue from victory in sport must be prepared to forgo the moral adulation (and perhaps the financial reward) that goes with it.

The moral responsibility associated with athletic victory assumes what I call *athlete agency* – the idea that the athlete herself is the primary cause of her performance. The concept is a variant of human agency, which can be defined as the ability to act with certain intentions and/or to be the cause of certain outcomes.[28] Metaphysically speaking, the concept of human agency is fraught—attached as it is to such perennial problems as free will and intentionality.[29] But we need not resolve these philosophical puzzles to connect the athletic concept of deserved victory with factors under an athlete's control.[30] The intuition implied by the principle of equal opportunity, a fundamental feature of the metaphysics of sport itself, is that we want *as much as possible* for the athlete himself to be the cause of his own performance because this is what makes him worthy of praise or blame.

Let me pause for a moment to address some anticipated challenges to the idea of athlete agency I am promoting here. Critics will say that the decision to take drugs may also be an act of athlete agency, maybe even athletic virtue, as long as it is voluntary and informed. The proportion of my performance due to my choices of equipment, supplements, or drugs is just as human as the proportion due to training and healthy diet; it is only the pre-existing ban on such substances and measures that casts moral derision on them.[31] I grant that performance enhancing

---

[28] Markus Schlosser, "Agency," *The Stanford Encyclopedia of Philosophy* (Fall 2015 Edition), ed. Edward N. Zalta.

[29] For a recent attempt to resolve the problem, see Erasmus Mayr, *Understanding Human Agency* (Oxford University Press, 2011).

[30] Compare D. Pereboom, *Living without Free Will* (Cambridge U. Press, 2001) 3: "an action is free in the sense required for moral responsibility only if it is not produced by a deterministic process that traces back to causal factors beyond the agent's control.".

[31] For arguments along these lines, see W.M. Brown, "Ethics, drugs, and sport," *Journal of the Philosophy of Sport* 7:1 (1980), 15–23.

substances and techniques are the product of human beings, that athletes may choose to adopt them freely and intentionally, just as they choose to adopt a certain strategy, and that sports are set up to reward superior athletic performance. There is a distinction, however, between EPO being a product of human ingenuity and the athlete's performance being, as much as possible, a product of their own agency.[32]

The idea behind athlete agency is for the athlete herself to be the direct and active cause of her athletic performance; her decision to use EPO, even if informed and voluntary,[33] makes her at best an indirect cause of the proportion of her performance that is attributable to the increased hematocrit caused by the drug. Even when the technology in question *is* the product of the same athlete's engineering skill and creativity, as was the case with cyclist-engineer Graeme Obree's hour-record in cycling,[34] the performance advantage gained by it by it was due to increased aerodynamic efficiency, not the athlete's agency. Let me illustrate with a thought-experiment. Imagine the record-setting Obree racing against himself on a normal bike in a legal position and winning by 30 seconds. That margin of victory would be attributable not to the athlete – who in this thought experiment is

---

[32] I also deliberately avoid the criterion 'natural' here, which seems to me to present more problems than it solves. By focusing on human agency, I can link the spirit of sport with the humanism of Olympism, which is to say its social and political goals, rather than any implied conception of what is or is not "natural."

[33] And while we're on the topic of informed consent. Geeraets, "Ideology," 260 argues that consent to the code is not actually voluntary because there are no good alternatives (if you're already committed to a sport) or, if you are not yet committed, you must be a minor and unable to consent voluntarily. It seems to me that the same claim can be made about any sports rule, including the ban on using your hands in soccer.

[34] A remarkable story; see Graeme Obree, *Flying Scotsman: Cycling to Triumph Through My Darkest Hours* (Boulder, CO: Velo Press, 2005), or the film of the same name.

identical to the athlete he defeats – but rather to the advantages provided by his equipment. The principle of athlete agency seeks to reduce or eliminate such advantage and maximize the extent to which the athlete is the direct and active cause of his performance.

Spirit of Sport and Inefficiency

To reiterate, the "spirit of sport" understood as the "essence of Olympism" envisions athletic competition as a means to the end of personal and social human development. As such, its goal is not to achieve ever-improved sports performances, but rather ever-improved people and communities. To achieve such social goals, sport must emphasize athlete agency. The Olympic motto, *citius, altius, fortius* (faster, higher, stronger) may "express the aspirations of the Olympic Movement," as it says in the Olympic Charter,[35] but it is not part of the Fundamental Principles of Olympism and does not describe the Olympic Movement's goals. If the goal of Olympic sport was really to see how high a person can go, it would allow the use of rocket ships. As it is, Olympic contests adjudicated according to height limit the use of technology to vaulting poles, and only then because that event presents a distinct set of challenges from the high-jump. As a matter of fact, limitation of performance-enhancing technology is imbedded into the fundamental nature of sport.[36] As Bernard Suits observed decades ago, sports are essentially "the voluntary attempt to overcome

---

[35] Olympic Charter (2018) 23.

[36] Loland, "Performance-enhancing drugs," 11, correctly appeals to the structure of sport to defend his interpretation of its spirit. Pointing out that sports rules are "systems of constraints and restrictions designed to cultivate particular sets of human abilities and skills," he identifies a norm of fair equality of opportunity (FEO) implied by the elimination of or compensation for "non-relevant" inequalities in sport. I add that what is distinctive about regulated "non-relevant" inequalities such as sex, weight, finances, and technology is not whether they are natural, but rather whether they are a product of the athlete's agency and therefore her moral responsibility (Reid, "Responsibility," 23).

unnecessary obstacles,"[37] where "rules prohibit use of more efficient in favour of less efficient means."[38] The reason that technological efficiencies that reduce athlete agency are discouraged or even banned in sport is that prescribed inefficiencies create challenges, which push human beings to improve themselves – and not just in terms of athletic performance.[39] Given that human improvement is the goal of Olympism and therefore "the spirit of sport," the *inefficiencies* of sport must be preserved.

The problem with performance-enhancing technologies, fundamentally, is that they attempt to overcome a sport's prescribed inefficiencies by some means other than the human virtues those obstacles were intended to stimulate.[40] The sport says I have to get from A to B as quickly as possible, then proscribes any means more efficient than travel by foot. If I put plastic springs in my shoes or ingest a substance that allows my blood to carry more oxygen than it normally would, I may complete my task more efficiently, but I will not have achieved any higher level of the human development sought by Olympism, even if I win. In fact, insofar as my margin of victory is due to some factor other than the human development sport is supposed to encourage, I may deprive a competitor more deserving of the victory in terms of moral responsibility. Indeed, in sports like professional cycling long associated with doping, victory can be as much a cause for moral suspicion as it is for moral praise. And often the moral suspicion is not specifically that the cyclist broke the rules, as the

---

[37] Suits, *Grasshopper*, 55.

[38] Suits, *Grasshopper*, 54.

[39] I exclude improved technique, such as a more efficient swimming stroke, from the category of efficiencies to be discouraged, since they consistent with the prescription of inefficiencies. Thanks to Charles Stocking for prompting this clarification.

[40] My argument that the purpose of inefficiency is to promote human virtue can be found in "Performance-Enhancing Technologies and Olympic Fair Play," in this volume.

boos directed at Chris Froome the 2018 Tour de France illustrate.[41] Such moral suspicion and reluctance to praise certain cases of athletic success derive from the idea that something other than athlete agency accounts for it. It also shows that victory reaps much (if not all) of its value from its association with virtue.

Although the "spirit of sport" should be used as a criterion to determine which techniques and substances should be legal to use, it is not itself a matter of legality. In other words, a substance or technique does not comply with the spirit of sport by virtue of its being legal, the way Froome's use of Ventolin was legal if it stayed under the predetermined threshold for therapeutic doses.[42] This is why abolitionists are wrong when they claim that the moral problems associated with doping will be eliminated if the ban is simply lifted. Participants in the social practice of sport tend to have similar moral intuitions about illegitimate means of performance-enhancement; even convicted dope-cheats affirm the same intuition when they point out that they still had to train as hard as their competitors, or claim to have been coerced by the belief that their competitors were doping so this was the only way to "level the playing field." A similar moral intuition applies to equipment. I remember Greg Lemond saying in a personal interview, "the cyclist who won the race would still have won even if he was riding the last placed rider's bike." The fact that his statement conflicts with the logic of sports equipment marketing, including ads that Lemond himself was appearing in at the time, may help to explain why the principles of inefficiency and equality of opportunity embedded in the very structure of sport, are so easily forgotten or overlooked. Efficiencies threaten the spirit of sport by undermining athlete agency.

---

[41] For more on the Froome case see, for example, William Fotheringham, "Chris Froome given little sympathy as Team Sky get a sense of déjà vu," in *The Guardian*, July 7, 2018.

[42] Or the way blood transfusions were legal when used by the United States cycling team at the 1984 Olympics. For a detailed account of the case, see David F. Prouty, *In Spite of Us* (Brattleboro, VT: VeloNews, 1988) 121-71.

VI. Justice as Fair Play

Spirit of Sport and Accessibility

The expense and exclusivity of high-tech performance enhancers highlights another overlooked aspect of the spirit of sport: accessibility. Every athlete has equal access to her own agency (so to speak), but not every athlete has equal access to external resources that improve performance. Recalling that the Olympic Movement is global, and that the goal of Olympism is not just individual human development but "promotion of a peaceful society," rules-makers need to be especially sensitive to performance advantages that can be bought. Huge economic disparities among countries and individual athletes routinely threaten the principle of Equal Opportunity and undermine the ideal of athlete agency. The same is true of technological innovations that are provided exclusively to one athlete or team. The notion of being able to buy an advantage helps to fuel the sponsorship economy in many modern sports, but it is contrary to the "spirit of sport" understood Olympically. Most sports, like cycling, have rules that prohibit the use of equipment that is not available on the consumer market. Others, such as bobsleigh, allow proprietary equipment. Olympic sailing, meanwhile, uses strictly-defined classes which all but eliminate performance differences between boats thereby increasing the proportion of the performance due to athlete agency.

Indeed, the sport of sailing provides a good illustration of the reasons why Olympic sport, at least, should limit performance aids to resources widely available across the globe. The America's Cup may be more prestigious than Olympic sailing races, but that event allows—even emphasizes—boat design and engineering. As a result, only the wealthiest and most technologically-advanced teams are able to compete.[43] In their long history, which goes all

---

[43] Olympic Bobsleigh resembles the America's Cup in privileging wealthy and technologically-advanced competitors. The nations winning the most historically are: Germany, Switzerland, and the United States. See "All-time medal table for bobsleigh in the Winter Olympics as of 2018, by country," *Statista*, 7/26/2019.

the way back to the 8th century BCE, the Olympic Games have witnessed repeated attempts by the upper classes to use their wealth and privilege to gain advantages in sport. In ancient Greece, for example, after lower-class athletes began winning victories in "gymnic" events like running and wrestling, the elites introduced equestrian events—in which the owner of the horse received the victor's wreath—in order to preserve their access to victory.[44] The current push to allow performance-enhancing technologies in sport in the name of such "human" values as freedom and autonomy, appears to me to be motivated rather by wealthier and more technologically-advanced nations attempting to exploit those advantages in the Olympic Games and other sports.[45] The Olympic Movement can promote athlete agency and the spirit of sport in an international context by emphasizing basic, widely accessible sports like running and soccer, while minimizing the effect of economic advantage in sports like sailing, cycling, and bobsleigh.

The Olympic Movement may never be able to define the "spirit of sport" in a way that allows for easy application. In fact, efforts to codify such a concept may well lead to disaster, as with the aforementioned case of "amateurism." We *can* make an effort to better understand and clarify it, though, and that is what I am trying to do in this paper. I think that confusion about the "spirit of sport" criterion derives from a lack of interest in Olympism and a lack of perspective about the objectives of the Olympic Movement and of sport itself as a human practice. The "spirit of sport" is not just about doping, rules, or sport—it is about promoting human agency by preserving inefficiency and providing accessibility. A good way to apply the "spirit of sport"

---

[44] See, for example, Golden, *Greek Sport and Social Status*, 5 ff.
[45] See Lopez Frias, "Unnatural Technology," 291 f. for a thoughtful overview of the problem. For my own part, I do not deny that freedom and autonomy are human values, but I wonder why people would try to express them in an essentially rule-governed social practice like sport.

criterion is simply to prohibit substances and techniques that decrease the proportion of athletic performance attributable to the athlete's agency and to permit and even encourage things that increase that proportion.

Obviously, my clarification of the "spirit of sport" in terms of athlete agency does not provide the kind of sharp definitional boundaries that make regulation (as well as gaming the system) easy. Decisions about individual techniques and substances will need to be made by a committee of judges with experience and knowledge of sport and its history. For example, we might perform my thought experiment in which an athlete competes against herself to determine whether an energy drink undermines athlete agency and conclude that it does because she runs a marathon ten seconds faster than she would have consuming only water; we might even conclude that water undermines athlete agency compared to nothing. A knowledgeable committee using all three of WADA's criteria, however, is very unlikely consider the drink a sufficient threat to athlete agency to justify its ban. The spirit of sport is one of three *criteria* for deciding what should be banned, not a strict definition. My hope is that understanding the spirit of sport in terms of human agency will help rules committees justify the bans on things that threaten values that underpin Olympic sport.

Conclusion

I admit that my understanding of the "spirit of sport" in terms of athlete agency, combined with my claim that modern sport is dominated by an "Efficiency Ethos," may seem apocalyptic. But I am not at all a nihilist when it comes to sport and its spirit. I believe that sport is a great teacher of its own intrinsic value, especially for those who participate in it. This is why most athletes understand that technological efficiency may sell products, but it also undermines sport's values and threatens the crucial connection between victory and virtue. Even with the all the ills that sport in general and the Olympic Games in particular have experienced in the last century or so, both remain an important part of modern life. Perhaps they are so familiar now that we no longer feel the need to question their purpose or aspirations. We may even wonder why modern societies push for ever more social liberty while insisting on draconian rules in sport. At least, I hope we wonder. Because it only by wondering about the nature and purpose of sport and the Olympic Games that we can open ourselves up to the answers, which happily can be found embedded within them.

Section VII
Peace and World Community

20. The Political Heritage of the Olympic Games[1]

The political goal of the Modern Olympism is clearly stated in the *Olympic Charter*: "to place sport at the service of the harmonious development of man, with a view to promoting a peaceful society concerned with the preservation of human dignity"[2] This goal hasn't changed in the 100+ year history of the modern Games; indeed it was inspired by the 1,000+ year history of the Ancient Olympic Festival. But we now know that some 19th century European revivalists manipulated Hellenic ideals to suit their own upper-class agendas,[3] and we may wonder i the Games' political heritage has any relevance to the modern Movement at all. Today's Olympic challenges include discrimination based on religion and gender, cultural hegemony and sabre-rattling among the rich and powerful, and environmental degradation.

The ancient Olympic Games may have fostered peace in antiquity, but it is hard to see how a religiously and culturally homogeneous festival that excluded females, foreigners, and slaves can teach any lessons to its younger, secular, cosmopolitan descendent. A closer look reveals, however, that ancient and modern Olympic politics are not so different as they seem. The ancient Olympic Games were successful precisely because they used sport to effectively address issues of social discrimination and national rivalry, while inspiring diverse individuals to unite for a common cause. If the modern Olympic Movement wishes to achieve its political goals, it should understand the relevance, risks, and possible rewards of its ancient political heritage.

National Rivalry

One of the first political criticisms to be made of the modern Olympic Games is that they preach internationalism but serve the

---

[1] Previously published in *Olympic Ethics and Philosophy*, eds. Mike McNamee and Jim Parry (London: Routledge, 2012): 6-20. Reprinted with permission. All rights reserved.
[2] Olympic Charter (2010), 11.
[3] Chatziefstathiou & Henry, "Hellenism and Olympism," 24-43.

national interests of a wealthy few. The Movement has its origins and base of operations in Europe, its governing members are overwhelmingly European, and its economic backbone is predominantly American. Because of the size of the Games and the infrastructure required to host them, the Olympic Games almost always take place in large, wealthy, Western cities. Even Olympic sports, with very few exceptions, are Western in origin and, arguably, in terms of the values they promote. So rather than the cosmopolitan utopia envisioned by the Olympic Charter, what we seem to have in reality is a playing field tilted to favour the West and wealth; a mechanism for reinforcing existing power structures and for promulgating the cultural values of the rich. To some degree this reflects the ancient use of athletics; they were a part of the hegemonic Hellenism spread by Alexander the Great and others. At the same time, however, the intrinsic values of Olympic sport do promote the common interests of humanity rather than the particular interests of nations and individuals.

Historically, this is a legacy of the religious orientation of the Games. Ancient Olympia was a religious sanctuary long before it began hosting athletic contests. As such, it was not regarded as the possession of any nation, city, tribe, or individual; rather it was the possession of the relevant god or gods.[4] Olympic soil was, therefore, politically neutral. Even though city states such as Pisa or Elis served as official custodians of the site, and later the Games, it was never understood to be "theirs" in the political sense. The "ownership" was attributed instead to the Olympian deities, whose supremacy was thought to overwhelm social and political distinctions among human beings. This religious setting produced among those gathered a sense of human commonality and community in contrast to the divinities upon whose goodwill they believed their own wellbeing to depend. When Hellenes from diverse tribes throughout the surrounding area came to Olympia to worship common gods, they were expected to leave their ethnic and political differences outside the walls. Indeed, the

---

[4] Burkert, *Greek Religion*, 95.

introduction of athletics into the Olympic sanctuary may have been motivated by the need to preserve this sense of equality before the gods despite these individual and cultural differences.[5]

Sometime around the 8th century BCE, a footrace was staged at Olympia to decide who would light the sacrificial flame.[6] In a politically homogeneous community, that honor would be given to the person at the top of the acknowledged social hierarchy—usually the king. But at Olympia, diverse groups with rival hierarchies were present; the footrace therefore provided an impartial means for selecting an honoree. One could interpret the race as offering a chance for the god to choose his favourite from among the competitors—similar to the way Homer's *Iliad* describes divine interference in athletic contests (book 23). Or, one could interpret the footrace as a "scientific" approach to answering a question about human worthiness, one based on observation of actual performance rather than presumptions about inherent supremacy. Either way, what athletics brought to Olympia, was a peaceful, publicly observed, and essentially cooperative means of settling competing claims to honour in a diverse setting.[7] To be sure, each faction supported their native athletes, wishing for their victory and the defeat of their rivals. But because they all witnessed the selection of the winner through the relatively just and impartial process of a footrace, there was acceptance of the result and perhaps even a grudging appreciation for the virtue displayed by all of the competitors in the contest—whatever their ethnic origins

As a matter of fact, this competitive-cooperative dichotomy characteristic of sport reflected the political situation of small Greek city-states around the 8th century BCE. These city-states viewed themselves much as individual nations view themselves

---

[5] On equality before the gods, see Burkert, *Greek Religion*, 53.
[6] This is based on a passage in Philostratus (*Gymnasticus* 5). On the official founding date of the Games. See Panos Valavanis, "Historical Origins of the Olympic Games," 141-5.
[7] See "Running Towards Truth in Ancient Olympia," in this volume.

today: as politically independent and ethnically distinct from their neighbours. Because of their close physical proximity, they were inevitably in competition with one another for scarce natural resources. At the same time, however, they needed to cooperate to facilitate economic trade and to form military alliances with their neighbours.[8] Athletic competition, likewise, takes place within a context of cooperation where rival parties agree to contest rules, jointly supervise the proceedings, and affirm (however reluctantly) the validity of the results. So, for example, when an Athenian and a Spartan wrestled in the Olympic Games, they expressed a cultural and political rivalry while demonstrating cooperation by following the agreed upon structure of rules.

The political neutrality of contest rules also may have been inspired by the religious context of the ancient Games: the goal of the festival was to propitiate the god, for the benefit of the entire community, rather than any particular political figure or group. It was in everyone's interest to make an honest selection—one that would in fact please the supreme mind of Zeus. Meanwhile, the willingness of free and often noble men to subject themselves to the politically neutral rules of sport (and even to be flogged publicly in case of violations) laid the groundwork for the social and political revolution that we now call democracy.[9] Sports rules force us to treat our competitors as equals: all runners set off from a common starting line, wrestlers draw lots to determine their matches, chariot starts are staggered to compensate for the difference in distance to the common turning post. These equalizing rules, in turn, make possible the demonstration of athletic superiority. The politically revolutionary images of Jesse Owens and Luz Long at the 1936 Olympics in Berlin exhibit the Modern Games' ability to reconstruct this scenario. Owens, an African American denied complete civil rights in his own country, became close friends with his German rival, Long, who had been

---

[8] Hansen, *Polis*, 114.

[9] This is the argument of Miller, "Naked Democracy," 277–96. See also "From Aristocracy to Democracy" in this volume.

weaned on the racist ideology of Nazism. Sport, by its structure, allows for the expression of rivalry and difference while demanding respect for cooperation and similarity.

Indeed Olympic sport did this more reliably than conventional politics in antiquity. The so-called Olympic Truce or *ekecheiria*, which protected pilgrims travelling to the games and the competition area itself from military aggression, was generally (although not universally) respected. Because the varied city-states who participated in the games were often at war with one another, the Olympic festival provided a safe place for them to negotiate with enemies, form alliances with friends, and perhaps even pray to the gods for victory in full view of their rivals. The association between Olympic Games and peace, a central theme of modern Olympism, was probably more a by-product of the social dynamics of sport and human contact than a conscious goal of the festival.[10] Nevertheless, the religiously motivated political neutrality of Olympia and of the Games that were held there provided an opportunity for ancient Hellenes to peacefully express their differences while affirming certain commonalities. In this way, Olympia provided an ideal political model in which cooperation facilitated healthy competition among city-states without favouring one over the other.

The global scope of the Modern Olympic Movement and its political goals need not entail that the ancient Games' political process is irrelevant today. To be sure, the process whereby diverse competitors settle competing claims to superiority by submitting to a fairly administered set of common rule still obtains, as does its political benefit. One big difference in the Modern Games, however, is the absence of a religious context and of any god or set of gods that could command the common respect of the whole world the way Zeus and his cohorts reigned in ancient Olympia. There are, however, common ideals and even common causes capable of transcending national and cultural concerns — and that was really what the religious context contributed to

---

[10] Reid, "Olympic Sport and Its Lessons for Peace," in this volume.

ancient Olympia's political goals. In the modern context, Olympic "neutrality" needs to be pursued first, through improved ethnic and gender balance in the IOC membership, as well as other international sports governing bodies. With the tradition of lifetime appointments, this is a slow process, but charges of political, as well as cultural and commercial bias among governing members is foundational to the continued health of the Olympic Movement.

Second, the political neutrality of the Olympic site is essential to its political effectiveness. One solution is to establish a permanent Olympic site, as they had in ancient times; but the size of the modern Games and the cultural learning that results from their global journey weigh against that option. It is hard to imagine any place on the globe that might be considered neutral by all the world's peoples; even a return to the historical site of Olympia or (more practically) to Athens may do more harm than good, both to the host country and the rest of the world's sense of inclusion. The current method of choosing different sites around the globe by means of competitive bid seems most promising; but as ancient practice shows, this competition needs to be as fair and perspicuous as the athletic competitions. The criteria for victory should be public and fair, and efforts should be made to maximize the number of eligible cities, not least by minimizing or subsidizing the costs involved in making a bid. Reducing the size of the Games, furthermore, would increase the number of cities in places like Africa and South America capable of hosting the Games. Furthermore the bid and selection process should be as open and public as possible—the televising of final presentations is a step in the right direction. Sport itself teaches us that the result of competitions that pit nations against each other can be accepted peacefully as long as they are perceived as fair.

Finally, the list of sports and events should be made more international.[11] The current list, while coming close to achieving

---

[11] A complete argument for this is made by Jim Parry, "Sport and Olympism," 188-204.

gender equity, is still very heavily dominated by sports of Western origin. The reasons for this may be historical rather than philosophical and it can be argued that such quintessentially Western sports as baseball are nearly as important in Eastern cultures, such as Japan, as they are in Western cultures. It is equally true that the few Eastern sports introduced into the program, specifically judo and taekwondo, have been effectively embraced by Western culture. Current criteria for Olympic sport recognition and selection include the sport being practiced in a large number of countries and continents,[12] and the forces of globalization tend to privilege the spread of already established and income-producing Western sports. In fact, the latest winners in the Olympic sport selection game were golf and rugby sevens. Perhaps the IOC should exercise its ability to challenge the established sporting hierarchy by recognizing more traditionally Eastern sports, thereby promoting their development worldwide and educating the West about the values that underpin them. The Olympic Games' power to promote world community depends upon an aura of neutrality, which demands an effort to increase internationalization and fair competition.

Social Discrimination

Although the religiously motivated neutrality of the ancient Olympic Games provided terrain for healthy national competition that preserved respect for ethnic difference, Olympia's record on respecting social difference is far from stellar—at least at first glance. Females, foreigners, and slaves were explicitly excluded from the Games, and among free males, victory remained more or less the privilege of wealthy aristocrats who had the money and leisure time for training and competition. Competitors at the Olympic Games swore an oath that they had trained faithfully for at least ten months and were required to spend the month before the Games at Elis training under the supervision of special

---

[12] There are 33 criteria divided into seven categories. *Factsheet: The Sports on the Olympic Program* (Lausanne, 2008), 1.

VII. Peace and World Community

judges.[13] Nevertheless, there is evidence that the Games worked against social discrimination and may even have laid the groundwork for democracy by changing the conception of aristocracy.[14] The athletic and intellectual prowess demonstrated by non-nobles at the Games transformed the idea of *aretē* (virtue) and *aristeia* "being the best and outdoing all others"[15] away from something acquired at birth and toward something that could be trained. That change transformed sport into a vehicle for social and economic mobility.

Beginning in the 6th century BCE, records show a major change in the provenance of Olympic victors. Whereas earlier winners had come from various city states in the Peloponnese and other parts of the Greek mainland nearby Olympia, the 6th and 5th centuries were dominated by athletes hailing from Magna Graecia, i.e. Greek settlements in southern Italy, northern Africa, and Asia Minor.[16] To some degree, this simply reflects political changes—the settlements were self-governing city-states formed for a variety of reasons including overpopulation, internecine rivalry, and the facilitation of foreign trade. In some cases nobles were sent to found the settlements; Sparta even sent an Olympic champion to attract settlers, and perhaps divine favour.[17] But most of Magna Graecia's champions were home-grown; their success not a matter of noble blood but rather of training. Like anyone who leaves home to settle in a far-off land, the Greeks who settled overseas must have been in some way socially marginalized. Just as former French and British colonies take special pleasure in athletic victories over their former masters, there must have been a special motivation for Greek colonists to succeed at Olympia. Although Greek colonies were politically independent, we might suppose

---

[13] Golden, *Sport and Society in Ancient Greece*, 15-16.
[14] See "From Aristocracy to Democracy" in this volume.
[15] This phrase *"aien aristeuein kai upeirochon emmenai allon"* comes from Homer's *Iliad* 6.208, and 11.784.
[16] N. Spivey, *The Ancient Olympics*, 170.
[17] The colony was Cyrene in 630 BCE and the athlete was Chionis of Sparta. Pausanias, cited in Spivey, *The Ancient Olympics,* 182–183.

that they desired to prove their authentic Greekness in the heart of the motherland.

The success of these athletes, insofar as it depended on training, grated on traditional aristocratic sensibilities. The belief had been that true aristocrats didn't need to train to become athletes and they didn't need to study to be intellectuals. In Homer's *Odyssey* the hero proves his nobility through untrained athleticism. Washing up a weakened castaway on the shores of Phaeacia, Odysseus responds to the insulting implication that he may be a businessman rather than a king by slinging a discus farther than all the locals.[18] Back in Ithaca, his queen and subjects fail to recognize him until he levels a low-class rival in boxing, strings the gigantic royal bow, and shoots an arrow through the narrow column formed by the sockets on row of axe-heads.[19] The belief that excellence is a matter of inheritance is also reflected in Pindar's 5th century BCE victory odes, which routinely attribute a champion's success to his noble ancestry and its attendant divine favour. In fact, the belief that aristocrats shouldn't have to train shows up in the early modern Olympic ethos against the employment of coaches—as artfully illustrated in the movie *Chariots of Fire*.

Of course, aristocratic Olympic victors did train and they did employ coaches—often at considerable expense, but almost never with public acknowledgment.[20] Very likely they did this in response to the challenge provided by lower-class athletes, especially those from the colonies who had a history not only of training bodies, but minds and souls as well. A likely source for this ethos is Pythagoras of Samos, who emigrated to the colony of Kroton in 532 BCE, perhaps after having met the young wrestler

---

[18] Homer, *Odyssey* 8.100-233.
[19] The boxing episode is in book 18, the archery contest in book 21.
[20] Explains Nicholson, *Aristocracy and Athletics*, 21: "what motivated anxiety about professional trainers was that, by appearing to add new abilities such as skill to their pupils, they threatened the idea that the qualities on which victory depended were inherited."

VII. Peace and World Community

Milo at that summer's Olympic Games.[21] Literary accounts of Pythagoras and Pythagoreanism are conflicting and controversial, but there is general agreement that they promoted philosophy as a way of life emphasizing balance, harmony, daily exercise, and a healthy diet.[22] A common story about the Pythagorean athlete Milo's training describes him lifting a calf every day until it became a bull—a clear reflection of progressive resistance training. By some accounts Pythagoras was already an athletic trainer in Samos before he came to Kroton, perhaps attracted by its reputation for medical research and athletic success.[23] Indeed Kroton was so dominant in the Olympic Games that the top 7 finishers in the sprint race of 576 BCE all hailed from that single city—a phenomenon that gave birth to the proverb that "he who finishes last of the Krotonites is first among the rest of the Greeks" (Strabo 6.1.12).

Whatever the details of Pythagoras' involvement, the athletic excellence of Krotonites and other colonists is undisputed. Furthermore, because of the enduring association between athletic excellence and *aretē* (virtue), the realization that athletic success could be trained may have inspired the idea that *aretē* could also be trained. This is certainly the attitude that we find in the classical philosophy of Socrates, Plato, and Aristotle; it may also explain these philosophers' presence in Athens' gymnasia. Though he himself never competed in the Olympic Games, Plato had an athletic background and is said to have been deeply inspired by Pythagoreanism. Indeed it was after his first trip to Magna Graecia, which may well have included a visit to Kroton (and definitely included contact with Pythagoreans such as Archytas of

---

[21] Michele Di Donato, "La Scuola Pitagorica e la Nascita della Ginnastica Educativa." *Alcmeone* 1(1977): 11-21. Reprinted in Teja and Mariano, eds. *Agonistica in Magna Grecia: La Scuola Atletica di Crotone* (Calopezzati (CS): Edizioni del Convento, 2004), 45. Di Donato believes that Milo might have met Pythagoras at Olympia in 532, the year of his first wrestling victory in the adult category.

[22] A source considered reliable is Iamblichus, *The Pythagorean Life*.

[23] Di Donato, "La Scuola Pitagorica," 45.

Tarentum) that he set up his philosophical school in the Athenian gymnasium called the Academy.[24] Perhaps Plato was actually following the tradition of Pythagoras, who is said to have recruited his students among athletes at the gymnasium.[25] In any case, it is likely that the revolutionary idea that excellence (in athletics and in moral virtue) is a matter of training rather than noble birth has its roots in the Olympic Games, especially the success of free-thinking colonists from Magna Graecia.

Why, it may be asked, if the ancient Olympic Games were such a beacon for opportunity and intellectual exchange, did they continue to exclude females, foreigners, and slaves? A primary response is that these ancient exclusions simply reflect the contemporary social prejudices, as similar exclusions in the early modern Games do. But the situation in Olympia was complicated by the same religious dimension that helped inspire the Games' revolutionary impartiality. Since the main purpose of the contest was to select a symbolic sacrifice that would motivate the god to provide benefits to the community, it is unlikely that a foreigner would fit the bill. Foreigners here would be defined not so much by their national origin as by their religious or cultural beliefs. Indeed one of the tests for Greekness was simply the ability to speak Greek. As the "community" in question expanded in the Roman period, the eligibility pool expanded accordingly. Since the community of the modern Olympic Games is quite explicitly the world, there are no longer any foreigners to exclude.

As for slaves, another basic principle of religious sacrifice is that you give up your best. The animals sacrificed are always the highest quality, never the weakest of the herd. Not only were most slaves foreigners, they were generally not cared for in a way that would allow them to achieve athletic excellence. And even if a slave happened to be a champion athlete (perhaps one captured in war), it would be religiously unacceptable to offer him rather than

---

[24] For more Plato's Academy, see Reid, "Plato's Gymnasium" and "Sport as Moral Education in Plato's *Republic*."

[25] Iamblichus, *The Pythagorean Life*, 6-7.

VII. Peace and World Community

"the best" of a community's citizens to a god in sacrifice. Notably, ancient Rome routinely used slaves as athletes—especially as gladiators and the drivers of chariots. This reflects the diminished religious importance of those games as well as the political objective of demonstrating the power of the Emperor as the unquestioned commander of these skilled fighters.[26]

The case of female exclusion from Olympia is perhaps the most complicated. Again, the primary reason for it seems to be religious. At some point, the Olympic Games were dedicated to Heracles (who, upon at least one mythological account is their founder) and females are traditionally excluded from his cult.[27] Inscriptions suggest, meanwhile, that females did compete in the other Panhellenic festivals of Delphi, Isthmia, and Nemea; as well as important local festivals such as the Dionysia and Panathenaia; there is even an ancient inscription in which a father boasts of his daughter's victories, including one over the boys:

> Hermesianax son of Dionysios, citizen of Kaisarea Tralles as well as of Athens and Delphi, dedicates this to Pythian Apollo on behalf of his daughters who hold the same citizenship: For Tryphosa, who won the Pythian Games when Antigonos and Kleomachidas were *agonothetai*, and the following Isthmian Games when Iouventios Proklos was *agonothetes*, in the stadion, first of the virgins. For Hedea, who won the chariot race in armor at the Isthmian Games when Cornelius Pulcher was *agonothetes*, and the *stadion* at the Nemean Games when Antigonos was *agonothetes* and at Sikyon when Menoitas was *agonothetes*. She also won the *kithara*-singing in the boys' category at the Sebasteia in Athens when Nouios son of Philinos was *agonothetes*. For Dionysia, who won the Isthmian Games when Antigonos was *agonothetes*, and the games of

---

[26] For more on this contrast, see Reid, *Athletics and Philosophy in the Ancient World,* 109-225.
[27] Mouratidis, "Heracles at Olympia," 41-55.

Asklepios at sacred Epidauros when Nikoteles was *agonothetes*, in the *stadion*.[28]

At Olympia there were footraces for girls called the Heraia that took place on the same track but at a different time from the Olympic Games. These races may have had their origin in a footrace to choose a priestess for Hera, whose cult at Olympia seems to predate even that of Zeus (Pausanias: 5.16.2). We also know that there were females in Pythagoras' schools as well as Plato's Academy, that Sparta had a comprehensive program of physical education for girls, and that Plato suggests something similar both in *Republic* and *Laws*. All this is not to suggest that females were treated equally with males in ancient Greek athletics— I would not even make that claim about sports today— rather it is to point out females did participate in athletics in Ancient Greece. I believe furthermore that the virtues females displayed in ancient athletics provoked wonder about their capacity for "masculine" virtue, as evidenced by the myths of the Amazon warriors and the athletic female Atalanta, who was known for outrunning and outwrestling her male suitors.[29]

The Olympics' political heritage when it comes to social discrimination, then, is that presumptive exclusion runs contrary to the logic of properly selecting of worthy victors; in other words, the only way to ensure that the winner is actually the best is to maximize the opportunities to participate in the contest. The discovery that athletic excellence could be trained (and was therefore available to those without the benefit of noble birth) expanded ideas about who might be capable of it. Soon the idea emerged that general human excellence could be trained, and this led to the formation of schools and gymnasia that would train it. The exclusion of individuals from the opportunity to achieve excellence was, in this particular context, an exclusion of

---

[28] SIG #802, 47 CE, Delphi: Translation Miller 2012, #162. For a full account see Scanlon, *Eros and Greek Athletics*, chapters 4-7.

[29] For a fuller discussion, see Reid, "Aristotle's Pentathlete" *Athletics and Philosophy in the Ancient World*, 191-2.

individuals who could potentially bring glory and benefits to the entire community. It was in this way that the logic of Olympic sport worked against discrimination and provided social opportunity for those otherwise marginalized.

The Modern Olympics has its own history of social exclusion; in fact class-based social exclusion was arguably a key motive in the Games' revival. Today, athletes of both genders and all social classes are welcomed at the Games. It is tempting to call this a triumph of sports logic, but the reality is that exclusion persists in the Modern Games. The ancient discovery that athletic excellence can be trained has continued in modern times to motivate the recruitment of athletes from the lower social classes, but it hasn't always resulted in the inclusion of those athletes into the more privileged strata of society. Today we conceptually separate athletic skill from overall human virtue, sometimes to the extent of assuming that talented athletes must be intellectually deficient. The result is that athletes from lower or marginalized classes may earn fame and fortune from playing sports, but they rarely earn acceptance as highly valuable members of society and often they are discouraged from taking advantage of the opportunities, educational and otherwise, that would promote a more well-rounded excellence and better economic opportunities later in life.

Instead, the financial advantages afforded to athletes tend to be concentrated among a very small group of sports and their stars (Olympic examples would include basketball, soccer, and tennis). The success of these heroes encourages many young people to try and use sport as a social and financial ladder, despite the statistical improbability that they will ever receive even adequate compensation as athletes, much less the spectacular salaries of the famous few. This phenomenon produces within sport the same gross economic disparities found in the contemporary globalized economy.[30] These disparities, in turn, work against sport's

---

[30] For more, see Deane Neubauer, "Modern Sport and Olympic Games: The Problematic Complexities Raised by the Dynamics of Globalization," *Journal of Olympic History* 19:1 (March, 2011), 19.

potential to bridge the economic divide by denying even promising athletes in very poor countries the support they need to fulfill their athletic potential. The IOC recognizes this problem and has formed the Olympic Solidarity Commission in an attempt to address it. Olympic Solidarity distributes a share of television revenues to support the development of events, coaching and facilities for athletes in underdeveloped regions, and sponsors "scholarships" for individual athletes to help with training and travel expenses; its 2009-2012 budget is 311 million U.S. dollars.[31] The importance of this organization to the ideal of equal opportunity cannot be overstated. Economic disparity remains an enormous challenge for the Olympic Movement and globalization, which favors those already advantaged, threatens to make the problem worse.

The issue of female participation in the modern Games might seem easy to solve in comparison to economic disparity. But it is, in a sense, more complex, because it pits the value of women's rights against that of respect for cultural diversity. The IOC may have equalized the number of men's and women's events, but even if they reach the loftier goal of an equal number of male and female athletes (45% in 2016),[32] it would not represent true equality of opportunity for women in sport. The *Olympic Charter* declares sports participation to be a human right,[33] but as long as the regulations of sports like Beach Volleyball require females to play in bikinis, women in many countries will forego their right to play that game for cultural reasons.[34] Even when revealing uniforms are not required by rules, they may be necessary for competitive performance and inclusion in a particular sport's culture. Given that the practice of nudity in ancient athletics has been identified as one of the factors that helped sport to level down social classes,

---

[31] Olympic Solidarity, *Where the Action is: 2009-2012 Quadrennial Plan* (Lausanne, IOC: 2009), 10.
[32] IOC, *Factsheet on Women*, 4.
[33] Olympic Charter, 2010, 11
[34] See Charlene Weaving, *"The Burning Flame Within,"* 228-41.

it is unsurprising that uniforms should be a source of self-imposed social exclusion today. On the other hand, ancient athletic nudity shows the extent to which sport was regarded as a place where social and cultural differences were temporarily put aside. Respect for cultural traditions must not be an excuse for failing to address the issue of female participation in sport or society. Participation is a necessary prerequisite for sport to do its work in eroding social difference.

Common Purpose

A third contention against the modern relevance of the ancient Olympic political heritage is that the global challenges of promoting world peace and combating environmental degradation are simply too great to compare with the politics of ancient Greece. To be sure, the internal squabbles of the ancient Hellenes were more localized, but the ability demonstrated by Olympic sport in ancient times to erode discriminatory tendencies and promote mutual respect is hardly irrelevant to the modern Olympic Movement's goals. Indeed, the goals of peace and environmental sustainability are just the kind of common purpose for which the ancient Games proved to be an effective vehicle. A third key aspect of Olympic political heritage is the phenomenon of inspiring groups with diverse interests (city-states or nations) to work together for a common goal.

The original common goal at Olympia, as we have already observed, was religious—specifically the propitiation of gods who were expected to respond with concrete benefits such as bountiful harvests, cure from disease, and victory in war. This is very different from the economy of modern sports, which focuses on ticket sales and television rights. As I have argued elsewhere, however, the continued use of sport as part of social service projects, both by individual athletes who set up and serve charitable foundations, and through the phenomenon of charity sports events, reflects the ancient religious heritage of the Games.[35]

---

[35] See Reid, "Olympic Sacrifice," in this volume.

But the common political purposes served by the Olympic Games are not limited to social services or even to peace. In fact the most famous common purpose attributed to the ancient Olympic Games is the loose military alliance that allowed otherwise rival Greek city-states (including Athens and Sparta) to defeat Xerxes' army in the Persian Wars. Arguably, the Greeks' participation in the Olympics formed the basis for this cooperation, but there was more to it than sport and religion.

The ancient Greek tradition of philosophical dialogue, especially among intellectuals from distant lands, may also be indebted to the Olympic Games. The earliest philosophers came mostly from city-states in Asia Minor who participated in the Olympic Games; it is likely that the Games provided for them an opportunity to present and exchange ideas in the atmosphere of cooperative competition discussed above. Sports metaphors and comparisons between athletic contests and philosophical dialogue are common in ancient Greek philosophy.[36] Plato, perhaps the most athletic of ancient philosophers, is said to have attended the Games regularly as a spectator. By the 4th century BCE Sophists and orators were a fixture at the games and may even have established for themselves a kind of informal competition. In Plato's *Hippias Minor*, the sophist from Elis (a city which oversaw the Olympic Games) describes himself as an Olympic competitor and Socrates compares him with the "athletes of the body" (364a). We have no records of Olympic contests for intellectuals, but there are other forms of success.

Many Olympic speeches stressed Panhellenic unity. The orator Lysias spoke against the tyrant Dionysios in 388 BCE, encouraging all Hellenes to join forces against him. Other rhetoricians, including Gorgias (392 BCE) and Isocrates (380 BCE) gave "Olympic Orations" that stressed Panhellenic unity. In his speech, Gorgias compared the art of rhetoric to Olympic contest, and a statue of him was erected at Olympia, following the tradition

---

[36] For an interpretation of Socratic philosophy as athletic contest see Reid, "Athletic Competition as Socratic Philosophy," 73-77.

for athletic champions. The exchange of ideas at Olympia was as politically important as the exchange of boxing blows; maybe more important. The Games provided the opportunity and means for intellectual communion. Perhaps the philosophers, historians and others travelled to Olympia as part of the official delegations from their cities, perhaps they paid their own way in the hopes of attracting lucrative commissions from the wealthy aristocrats racing horses there. In any case, this open exchange of ideas brought scholars together with politicians, educators, and other government officials in such a way that the complexity of common problems encompassing many diverse perspectives could be hashed out in an atmosphere of peace and mutual respect. The best example is the Panhellenic truce of 481 B.C.E., negotiated at Olympia, which put an end to internal conflicts, at least until the end of the Persian Wars.[37]

Unfortunately political dialogue at recent Olympic Games has been anything but civil and cooperative. The protests and occasionally violent attacks on the Olympic torch in 2008 come to mind immediately. Rather than a spirit of cooperation, there seems to be a standoff between those who uncritically promote the Games and their ideals, and those who view them as a force of unmitigated evil. Interestingly, this reflects today's contrasting attitudes towards globalization: those who see it as progress versus those who see it as a disaster.[38] Due at least partially to the commercial interests of its sponsors, the IOC's reaction to these clashes has been one of avoidance. The 2008 torch route was detoured around protesters (and patiently waiting fans) in San Francisco and the international portions of the torch relay have been discontinued indefinitely. Meanwhile, political speech at the Games is often relegated to protest zones, where it largely goes unheard. The political heritage of the Games calls instead for peaceful dialogue, especially on issues of mutual concern. The

---

[37] Crowther, "The Ancient Olympics and Their Ideals," 21.
[38] A dynamic explained by Neubauer, "Modern Sport," 22-23.

Olympic Movement should not avoid this dialogue for commercial or other reasons; rather it should encourage it.

We observed that the ancient Games were characterized by commitment to a common purpose; it may be difficult to imagine a modern global analogue, but environmental sustainability is a propitious example. In the 1990s the IOC began defining and envisioning its commitment to the environment as a third pillar, alongside sport and education. It developed its own Agenda 21, as part of the United Nations' effort to promote sustainable development. The IOC saw its environmental commitments as a logical outgrowth of Olympism's promotion of "the harmonious development of man,"[39] noting that the environment, like Olympic sport, transcends geographical borders and ideological difference.[40] Sustainability requires a cooperative global effort and the Olympic Movement can take a leadership role. Instead of dedicating the Games to the gods like ancients, or to the glory of sport like the modern, we might dedicate them today to the glory of the Earth and to the health and wellbeing of all its inhabitants. Not only can the Olympic Movement model environmental responsibility, they may sponsor and support peaceful dialogue on the issue during the Games, garnering the World's attention and modeling constructive solutions.

Current Challenges

Reading the Olympic Charter, one might get the impression that the IOC views itself as apolitical or even anti-political. Part of its "Mission and Role" is "to oppose any political or commercial abuse of sport and athletes."[41] IOC members swear an oath to keep free of political influence,[42] National Olympic Committees are

---

[39] J.A. Samaranch, "Foreword," *Olympic Movement's Agenda 21* ed. IOC Sport and Environment Commission (Lausanne: IOC, 1999), 7.

[40] Klaus Topfer, "Foreword," *Olympic Movement's Agenda 21* ed. IOC Sport and Environment Commission (Lausanne: IOC, 1999): 9-10.

[41] Olympic Charter (2010), 15.

[42] Olympic Charter (2010), 31.

instructed to resist political pressure,[43] and political demonstrations are prohibited at Olympic sites.[44] At the same time, the Olympic Movement's goals of peace and human dignity are explicitly political. The difference is that they want these goals promoted through sport rather than government. This vision reflects the political heritage of the ancient Games, which was religious in orientation but nevertheless had profound political effects precisely for the promotion of respectful competition, human potential, and group cooperation.

The modern world is different from the ancient in myriad ways, and the modern Olympic Games are accordingly different from their ancient predecessors. But there is value in coming to understand how the ancient Games functioned politically if the Modern Games are to be an effective political tool. We must remember that the best method of diffusing national rivalry is to be as neutral as possible. Just as Olympia had shrines to a variety of gods, the Olympic Games should include sports and recruit governing members from a variety of cultures and perspectives. Since the Games' ability to combat social discrimination depends on equal opportunity, we need to pay special attention to economic disparity. Finally, since the free exchange of ideas facilitates cooperation in common tasks, th Games should incorporate forums to address such issues as environmental sustainability - with an emphasis on peaceful dialogue among divergent perspectives. The political achievements of the ancient Olympic Games may not have been intentional, but nor were they a matter of luck. The modern Olympic Movement's political success and failure should not be a matter of luck either; it requires, among other things, an understanding and appreciation of the Games' ancient political heritage.

---

[43] Olympic Charter (2010), 62.
[44] Olympic Charter (2007), 98.

21. Olympic Sport and Its Lessons for Peace[1]

To the ancients, an Olympic victory was imagined as a visit from the winged goddess *Nikē*, who swooped down from Olympus to briefly bless the mortal athlete with a divine crown of sacred olive leaves. To us moderns, Olympic victory is more likely to be associated with Nike, the multi-national mega-company, which swoops down from Wall Street to briefly bless the athlete with a fat paycheck and temporary status as a corporate shill. Just as the corporate Nike differs from the goddess after whom it is named, the modern Olympic Games differ in important ways from their ancient Greek ancestor. Nevertheless, the modern Olympic movement should take its ancient inspiration seriously. After all, the ancient festival boasts a nearly uninterrupted millennium-long history, while modern Games already have been stopped twice by war in the relative infancy of their first century. For a movement that proclaims one of its central goals to be peace, that does not seem the most auspicious of beginnings. Do the ancients have any lessons to teach us moderns about the relationship between sport and peace? Or is the Olympic ideal of peace, like the ancient goddess *Nike*, merely a rhetorically convenient marketing tool to be exploited for power and profit?

In what follows, I suggest that we can learn from the ancient association between Olympic Games and peace because that association derives not merely from mythology and rhetoric, but also from particular (and perhaps unexpected) effects of athletic competition itself. I think that Olympic sport *taught* the ancient Hellenes something about peace by obliging them to set aside their conflicts, treat others as equals, and tolerate differences. These aspects of Olympic sport depend partly on cultural particularities from ancient Greece, but they continue to manifest themselves in the structure of modern games. As such, the Olympic Games retain

---

[1] Previously published in *Olympic Truce: Sport as a Platform for Peace*, eds. K. Georgiadis & A. Syrigos (Athens: International Olympic Truce Center, 2009) 25-35, and *Journal of the Philosophy of Sport* 33:2 (2006), 205-13. Reprinted by permission. All rights reserved.

the potential to teach us similar lessons—as long as we are willing to listen. This requires us to do more than recount what our predecessors *did*, it demands that we ask the question *why* they did it, and that we seek common ground between their reasons and ours. The goal of this paper is to discover enlightening intersections in the relationship among ancient Greek culture, Olympic sport, and the philosophical ideal of peace that emerged at the onset of the modern age. It seeks to revive the lessons inherent in the Olympic tradition so they may continue to help us in the struggle for peace.

Olympic Peace: An Ancient Paradox

The ideal of Olympic peace is paradoxical—typical of the Delphic Oracle that is said to have proposed it.[2] What on earth makes anyone think that international peace and good will can be promoted through competition among national teams? Although the *Olympic Charter* states explicitly that the Olympic Games are competitions between athletes and not between countries,[3] there is no denying that the games provide a stage for the expression of international rivalry and conflict, which potentially breeds nationalism and divisiveness. Some would say that the Olympic movement should remove all pretense of promoting peace and admit its status as a sports-entertainment product that profits by manipulating nationalistic emotions and staging mock battles among political foes. As a political tool, the Olympic Games have at best a checkered past. There's no denying that if peace is in fact an Olympic goal, the Games have fallen well short of the mark in both ancient and modern times. Of all the Olympic ideals inherited from the ancients, peace is perhaps the most puzzling.

Ancient Greece itself was hardly a beacon of peace and concord. Their society was at least as warlike as ours, and the Olympic games featured cultural and political rivalries just as bitter as those seen today. Contests between Spartans and Athenians, between mainland Greeks and those hailing from Sicily

---

[2] Pausanias 5.4.5-6

[3] *Olympic Charter* (2004) Rule 6.1.

or Asia Minor, were no doubt as emotionally charged as the 20th century battles between France and Germany, China and Taiwan, or the USA-USSR. Political rivalries certainly compromised contests on occasion in antiquity, as they did in Hungary's bloody water-polo match against the USSR in 1956. And there's no denying that the sanctuary at Olympia was filled with dedications of weapons and armor: thanks to Zeus for success in war.[4] As classicist Nigel Crowther observes, ancient visitors witnessing all those martial dedications would be much more likely to correlate Olympia with war rather than peace.[5]

Nonetheless, the ancient Olympic festival somehow developed an association with peace.[6] The promotion of friendship and unity among the Greeks was explicitly identified as the reason Heracles had founded and Iphitos had revived the Olympic Games.[7] Although such mythology better reflects the wishes of its creators than historical reality, it can be concluded from the existence of these myths that the peace association was at some point taken quite seriously, even if it was not the historical reason for the inauguration of the Games. The historical record suggests

---

[4] A.E. Raubitschek, "The Panhellenic Idea and the Olympic Games," in *The Archaeology of the Olympics,* ed. W. Raschke (Madison: University of Wisconsin Press, 1988), 36. Olympia was not distinctive in this regard, such dedications were normal for sanctuaries dedicated to Zeus. Crowther, "Ancient Olympics," 17, notes that intellectuals such as Plato opposed the dedication of arms taken from Greeks (*Republic* V 496e-470a).

[5] Crowther, "Ancient Olympics," 17.

[6] It may be objected that this ancient idea is importantly different from peace as understood in modern times. When thinkers like Plato praise peace, they are thinking about internal harmony and concord, rather than the absence of war. As we shall see however, the concept of internal concord and international peace come together when one talks about the expansion of communities and especially the concept of a world community or *cosmopolis*.

[7] For the Heracles story, see Pindar *Olympian* 10.30-60, the Iphitos story is repeated by Pausanias at 5.4.5.

that the peace association grew stronger as the games matured. Orators including Gorgias, Lysias, and Isocrates preached Panhellenism to festival crowds, Olympic officials were used as ambassadors of peace, and there is evidence of a court being set up at Olympia to mediate disputes among Greek city-states.[8] Although the ancient Games failed to eradicate war, they tirelessly declared their truce and brought diverse people together to engage in rule-governed, non-violent struggle.[9]

Indeed the Games' ability to promote an atmosphere of friendship and solidarity among otherwise diverse (and often warring) peoples may be their most remarkable (and perhaps unexpected) legacy. The athletic contests at Olympia were primarily intended for the religious purpose of attracting pilgrims and (especially) the attention of the gods. The effects of such gatherings transcended the religious, however, and apparently resulted in feelings of community and solidarity among those gathered. Athletes were supported, rewarded, and rooted on by their particular city-states, but the overall emphasis at Olympia was on everyone's common Hellenicity. As Burkert observes, to go to Olympia was in some sense, to be Greek.[10] Most likely it was the atmosphere and attitudes created by the religious-sports festival that generated the Olympics' association with peace, as well as the pacifist myths about its origins. Notably, our sources for these myths come centuries after the Olympic Games began; Pindar writes around the 5th century BCE and Pausanias writes in the 2nd c. CE. The drive for Hellenic unity was especially strong around the time of the Persian Wars (500-449 BCE). Peaceful reconciliation

---

[8] Crowther, "Ancient Olympics," 19.

[9] Here I am using the term 'violence' to contrast games with war, in which the objective of the activity is to kill or disable one's opponent. Although such ancient sports as boxing and pankration were brutal, and sometimes resulted in death, death was not the intention of the contest and in some cases the dead man was posthumously awarded the victory. Pausanias 8.40.2-5.

[10] Burkert, *Greek Religion*, 130.

was also a popular theme for Olympic orations during the Peloponnesian War (431–404 BCE).

The association between Olympic Games and peace was made explicit in the modern *Olympic Charter.* Its "Fundamental Principles of Olympism," identifies the promotion of "a peaceful society" as one of its primary goals.[11] Further, part of the "Mission and Role of the IOC" is to "to cooperate with the competent public or private organizations and authorities in the endeavor to place sport at the service of humanity and thereby to promote peace.[12] These are vague assertions that leave little guidance by way of method. A clue might be derived, however, from Fundamental Principle #4, which defines "Olympic spirit" in terms of mutual understanding, friendship, solidarity and fair play.[13] Perhaps this is where Olympism and pacifism meet since these qualities are associated not just with the practice of sport but also with the philosophies of peace that emerge in the modern age. A closer look at this relationship will reveal that Olympic-style sport can cultivate peaceful attitudes in three ways: first, by carving out space and time for putting aside conflicts (truce/friendship); second, by treating individuals as equals under the rules of the game (equality/fair play); and third, by tolerating and even celebrating differences (mutual understanding/solidarity). The Olympic Movement's most valuable contribution to peace comes at a grassroots level—the cultivation of peaceful attitudes through the image of its festival and the playing of its games.

Truce & Sanctuary

The first lesson that Olympic Games can teach us about peace is that a time and place has to be set aside for it. Philosophers disagree about whether peace is a natural state for humanity. Thomas Hobbes famously declared mankind's natural state to be one of warring enemies in a world dominated by "scarcity and

---

[11] Olympic Charter (2004), 9.
[12] Olympic Charter (2004), 11.
[13] Olympic Charter (2004), 9.

fear."[14] The Renaissance Christian Erasmus countered that every sort of being has an innate sense of peace and concord.[15] In the ancient Greek tradition, Hesiod declared strife to be the basis of human life itself, but he distinguished the good strife that motivates competition from the bad strife that fosters war.[16] He also hearkened back to a mythical Golden Age (succeeded in Olympic style by Silver and Bronze ages) during which humanity thrived without war.[17] We all seek that Golden Age of peace and thriving, recognizing it as a higher expression of our humanity than the war and enmity. Because such a condition is rarely part of our day-to-day lives, deliberate efforts at peace have to be made. We must intentionally carve out times and places where conflict is set aside in order to achieve this higher purpose. So far, so good, but how on earth did athletic contests become that kind of place?

The initial answer is a religious one. Ancient Greek religious sanctuaries were considered the property of the gods, specifically marked off from the realm of day-to-day life. Sanctuaries hosted sacrificial rituals in which the gods' favor was symbolically exchanged for some kind of gift.[18] The success of such exchanges depended of course on attracting the gods' attention. Perhaps it was for this reason that athletic games were at some point added to the sacrificial ritual at Olympia—such a spectacle would attract gods and mortals alike. Like every other religious ritual, the Olympic Games were separate from worldly concerns and conflict. The Olympic sanctuary was a special place in which diverse peoples, who might otherwise be strangers or even enemies, came together for a common purpose. Athletic space can also be interpreted as a kind of sanctuary, set apart from the everyday. One may view the basketball courts or soccer ground in a turbulent

---

[14] Thomas Hobbes, *Leviathan* (Indianapolis, IA: Library of Liberal Arts, 1958), 107.

[15] Erasmus, "The Complaint of Peace," in *The Essential Erasmus*, trans. J.P. Dolan (New York: Mentor Books, 1963), 178.

[16] Hesiod, *Works and Days*, 11-26.

[17] Hesiod, *Works and Days*, 5.106-201

[18] Mikalson, Ancient Greek Religion, 25.

neighborhood as providing an oasis—a place where quarrels must be suspended, enough at least to make the game possible. Although Olympic sport has lost its religious purpose, it can retain its status as sanctuary. Sport should mark off a time and place where we deliberately put aside Hesiod's bad strife in order to engage the good strife of athletic competition.[19]

The ancient Greeks' ability to compete peacefully, even with their enemies, may have roots even deeper than religion, in venerable Hellenic tradition of *xenia* or hospitality. *Xenia* requires that Greeks welcome the stranger and provide for his basic needs—all before knowing anything about him. It was a kind of unwritten pact among human beings, with obligations for the guest as well as the host, which was believed to be enforced by the same god to whom the Olympic Games were dedicated: Zeus.[20] The tradition of *xenia* shows the importance of overcoming such common human sentiments as fear and hostility in the face of a stranger. Doing this effectively clears out a space where the roots of friendship and brotherhood can take hold. It is a kind of interpersonal truce, the importance of which was not lost on

---

[19] Burkert, *Greek Religion*, 248. To be sure, many fail to acknowledge this separation. Fans and even athletes may attempt to transfer worldly conflicts to the arena. An analysis of these cases is not the purpose of this paper; I will only observe that this is ineffective and even an abuse of sport. Although efforts such as Ping-Pong diplomacy may have some political value, real political conflicts will never be resolved by the results of athletic contests.

[20] *Xenia* is illustrated by the myth of Baucis and Philemon, which recounts the gods Zeus and Hermes, disguised as a travelers, being turned away from house after house before taking refuge with the poorest couple in town. The couple generously shared what little they had and by morning their house was transformed into palace and they never wanted for anything again. See E. Hamilton, *Mythology:* (New York: Warner, 1942) 115-7. *Xenia* is also demonstrated in Homer's *Odyssey*, where the Phaeacians welcome the stranger Odysseus to a feast and friendly athletic games 8.546-7), while the Cyclops and suitors dishonor the unwritten pact and suffer accordingly.

modern thinkers such as Immanuel Kant, who declared "universal hospitality" to be the third definitive article in his plan for perpetual peace among nations. No doubt aware of the ancient Hellenic tradition, Kant understood it to be guaranteed not by gods in the limited space of an Olympic festival, but by the fact that all human beings share common ownership of the earth's surface.[21] The contemporary philosopher Jacques Derrida affirms both the ancient and enlightenment conceptions of hospitality, identifying its importance not just to peace but to ethics. Says Derrida, "ethics is hospitality."[22]

As a Panhellenic event attracting participants from a variety of city-states, the ancient Olympic festival took the religious, athletic, and cultural idea of sanctuary to an "international" level. The vehicle necessary for such a gathering was an official truce, known as *ekecheiria*, which allowed people from all over the Hellenic world to travel safely to Olympia. The Olympic truce did not, as is sometimes claimed, put an end to wars. Its main function was the protection of pilgrims traveling to and from the festival, but even this limited function makes it clear that the communal festival was regarded as *more important* than the worldly conflicts between city-states.[23] The truce shows that festival trumped war; rendering the latter a baser activity (at least in the imagined opinion of the gods). In practice, the large and diverse gatherings at Olympia provided important opportunities social and intellectual interaction. Of course, the religious dimension of the ancient games helped to "enforce" the truce, and of course, it was not fail-safe. In 364 BCE, a battle took place within the sanctuary

---

[21] Immanuel Kant, *Perpetual Peace and Other Essays*, trans. T. Humphrey. (Indianapolis, IA: Hackett, 1983), 358.

[22] J. Derrida, *On Cosmopolitanism and Forgiveness* (London: Routledge, 2001), 17.

[23] Finley & Plecket, *The Olympic Games*, 98. Scholars may be confusing the Olympic truce with the Panhellenic truce of 481 BC, perhaps negotiated at Olympia, which did put an end to internal conflicts, at least until the end of the Persian Wars. See Crowther, "Ancient Olympics," 21.

during the games.[24] But truce violations were notable for their rarity, and the effectiveness and duration of the ancient Games and their truce stands as a practical demonstration of endurance in struggle for peace.[25]

The modern Olympic Truce is even more ambitious than the ancient. Invoked with formal endorsement from the United Nations for all Games since 1993, the truce demands that nations follow the athletes' example and put aside their political differences at least for the duration of the Games.[26] Although the modern truce usually fails its goal of stopping conflicts worldwide, its successes have been remarkable. A brief cease-fire in Bosnia during the Lillehammer Games, for example, allowed an estimated 10,000 children to be vaccinated.[27] More visibly, the Olympic teams of North and South Korea have marched together under one flag during various Opening Ceremonies. Ultimately, the point of truce is one of "opening windows of opportunity for peace."[28] Like the Olympic festival, and ideally like sport itself, truce creates a time and place where conflicts are set aside and culture of peace may have a chance to take root. Just as *xenia* required ancient Hellenes to make space and bring out their best for the stranger, the Olympic games cultivate peace by making a space where we might bring out our best as human beings.

Equality & Fair Play

The second lesson that Olympic sport can teach us about peace is that we must, on some level, recognize one another as equals. This principle may also derive from the religious origins of the Games, since differences among human beings were regarded as insignificant in comparison with our collective inferiority to the gods. A more direct influence was the simple fact that athletic contests consider competitors equal under their rules. Scholars

---

[24] Drees, *Olympia*, 154.
[25] Miller, Ancient Greek Athletics, 225.
[26] Briggs, et. al., *16 Days*, 16.
[27] Briggs et. al., *16 Days*, 29.
[28] Briggs et. al., *16* Days, 19.

have postulated that the function of athletic contests within the ancient Greek religious festival was to select a single "best" winner, who would then be symbolically sacrificed to the god.[29] The tokens of victory explicitly associate athletic victors with the victims of ritual sacrifice.[30] In order to perform such a scientific testing function, games must provide contestants equal opportunity. This athletic equality stood in stark contrast to the highly stratified societies from which most ancient athletes hailed. Some scholars believe that athletic equality may have influenced the development of democracy in ancient Greece. Noting that a free man would subject himself to the public punishment if he violated the rules of the contest, archaeologist Stephen Miller concludes that *isonomia,* or the concept of equality before the law, may be the greatest "creation" of ancient athletics.[31]

In our modern world where international law is already a fledgling reality, the idea that athletic games could be at the root of such a concept may seem strange. But it's hard to name another place where citizens from different communities governed by different laws get together and agree to be guided by one set of rules. Quite simply sport is not possible unless competitors submit to a common set of rules, which defines them as equals. It is worth noting that at time of the first Modern Olympic Games (1896), there weren't standardized international sports rules. Competitors in the triple jump, for example, used contrasting styles since the rules did not specify how the jump should be made.[32] It was in fact the establishment of the Olympic festival that led to the founding of most international sports federations and the subsequent

---

[29] Sansone, *Greek Athletics,* 40 f.

[30] Burkert, *Greek Religion,* 56.

[31] Miller, *Ancient Greek Athletics,* 233. Not only did ancient competitors compete under common rules, recent archaeological evidence suggests that the ancient *hoplitodromos* (race in armor) used standard equipment that was stored at the stadium (33).

[32] K. Georgiadis, Olympic Revival: The Revival of the Olympic Games in Modern Times (Athens: Ekdotike, 2003), 175.

standardization of the rules.³³ It may be objected that this standardization of rules amounts to nothing more than cultural hegemony, an agreement merely forced upon competing parties by stronger authorities. Like the *Pax Romana,* this would be more the imposition of power than the cultivation of peace, but participation in athletic contests is by definition voluntary.³⁴

The fact is that athletic participation levels down social hierarchies. No matter the competitors' social or political status, the rules of the contest treat them as equal to one another and, in a sense, force them to treat each other as "equal under the law." The nudity of ancient athletes may be the most vivid illustration of this principle. As Miller puts it, "Once clothes are stripped off the human figure, it is difficult to distinguish the rich from the poor, the smart from the dumb, the aristocrat from the king or the democrat."³⁵ Perhaps more significant in the social context of the ancient games, competitors faced the possibility of being flogged in public for rules violations. Since flogging was a shameful punishment, normally reserved for slaves, a free and possibly even noble man's willingness to risk such shame is strong evidence of the atypical equality associated with Greek athletics.³⁶

The importance of equality under the law is reflected, among other places, in Immanuel Kant's important 18th century essay *Perpetual Peace.* There, Kant proposes a civil contract among nations, akin to the traditional concept of a social contract, in which individuals give up just enough personal freedom to secure the much greater freedom provided by peace.³⁷ This submission to

---

³³ A. Guttmann, *The Olympics: A History of the Modern Games* (Chicago: University of Illinois Press, 2002), 16.

³⁴ It has been argued that the Olympic Games are biased toward European and North America culture, particularly in their selection of sports. Although limitations on the number and nature of Olympic sports inevitably narrows athlete's choices, it does not eliminate the fact that sports participation is voluntary.

³⁵ Miller, "Naked Democracy," 283.

³⁶ Miller, Ancient Greek Athletics, 233.

³⁷ Kant, Perpetual Peace, 357.

VII. Peace and World Community

common laws is viewed as completely voluntary because it is completely rational. Since the world itself is limited in terms of space, rational nations must secure their freedom by making agreements with others to live together in peace. The nation who refuses such an agreement must be either irrational, or more interested in power than peace. Plato's *Republic* (351b f.) argues likewise that peace within the city must be based on adherence to purely rational laws. Justice is identified with the harmonious function of an individual or a community, and injustice leads inevitably toward discord and civil war; it makes the community an enemy of itself.[38]

Today's athletes may submit to the common rules of sport grudgingly, especially where personal or political differences exist, but they *must* enter the agreement in order to have the chance of victory. That drive for victory on a team level no doubt pushed the racial integration of sport, and is currently pushing female participation in athletics—even where cultural obstacles exist. Says Olympic Scholar Nikolaos Nissiotis, "sports competition transforms human aggressiveness—a biological, essential momentum which expresses the desire to dominate the other—into a means of sociable relations."[39] Sport allows us to express our differences, maybe even our anger, while still respecting our status as equals. Perhaps even more important for the goal of peace, international contests such as those in the Olympic Games provide an educational spectacle in which the world sees diverse people treating each other as equals and voluntarily submitting to common rules. Indeed Olympic competition illustrates the paradoxical ideal of competitive striving within a cooperative

---

[38] Both Kant and Erasmus follow the Greek philosophical tradition of connecting politics with morality. Kant points (famously) to universal human reason as the basis for a common morality (*Perpetual Peace*, 359). In other words, whatever our national, cultural, or even personal differences, we are all subject to moral laws derived from universal human reason.

[39] N. Nissiotis, "The Olympic Movement's Contribution to Peace," in *International Olympic Academy Proceedings* (1985): 59.

framework. So the second lesson about peace Olympic games teach us is to treat one another as equals.

Tolerance & Cosmopolitanism

The lesson of equality through sport leaves us with a paradox. Aren't contests all about finding winners? Aren't they designed to bring inequalities? Within this paradox lies the Olympic Games' third lesson about peace: we must learn to respect our differences. The roots of this lesson lie most probably in the nature of the ancient site itself. Although Olympia was dedicated primarily to Zeus, it hosted altars to an immense variety of gods and heroes. Further, it was a Panhellenic site, serving not just a single city or region, but the diverse panorama of peoples and cultures within the ancient Greek world. Every four years during the Games, the small valley space was packed with a huge variety of visitors. By coming to Olympia for common worship, feasting, and athletic competition, this group created a new community—one more culturally and politically diverse than the communities from which they traveled. A modern might call this Olympic community 'multicultural'; although the ancients had their own word: 'cosmopolitan'. In any case, Olympia and other Panhellenic festivals seem to have helped diverse groups tolerate their differences and identify themselves as "Greek."[40] It's likely that Olympic style sport facilitated this unification.

Engagement in athletic competition with a someone different in any number of ways helps not only to overcome stereotypes and confirm our common humanity, but perhaps more important it can help us to tolerate and even appreciate our differences. Imagine a pair of wrestlers, one Athenian one Spartan, raised from birth to distrust the other. During the close-fought match, however, the stereotypes fade away because the sport requires them to respond

---

[40] Of course the unification of "The Greeks" includes many other factors, not least of which is the story of Troy. There is an historical correlation, however, between the popularity of Panhellenic festivals including Olympia, and the Greeks' victory in the Persian war.

to each other, not as Athenian or Spartan, but as wrestlers. Ideally they might even come to appreciate their differences as wrestlers; perhaps one relies on strength and endurance, the other on speed and technique. As soon as they begin to evaluate one another in terms of their personal qualities, however, they begin to evaluate one another as people do *within* a single community. At this point, the Athenian and the Spartan have not lost their identities as Athenian and Spartan, nor has one absorbed the other into his culture; what has happened is that their idea of community has expanded to include persons and cultures that were previously excluded.

This intellectual community-expansion reflects the ancient concept of cosmopolitanism or world-citizenship. This idea bloomed when the Socratically-inspired philosophy of Greek Stoicism faced the unprecedented racial and religious diversity of the Roman Empire. Both the Emperor Marcus Aurelius and the slave Epictetus embraced the essential unity of all mankind. Stoics viewed humanity as something like a single organism that depends for its health on the well-being of all its parts.[41] The stoic philosophers themselves hailed from every edge of the empire and must have found as much strength in their cultural diversity as philosophical agreement. Their cosmopolitanism did not advocate a withdrawal from particular communities (or even from participating in their communities' wars), rather it posited a higher human community of which each individual is simultaneously a part. The sentiment is echoed by this description of Diogenes of Sinope (who is said to have coined the term 'cosmopolis'):

> He would ridicule good birth and fame and all such distractions, calling them showy ornaments of vice. The only true commonwealth was, he said, that which is as wide as the universe.[42]

---

[41] W. L. Davidson, *The Stoic Creed* (Edinburgh: T. & T. Clark, 1907), 165.
[42] Diogenes Laertius: II/II.19

Stoic cosmopolitanism, like the Olympic father Pierre de Coubertin's sincere internationalism,[43] did not depend on insulation from or imposition of one culture over another, rather it sought to engage different cultures on some sort of common ground. Athletic arenas are one such common ground, the valley of Olympia was another, eventually all of Hellas became a larger common ground, and by the time Kant writes about international peace, the idea has expanded even further. Allowing that nations may have particular borders and interests, Kant argued that all human beings nevertheless share common ownership of the earth's surface. The globe itself is a kind of bordered community in which all human beings are entitled to certain basic rights, which Kant described as "cosmopolitan."[44] It may be daunting to imagine a true world community, but the Modern Olympic Games have been remarkably successful at presenting at least the image of one. Olympic sport continues to emphasize commonalities while celebrating differences. Nissiotis describes the Olympic Games as "a world community beyond any kind of discrimination and hatred."[45] The Olympics best illustrate their cosmopolitanism spirit when the athletes abandon national ranks and enter the closing ceremonies as one world made of many diverse individuals and groups. Olympic sport's third lesson about peace is that we can live with and even respect our differences.

Conclusion

Those who dream and write about ideal societies where peace prevails are frequently accused of uselessly building castles in the sky; but most often they are fully aware that the complete ideal is unrealizable. Throughout his plea for peace, Erasmus laments the warring he finds ubiquitous among mankind—even among professors in the University and monks in the monastery.[46] Saint

---

[43] This term is explained by Morgan, "Cosmopolitanism," 88, based on an interpretation of a variety of Coubertin's texts.
[44] Kant, *Perpetual Peace*, 358-60.
[45] Nissiotis, "The Olympic Movement's Contribution to Peace," 58.
[46] Erasmus, "Complaint of Peace," 182.

Augustine is so frustrated by the problems of worldly conflict, he finally consigns true peace to the afterlife.[47] And Kant ends *Perpetual Peace* with the declaration that making a just and peaceful world is a duty, "though only through an unending process of approximation to it."[48] In philosophy, peace is always an ideal—but one worth striving for. What's remarkable about the Olympics and peace is that the two came to be associated with one another at all. In this paper I have suggested that the connection develops out of certain aspects of Olympic style sport. Although the aspects derive from the particular cultural heritage of the Games, they still endure today. Olympic sport can teach us three lessons about peace: first, that we must deliberately set aside a time and place for it; second that we must recognize others' equality; and third, that we must respect one another's differences within the larger world community. Whatever the Olympic Movement's political ambitions for international peace, the cultivation of harmony and concord among individuals in any size community should be recognized as a valuable and lasting gift contribution to the struggle. As Saint Augustine put it, "Any man who has examined history and human nature will agree with me that there is no such thing as a human heart that does not crave for joy and peace."[49]" Let the Olympic Games be more than an expression of this craving, let them be an instrument of peace—one that provides the opportunity for the peaceful values inherent in sport to offer their lessons in a violent, cynical, and increasingly small world.

---

[47] Augustine, "City of God," in *Medieval Philosophy*, eds. F. Baird & W. Kaufmann, 95-123 (New Jersey: Prentice Hall, 1994) 123.

[48] Kant, *Perpetual Peace*, 386.

[49] Augustine, "City of God," 115.

22. Olympic Sport and Globalization[1]

The ideal expression of harmoniously globalized sport may be the closing ceremony of the Olympic Games. Instead of marching into the stadium as orderly, uniformed regiments lined up behind their countries' flags, the athletes abandon national ranks and burst into the stadium in a colorful, cacophonous, joyful swarm. Gymnasts perch on the shoulders of weightlifters, victors offer an up-close look at their newly won medals, Korean swimmers pose to have their pictures taken with American basketball stars. It is a welcome image of a globalized world, but it wasn't part of the original Olympic plan. Rather it was the suggestion of a local 17 year old named John Ian Wing during the 1956 Melbourne Games. "The march I have in mind is different than the one during the Opening Ceremony and will make these games even greater," stated Wing in a letter to Games' officials. "During the march there will only be 1 NATION. War, politics and nationality will be all forgotten, what more could anybody want, if the whole world could be made as one nation."[2] In fact, the world in 1956 and even athletes' behavior at the Games had been characterized less by harmony and more by simmering political tension and bitter national rivalry. Infamously, a water polo match between Russia and Hungary had to be cancelled because of fighting that tinged the pool water with blood. Sport may seek to promote international harmony, but the reality often falls far short of the ideal.

The relationship between sport and globalization is at once ancient, modern, and futuristic. It derives from the phenomenon of the Ancient Olympic Games, the religious purpose of which had the (probably unintended) effect of pacifying and unifying diverse and often warring tribes in the ancient Mediterranean. It is

---

[1] Originally published in *Introduction to the Philosophy of Sport* (Lanham, MD: Rowman and Littlefield, 2012). Reprinted with permission. All rights reserved.

[2] John Ian Wing, "Letter saved the Games," (National Library of Australia, Papers of Sir Wilfred Kent Hughes, NS 4856/series 19).

replicated in the philosophical underpinnings of the Modern Olympic Games, which were inspired by the ideals of the European enlightenment. And it is futuristic in that international and especially Olympic sport functions as a kind of trailblazer for the political future of a globalized world. The term 'globalization' refers primarily to "fundamental changes in the spatial and temporal contours of social existence."[3] Advances in travel and communication technology have been "shrinking the world" and increasing contact between people despite geographical and cultural distance for some time. Olympic-style sport has long been at the forefront of this process. Increased intercultural contact through trade and shipping even had a hand in the development of the ancient Olympic Games,[4] and developments in telegraph and train technology helped to motivate the first Modern Olympic Games in 1896.[5] In recent years we have experienced an acceleration of the globalization process and, predictably, international sport and the Olympic Games in particular seem to have embraced the phenomenon.

Spectators in every corner of world can experience and discuss sporting events live through television and internet technology. Roughly 70% of the world's population, 4.7 billion viewers in all, watched the 2008 Beijing Olympics on television.[6] Relatively cheap and increasingly quick transportation makes it easier for athletes at almost every level to play with competitors from different cultures and backgrounds. It has also made professional sports an exportable product. America's National Football League plays annually in Europe. The Tour de France routinely starts in foreign countries. Its rival, the Giro d'Italia has

---

[3] William Scheuerman, "Globalization," *The Stanford Encyclopedia of Philosophy* (Summer 2010 Edition), edited by Edward N. Zalta.

[4] Reid, "Sport, Philosophy, and the Quest for Knowledge," 42.

[5] Baron Pierre de Coubertin, quoted in Foundation for the Hellenic World, "The revival of the ancient Olympic Games," *From Ancient Olympia to Athens of 1896*, 2011.

[6] The Nielsen Company, "Beijing Olympics Draw Largest Ever Global Television Audience," *Nielsenwire*, September 8, 2008.

even considered a start in Washington D.C. Formula-One car racing, once a strictly European affair, loads its cars and equipment on planes and flies off to compete at tracks as far flung as Bahrain, India, and Malaysia. Even when leagues don't travel, their athletes do. European Football, American Basketball, and even Japanese Sumo includes athletes from outside the geographical region, often from the other side of the globe. Indeed sport may involve more interaction among culturally diverse people than any other human activity. In that sense, it can teach us something about globalization—but the lesson isn't always positive. What can we learn about globalization from sport and how can sport's values be protected from its dangers?

Globalization: The Reality

For all its potential benefits, globalization brings with it some serious problems, not least of which is its tendency to benefit the wealthy and powerful, who in turn often try to impose their cultural paradigm upon the rest of the world. As far back as 1950, the philosopher Martin Heidegger worried that the removal of distance between people, rather than increasing possibilities for richer interaction, would homogenize our differences into one bland experiential mass.[7] What would the Olympic Games be if the cultural diversity of the athletes was eliminated and the only difference that remained was the color of their uniforms? The philosophical vision behind the Olympic Games is cosmopolitan, based on a vision of global community. Its stated goal is "to place sport at the service of the harmonious development of man, with a view to promoting a peaceful society concerned with the preservation of human dignity."[8]

In practice, however, the global playing field of sport seems tilted toward the West and toward wealth. It is a mechanism well-adapted for reinforcing existing power structures and promulgating the cultural values of the elite. The Olympic

---

[7] Martin Heidegger, *Poetry, Language, Thought*, (New York: Harper & Row, 1971), 166.
[8] Olympic Charter (2010), 11.

Movement, like most of international sport, is dominated by Western cultures, especially North America, Great Britain, and Western Europe. This is seen not only in the selection of host cities (including Beijing, the Summer Games have ventured just three times outside the West), but also in the cultural origin of the Olympic sports and, perhaps most visibly, in the ethnic makeup and political orientation of the IOC itself.

The Olympic Movement is sometimes accused of being Eurocentric despite its universalistic ideals. This is not to say that the organization self-consciously privileges Europe or the West, but rather that its perspective is conditioned by a European heritage and set of assumptions that are not always shared by the rest of the world. Indeed, the *understanding* of what universalism is differs around the world. In the philosophical heritage of Europe, for example, following figures such as Descartes and Kant, there is a one-size-fits-all understanding of universal truth. Even complex ethical concepts are thought reducible to purely rational formulas that can be communicated to and applied by everyone.[9] The philosophical heritage of China and most of Asia, by contrast, tends to think of universal truth as something inexpressible, able to accommodate diverse expressions.[10] The problem is not that the world contains different and sometimes incompatible viewpoints. The problem is failing to acknowledge this. In the current era of globalization, where the wealthier and more powerful countries of North America and Europe tend to dominate economics and politics, it is easy for the West to think of their own heritage and values as the universal standard.

This phenomenon can be especially frustrating as it extends to political ideals. In the West, liberal democracy—in particular the rule of law—is often seen as the only acceptable form of government. Jim Parry observes that Western liberals who insist on individual autonomy (i.e. autonomy-based liberalism) cannot tolerate illiberal cultures (i.e. those who do not allow individual

---

[9] A key example is Kant's categorical imperative.
[10] Reid, "East to Olympia," in this volume.

autonomy). Rights-based liberalism, by contrast, "protects all cultures that provide their members with a decent environment and life chances."[11] Even so, it is hard to know the appropriate limits of tolerance across cultural boundaries. Democracy presupposes feelings of trust, commitment, and belonging that are hard to find at an international level.[12]

At the same time, it can be difficult to sort out how much of one's resistance to foreign politics is merely cultural and how much is moral. Many believe morality itself is conditioned by cultural differences, or that ethics is completely relative. But uncritical acceptance of all cultures (however abhorrent their practices) is not politically responsible. Parry sees it as a kind of concealed ethnocentrism. "It is not true that to respect other cultures is to abstain from criticizing them," he explains. "Rather relativism is a kind of disrespect—failing to apply to others (denying to others) the standards of justification and argument we apply to ourselves."[13] Tolerance of cultural difference, then, is only respectful up to a point. A community with no moral standards is not a community at all. What we need is a community that respects cultural difference while upholding some mutually-acceptable standards of morality.

Sport may provide a model for this insofar as it promotes general principles of justice such as equal opportunity and fair play, while making room for diverse styles of play. But even as individual athletic contests offer level playing fields and common starting lines, equal opportunity is far from reality in the global village. Huge economic disparities between countries and within countries challenge the ideals of distributive justice. National teams are far from equal in terms of facilities, coaching, medical support, even funding for travel. The IOC commission on Olympic Solidarity tries to overcome these international disparities by distributing a portion of the Games' television revenue to the

---

[11] Parry, "Sport and Olympism," 194.
[12] Scheuerman, "Globalization"
[13] Parry, "Sport and Olympism," 197.

National Olympic Committees most in need, but the demand is huge and the resources are limited.[14]

The euphoric spectacle of the Olympic Games should not lull us into thinking that global athletic competition is really fair. The tables that rank countries according to medals won, for example, embody none of the principles of fairness expected in sport. The teams do not have the same number of athletes and they do not compete in all the same events. Olympic medal table rankings, furthermore, correlate more reliably with GDP (an indicator of size and wealth) than any other variable.[15] Countries may proudly outperform their predicted rankings and athletes from relatively small and poor countries like Jamaica may come to dominate competitors from larger and wealthier neighbors—but this neither rectifies nor justifies globalization's tendency to favor those who, to use a popular sports metaphor, were born on third base but thought they hit a triple.

It is also worth remembering, from a cultural point of view, that the traditions and ideals of the West, particularly Europe and the USA, continue to dominate Olympic sport. The image of women in skimpy bikinis playing beach volleyball in a stadium as a mixed crowd of males and females looks on may seem emblematic of a laid-back California attitude toward sports. In many cultures, however, such a spectacle is at best immodest and at worst, grounds for serious punishment. It may be tempting to declare that such cultures repress women, deny human liberty, and need to rise to the standards of the international community. But there is a real risk that such sentiments are ultimately cultural hegemony—the imposition of the values of the dominant class upon all others. Cultural hegemonists, furthermore, need to be careful of what they wish for because the dominance of one particular culture—no matter how rich and valid it is—may cause the demise of other local cultures and of cultural diversity in general. It is hard to imagine *any* single culture being so great that

---

[14] IOC, "Olympic Solidarity Commission," *Olympic.org*, 2011.
[15] Bernard and Busse, "Who Wins the Olympic Games," 413-417.

no other cultures are needed or desired. I really love Italian cuisine, but I would never wish that all other cuisines should disappear, leaving me with only one choice. Just as we value a variety of culinary styles and traditions, we may value variety in other cultural products such as art, music, literature, even sport.

Multiculturalism: The Method

Multiculturalism responds to globalization by appreciating cultural diversity and seeking to preserve it, even while working toward common principles like justice and fairness. Sport provides good examples of this. In World Cup soccer, for example, teams play according to a common set of rules while exhibiting a variety of culturally-specific styles. Aesthetic rather than pragmatic values are often demonstrated in the play of teams from South America. Meanwhile, teams from Northern Europe are expected to play more conservatively and defensively. Part of the beauty of the tournament comes from the diversity of playing styles and it would be a shame if pressure to win dictated a single successful style of play.

Globalization, like sport, carries this risk of homogenization not least because it diminishes the isolation of communities. Words and images from outside a community inevitably arrive inside while words and images from inside a community inevitably make their way outside. The development of social media has accelerated this phenomenon and helped to attract international attention to previously ignored oppression in countries around the world. Sports, however, are also communities in themselves—practice communities—and that means that they can value diversity within their community even as its boundaries remain porous. In other words, the soccer community can value and preserve diverse styles of play even while promoting one common game.

It is important to distinguish between strangeness and difference. Declaring something strange is not just to say that it is different, but it also expresses an emotional reaction of puzzlement or even repulsion. Valuing diversity, by contrast, involves expressing a reaction of acceptance and curiosity toward new and different ways. Within sport this means, first of all, the acceptance of multiple interpretations of a game. Let the South Americans play "beautiful" soccer and North Europeans play conservative soccer, and try to ensure that diverse styles are encouraged by the rules. Let us not call one style of soccer strange—even if it turns out to lead to fewer victories. Let us try to appreciate the different values and objectives that different people bring to the game.

Multiculturalism may also mean temporarily setting aside intercultural debates to make athletic interaction possible. For example, some people regard the Muslim requirement of head coverings for women as a form of unjust oppression. The Iranian women's soccer team was forced to forfeit a qualifying match and give up its chance of competing in the 2012 Olympics because they insisted on wearing headscarves, which go against the international soccer federation's rules.[16] It is certain that the wearing of headscarves is not a violation of human rights and the rule prohibiting them is not fundamental to the game of soccer. Why not make an exception to the rule, or rewrite it in such a way that allows Muslim women to play soccer and observe their religious beliefs? If the motivation for the rule is safety, work to develop a safe headscarf. A multicultural sporting community that values diversity must make an effort to encourage it.

The Olympic Movement values diversity, but it must not interpret its own ideals so narrowly that they become an obstacle. Jim Parry maintains that the *concept* of Olympism, understood at a high level of generality, may admit of diverse interpretations or *conceptions* which bring the concept to life in particular contexts.[17] Multiculturalism in the Olympic Movement must be a concerted effort. Not only should athletes, officials, and IOC members represent a variety of cultural backgrounds and perspectives, the program of sports itself should show more cultural variety. Judo

---

[16] Thomas Erdbrink, "FIFA bans headscarves for Iranian women's soccer team," *The Washington Post,* June 6, 2011.

[17] Parry, "Sport and Olympism," 191.

and Taekwondo are the only two sports on the current Olympic program with a non-western origin, and even they had to be adapted to a Western-style scoring system to be accepted.

New sports are considered for the Olympic program based on such criteria as history and tradition, universality, and popularity. This system seems to set the cart before the horse in multicultural terms since sports tend to become popular and universal *after* they are accepted into the Olympics. Parry suggests a compensatory policy according to which one popular sport from each continent would be included in the official program.[18] This would combat globalization's tendency to homogenize sport while serving the Olympic Movement's cultural education goals. It is a multicultural solution to one of globalization's problems.

Sustainability: The Common Cause

One thing that underpinned the ancient Olympic Games' success at unifying and pacifying diverse Hellenic tribes was the sense that they were working toward a common cause. In their case, the cause was religious. The ancient games were a form of worship designed to propitiate common gods and therefore receive such collective benefits as abundant of harvests and healing from illness. This worthwhile religious purpose inspired a ban on attacking worshippers in transit to the site, known as the *ekecheiria*. In some years, the *ekecheiria* was extended to a temporary suspension of military hostilities.[19] Even when wars continued, however, delegations from the tribes could meet safely at Olympia and for that reason it was a good place to negotiate peace-treaties. In fact all kinds of intellectuals and politicians met and debated common issues at the ancient Olympic Games. Many of the most famous orations dealt precisely with Panhellenic unity and the importance of working together rather than against one another. An Olympic Truce is still called every four years and the United Nations passes a resolution endorsing it, but its success in stopping wars is, at best, limited. The Olympic Games would benefit from a

---

[18] Parry, "Sport and Olympism," 202.
[19] Crowther, "The Ancient Olympics,"11.

common global project akin to the religious cause that united the ancient Greeks. The issue of environmental sustainability seems perfect and, indeed, it has been adopted by the Movement as a third objective alongside sport and culture.

Sustainable development can be defined as a strategy that "meets the needs of the present without compromising the ability of future generations to meet their own needs."[20] Given the global effect of environmental degradation, sustainability requires a global response. Says William Scheuerman, "dogmatic insistence on the sanctity of national sovereignty risks constituting a cynical fig leaf for irresponsible activities whose impact extends well beyond . . . those countries most directly responsible."[21] Common ground among nations, including some agreement about the nature of moral responsibility, must be found if the world is to find an effective solution to its environmental challenges. A system of liberal democracy confined to nation-states is not well placed to deal with this problem. Indeed, continued environmental degradation potentially erodes democracy by undermining its legitimacy and perceived effectiveness.[22] This may seem an issue far removed from sport and Olympism, but after the United Nations, the Olympic Games may provide one of the best forums for international discussion and debate. The IOC's Sport and Environment Commission seeks to make the Olympic Games a model of sustainability,[23] not least by using environmental criteria to select host cities and by subjecting the Games themselves to scrutiny from NGOs and the media.

Of course modeling is a form of education and the practice of sport can itself better model an ideal of sustainability. Observing that the Olympic motto *citius, altius, fortius* (faster, higher, stronger) suggests unlimited growth in human performance,

---

[20] World Commission on Environment and Development, *Our Common Future*, (Oxford: Oxford University Press, 1987), 8.

[21] William Scheuerman, "Globalization."

[22] William Scheuerman, "Globalization."

[23] IOC, "The Sport and Environment Commission," *Olympic.org*, 2009.

despite the limited nature of human bio-motor abilities, Sigmund Loland sees a reflection of the ecological crisis, which is caused by the pursuit of unlimited growth of wealth and population on a planet with limited natural resources.[24] Sports that focus on absolute records, like the 100-meter dash, the 50-meter freestyle swim, or the kilometer time trial in cycling, are the least sustainable because they are the least complex. They try and replicate identical testing conditions and leave pure performance as the only variable. It is no coincidence that these sports also have an increased incidence of drug use and other performance-enhancing techniques. Sports like basketball, where a variety of skills and techniques are demanded are more sustainable.

Loland sees a solution to this problem in increasing the diversity and complexity of less-sustainable sports.[25] For example, why not vary the surface and other external conditions faced by sprinters? Why not test the swimmers not only in pools, but also in open water? Rather than ranking athletes by single record performances, why not keep track of their consistency over a season under different conditions? Rethinking sport would in this way give us a chance not only to improve sustainability but also to address collateral issues such as economic disparity. Why not privilege sports that require less equipment and facilities, eliminating those, such as equestrian sports, accessible only to the wealthy? The guiding principle for reforming sport need not be original. It can be intrinsic sporting values such as fairness; they just need to be rethought globally.

The values required to implement environmental sustainability integrate well with the internal virtues and values of sport. In his foreword to the Olympic Movement's Agenda 21 statement on Sport for Sustainable Development, Klaus Topfer of the United Nations Environment Program (UNEP) points out that the environment is like sport in that it knows no borders, transcends ideological cleavages, and does not recognize artificial

---

[24] Loland, "Record Sports," 130.
[25] Loland, "Record Sports," 138.

distinctions between North and South or East and West, but is one and indivisible.[26] It is not enough to say that sport, like the environment, needs to be open to everyone. Foundational sports principles such as equal opportunity and the level playing field need to be reconceived globally. This entails an effort to overcome social inequities by working to improve the socio-economic condition of the least advantaged.

The first objective of Agenda 21 states that "Sustainable development is only conceivable if accompanied by the satisfaction of those cultural and material needs that are essential for all individuals to live with dignity and play a positive role in the society to which they belong."[27] Likewise Agenda 21 asks sport to battle social exclusion by "promoting sports activities by groups of individuals who are excluded from them for reasons of economic resources, sex, race or caste."[28] Not only is inclusion part of the logic of sport—the most able victor can only be found if all candidates compete—it is fundamental to sustainability, which demands that resources are managed in a way that allows everyone to live with dignity. The Olympic Games' international visibility put it in an ideal position to model sustainable values— values which in any case are characteristic of sport.

Peace: The Goal

The political goal of the Olympic Movement and, ultimately, all international sport is peace. This goal is viewed as an inheritance from the ancient Olympic Games which, as we have already seen, declared an effective truce to protect travelers and played an important role in the unification and internal pacification of the Hellenes. I have argued that this association between the Olympic Games and peace was probably more a by-product of the social dynamics of sport and human contact than a conscious goal of the ancient festival.[29] Specifically, the athletic

---

[26] IOC, *Agenda 21: Sport for Sustainable Development* (Lausanne: 1999).
[27] IOC, *Agenda 21*, 23-4.
[28] IOC, *Agenda 21*, 26-27.
[29] Reid, "Olympic Sport and Its Lessons for Peace," 205.

festival required people to set aside their conflicts, at least for a limited period of time. It required them to treat strangers and rivals as equals—at least with respect to the rules of a particular contest. And it encouraged them to tolerate their differences, at least well enough to inhabit a small river valley at close quarters during the summer heat. In short, the ancient Olympic Games used sport to motivate people to make a special effort to live together in a small space. Insofar as globalization represents the virtual shrinking of social space, the values of Olympic sport may help us to deal with this challenge.

The first element is the demarcation of a common space within which political conflicts are put aside. Such extraordinary spaces are part and parcel of play activities—that is, they are set off from the ordinary workaday world. In ancient Olympia the relevant space was religious, a sanctuary bounded by a wall called the *Altis*. The modern Games use decoration and ceremonies along with the burning of the Olympic flame—to transform whole cities, at least temporarily, into special kinds of places. Anyone who has ever attended an Olympic Games can attest to this change. The important thing, however, is that it is recognized as a place where worldly conflicts are temporarily set aside and a special effort is made to interact both competitively and cooperatively despite human differences. Hopefully we will come to appreciate these differences, or at least to learn from them, as we occupy this intercultural space. Most important, as on the field of sport, we must treat others as equals under the rules no matter our personal feelings of like and dislike.

It must be said that international athletics, as practiced, could do a much better job of engaging athletes, coaches, officials, and even spectators in these peace-promoting aspects of sport. As Bruce Kidd observes, very few athletes are encouraged to take part in the extraordinarily rich opportunities the Olympic Movement provides for cultural education and exchange.[30] Athletes with

---

[30] Bruce Kidd, "Taking the Rhetoric Seriously: Proposals for Olympic Education," *Quest* 48 (1996), 85.

early events routinely skip the opening ceremony and often leave town before the closing ritual. Many refuse to live in the Olympic village, which itself could be better integrated by having athletes of different countries actually room together. Some are even advised by medical staff to avoid shaking hands with competitors for fear of contracting illness.[31]

The obvious obstacle is that many athletes are so focused on their performance that they eschew anything that might interfere with it, no matter how culturally valuable. Ironically, some of the star professional athletes for whom the Olympics is not a primary athletic objective seem to take best advantage of the cultural opportunities of the Games. It is not all the athletes' fault, however. As Kidd points out, "[R]elatively little effort is made to use the common language and experience of Olympic sports as a first step toward helping participants consciously navigate the divides of culture, be they structured by religion, ethnicity, class, or gender."[32] The educational potential of sport, on the international level as well as the local, is not automatic and must be intentionally pursued with at least as much enthusiasm as victory is pursued.

As a solution Kidd proposes an "Olympic Curriculum" focused not just on competition but also education, emphasizing intrinsic sport values like fair play, including competitors from different backgrounds, instructing athletes on the health risks of intensive training, cultivating an awareness of the history, geography, and environmental influence of their sports, and developing the skills of intercultural communication, including foreign language. The curriculum would include community service, and honors and ranks would be based on overall achievement rather than mere athletic performance.[33] Those who find such a transformation of sport implausible, should ask themselves why, given the curricular demands already placed

---

[31] Glen Levy, "British Athletes Told to Avoid Shaking Hands at the Olympics," *Time Newsfeed*. March 6, 2012.
[32] Kidd, "Taking the Rhetoric Seriously," 86.
[33] Kidd, "Taking the Rhetoric Seriously," 89.

upon athletes in universities? The obvious objection is, again, that elite athletes are too focused on performance to take advantage of the intercultural opportunities provided by international sports. This, of course, begs the question of the *purpose* of international sport. If its goal is peace and if its peace-promoting ability depends on intercultural communication, why are we neglecting that in order to achieve ever greater performances? What good does adding another centimeter to the pole vault record really do for society? If it is indeed too much to ask of elite athletes to focus on high-level sport and peace-politics too, perhaps the Olympic Movement is to some degree wasted on them.

A very successful form of peace-promoting education is offered by the International Olympic Academy. This organization, housed in Ancient Olympia, Greece brings together students from all over the world to live and play together. I have participated in the Academy's session for postgraduates on three separate occasions and I can say from experience that the peace-promoting ideals of international sport are ably disseminated there. First of all, the Academy is an extraordinarily beautiful campus set apart from ordinary life at the foot of the ancient Mount Chronion. Students know to put aside their differences while they are there. Roommates often come from countries with a history of conflict and rivalry. Mornings are generally spent in the classroom while afternoons involve various sports activities. Students treat each other as equals in these activities, whatever their differences in academic preparation or language capacity and whatever their level of athletic ability. At the IOA, unlike the Olympic Games, males and females compete together. The evenings are devoted to cultural exchange, with students presenting their home countries' history, traditions, food, and drink. They don't always like one another, but they learn to live together and even appreciate their differences, often forming close bonds that last well beyond their time at the Academy.

The point here is that sport's response to globalization need not be limited to the utopian image of the Olympic closing ceremony. More specific things can be done. Globalization provides not just great opportunities for sport but also serious challenges. A key sport value is equal opportunity, but globalization has historically favored the rich and powerful. Sport needs to be intentional about countering this tendency by providing opportunities for those less fortunate and by including those conventionally excluded. Another key risk of globalization is the loss of diversity, the homogenization of sport and culture more generally. Sports can be understood metaphysically as communities and, as communities, sports are capable of valuing and promoting diversity. Soccer should continue to celebrate different styles of play, and multi-sport festivals like the Olympic Games should promote non-traditional sports. Furthermore cultural differences, such as the wearing of appropriate headscarves by Muslim women should be tolerated so long as it does not interfere with the fundamental principles of sport.

Sport should be a partner and a model for global projects such as sustainable development. This entails less emphasis on records at the narrow end of the sport-selection cone, and more emphasis on inclusive participation at the wide end of the cone. Finally, sport should work toward peace by providing an appropriate space where people can meet as equals, setting aside conflicts, tolerating and maybe even celebrating their differences. Athletes should be encouraged to take advantage of these opportunities for cultural exchange; and at the same time these opportunities should not be limited to athletes. As the example of the International Olympic Academy shows, the international political potential of sport may be best expressed through the play and interaction of non-elite athletes or even non-athletes who nevertheless can take part in the Olympic dream.

Section VIII
Olympism East and West

23. Olympic Virtue between East and West[1]

Despite the rich philosophical heritage of the East, Olympism's connection between athletics and education for character more commonly associated with the West. Classical Eastern philosophy does focus on virtue, but it seems to exclude sport as a means of cultivation since the Confucian is uninterested in victory and the Daoist seeks passivity and avoids contention. A closer look reveals, however, that Eastern conceptions of virtue have much in common with those of Ancient Greece so often linked to Olympic philosophy. Combining research in the history and philosophy of sport with analysis of such texts such as the *Analects* of Kongzi (Confucius), Laozi's *Daodejing*, Plato's *Republic* and Epictetus' *Handbook*, this essay argues that the enlightened practice of Olympic sport has the potential to cultivate qualities common both to *de* and *aretē*.

Some of my deepest thinking about the comparison between Eastern and Western philosophy of sport was inspired by a lazy student's answer on an essay test. Our textbook had distinguished Eastern from Western-style sports according to their underlying philosophies: Eastern sports were associated with passivity, collectivism and spirituality, while Western sports were characterized by aggression, individualism and instrumentalism. The student, who, as usual, hadn't read the book, nevertheless presented a strong argument for the opposite case. He contrasted (what he saw as) the violent, individualistic and self-serving nature of Eastern martial arts such as karate with the Western preference for team sports, such as football, that emphasize cooperation, team spirit and community representation. His answer made me wonder whether the differences between Eastern and Western sports were less fundamental than their stereotypical representations would suggest. And this question made me

---

[1] Originally published as "Athletic Virtue: Between East and West" in *Sport, Ethics and Philosophy* 4.1 (2010): 16:26. Reprinted with permission, all rights reserved.

wonder whether the differences between Eastern and Western philosophy were likewise less profound than commonly thought—especially as they apply to sport. After all, both Daoism and Confucianism focus on virtue, while Classical Greek virtue ethics underpin the "Western" conception of sport.[2]

Could it be that the virtue potentially cultivated by the practice of Olympic sport is valued in Eastern and Western traditions alike? This essay is a comparison of classical Greek and Chinese ideas about virtue applied to the practice of sport, where 'sport' is understood to include Olympic-style athletic games as well as martial arts, dance and related activities such as *t'ai chi* and *chi gong*. I will begin with well-known contrasts between Eastern and Western traditions, specifically the issues of struggle versus effortlessness, external rewards versus internal harmony and individualism versus collectivism. The comparisons will result in a breaking down of contrasts which affirms common ground without homogenizing out important distinctions. We will find not only that Eastern and Western philosophical traditions have much in common that is relevant to sport, but also that they contain important differences, which might be instructive to both sides as we deal with the challenges of globalization.

De vs. Aretē

The first question to be examined is whether the concept of virtue is itself compatible between the traditions. Do the Confucian and Daoist conceptions of *de*, already quite distinct from one another, bear any resemblance to the Classical Greek conception of *aretē*? The historical connection between *aretē* and athletics was derived partly from aristocratic values such as *kalokagathia* (being both beautiful and good) and *aristeia* (a drive to be the best and

---

[2] I place 'Western' in scare quotes because I regard it as controversial that ancient Hellenic philosophy is characteristically Western rather than Eastern. Like the location of Hellas itself, I think it is best represented as 'between East and West'. For a full account of this thesis see Evangeliou, *Hellenic Philosophy*.

outdo all others).³ These ideals grew out of an intensely competitive culture in which authority was routinely challenged (witness Achilles' defiance of Agamemnon in Homer's *Iliad*), and where lucrative prizes were awarded to those who proved their competitive worth. Confucianism and Daoism emerge from an equally warlike age in China, but rather than associating *de* with challenge to authority, they advocate introspection, non-contention, and sometimes social withdrawal. To the extent that *de* is associated with sports and physical movement, it is in reference to personal development or gentlemanly manners in traditional activities such as archery, chariot racing, and court games.

Despite this contrast, however, both *de* and *aretē* turn out to be similar kinds of things. They are both understood as a kind of power in the soul; what the Greeks called *dynamis* and sinologist Arthur Waley translated as "moral force."⁴ In both traditions, this soul-power is connected with the body: for the Chinese because they made no strict distinction between body and soul, and for the Greeks because bodily movement (*kinēsis*) was a product of the soul and therefore a means both to cultivate and to demonstrate the health of one's soul.⁵ Plato, who was himself a competitive wrestler, accordingly makes extensive physical training part of his educational programs for *aretē*, and indeed athletic activities were a common part of young Hellenes' lives.⁶ In Kongzi's milieu, by

---

[3] Homer, *Iliad* 6.208 and 11.784.

[4] On *dynamis* and *areté*, see Plato, *Republic* 477bc, 430b. Waley, *Three Ways of Thought*, 33 says that *de* "is a force or power closely akin to what we call character and contrasted with *li*, 'physical force'."

[5] For the connection between *kinesis* and *psyche*, see Plato *Phaedrus* 245c-246a; *Laws* X 894c; *Sophist* 254d; and Aristotle *De Anima* 413a-b, 432a-433b.

[6] Plato, *Republic* 410b-412a, Plato explains that physical training is used in combination with music and poetry to balance and harmonize the rational and spirited parts of the soul. In particular, gymnastics arouses the spirited part of the soul and keeps a philosopher from becoming too weak and soft. For an analysis see Reid, "Sport as Moral Education in Plato's *Republic*."

contrast, the task was not to challenge leaders' authority, but rather to convince them to act virtuously for the good of the community as a whole. Whereas Greek *aretē* is conceived as a means of overthrowing others, Chinese *de* seems to function more like a magnet that naturally draws others in, obviating the need for force. In response to a question on how to govern people Kongzi says, "What need is there for executions? If you desire goodness, then the common people will be good. The Virtue of a gentleman is like the wind, and the Virtue of a petty person is like the grass—when the wind moves over the grass, the grass is sure to bend" (*Analects* 12.19).[7]

This contrast between competitive and magnetic models of virtue derives more from cultural context than deep conceptual differences. It is fair to say that Eastern and Western traditions alike expect virtue to wield both competitive advantage and inspirational power. What is Plato's depiction of Socrates, if not an attempt to inspire others toward *aretē*? And why did the Chinese assign civil service jobs on the basis of competitive examination if they didn't think virtue could be tested and contested? Likewise, the differences between particular virtues identified as parts of *de* and *aretē* are grounded primarily in cultural rather than conceptual differences.[8] In both traditions virtue is ultimately unified, with the parts working together to make up the whole.[9] In neither Greek nor Chinese philosophy is virtue inherited from ancestors or transferred from teachers to students. Nor does either tradition think that virtue is specific to a particular culture, race, or ethnicity.

---

[7] See also *Analects* 12.17: "To 'govern' [*zheng*] means to be 'correct' [*zheng*]. If you set an example by being correct yourself, who will dare to be incorrect?"

[8] The cardinal Platonic virtues are: *eusébeia* (respect), *andreia* (courage), *sophrosyne* (self-discipline), *dikiaosyne*, (justice), and *sophia* (wisdom); Aristotle has a much longer list. In Confucius we find *ren* (humanity, benevolence), *xiao* (filial piety), *yi* (righteousness), *li* (ritual, propriety) and *chih* (wisdom).

[9] For Plato's unity of the virtues see Penner, "Unity of Virtue." For Confucius, see *Analects* 17.8

Philosophers on both sides of the world conceived of virtue as a perfection of universal human traits, what the Confucian philosopher Mengzi (Mencius) called "sprouts,"—as natural as the four limbs—which are developed through activities requiring discipline and effort. [10] But even if *de* and *aretē* are both forms of psychic power cultivated through training, it does not follow that the desired states of virtue resemble one another, much less that athletics might be a means toward those ends.

Struggle (Agōn) vs. Effortlessness (Wu-wei).

For starters, let us compare the Hellenic view of life as essentially struggle (*agōn*) with the Chinese view of life as essentially peaceful and harmonious. In the former context, virtue is associated with power and courage, while the latter context emphasizes yielding and acceptance. The Chinese idea of *wuwei*, 'non-action' or 'effortlessness', is valued in both Confucian and Daoist traditions, even though they disagree about its exact meaning. Laozi often expresses the ideal specifically as non-contention: "Only do not contend, and you will not go wrong."[11]

---

[10] Mencius 2A6 "From this we can see that if one is without the heart of compassion, one is not a human. If one is without the heart of disdain, one is not a human. If one is without the heart of deference, one is not a human. If one is not without the heart of approval and disapproval, one is not a human. The heart of compassion is the sprout of benevolence. The heart of disdain is the sprout of righteousness. The heart of deference is the sprout of propriety. The heart of approval and disapproval is the sprout of wisdom. People having these four sprouts is like having four limbs. To have these four sprouts is to say of oneself that one is unable to be virtuous is the steal from oneself. To say that one's ruler is unable to be virtuous is to steal from one's ruler. In general, having these four sprouts within oneself, if one knows to fill them all out, it will be like a fire starting up, a spring breaking through! If one can merely fill them out, they will be sufficient to care for all within the Four Seas. If one merely fails to fill them out, they will be insufficient to serve one's parents."

[11] Laozi *Daodejing* #8 trans. Addiss & Lombardo.

But it would be rash to conclude that Laozi's non-contention entails avoidance of athletic games. After all, he associates non-contention with victory.[12] More likely his point is akin to the Stoic mantra of not desiring what one cannot control. As Epictetus says, "you are invincible if you never enter a contest in which victory is not under your control."[13] Both Stoics and Daoists would define victory not in terms of the contest outcome itself, but rather according to factors under their control. Insofar as we use sport to learn about ourselves: our potential, our limitations, our relationships with others and the natural world; we may compete without contending and cultivate virtue as a result.

Wuwei also manifests itself in competition through the familiar martial arts tactic of using opponents' aggression against them. The Daoist lesson is one of strength in yielding. "The accomplished person is not aggressive," says Laozi.[14]

> The most fruitful outcome
> Does not depend on force,
> but succeeds without arrogance
> Without hostility
> Without pride
> Without resistance
> Without violence."[15]

Likewise, the courage (*andreia*) constituent of Hellenic *aretē* is not mere boldness; it is always coupled with self-control or *sōphrosynē*. The important thing in *agōn* is to act in accordance with wisdom, in fact Plato (*Republic* 430b, 442c) describes virtue partly in terms of the spirited part of the soul being able to follow reason's lead. Socrates' historic *retreat* in the battle of Delium can be seen as an example of *wuwei* virtue that saved many lives and so enabled the

---

[12] Laozi *Daodejing* #73"The Way does not contend but is good at victory; Does not speak but is good at responding;Does not call but things come of their own accord. (trans. Ivanhoe)

[13] Epictetus, *Handbook* #19, trans. Carter.

[14] *Daodejing* 68 trans. Addiss & Lombardo.

[15] *Daodejing* 30 trans. Addiss & Lombardo

Athenians to fight another day.[16] Socrates also displays virtuous non-action in response to the immoral government command that he bring Leon of Salamis to trial; the philosopher simply went home (Plato, *Apology* 34b-f). It turns out that yielding and non-action may be as important for Western *agōn* as they are for Eastern harmony.

But what is most familiar to athletes about the concept of *wuwei* is that achieving effortlessness is anything but effortless. Usain Bolt's 100 meter world record in the Beijing Olympics was the picture of effortlessness, but only the most naïve would believe that this state of excellence was achieved without effort. It takes a lot of work to arrive in the place where one can act in complete harmony with nature. We may compare the cultivation of *wuwei* to the acquisition of language: it is learned with difficulty at first but eventually fluency is achieved, and for some, even poetic eloquence at last becomes effortless. By his own account, it took Kongzi seventy years to achieve the state where his "heart's desire" was congruent with propriety.[17]

For Laozi, the endeavor faces backwards towards one's original state of virtue—a kind of de-civilization process that runs counter to conventional ideas of effort and achievement but presents its own challenge nonetheless. Any athlete who has striven to achieve a clear mind by "not thinking" or to achieve self-control by "not attacking" but rather letting the play come to him knows the challenge implied by the concept of *wuwei*. In both Eastern and Western traditions, virtue is a hard-won state within which moral action becomes effortless because one always desires the right thing. In Platonic ethics, this phenomenon is dubbed the denial of *akrasia* or weakness of will. As Zhu Xi remarks in

---

[16] A historical event recounted at *Symposium* 221ab.
[17] *Analects* 2.4 The Master said, "At fifteen I set my mind upon learning; a thirty, I took my place in society; at forty, I became free of doubts; at fifty, I understood Heaven's Mandate (*ming*); at sixty, my ear was attuned; and at seventy, I could follow my heart's desire without overstepping the bounds of propriety."

commenting on *Analects* 14.4, "when [the Good person] sees what is right to do, he simply must do it."[18] Although Olympic sport can hardly claim to teach the kind of moral effortlessness associated with de and *aretē*, it does teach us that patient training can bring us to a state in which the right athletic actions become second-nature.

External Rewards vs. Internal Harmony

Perhaps the intended purposes of *de* and *aretē* are different. At first glance it might seem that Hellenic *aretē* derives its worth from concrete, external rewards such as victory in war, physical beauty, even holiness—traits which translated into practical benefits for and from one's family and city. Indeed the Greek preoccupation with the aesthetics of the athletic body is rarely replicated in Chinese art or poetry, and the practical military benefit of athletic training seems more or less disconnected from Eastern discussions about virtue. Far from associating *de* with practical benefits, both Daoism and Confucianism constantly warn against the desire for praise or profit. Says Laozi, "The worst calamity is the desire to acquire."[19] Kongzi actually distinguishes the virtuous person from the non-virtuous by explaining that the former "understands rightness" while the latter "understands profit."[20] He adds that good people feel at home in goodness whereas others pursue virtue only in the hopes of profiting from it.[21] *De* seems to be an end in itself whereas *aretē* is understood as a means to external rewards.

But again this distinction breaks down under scrutiny. As far back as Homer, the suggestion is made that good athletes are not always good soldiers (*Iliad*, 23.741-752). Gymnasium culture in Greece had a military function, but athletic festivals were primarily religious in nature and the *aretē* associated with athletics

---

[18] Zhu Xi qtd. in Slingerland,113.
[19] *Daodejing* #46, trans. P. Ivanhoe
[20] *Analects* 4.16, trans. Slingerland
[21] *Analects* 4.2, tras. Slingerland

was valued first and foremost for its intrinsic worth.[22] Indeed it was a sign of value and dignity to engage in activities for their own sake (music and philosophy included); the mythical Prometheus' gift of divinity made such activities possible, thereby distinguishing human beings from other animals who act only as a means to survival. Although famous Greek athletes were well compensated (as are, for example, modern artists) it does not follow automatically that external reward is what motivated them.[23] Kongzi' and Laozi's chastisements against fame and acquisitiveness are less an exhortation to poverty than a warning about misplaced motivations. In that sense they reflect Socrates' shaming of the Athenians for their "eagerness to possess as much wealth, reputation, and honors as possible" rather than virtue. He explains that virtue does not come from wealth, but that wealth and "every other good for mankind" comes from virtue (Plato, *Apology* 29de). The primacy of virtue over such external concerns as wealth and fame is common to both Eastern and Western traditions.

Of course the reality in ancient Greece and most of the modern world (East and West) is that Olympic success can lead to increased wealth and social prestige, and as a result it is often undertaken in hopes of those rewards. Similar desires no doubt

---

[22] Indeed, Plato has Socrates compare as "counterparts" proper engagement in philosophic argument with proper participation in physical training at *Republic* 539d. His point here is that those who use argument for the "sport" of defeating others rather than the higher goal of finding truth and leading a virtuous life, are akin to those who practice athletics for *philonikia*, the love of victory, rather than the pursuit of personal excellence or *aretē*. Plato feels that the former are not worthy of the name "philosopher" – are the latter worthy of the name Olympian?

[23] Prizes are inherent in the very idea of athletics, which shares its etymological root with the word for prize: *athlon*. But prizes can take forms other than the monetary and social benefits derided by the philosophers. In any case, participation in prize games is compatible with the motivations advocated in both traditions.

motivated many of Kongzi's followers; today pilgrims actually pray and sacrifice to him at temples, hoping for success in their exams and lucrative careers. The philosophical point is that the best (and statistically more likely) benefits of athletic activities are intrinsic—specifically the cultivation of virtue or character. And, as the Stoic Epictetus explains, pursuing virtue may bring fame and fortune in its wake, but those who pursue fame and fortune we will never achieve virtue (*Handbook*, #1). Says Kongzi, "Do not worry that you are not recognized by others; worry rather that you yourself lack ability."[24] Mengzi (4B18) adds that "gentlemen are ashamed to have their reputation exceed what they genuinely are." And Laozi points out that the virtuous person acts without expectation of reward.[25] In both traditions, virtue turns out to be inward-looking. The harmonious flow of blood (*xue*) and energy (*qi*) valued in the East, resembles the harmonious function of Plato's tripartite soul. And the Hellenes' aesthetic appreciation of the muscular athletic body, derives from their belief that such physical beauty expresses a harmonious and beautiful soul. Both *de* and *aretē* are internal qualities which can be cultivated through physical movement: whether Confucian ritual (*li*),[26] Daoist martial arts,[27] or Hellenic gymnastics. In both Eastern and Western traditions, however, the desire for external reward interferes with the cultivation of virtue.

---

[24] *Analects* 14.30, trans. Slingerland

[25] "To produce without possessing;/To act with no expectation of reward;/To lead without lording over;/Such is enigmatic Virtue!" (Laozi, 51, trans. P. Ivanhoe)

[26] See Brownell, *Training the Body,* 125: "They make use of a principle recognized by Confucius fifteen hundred years before Bourdieu: when structured body movements are assigned symbolic and moral significance, and are repeated often enough, they generate a moral orientation toward the world that is habitual because the body as a mnemonic device serves to reinforce it."

[27] Daoist martial artists use movement to cultivate *qi*, the "floodlike energy" Zhuangzi takes to be source of virtue "Zhaungzi" in Ivanhoe & Van Norden, 365.

Individualism vs. Collectivism

One reason external concerns interfere with virtue in Eastern philosophy is the famed collectivism of that tradition. Says Mengzi(1A1), "if righteousness is put behind and profit is put ahead, one will not be satisfied without grasping from others." Daoism too, despite its occasional advocacy of social withdrawal, associates virtue with benevolence. "Sages do not accumulate," says Laozi. "The more they do for others, the more they have; the more they give to others the more they possess."[28] Echoing Buddhist metaphysics, Zhuangzi goes so far as to eliminate distinctions between oneself and the world, "Heaven and earth were born when I was born;" he says, "the ten thousand things and I among them are but one thing."[29] It is said that, in general, Easterners defer to group interests while Westerners affirm the primacy of the individual. The observation has even been offered as an explanation for the relative absence of sport in Asian history: activities that select and exalt a single winner while causing those defeated to "lose face" in public seem antithetical to the community orientation of the East. At the 2008 Beijing Olympics, Western journalists expressed surprise at Chinese athletes who had the temerity to show individual joy at their victories. But are such displays evidence that modern Chinese have lost touch with their collectivist heritage? And are Western athletes as individualistic as charged?

To be sure, there is an important contrast between the loose collection of independent city-states we now call ancient Greece, and the relatively stable and structured empires of ancient China. The Hellenic model of open competition in athletics, drama, rhetoric, even philosophy has no ancient counterpart in the East. However, the function of athletics in the ancient West was to bring diverse states together and inspire cooperation, most notably in

---

[28] Laozi, 81 trans. P. Ivanhoe
[29] Zhuangzi qtd. in Waley, 9.

the case of the Persian Wars.[30] Furthermore, the success of individual athletes brought glory to their families and their city-states, inspiring a sense of representation and service that overshadowed individual interests. Indeed Western sports have retained this communitarian function, not least by focusing on teamwork even in "individual sports" such as athletics, cycling, or gymnastics. American gymnast Kerri Strugg was lauded for vaulting on an injured leg to help her team win gold at the 1996 Olympic Games. Meanwhile the honor of representing one's club, school, city, state, or country remains a prime motivator for modern athletes—Eastern and Western. We can say that participation in sports helps athletes to appreciate the political tension between individual and community—whichever side of that equation their cultural heritage favors.

Enlightened athletes rightly celebrate their individual achievement, but they should also exhibit the humility that comes from knowing that there is no such thing as *purely* individual achievement. For the ancient Greeks, this humility is reflected in the posture and expression of athletic statues. For modern athletes it is expressed in kind gestures towards their opponents, and the symbolic sharing of victory with their country, team, and sponsors. Again, the experience of sport ought to foster humility, not least because athletes must constantly deal with failure. And humility is foundational to both *de* and *aretē*. Says Laozi, "Because *Dao* never considers itself great, it is able to perfect its greatness."[31] Likewise Socrates' wisdom derives from an awareness of his ignorance (Plato, *Apology* 21d); indeed the Greek term *philosophia* indicates the love of wisdom in contrast to the presumed possession of it. "To know that one does not know is best;" concurs Laozi. "Not to know but to believe that one knows is a disease. Only by seeing this disease as a disease can one be free of it."[32] One

---

[30] For more on the political function of the ancient Olympic Games, see Reid "Olympic Sport and its Lessons for Peace."

[31] *Daodejing*, 34, trans. P. Ivanhoe

[32] *Daodejing* 71, trans. P. Ivanhoe

of the greatest gifts that athletics can give is an opportunity to understand our individual imperfections and to appreciate the brevity of our moments of excellence—excellence that depends upon and should be shared with our communities. The truth is that human experience requires both individual and collectivist perspectives and sport can help us to improve our awareness of both.

Conclusion

So what are the virtues common to *de* and *aretē* cultivated by athletics? The answer is not a list of particular terms such as courage, benevolence, and honesty. Just as different languages carve up the world differently by assigning names to different pieces of it, the important thing is to understand the whole rather than aligning its various parts. Let us focus on what is common to Eastern and Western conceptions of virtue. First, virtue is an excellence of the natural person available to anyone who pursues it. Second, this excellence is cultivated by training, which may involve effort and struggle, but in its maturity virtue approaches effortlessness by achieving harmony between oneself and one's world. Third, although virtue is associated with external wealth and honors; the pursuit of the latter must be guarded against because it interferes with the attainment of the former. Fourth, virtue involves both individual achievement and community engagement, thus reflecting the natural state of humanity.

Participation in Olympic sports, recreationally or competitively, individually or as part of a team—has the potential to cultivate these virtuous qualities as long as it achieves the following: first, the chance to participate must be open to everyone and the rules of the sport must reflect the principle of equal opportunity—this reflects concern with the cultivation of virtue; second, the emphasis should be on process rather than results; both athletic and moral effortlessness come only as the result of patient training; third, learning and personal development should always take precedence over prizes and honors in the enlightened practice of sport; fourth, the athlete should experience both individual and collective responsibility, combining the exuberance appropriate to hard-won achievement with the humility appropriate to a realistic understanding of human interdependence. None of these considerations requires us to change sport itself, or even to downplay cultural distinctions. Rather they ask us to appreciate and emphasize those aspects of sport that provide a common foundation for ethical agreement among cultures. Wushu (Chinese martial arts) should not become more like boxing any more than Laozi should be more like Plato — or even more like Kongzi, for that matter. The goal is not to homogenize sport or philosophy or even conceptions of virtue. The point is to recognize that the enlightened practice of sport has the potential to cultivate aspects of virtue common to East and West, and these common values may provide a foundation for ethical interaction in this rapidly shrinking world.

24. East to Olympia[1]

By going to Beijing in 2008, the Olympic Games may seem to have ventured farther than ever from their cultural origin in ancient Olympia, Greece. This may be viewed as a triumph—but a triumph of what? Some may see it as a victory for Western cultural imperialism; others as a victory for Olympic multiculturalism. But it is best seen as an opportunity for the Eurocentric Olympic Movement to counterbalance its Western values and ideals with those of China and the East,[2] thereby re-centering its philosophy between East and West, and redirecting Olympism back toward its origins in ancient Greece. This process does not require changes to the "Fundamental Principles of Olympism," but rather an expanded understanding of how that language may be understood from diverse cultural perspectives. The effort by Easterners and Westerners alike to "re-center" our understanding of Olympic philosophy will serve the Movement well as it tries to find common ethical and philosophical ground among diverse cultures in this age of globalization.

Olympism's stated goal, "to place sport at the service of the harmonious development of man, with a view to promoting a peaceful society concerned with the preservation of human dignity,"[3] can hardly be called Eurocentric or even Western, but the pursuit of that goal is hampered by interpreting Olympic philosophy exclusively from a modern European perspective. The ancient Hellenic philosophy from which Olympism derives is not a characteristically Western product. Rather, it is a "centrist" perspective that resulted from a need to mediate among diverse Hellenic cultures in the ancient Mediterranean world. This philosophy contained, in its original form, many characteristics

---

[1] Originally published in *Olympika: The International Journal of Olympic Studies*, 19:1 (2010), 59-79. Reprinted in V. Girginov, ed, *Olympic Studies* (Abingdon: Routledge, 2014). Reprinted with permission.

[2] By "Eastern" ideas, I mean those linked specifically to Laozi and Confucius, which had a seminal influence throughout the region.

[3] Olympic Charter (2007), 11.

now associated with the East.⁴ By examining the language of Olympism through the divergent lenses of modern European, ancient Chinese, and ancient Hellenic ideas, I hope to recast Olympic philosophy in a new and ecumenical light. This more flexible and cosmopolitan understanding of Olympism not only better reflects the Movement's ancient Hellenic heritage, but also better serves its current multicultural goals. In honor of the Olympic Games' first visit to China, let us take this opportunity to move Olympic ideology East toward Olympia.

Philosophy: The Way is not the only way

"Olympism is a philosophy of life." So begins the Olympic Charter's statement of fundamental principles.⁵ In the attempt to consider Olympic philosophy from both Eastern and Western perspectives, begin with the meaning of philosophy itself. What does it mean to have a "philosophy of life"? Should everyone in the Olympic Movement have the same philosophy of life? Can philosophy transcend cultural differences?

Rene Descartes, the "father" of modern Western philosophy, thought of himself as a "citizen of the world"⁶ and regarded his work as culturally transcendent because it used what he thought were the culturally unbiased tools of reason and logic to uncover universally-valid truths. For him, "the power of judging well and distinguishing true from false—which we properly call 'good sense' or 'reason'—is naturally equal in all men."⁷ Despite the gender exclusion implied by his language, he seems at least to have meant that reason was universal across cultures. Descartes' method, which he called *scientia,* was to reject everything he previously believed because it might be prejudiced by unreliable sense-data, and then to rebuild knowledge by solely rational means from the cornerstone of one logically irrefutable truth.

---

⁴ See C. Evangeliou, *Hellenic Philosophy.*

⁵ Olympic Charter (2007), 11.

⁶ In his early writings, Descartes used the pseudonym "Polybius, citizen of the world." Descartes, *Philosophical Writings,* vol. I, 2 n.1.

⁷ Descartes, "Discourse on Method," *Philosophical Writings,* 111.

Because modern Western philosophy traditionally viewed its project as objective and universal, it tended to regard its conclusions as correct, certain, and paradigmatic examples for all to follow. Conflicting theories would be methodically tested according to rational standards in a competitive "marketplace of ideas" and the last one standing would be the truth—or at least the closest thing to truth that we can muster. From the perspective of modern Western philosophy, then, Olympism articulates a monolithic truth to be understood in only one correct way through the universal tool of reason. But is pure rationality the only way to think about Olympic philosophy?

In the Eastern philosophical tradition, truth need not have one exclusive expression. In fact, the attempt to nail down certainty by articulating or "naming" things is believed to lead away from the truth. It would seem from the Eastern perspective that truth itself is intrinsically mysterious; hence the opening of the *Daodejing*,

> A Way that can be followed is not a constant Way.
> A name that can be named is not a constant name.
> Nameless, it is the beginning of Heaven and earth;
> Named, it is the mother of the myriad creatures
> And so,
> Always eliminate desires in order to observe its mysteries;
> Always have desires in order to observe its manifestations.
> These two come forth in unity but diverge in name,
> Their unity is known as an enigma.
> Within this enigma is yet a deeper enigma.
> The gate of all mysteries.[8]

It is often pointed out that Laozi's *Daodejing* is the text most translated into English from Chinese. It is arguably the most

---

[8] Laozi, "Daodejing" 1.1., trans. P. Ivanhoe in *Readings in Classical Chinese Philosophy*. All quotations from the *Daodejing* are from this source unless otherwise indicated.

famous and influential work in Asian philosophy, but the best explanation for its great number of translations is more likely the fact that the original Chinese is so richly ambiguous that it accommodates an enormous variety of interpretations.[9] From the Western perspective, truth can be reliably analyzed and clarified without variation, but from the Eastern perspective, dissected truth risks losing its veracity.

Much of ancient Chinese philosophy takes the form of poetry, parable, or aphorism rather than exposition. The traditional method of study was to take a bit of text and discuss its various meanings in a small group. All interpretations were not equal; the Master had authority, and some understandings were deemed better than others. Authoritative commentaries are still used to navigate the texts. But the object of traditional Chinese philosophy was not to win the argument, or even to articulate a universally valid interpretation; divergent understandings of a common text were accepted (within limits) and even encouraged. Consider the later Chinese thinker Zhuangzi's hypothesis:

> Suppose I am arguing with you, and you get the better of me. Does the fact that I am not a match for you mean that you are really right and I am really wrong? Or if I get the better of you, does the fact that you are not a match for me mean that I am really right and you are really wrong? Must one of us necessarily be right and the other wrong, or may we not both be right or both be wrong?"[10]

Unlike the zero-sum game of Western philosophy, Eastern thought allows for multiple understandings of a single truth to be correct.

Given the multicultural ambitions of the modern Olympic movement, a philosophical model that accommodates diverse interpretations without collapsing to relativism may be attractive

---

[9] Sarah Allan, "Introduction" in Lao-Tzu, *Tao Te Ching* trans. D.C. Lau (New York: Everyman, 1994), xxi.

[10] Zhangzui qtd. in Waley, *Three Ways of Thought in Ancient China* (Stanford: Stanford U.P., 1939), 10.

indeed.¹¹ The Olympic Movement is expected to serve common goals and values in this age of globalization, but at the same time it seeks to affirm and celebrate cultural diversity. Accordingly, its philosophy must establish common ground without demanding a perfectly uniform articulation. This sort of philosophical model would better reflect Olympism's ancient Hellenic heritage (which also communicated ideas through such ambiguous media as poetry, parable, and aphorism). Laozi's resistance to "naming" the Dao and his characterization of it as "enigma" and the "gate of mysteries," reflect the foundational principles of Hellenic philosophy: uncertainty and wonder.¹² The paradigmatic Hellenic philosopher, Socrates, claimed that his wisdom was simply awareness of his ignorance, expressing an attitude that goes back at least as far as Pythagoras and gives the Greek word '*philosōphia*' its meaning.¹³ Philosophy means "love of learning," and in its ancient expression reflects a disposition or spirit rather than a crusade for universal truths.¹⁴

The emphasis in the ancient Chinese and Hellenic traditions is upon process and dispositions rather than results. Socrates did not articulate universal truths, and he did not write at all. Plato's Socratic dialogues aim to show readers their ignorance rather than to communicate knowledge. At *Apology* 23b, Apollo's oracular proclamation that no one is wiser than Socrates is interpreted by the philosopher to mean that "the wisest of you men is the one who realizes, like Socrates, that in respect of wisdom he is really

---

¹¹ Parry, "Sport and Olympism," 192, says Olympic values "articulated at a high level of generality, will admit of a wide range of interpretation, but they nevertheless provide a framework that can be agreed on by social groups with very differing commitments."

¹² See C. Evangeliou, "Philosophy, Human Wonder and Hellenic *Logos*," *Skepsis* II (1991), p. 29-41.

¹³ Socrates' statement is at *Apology* 23b. The story about Pythagoras comes from Diogenes Laertius, 1.12.

¹⁴ The origin of such a crusade for universal truth may be traced back to early Christianity See Evangeliou, *Hellenic Philosophy*, 64-74.

worthless." This Hellenic spirit fits perfectly well with Laozi's description of the Daoist sage in *Daodejing* 71:

> To know that one does not know is best;
> Not to know but to believe that one knows is a disease.
> Only by seeing this as a disease can one be free of it.
> Sages are free of this disease;
> Because they see this as a disease, they are free of it.

Likewise Confucius identifies "love of learning" as his own characteristic virtue.[15] "Love of learning" is the disposition that prevents such important qualities as trustworthiness from becoming vices—in this case "harmful rigidity."[16] Furthermore, it is a virtue that promotes engagement with others. As Confucius says, "Do I regard myself as a possessor of wisdom? Far from it. But if even a simple peasant comes in all sincerity and asks me a question, I am ready to thrash the matter out, with all its pros and cons, to the very end."[17] Desire for learning based on awareness of one's ignorance is common to Eastern and Hellenic philosophy and crucial to an Olympic attitude of welcoming diverse ideas.

The Eastern emphasis on disposition and process rather than results not only serves philosophical projects, but also athletic ones. Modern Olympic sport has suffered from an obsession with quantifiable results that often leaves the values of Olympism behind. Success at the Olympic Games should not be defined narrowly in terms of medals and records, but rather the cultivation of virtues and ideals, such as the "Olympic Spirit…of friendship, solidarity, and fair play."[18] Confucius identified ritual as the primary means for cultivating appropriate dispositions and the

---

[15] Confucius, *Analects* 5.28: "In any village of ten households there are surely those who are as dutiful or trustworthy as I am, but there is no-one who matches my love of learning."

[16] Confucius, *Analects* 17.8 "Loving Goodness without balancing it with a love for learning will result in the vice of foolishness"

[17] Confucius, *Analects*, trans. A. Waley 9.7. Socrates expresses a similar willingness to discuss with anyone.

[18] Olympic Charter (2007) 11.

Olympic Games are already rich in meaningful rituals, such as the athletes' and officials' oaths, the lighting of the flame, or even the informal tradition of mixing different nationalities together in the closing ceremony. More important, emphasis on process rather than results allows for multiple interpretations of success.[19] It is this elasticity that serves as the first key distinction between analytic Western philosophy and traditional Eastern and Hellenic philosophy. Confucius' declaration that "The [sage] is true, but not rigidly trustworthy" may seem lax at first glance to Westerners.[20] Nevertheless, it better reflects the humility characteristic of Olympism's ancient heritage and better serves the Olympic movement's modern multicultural goals.

Metaphysics: The Parts and The Whole

After stating that "Olympism is a philosophy of life," the first fundamental principle describes its vision of that life as one "exalting and combining in a balanced whole the qualities of body, will and mind."[21] From the Eastern perspective, the emphasis in

---

[19] This is especially important since the medal count is so closely linked to GDP that most countries cannot hope for conventional success. Says Waley, *Three Ways of Thought*, 36: "Success is a theme seldom dealt with in the *Analects*; for it is well known that the Way 'does not prevail in the world,' and the merits of the true *chün-tzu* are not such as the world is likely to recognize or reward."

[20] Confucius, *Analects* 15.37, see also 19.11: "As long as one does not transgress the bounds when it comes to important Virtues, it is permissible to cross the line here and there when it comes to minor virtues.'" Mencius 4.17 illustrates with this example: "Chunyu Kun said, 'That men and women should not touch in handing something to one another—is that the ritual?' /Mengzi said, 'It is the ritual.'/Chunyu Kun said, 'If your sister-in-law were drowning, would you pull her out with your hand?'/ Mengzi said, 'To not pull your sister-in-law out when she is drowning is to be a beast. That men and women should not touch in handing something to one another is the ritual, but if your sister-in-law is drowning, to pull her out with your hand is discretion."

[21] Olympic Charter (2007), 11.

this statement rests squarely on the phrase "balanced whole." As reflected in *yin-yang*, the best-known symbol of Chinese thought, existence is perceived inclusively as a harmonious collection of complementary opposites—the emphasis is on the whole and not on the parts. The Western analytical tradition (just as its name suggests) focuses on analyzing, or to use Descartes' locution, "dividing up into the smallest possible parts."[22] Hence Westerners tend to conceive of humanity in terms of individual persons composed of separate minds and bodies, or, as specified in the first fundamental principle of Olympism: "body, will, and mind." [23] Although Eastern and Western metaphysics do not necessarily contradict one another, they approach the study from deeply contrasting perspectives. The more holistic Eastern understanding of reality might serve the Olympic Movement better than the analytical Western approach has.

The most relevant example of Western analytic attitudes challenging the spirit of Olympism is indeed the view of persons as separate bodies and minds. This view is not uncommon, it is found even among the ancient Hellenes, but modern Western philosophy's epistemological ranking of mind over body hinders the Olympic cause. Descartes' search for an irrefutable cornerstone upon which to build certain knowledge yielded the famous statement, "I think, therefore I exist."[24] Since it is logically impossible to think without at the same time existing, Descartes

---

[22] Descartes, "Rules for the Direction of the Mind" #13, in Cottingham, Stoothoff, and Murdoch, eds., *Philosophical Writings*, vol. I, 51.
[23] The addition of "will" probably reflects contemporary ethical discussions about human will as the seat of moral responsibility.
[24] Descartes, "Second Meditation" 25, in *Philosophical Writings*, vol. II, 17. "I think therefore I exist" is a paraphrase of Descartes' main point in the Second Meditation, not an exact quotation. While giving a series of lectures in Beijing, I asked the class whether anyone had heard of Descartes. A Chinese student raised her hand and said, "We think therefore we exist." I was delighted both that she could quote Descartes, and that she had added an Eastern spin by replacing his "I" with a collective "we."

took the act of thinking, and therefore his mind, to be the one most certain aspect of his existence—infinitely more certain than ideas about his body, which inevitably depended upon unreliable senses. Our bodies might be figments of our imaginations, existing as in a dream. But even if his entire existence is a dream, it would still be true that Descartes was thinking when he had this idea.

So modern Western philosophy tended to view the mind and its characteristic act of thinking as really distinct from—and more important than—the body, other persons, and nature itself. And sport, associated with the body, suffered accordingly in terms of importance and worth. Olympism's attempt to "exalt" sport by combining body with will and mind may be a reaction to this hierarchy. The attitude persists, however, that athletes are seen as less valuable to society than intellectuals. Professional athletes receive high salaries because they are regarded as entertainers, but they are not considered essential to the community as educators, engineers, and economists are. Meanwhile, the Olympic Games' moral and political ideals remain disassociated from (and somehow subordinated to) the prowess of its athletes. Even the Movement occasionally downplays its educational and political ambitions, describing itself simply as a sports festival. Dividing things into parts seems an inevitable prelude to ranking those parts according to value. The Western ranking of mind over body has caused sport to be taken less seriously by outsiders, and even to take itself less seriously as a socially valuable activity.

Eastern thought does not overturn this hierarchy; neither ancient nor modern China grants athletes much prestige. But the reason is not a separation of mind and body, nor a separation of the physical from the spiritual. What Eastern philosophy offers is a holistic picture of the human being that emphasizes internal harmony over external muscularity. Westerners tend to think of the body structurally, in terms of flesh and bones, muscles and levers, whereas Easterners focus on the internal flow of blood *xue* and energy, *qi*.[25] Westerners tend to associate thought with the

---

[25] Akio Inoue, "Critique of Modern Olympism," 165.

VIII. Olympism East and West

brain, while the ancient Chinese located thought in the middle of a body, associating it with the "heart-mind" and sensations in the belly.[26] In philosophical terms, the root or seed of virtue (*de*), intimately connected with the Way (*Dao*), resides within and is cultivated partly through physical movement. Confucians perform ritual (*li*) in order to "remember" the *Dao*,[27] while Daoist martial artists use movement to cultivate *qi*, the "floodlike energy" Zhuangzi takes to be the source of virtue.[28]

Ancient Hellenic philosophy generally shares the Western distinction between the spiritual mind or soul (the word *psychē* designates both), and a less important material body. What is different is that ancient Hellenes thought of bodily movement as a product of the *psychē* (mind/soul),[29] and in Plato's case at least, sought to train the *psychē* for virtue—as the Chinese did—partly through bodily movement. In the *Republic*, an educational program in gymnastics is established "chiefly for the sake of the soul" (410bc) and athletic contests are used to help determine worthiness for advanced study.[30] The related Platonic doctrine that the knowledge sufficient for virtue is "recollected" rather than acquired also reflects Chinese holism. By emphasizing a strong metaphysical connection between mind and body, Olympism can

---

[26] See Waley, *Three Ways of Thought*, 44.

[27] Brownell, *Training the Body for China*, 125: "They make use of a principle recognized by Confucius fifteen hundred years before Bourdieu: when structured body movements are assigned symbolic and moral significance, and are repeated often enough, they generate a moral orientation toward the world that is habitual because the body as a mnemonic device serves to reinforce it."

[28] "Zhaungzi" in Ivanhoe and Norden, eds., *Readings in Classical Chinese Philosophy*, 365. All quotations from the Zhuaungzi are from this source unless otherwise indicated.

[29] For Homer, the *psychē* was life itself and the word for body, *soma*, signified a corpse—a body lacking in movement because its *psychē* had escaped it at death. See B. Snell, *The Discovery of the Mind in Greek Philosophy and Literature* (New York: Dover, 1982), 8-22.

[30] See Reid, "Sport and Moral Education in Plato's *Republic*," 160-175.

downplay the Western tendency toward analysis and hierarchy in favor of the Eastern tendency toward combination and harmony. In this way it may achieve the "balanced whole" that best reflects its Hellenic heritage and serves Olympic goals.

Ethics: Rules and Virtue

The second sentence of the first fundamental principle of Olympism explains its ethical vision: "Blending sport with culture and education, Olympism seeks to create a way of life based on the joy of effort, the educational value of good example and respect for universal fundamental ethical principles."[31] From the Western point of view, the key phrase here is "universal fundamental ethical principles." The discovery and articulation of such principles was the focus of modern (especially 19th century) European ethical philosophy. Immanuel Kant's categorical imperative, by definition a statement that articulates a universal obligation, is an excellent example. In its first formulation Kant's categorical imperative was expressed as a rule: "Act only according to the maxim whereby you can at the same time will that it should become a universal law."[32] Kant took his imperative to be infallible, unavoidable and applicable to all humanity because it was derived from the goodness of the will and ultimately from reason.[33] In effect, it was an attempt to raise individuals above personal feelings and particular concerns that could not be justified in a universal (and hence ethical) way.

As a theory, Kant's universal rationalism fits well with Olympic ideology. The vision of world peace seems to demand the articulation of principles and implementation of rules that transcend cultural differences by deriving their authority from reason. In practice, however, unbiased application of any rule is difficult. For example, Kant made a strong theoretical case that

---

[31] Olympic Charter (2007), 11.
[32] Kant, *Grounding for the Metaphysics of Morals*, 421.
[33] Kant, *Grounding for the Metaphysics of Morals*, 411: "principles should be derived from the universal concept of a rational being in general, since moral laws should hold for every rational being."

lying could never be justified on his system, but his defense of telling the truth to a murderer about the location of a potential victim was unconvincing even to the most sympathetic.[34] Nevertheless, a typical Western interpretation of Olympism is that there are universal fundamental ethical principles such as fairness, which can be expressed in concrete rules such as the common starting line. Just as Descartes began from his *cogito*,[35] Western ethical thought tries to begin with an irrefutable ethical principle and then apply it to individual cases by developing specific rules.

The danger is when those in power impose their paradigm upon the "uncivilized" by punishing or excluding those who don't follow the rules. Arguably the very founding of the IOC was the invention of a bureaucracy to exemplify and enforce these universal principles. Conveniently it was an aristocratic bureaucracy who could back up their principles with worldly power. Inconveniently, however, the group tended to confuse the values of their particular culture and social class with the universal principles they were supposed to be promoting. Consistent with the Western spirit of modernism and colonialism, the wealthy Europeans at the IOC interpreted Olympism as a civilized ideology to be disseminated for the benefit of a largely uncivilized world. The "educational value of a good example" would be understood here as setting up a paradigm of European aristocracy to which youth around the world would aspire to conform.

A specific example of Western philosophical universalism collapsing into social imperialism is the sad history of Olympic amateurism. The worthy idea that sports participation should be voluntary and intrinsically rewarding was instantiated into increasingly complex sets of rules that had the effect of excluding all but the wealthy or well-connected. The virtuous ideal of autonomous athletes playing for the love of the game devolved

---

[34] Kant, *Grounding for the Metaphysics of Morals*," 63-7.

[35] *Cogito* is shorthand for "I think, therefore I am" or in Latin, "*cogito ergo sum.*" Descartes identified this statement as the one irrefutable thing he could claim to know with certainty.

into a rule-culture that rewarded those who found loopholes and financially exploited those who did not. The phenomenon of "shamateurism" is a legacy of Western ethics that might have been foreseen by Eastern philosophy. Says Laozi (*Daodejing* 57),

> The more prohibitions and rules,
> The poorer people become…
> The more elaborate the laws,
> The more they commit crimes.

Confucius (*Analects* 4.11) agrees that those lacking virtue respond to legislation by thinking only about exemptions. Excessive rules and regulations, like those that enforced the amateur Olympic code, inspire the search for loopholes and exceptions rather than aspiration toward whatever noble spirit inspires them.

The traditional Eastern focus on virtue rather than rules in ethics may better serve Olympic ideals, not least because it concentrates on personal perfection rather than the correction and control of others.[36] Virtue (*de*) is understood as a kind of "moral force" that is contrasted favorably with physical (and especially martial) force. The seeds or "sprouts" of virtue are found naturally in every human being; the Confucian philosopher Mencius compares having them to having the four limbs (2A6). In keeping with the agricultural metaphor, virtue is cultivated within individuals rather than taught or transmitted from outside. Reflecting Olympism's "educational value of a good example," Confucius says one can always "find a teacher" either by emulating good people, or being reminded by bad people "of what needs to be changed in myself" (*Analects* 7.22)[37] Because the

---

[36] The exception that proves the rule of ancient Chinese philosophy's focus on virtue is a tradition called "Legalism" which focuses precisely on law and punishment. See A. Waley, *Three Ways of Thought*, 152-196.

[37] Confucius. See also *Analects* 4.17: "When you see someone who is worthy, concentrate on becoming their equal; when you see someone who is unworthy, use this as an opportunity to look within yourself."

"teacher" here is not an external authority, and the lesson learned is not a fixed formula, the Eastern virtue ethics model evades some of the pitfalls of modern Western ethics. The ethical "principle" of virtue (*de*), *is* universal, but it cannot be articulated as a formula or enforced like a code. The common ethical denominator is simply our humanity.

An ethical theory focused on virtue rather than rules also promotes freedom both from material temptation and from the approval of others. In this way it reflects the Hellenic ethical tradition embodied in Socrates' chastisement of the Athenians for their "eagerness to possess as much wealth, reputation, and honors as possible, while you do not care for nor give thought to wisdom, or truth, or the best possible state of your soul" (Plato, *Apology*, 29d). Socrates believed that the cultivation of virtue demands liberation from merely social concerns. As the Stoic Epictetus, an admirer of Socrates, warned, if we concentrate on virtue we may also achieve wealth and social status, but if we concentrate on the latter, we will never achieve the former (*Handbook*, #1). Confucius concurs: "[A sage] does not grieve that people do not recognize his merits; he grieves at his own incapacities"[38]

> To produce without possessing;
> To act with no expectation of reward;
> To lead without lording over;
> Such is Enigmatic Virtue![39]

---

[38] Confucius *Analects* 14.32 (Waley trans.) See also *Analects* 1.1, "To remain unsoured even though one's merits are unrecognized by others, is that not after all what is expected of a gentleman?" *Analects* 1.16: "The Master said, (the good man) does not grieve that other people do not recognize his merits. His only anxiety is lest he should fail to recognize theirs." and 15.18: "The Master said, A gentleman is distressed by his own lack of capacity; he is never distressed at the failure of others to recognize his merits"

[39] Laozi, *Daodejing*, 46, 10 (trans. P. Ivanhoe). The "desire to acquire" may be compared to the Hellenic idea of greed or *pleonexia*.

A philosophy focused on virtuous ideals (to which the IOC itself must live up to in its actions) will be more effective and more culturally transcendent than the institution of increasingly complex rules and regulations.

Both the ancient Chinese and Hellenic traditions acknowledge that virtue is hard to achieve. Says Confucius, "Goodness cannot be obtained until what is difficult has been duly done" (*Analects* 6.20). In ancient Greek thought, the path to virtue is described as arduous and uphill. Plato quotes Hesiod:

> Vice in abundance is easy to get
> The road is smooth and begins beside you,
> But the gods have put sweat between us and virtue.[40]

The process is aptly compared to athletic training. Once a state of excellence is attained, good actions flow effortlessly from it—not unlike an athlete in the "zone" who acts without deliberation and can do no wrong. Plato thought that a virtuous person could not help but act rightly.[41] Confucius identifies his highest level of philosophical development as a state in which his "heart's desire" harmonizes perfectly with propriety.[42] The Daoists practically equated this state of effortlessness (*wu-wei*) with virtue itself. Sometimes translated "inaction" or "passivity," *wu-wei* is nevertheless a state of strength. Like virtue itself, it is flexible and responsive to change—a principle that might well be adapted to serve the modern Olympic Movement. As Laozi explains in *Daodejing* (33, trans. Ivanhoe):

---

[40] Plato, *Republic* 364d. From Hesiod, *Works and Days* 287-89.
[41] This is often called Plato's denial of "*akrasia*" (weakness of will). Socrates' argues at *Protagoras* 355a ff. that if an agent has true knowledge of the right thing to do, he could not help but do it.
[42] Confucius, *Analects* 2.4: "At fifteen I set my mind upon learning; at thirty, I took my place in society; at forty, I became free of doubts; at fifty, I understood Heaven's Mandate (*ming*); at sixty, my ear was attuned; and at seventy, I could follow my heart's desire without overstepping the bounds of propriety."

> Those who know others are knowledgeable;
> Those who know themselves are enlightened.
> Those who conquer others have power;
> Those who conquer themselves are strong

Laozi's sentiment corresponds to the Delphic commandment "know thyself," taken by Socrates and Hellenic philosophy generally as the foundation of ethics. By looking inward toward virtue and personal excellence, the Eastern and Hellenic ethical traditions counterbalance the modern Western tendency to articulate and legislate "universal ethical principles." To be sure, both rules and virtue have their place in Olympism, but the Movement cannot limit itself to one or the other if it is to effectively face the challenge of finding common ethical ground among diverse cultural traditions. Indeed the Movement's leadership might start by looking at itself in the mirror.

Politics: Nature and Civilization

The second fundamental principle of Olympism states its political goal: "to place sport at the service of the harmonious development of man, with a view to promoting a peaceful society concerned with the preservation of human dignity."[43] From the perspective of modern Western philosophy, the promotion of a peaceful society depends upon the authority of a civilizing force, which uses law to overcome the natural state in which competing interests dispose us to violence. The British philosopher Thomas Hobbes famously described life within this "state of nature" as "solitary, poor, nasty, brutish, and short."[44] Accordingly, Westerners tend to envision the Olympic Movement's promotion of a peaceful society in terms pushing (and sometimes forcing) conformity to a political ideal through "civilizing" law and authority, just as modern Western ethics focuses on rules and punishment. The history of Western colonialism as well as the war in Afghanistan may be interpreted as evidence of this approach.

---

[43] Olympic Charter (2007), 11.
[44] Hobbes, *Leviathan*, 107.

Multiculturalism, however, poses special challenges to this top-down approach. Who holds the authority in a diverse world community? Who makes the rules? Who enforces them? How do we decide which model of civilization will rescue us from the chaotic and warlike "state of nature"?

These questions are less pressing from the Eastern perspective because there, the "state of nature" is characterized by harmony and peace. On this view, the promotion of a peaceful society depends on "going back" either to Confucianism's remote and idealized past, or to Daoism's uncorrupted childlike state symbolized by the image of an uncarved block.[45] Peace is not imposed upon a community through law and authority; rather the ideal leader exhibits *wu-wei*—a passivity that amounts to power by virtue of its concordance or harmony with nature. Says Laozi (*Daodejing* 68):

> The accomplished person is not aggressive.
> The good soldier is not hot-tempered.
> The best conqueror does not engage the enemy.
> The most effective leader takes the lowest place.
> This is called the *Te* of not contending.
> This is called the power of the leader.
> This is called matching Heaven's ancient ideal.

Daoism finds the greatest political strength in responsiveness and spontaneity, rather than force. "The supplest things in the world run roughshod over the most rigid," claims Laozi. "That which is not there can enter even when there is no space. This is how I know the advantages of *wuwei*!" (*Daodejing* 43 trans. P. Ivanhoe). The strength associated with aggression is bound to fail in this context. Violence amounts to weakness for Laozi because it begets further violence (*Daodejing* 30):

> Use Tao to help rule people.
> This world has no need for weapons,

---

[45] Clearly these ideal states differ, but both are regarded by their proponents as "natural."

Which soon turn on themselves.
Where armies camp, nettles grow;
After each war, years of famine.
The most fruitful outcome
Does not depend on force,
But succeeds without arrogance
Without hostility
Without pride
Without resistance
Without violence.

Confucius also condemns force as ineffective in *Analects* 2.3:

"If you try to guide the common people with coercive regulations and keep them in line with punishments, they will become evasive and will have no sense of shame. If however, you guide them with Virtue, and keep them in line by means of ritual, the people will have a sense of shame and will rectify themselves."

Both Laozi and Confucius advise leaders to concentrate on their own virtue rather than attempting to control their subjects.[46] "To demand much from oneself and little from others," counsels Confucius, "is the way (for a ruler) to banish discontent" (*Analects* 15.14). The idea is that a leader's virtues inspire similar behavior in his subjects, obviating the need for orders and punishments, or even knowledge of practical crafts such as agriculture.[47] This political ideal may be described as a virtue-culture; one in which

---

[46] Lloyd, *Ancient Worlds, Modern Reflections*, 45.

[47] See Confucius 13.4: "When a ruler loves ritual propriety, then none among his people will dare to be disrespectful. When a ruler loves rightness, then none among his people will dare not to obey. When a ruler loves trustworthiness, then none of his people will dare not to be honest;" 13.6: "when the ruler is correct, his will is put into effect without the need for official orders. When a ruler's person is not correct, he will not be obeyed no matter how many orders he issues."

the leaders' virtue has a magnetic effect that draws others in and inspires them to be and to do their best within the community. Virtue (*de*), says Confucius, "never dwells in solitude; it will always bring neighbours" (*Analects* 4.25). To illustrate, imagine a champion basketball team led by one great player whose excellence inspires everyone else to work hard and play their best. This model contrasts favorably with a Western-style rule-culture in which the coach tries to legislate good performances through strict regulations, such as required practices and dietary restrictions. The Eastern model of political philosophy is summed up in an image from nature: "The Virtue of the gentleman is like the wind, and the Virtue of a petty person is like the grass—when the wind moves over the grass, the grass is sure to bend" (*Analects* 12.19). Virtue's inspirational power is more influential than regulations, more powerful than violence.

The Olympic Movement's efforts to legislate and enforce its own values through punishment and exclusion have been unsuccessful. A renewed focus on inspiration through virtue—both the leaders' own and that of the athletes—may help the Movement to reach its goals. This was the model in ancient Greece, where a healthy skepticism about the reliability of *nomos* (law or convention) was combined with a deep respect for *physis*—nature in the sense of ultimate reality, much like the Chinese *Dao* or Way.[48] The ancient Hellenes saw harmony between virtue, politics and nature. Aristotle argued that "a city-state is among the things that exist by nature, [and] a human being is by nature a political animal" (*Politics* 1253a3). He added that a true city-state "must be concerned with virtue" because otherwise its laws are reduced to mere agreement and the community loses its ability to make people "good and just" (1280b5-12). In Plato's philosophy the just community resembles the virtuous soul, which itself moves in

---

[48] Lloyd, *Ancient Reflections*, 163. "Along with a strong sense of the objectivity of *phusis*, nature, went different views of …its antonym, where the term *nomos* covered laws, customs, conventions."

harmony with the heavens.[49] Later, the Stoics took living in accordance with nature to be their highest principle. The Olympic Movement's commitment to environmental sustainability emerges in this context as an appropriate effort toward "promoting a peaceful society;" one that reflects both Eastern philosophy and Olympism's own Hellenic heritage.[50]

Conclusion: The model of Harmony

The fourth Fundamental Principle of Olympism defines the Olympic spirit in terms of mutual understanding, friendship, solidarity, and fair play.[51] It is in this Olympic spirit that I have tried to view Olympism through the lens of Chinese philosophy. My goal is not to supplant the modern Western view — or any other view, for that matter. My goal is mutual understanding: becoming aware that even common values expressed in clear language can be interpreted differently by different people without losing their philosophical meaning. Just as Olympic athletes from diverse cultural backgrounds compete in a common arena, diverse understandings of Olympism can find common ground. And the winner of the contest in a given Olympiad, or even the dominant athlete in a given era, does not tell the whole story of the sport. To find meaning we must consider a panorama of perspectives and seek harmony among them. Confucius illustrates the phenomenon with music: "when it first begins, it resounds with a confusing variety of notes, but as it unfolds, these notes are reconciled by means of harmony, brought into tension by means of counterpoint, and finally woven together into a seamless whole. It is in this way that music reaches its perfection."[52] Likewise, the global Olympic community finds its own beauty and harmony within and not despite its diversity.

---

[49] Plato's *Republic* postulates three social classes that reflect this tripartite theory of the soul. The connection between virtue and planetary movement is found in *Timaeus* 47bc, 90d.

[50] See IOC, *Agenda 21*

[51] Olympic Charter (2007), 11.

[52] Confucius, *Analects* 3.2.

We have seen how Western metaphysics tends to break things down and concentrate on the parts, while Eastern philosophy focuses on interconnectedness within the whole. Western ethics embraces the language of universal obligation, defining its values through rules and commandments, whereas Eastern and Hellenic philosophy look inward toward cultivating virtue as a moral power. Likewise, Western politics uses law as a barrier to protect individual rights, while the Eastern and Hellenic models use virtue like a magnet to draw the community together and inspire right behavior. To be sure, examples reflecting the Eastern perspective are to be found in the West and vice versa. The point is not that one perspective is superior to the other or even that individual regions should privilege their particular heritages. The point is to *learn from one another*—to realize that true philosophy is a love of wisdom and learning; one that can cooperatively search after one truth and one "Way" without limiting itself to a single expression of its meaning. This is Olympism's Hellenic heritage; one that served Olympic ideals for over 1,000 years in antiquity.

By examining Olympism through the divergent lenses of East and West, we have seen that it accommodates both philosophies well—and that it may serve its multicultural goals by intentionally harmonizing these perspectives. The Movement should begin by taking an open attitude toward the beliefs and values of Asians, Africans, and others that it has heretofore tended to ignore—looking not to bring them under an established paradigm, but to engage them in the ongoing development of that paradigm. Next, it should rediscover virtue as a moral force and educational example by encouraging and rewarding both leaders and athletes who consistently act out Olympism's stated ideals. This requires special attention to the commercial aspects of the Games; if the Movement appears to care only about money, athletes and spectators will follow suit. Warns Mencius, "if righteousness is put behind and profit is put ahead, one will not be satisfied without

VIII. Olympism East and West

grasping from others."[53] The Games should also include more sports of non-western origin,[54] such as *wushu*, which, through the cultivation of *qi*, weaves minds, bodies, diverse individuals, and nature itself into a "balanced whole."[55] Finally, the Movement should intentionally exploit the power of its rituals to unify its community. The opening and closing ceremonies should be regarded not as mere entertainment, but as an opportunity to cultivate appropriate dispositions and to affirm the common cause of peace and understanding. The athletes' and officials' oaths, for example, are often deleted from commercial broadcasts—the IOC should work with entertainment executives to see that such tone-setting rituals are seen by more than the audience in the stadium.

At the Beijing Games, the Chinese put their own philosophical heritage in the service of Olympic ideals, for example by linking ideas from Confucius and Laozi with such Olympic principles as peace and friendship in the opening ceremony. But the effort must not stop with these Games and must not be limited to one nation or even one region. All members of the Olympic Movement need to work harder to develop a richer understanding of Olympism that embodies diverse perspectives on Olympic philosophy. Following the example of ancient Olympia, scholars from various nations should gather during the Games to exchange ideas and articulate common values. In this way, we may cultivate the unity that discourages violence and fosters peace. Ancient Chinese philosophers understood that such ideals carry within them their

---

[53] Mencius, in Ivanhoe, and Van Norden, eds. *Readings in Classical Chinese Philosophy*, 1A1.

[54] An argument also made by Parry, "Sport and Olympism" p. 201-2.

[55] See S. Ebrey, qtd in Brownell *Training the Body*, 241: "The human body was perceived as intimately connected with the world around it: the body and the environment mutually influenced each other, each being permeated with essences that circulated throughout the cosmos. The most important influence on both the cosmos and the body was the balance of yin and yang, which were the source of the universe, of life and death, and of health and illness in the individual parts and organs of the body."

own moral force; as is shown in the following conversation recounted by Mencius:

> He asked me abruptly "How could we get a world settlement?"
> "By unification," I said.
> "Who is capable of uniting the world?" he asked.
> "If there were a single ruler," I said, "who did not delight in the slaughter, he could unite the whole world."
> "And who would side with him?" he asked.
> "Everyone in the world," I replied.[56]

---

[56] Mencius, quoted in Waley, *Three Ways of Thought*, 91.

25. An American Philosopher at the Beijing Olympics[1]

The trouble with being a philosopher is that I look at the world through a lens of lofty ideals, and, perhaps inevitably, the world tends to fall short. The wonderful thing about being a philosopher is that I also find evidence of these lofty ideals in our world, and this fills my spirit with hope and enthusiasm. My visit to the 2008 Beijing Olympic Games brought both hope and disillusionment. Hope was found in the most unexpected places: the gift of a child, the tears of a millionaire, the ethereal glow of a shining moon. The disappointments were perhaps more predictable. The philosophical spirit behind Beijing's slogans: Humanistic (*renwen*) Games, Green Games, and High-tech Games, fell victim to overriding concerns about reputation, manipulation, and control. Ultimately, however, I think these Games succeeded for the same reasons all Games do: they brought diverse people together in an atmosphere of peace, reminding us all once again of our kinship and common humanity.

This essay compares ancient Chinese philosophical ideas with my experience in modern China at the 2008 Olympic Games. It might seem unfair to evaluate any modern reality according to philosophical ideals—but it is precisely by contrasting reality with ideals that we discover directions for improvement. There's no doubt that China is a country deeply focused on improving itself, and it will do well to draw on its extremely rich philosophical heritage as it seeks this improvement. Testament to the link that China sees between the Games and its ancient heritage is the fact that the Olympic Green was built in Beijing along the same auspicious north-west axis as the Forbidden City, Tiananmen Square, and sacred Temple of Heaven.

---

[1] Originally published in in Hardman and C. Jones, eds. *Philosophy of Sport: International Perspectives*, (Newcastle upon Tyne: Cambridge Scholars Publishing, 2010). 218-226. Reprinted with permission.

VIII. Olympism East and West

As a Western outsider, I hardly speak from a position of strong authority—either with respect to China's culture or to its philosophy. Furthermore, I recognize that it goes against Chinese custom for a visitor from distant lands to criticize her host. But with distance comes perspective, and so I offer these criticisms in friendship and admiration, not in effort to suggest Western superiority, but rather as a cooperative contribution to our communal efforts to better understand and improve this world as a whole.

"People's Games" or Police Games?

One of the strongest concepts from ancient Chinese philosophy, especially Confucianism, is the concept of leadership as virtuous sagehood. The idea is that a leader's virtues inspire similar behavior in his subjects, obviating the need for strict rules and harsh punishments. Says Confucius,

> If you try to guide the common people with coercive regulations [zheng] and keep them in line with punishments, the common people will become evasive and will have no sense of shame. If, however, you guide them with Virtue [te], and keep them in line by means of ritual, the people will have a sense of shame and will rectify themselves" (Analects 2.3).[2]

Daoism likewise associates forceful leadership with weakness. Says Laozi:

---

[1] See also Confucius, *Analects* 13.4: "When a ruler loves ritual propriety, then none among his people will dare to be disrespectful. When a ruler loves rightness, then none among his people will dare not to obey. When a ruler loves trustworthiness, then none of his people will dare not to be honest. The mere existence of such a ruler would cause the common people throughout the world to bundle their children on their backs and seek him out. Of what use then is the study of agriculture." Also and 13.6: "when the ruler is correct, his will is put into effect without the need for official orders. When a ruler's person is not correct, he will not be obeyed no matter how many orders he issues."

> Use Tao to help rule people.
> This world has no need for weapons,
> Which soon turn on themselves.
> Where armies camp, nettles grow;
> After each war, years of famine.
> The most fruitful outcome
> Does not depend on force,
> But succeeds without arrogance
> Without hostility
> Without pride
> Without resistance
> Without violence.[3]

This virtue-leadership philosophy belies a strong sense of humanism: a belief that human beings are essentially good. If people are inspired rather than threatened by their leaders, they will use their freedom to practice virtue and contribute to their communities.

Unfortunately the modern Chinese government seems to have forgotten the wisdom of its philosophical ancestors. The self-imposed epithet *"Renwen* (people's or humanistic) Games" suggests a spirit of respect and trust in the common people, but the reality in Beijing was often one of disrespect and distrust between the people and their leaders. Most often, this was justified in the name of "security." Applications to protest were routinely denied, as we know. But even the precise times and locations of public Olympic events, such as the cycling races or marathons, were at best hard to find and at worst misleading. Those lucky or persistent enough to be on the right sidewalk at the right time were closely guarded and controlled by a mega-force of police and security guards, not all of whom were in uniform.

My friend and I were part of a huge crowd that formed near Tsinghua University to watch the passing of the torch on opening day, but no torch ever passed and no-one knew which way to go. When we traveled across town to the old Beijing train station to

---

[3] Laozi, *Daodejing*, trans. Addiss & Lombardo, 30.

VIII. Olympism East and West

watch the opening ceremony on a big outdoor screen, we went through security only to find the screen turned off. "Too many people," a volunteer said with a shrug. To get to the men's bike race, my friend (who speaks fluent Mandarin) had to negotiate with guards literally miles from the course, then we (over)paid a taxi driver with an apparently illegal credential to drive us out there, only to be barricaded into a small area near the parking lot with the few other pesky spectators who dared to witness the race in person. At the start of the women's race, we met the Australian family of one of the riders who were fuming over the lack of access to their daughter and the event. Luckily their daughter spotted them as they yelled and waved from a distance and a sympathetic police supervisor let them come near the fence to hug her through the barricades. Actually, he wasn't too sympathetic, at the same moment he wheeled around and yelled at me to keep moving along the sidewalk.

Despite all these attempts to keep people away from the Games, the spirit of the Olympics, torch or no-torch, shined through. When crowds gathered and there was nothing else to see, we Westerners became the main attraction. Especially when we were wearing "Go China" headbands or stickers, Chinese people literally lined up to have their pictures taken with us. In some cases they may not have seen real-live Westerners before, and in others it was a rare chance to converse with native English speakers, or just to thank us for coming to Beijing. The most precious moment came when we were trying to hail a taxi after the "missing torch" debacle. A little Chinese girl, about 7 or 8 years old, came up to me with an Olympic mascot flag that said "Welcome to Beijing" on it. "Hello, how are you?" she said with a bright smile.

> "I am fine, how are you?" I replied, being careful to speak slowly and clearly.
> "I give you this flag," she said, handing it to me.
> "It's a nice flag," I said, afraid I misunderstood and not wanting to take it from her. "Is it yours?"
> "I give it to you," she insisted.

"Well, thank you very much, that's very nice! Can I give you a present?"
"Ok," she said twisting in that shy girlish way.
I pulled out my pin wallet and opened it up. I have been collecting and trading pins since the 1984 Olympics and I have a pretty good collection.
"Oooooh, very beautiful!" she said.
"Which one do you like the best," I asked.
She pointed to one with a skier on it and I took it out and gave it to her.
"Thank you. Welcome to Beijing! Bye bye,"

She ran back to her father, who was observing from a short distance. My friend said she thought the father told the girl to give me the flag as a way to teach his daughter about the spirit of giving and being nice to foreigners. I hope I made a good impression. Bringing people together so we can see that we are all human is what the Games are really all about—and it happened even at this crowded non-event, as the torch traveled overhead in a helicopter all in the name of security.

Harmony with or Manipulation of Nature?

Unlike Western philosophy, which sees nature as something opposed to civilization,[4] Eastern philosophy sees nature as a model. Daoism, in particular, seeks to return to an unspoiled, childlike state, characterized by the image of an uncarved block. The ideal leader exhibits a spontaneity or responsiveness called *wu-wei*, which derives its power from concordance or harmony with nature. Says Laozi

> The accomplished person is not aggressive.
> The good soldier is not hot-tempered.
> The best conqueror does not engage the enemy.

---

[4] The British philosopher Thomas Hobbes famously described life within this warlike "state of nature" as "solitary, poor, nasty, brutish, and short." *Leviathan Parts One and Two* (Indianapolis: Library of Liberal Arts, 1958): 107.

VIII. Olympism East and West

> The most effective leader takes the lowest place.
> This is called the *Te* of not contending.
> This is called the power of the leader.
> This is called matching Heaven's ancient ideal.[5]

The example is given of water's natural ability to erode even the hardest rock because it is soft and yielding. By harmonizing with nature, we channel its power and the flood-like energy called *qi*. Says Laozi, "the supplest things in the world run roughshod over the most rigid. That which is not there can enter even when there is no space. This is how I know the advantages of *wuwei*!"[6]

Modern Beijing's so-called "Green Games" seemed more like an attempt to manipulate nature than to harmonize with it. To be fair, Beijing's attempt to clean up their air and water for the Games was a very welcome change. After a sailing athlete became sick from falling into polluted water at a test event, the Chinese cleaned up the bay by hand. After Haile Gebrselassie withdrew from the marathon and other athletes threatened to compete wearing breathing masks, increasingly draconian efforts were made to clean up the air. Indeed, pollution angst almost overshadowed human-rights concerns in pre-Games media coverage. It seemed like everyone was staring at the gray hazy skies waiting to see if the Chinese government was actually strong enough to reverse decades of pollution in a matter of weeks.

The problem with this and other environmental measures is that they were short-term band-aids that poorly concealed long-festering wounds. Official Olympic spaces were clean and green, but outside things weren't nearly so pristine. Telltale smells emerged from places hastily hidden behind huge Olympic banners. We heard that the city's worst neighborhoods had actually been razed and that the poorest of its 15 million citizens had been sent away for the summer ("Reduce the size of the state,"

---

[5] Laozi, *Daodejing*, 68 (trans Addiss & Lombardo).

[6] Laozi, *Daodejing*, translation and commentary by Phillip Ivanhoe (London: Seven Bridges Press, 2002): 43.

advises Laozi).⁷ But I wonder how "green" Beijing will be once the banners come down and world quits watching?

The skies finally did clear up, apparently because of Mother Nature rather than in spite of her. We were walking under cloudy skies just south of Tiananmen (Heavenly Peace) Square, when the heavens opened up. There was thunder and wind and then it started raining cats and dogs. People scrambled for shelter and we ended up crowding under a subway station overhang with what seemed like hundreds of others, our umbrellas overlapping overhead and on the sides like the shields of a Roman phalanx. The gates to the station were locked to keep people from pouring in, so we just kept squeezing in tighter, united against the elements. I thought for a moment about the female cyclists who were still out racing in the mountains. It poured so hard that road began to look like a river, and a passing bus sent a small wave up over the curb and into our multicultural phalanx. The experience reminded me that whether we're battling nature or harmonizing with her, we all share this planet and must take mutual responsibility for its health. Wealthier countries such as China and the US can take the lead— if we work together to harmonize with nature, perhaps the rest of the world will be inspired by our example, just as Confucius said.

Technology trumps Tradition?

In its effort to return to nature, the *Daodejing* advises against the use of labor saving tools.⁸ On the surface, this advice would seem to fly in the face of Beijing's efforts to be the "High-tech Games." But I don't think its the use of technology *per se* that Laozi is opposed to, rather he worries that it may get in the way of cultivating virtue and thereby living a good life. The danger is that technology breeds admiration and perhaps envy for what someone has. As in Confucian philosophy, we end up worrying more about our wealth or reputation (or our reputation *for* wealth), than we do about self-improvement. "Do not be concerned that no one has heard of you," says Confucius, "but rather strive to

---

⁷ Laozi, *Daldejing,* trans. Ivanhoe, 80.
⁸ Laozi, *Daldejing,* 80.

become a person worthy of being known."[9] The idea is that those who strive for virtue may achieve wealth and a good reputation, but those who strive for wealth and reputation are unlikely to achieve virtue. Adds Laozi, "There is no greater calamity than not knowing what is enough. There is no greater fault than desire for success."[10]

There was no mistaking China's desire to display its technological success at the Games. The most conspicuous example of this was high-tech Olympic architecture, such as the "Bird's Nest" stadium and "Water Cube" natatorium. The idea seemed to be that these buildings, along with the performance of Chinese athletes and the flawless organization of the event, would put China on the map as a world player, erasing forever the image of the "sick man of Asia." Indeed it was the display on the technology behind these new venues that drew the most interest and enthusiasm from Chinese people at a special Olympic museum exhibit we attended. The displays on traditional sports and China's role in the Olympic movement were nearly empty in comparison. Just across from the Bird's Nest and Water Cube was a 6-star hotel complex shaped like a dragon with giant TV screens that could be seen from all over the city. But one has to ask, how many Chinese people can actually afford a 6-star hotel? And how many were forcibly displaced to make room for these buildings? Just as the high-tech swimsuits raise questions about whether new world records really reflect better swimmers, Beijing's high-tech architecture raises questions about whether China's advancement really reflects better lives for its people.

The pernicious idea that technology rather than personal virtue can make our lives better was perhaps best illustrated by Olympic sponsor Haier's exhibit entitled "One World One Home." This is a cutely commercialized version of the official Olympic slogan "One World One Dream" – there the dream is peace, but because Haier makes electric appliances, their version of the dream

---

[9] Confucius, *Analects*, 4.14
[10] Laozi, *Daodejing*, 46 (trans Addiss & Lombardo)

was a fully automated house. An army of enthusiastic English-speaking docents showed us how we could send text messages from our cell-phone to our air-conditioner, refrigerator, and security system to prepare for our arrival from work. They also showed us a virtual bedroom that would alter the light, temperature, even the scenery out our virtual window, to suit our particular preferences. My favorite was the virtual golf game, which allowed me to play golf without leaving the house. Of course, they didn't address the questions of what's really outside my window that I don't want to see, why I'm stuck in traffic coming home from work, who I need to keep out with the security station, or where the time went to go out for a real game of golf. True quality of life does not come from technology, and neither does respect on the world stage. China will need more than dazzling architecture, efficient organization, and Olympic medals to earn true respect. They must learn, as Laozi puts it, that

> The more they do for others, the more they have;
> The more they give to others the more they possess.[11]

Conclusions

The best thing about the Haier exhibit was that they gave me a souvenir pin. Not because I seemed to get something for nothing, but rather because pin-trading is a great participatory event. In an official pavilion, I found a Russian who had 13 different cycling pins I wanted—including two from 1968 and one from Munich 1972. I was afraid that I wouldn't have enough to trade, and he only found 9 pins among my collection that he wanted, but he let me take all 13 in exchange. Some people try to "profit" by trading only for more valuable pins. I prefer to be guided by "pin-karma." At the bike race a Chinese volunteer was fascinated by the pins I had on my lanyard. She pointed to one and I took it off, asking if she had one to trade, but she didn't understand so I just gave it to her. Then, at the end of the race, a Slovenian rider called me over

---

[11] Laozi, *Daodejing*, 81 (trans. Ivanhoe)

and offered a team pin—I asked which pin he wanted in trade, "None," he said, "I just want to give this to you" As Laozi says,

> The Way does not contend but is good at victory;
> Does not speak but is good at responding;
> Does not call but things come of their own accord.[12]

Ultimately, I think the Beijing Games fell short of their stated ideals. Issues of security and crowd control turned the People's Games into something more like the Police Games. The Green Games were more an attempt to manipulate Nature than to harmonize with it. And the High-tech games revealed a drive for wealth and reputation rather than improving lives. On the other hand, I think the Games succeeded according to Olympic ideals—which hardly depend on police, environmentalism, or technology. In their ancient Greek manifestation, athletes competed in the nude and spectators camped out in dry riverbeds. What made the Games great then—and now—is the same: it is the rediscovery of that simple human spirit that unites us all. In Beijing, I saw this everywhere: in the effortless elegance of Usain Bolt's 100 meter sprint, in the tearful joy of multi-millionaire Kobe Bryant on winning a medal worth 393 dollars, in the gift of a child on a crowded Beijing street, and in the beauty of a full moon that belongs equally to every one of us, shining through a clear black sky over the Bird's Nest stadium.

---

[12] Laozi, *Daodejing*, 73 (trans. Ivanhoe).

Epilogue

26. Why Olympic Philosophy Matters for Modern Sport[1]

A philosophy called "Marginal Gains" made Sir David Brailsford famous. It is credited with multiple victories in the Tour de France and Olympic Games, and has spread beyond cycling to other sports. It may now be the prevailing sports philosophy, but I would not call it an Olympic philosophy. For one thing, it is not a philosophy of what can be achieved *through* sport to benefit individuals and society, it is rather a philosophy of what can be achieved *within* sport to benefit teams and sponsors. For another, it is not inspired by ancient Greek history or philosophical ideals, but rather by a thoroughly modern focus on data, technology, and efficiency. The philosophy detaches athletic performance from its cultural and historical moorings then breaks it down into comprehensible quantities to be analyzed and optimized. The idea is to identify every miniscule factor that may influence athletic performance and improve it just slightly. All of these "marginal gains" then add up to a winning edge. For example, in the 23-day Tour de France bicycle race, staff drive ahead to replace each hotel's bedding with mattresses, sheets, and pillows optimized for each athlete. A kitchen on wheels also follows the race to prepare all the riders' meals. And data from each athlete's body and bicycle is gathered and analyzed – even during the race itself.

Let me be clear, I have nothing against Brailsford personally and no fundamental objection to his approach. Rather I offer him and his philosophy of Marginal Gains as an illustration of what I call the Efficiency Ethos that seems to pervade contemporary sport. And I argue that an Olympic Ethos is needed to balance it

---

[1] Originally published as "Why Olympia Matters for Modern Sport," *Journal of the Philosophy of Sport*, 44.2 (2017): 159-173, and *Reflecting on Modern Sport in Ancient Olympia*, eds. H. Reid and E. Moore (Sioux City, IA: Parnassos Press, 2017), 171-88. © 2017 Reprinted by permission of Informa UK Limited, trading as Taylor & Francis Group,www.tandfonline.com on behalf of International Association for the Philosophy of Sport – IAPS.

out. The ethos of a sporting community is important because it conditions the way we behave, explain, and understand our activities. Ancient and modern philosophers agree, furthermore, that we are in some sense free to choose the way we think about sport.[2] Alasdair MacIntyre has shown that sports are profitably thought of as communities in which the history and values of a given practice inform standards for merit.[3] Sports communities, in effect, choose what matters to them, and I argue that Olympic philosophy *should* matter to modern sports communities because it adds value to sport as a human practice. The Olympic Ethos is distinctively humanistic and virtue-seeking; as such it enhances the social and educational potential of sport.

The problem with the prevailing Efficiency Ethos is that it narrows down the goals and values of sport to the point of dehumanizing the practice. The Olympic Ethos counterbalances the Efficiency Ethos by reintegrating a historically humanistic philosophy of sport into the goods to be preserved and exalted within sporting communities. Sport Studies is fortunate to be a field where history and philosophy are usually taught together. They need to be integrated, however, in a way that seeks to understand more than just what our athletic ancestors *did*, but also how they thought about it and what they purported to gain from sport. Even according to the quantitative standards prized by modern minds, the Ancient Olympics' 1,000+ year history as a socially viable and meaningful activity easily outstrips, by many hundreds of years, any comparable modern practice. By understanding and incorporating the Olympic Ethos into sporting communities, we may rediscover the educational and cultural potential of sport today.

In this essay, I will show from the traditional philosophical perspectives of metaphysics, epistemology, aesthetics, ethics, and

---

[2] This is the flagship discovery of the phenomenologists, but the Stoics had already pointed it out in ancient times.

[3] A. MacIntyre, *After Virtue*, 177 says knowledge of a practice's history is necessary for recognizing its internal goods.

politics, how an ancient Olympic Ethos of sport contrasts with the modern Efficiency Ethos. I will reveal a holistic metaphysics that contrasts with an analytic one. I will show an epistemology that distinguishes knowledge and wisdom from mere information. I will describe an aesthetics that is autotelic rather than instrumental. I will outline an ethics in which sport serves the cause of virtue rather than the other way around. And I will point to a politics that promotes the common good by rewarding individual excellence. By drawing all these elements together, I will explain why Olympic philosophy matters for sport today.

Metaphysics

Aristotle called *Metaphysics* "first philosophy" because it is the foundational concern of philosophers—questions that come after (*meta*) the practical study of nature (*physis*). I would never claim that being had a different nature in ancient Greece than it does today, but how we think about being *has* changed. For the ancients, the cosmos was taken to be something whole and complete, so the emphasis in trying to understand it was on the connections among humanity, the natural environment, and the divine or spiritual realm. Furthermore, Aristotle wanted to know not just the material, formal, and efficient causes of a thing, but also its final cause—that is, its purpose and function within the cosmic whole (*Metaphysics* 996b1). Although the Olympic Ethos is distinctively humanistic, it recognizes that humanity cannot be understood independently of nature and divinity. For moderns, however, the emphasis in metaphysics is on analysis: breaking being down into the smallest possible parts and comprehending them individually. Humanity, as subject, is (perhaps hopelessly) disconnected from nature (which is regarded as an object) and divinity is set aside as something either reducible to nature or unknowable through science. Modern metaphysics breaks things apart, ancient metaphysics fuses them together.

Moderns will recognize Olympia's refreshing green pines and buzzing cicadas as the fortuitous consequence of a confluence of rivers, whereas the ancients interpreted its verdant landscape as permeated with divine life—the rivers Alpheios and Kladeos were themselves personified as gods and depicted on the pediment of the Temple of Zeus, inside of which the god himself was imagined to dwell. Human beings were likewise understood to be connected—not only with the living landscape and divine spirit upon which they thought their own lives depended—but also with one another in circles of friendship and community that ranged ever outward from family, to city, to nation, to mankind, and ultimately to nature and the gods. Although a distinction between mind and body was postulated by Plato and others, it was never so stark as Descartes' modern distinction was. For the ancients, the *psychē* (a word that encompasses both mind and soul) was what moved the body and gave it life—gymnastics in Plato's *Republic* is practiced specifically for the training of the *psychē* (410b-411e). An ancient athlete's soul was the primary source of his performance (which also depended upon his harmonious connection with nature and with the divine). Moderns, by contrast, not only privilege individuals over communities, they further subdivide humanity into mind, body, and spirit, while regarding the primary source of an athlete's performance as her body—even specific aspects of her body such as the length of her limbs, the quantity of her oxygen uptake, or the ratio between her strength and weight; in short, her physical efficiency in performing her athletic task. The ancient athlete was understood as part of a cosmic whole, the modern athlete is understood in terms of her measurable parts.

Our understanding of sport itself is also conditioned by this metaphysical contrast. As Allen Guttmann recognized decades ago, ancient sport was seen as a ritual while modern sport is conceived as a pursuit of records.[4] In its earliest Hellenic form, as a method of worship in hero cults, athletic contests were performed adjacent to or even upon the hero's tomb in an effort to awaken his or her life-giving spirit.[5] The hero's spirit was imagined as a conduit between human and divine that gave life even to

---

[4] Guttmann, *From Ritual to Record*.
[5] G. Nagy, *Ancient Greek Hero*, 0.§43

plants, as illustrated by the lush garden surrounding the athletic hero Protesilaos in Philostratus' essay *Heroicus*. Modern sports are generally not concerned with reuniting human, natural and divine spirits. Rather they serve to generate distinctions among human beings, to establish rankings and set records. Suits' definition of sport as "a voluntary effort to overcome unnecessary obstacles" applies to ancient and modern sports alike, but the Aristotelian final cause (that is, the purpose) of this phenomenon is conceived differently—and this difference has its roots in a holistic metaphysics focused on bringing things together versus an analytic metaphysics intent on breaking things apart.[6]

The metaphysical outlook behind the Efficiency Ethos in sport is aptly illustrated by Brailsford's approach to training. He breaks down athletic performance into its various scientific components and tries to develop new "cutting-edge" approaches in nutrition, biomechanics, genetics, equipment, aerodynamics, training, race strategy and sports medicine. Doping is explicitly shunned, but every legal advantage is pursued—including the consumption of legal performance-enhancing substances and, perhaps, the strategic exploitation of loopholes such as therapeutic use exemptions.[7]

The Efficiency approach is to challenge habit and tradition, while the Olympic approach is to reenact it – to perform a *mimēsis* of heroic virtue. When a great athlete like Milo of Croton emulated the feats of Heracles in a wrestling match in the stadium at Olympia, he might have been thought to activate the divine spirit or even to provoke an epiphany – the brief appearance of a god on earth. In the moment when the divine spirit, already latent in the natural environment, was personified through an athlete's peak

---

[6] Suits, *Grasshopper: Games*, 55.

[7] On the therapeutic use and threshold issue, see Fotheringham, "Chris Froome given little sympathy," *The Guardian*, July 7, 2018. Brailsford's team has not been without doping allegations, see T. Cary, "Sir Dave Brailsford faces mounting pressure as UK Anti-Doping chairman questions Team Sky chief's 'extraordinary' claims," *The Guardian*: 7 January, 2017.

Epilogue

performance, the boundaries between man and nature, between moral and immortal, between prosaic present and glorious past would seem to the ancient spectator to collapse and the cosmos would become whole again.[8] The metaphysics of the Olympic Ethos is holistic, of the Efficiency Ethos analytic. The Olympic Ethos connects human beings with each other, as well as with the natural and spiritual worlds. The Efficiency Ethos reduces athletes to quantifiable parts—an analysis that risks leaving their humanity behind.

Epistemology

Of course, the phenomenon of peak athletic performances causing an alteration in our sense of time and place still exists today—even for spectators—but we *think* about it differently. I had the fortune to be in the Bird's Nest stadium in Beijing the night that Usain Bolt won the 100 meter final, and I can tell you that there was a collective experience of euphoria in the stadium at that moment. The time was a world record, and I remember my friend commenting through a smiling stupor that he could have gone even faster if hadn't started pounding his chest before he crossed the finish line. The Efficiency Ethos in sport has not eliminated peak experiences in sport—even collective peak experiences of the kind that would have been interpreted as epiphanies in antiquity. Nor has it erased, as we said before, the fundamental desire for knowledge at the foundation of both sport and philosophy.[9] What has changed epistemologically is the *kind* of knowing we seek and the *means* of knowing we value. The Efficiency Ethos privileges quantitative knowing while the Olympic Ethos seeks qualitative knowing.

This contrast derives primarily from a difference in what we seek to know and why we seek to know it. The Olympic Ethos

---

[8] For a philosophical analysis of ancient athletics as reenactment of heroes see H. Reid, 2016, 'Athletes as Heroes and Role Models: An Ancient Model'. *Sport, Ethics and Philosophy*, 11:1, 40-51, DOI: 10.1080/17511321.2016.1261931.

[9] See "Running toward Truth in ancient Olympia" in this volume.

seeks knowledge (*epistēmē*) and wisdom (*sophia*); the Efficiency Ethos seeks objective information useful for gaining a competitive edge. Olympic Epistemology begins with wonder and seeks understanding—as Aristotle says of philosophy (*Metaphysics* 982b25)—not for the sake of any other advantage or utility, but for its own sake. To be sure, there are benefits to the understanding gained through sport just as there are benefits to the understanding gained through philosophy—knowledge and wisdom are essential to the exercise of human virtue, upon which happiness (*eudaimonia*) and even pleasure supervene (*Nicomachean Ethics* 1169a3-11). Sport may provide worldly goods like health, wealth, and admiration, but it is not for the sake of these things that I participate under the Olympic Ethos. Rather, it is in pursuit of a better qualitative and collective understanding of humanity, of the cosmos and of our role within it. In modern terms, we might call this experiential learning—it is not something easily quantified or reduced to a formula; it may be collective but never objective. It is an increased understanding and awareness that comes about through thoughtful experience – and because I am essentially an embodied social animal, it must be an embodied social experience. Usain Bolt's fantastic feat gave me a qualitative feeling of what humanity is capable of and how we are all interconnected.

For my friend at the Bird's Nest, who had been an Olympic-level track athlete and has technical expertise, the same experience was interpreted, in accordance with the Efficiency Ethos, quantitatively. The 9.69 was a world record, but it might have been a 9.68 or maybe even a 9.65 without the celebration. The goal is to go faster, to do everything it takes, to find out in how few seconds (actually, how few hundredths or even thousandths of a second) a human being can cover the admittedly arbitrary distance of 100 meters on a perfectly level optimized surface. Efficiency epistemology seeks an objectively-verified set of numbers uncontaminated by the vagaries of personality and environment; its goal is to set a record or to win.

The appeal of such quantitative knowledge is that it seems impartial, uncontaminated, and therefore true; the weakness is that it is narrow (almost to the point of meaninglessness) and unsustainable. As Sigmund Loland has pointed out, in record sports such as the 100 meter dash, the margin of difference keeps getting smaller, which makes the pursuit unsustainable in the long-term.[10] The kind of holistic understanding of self and cosmos sought in the Olympic Ethos has no such limitation. To be sure, quantitative knowledge-seeking is not logically incompatible with the qualitative knowledge sought under the Olympic Ethos. The structure of sport certainly encourages winning and reliably rewards technologically sophisticated training—the extraordinary success of Pythagorean athletes Olympics in the late 7th and early 6th century BCE is no doubt connected to such methods.[11] The difference is that their scientific training took place in a philosophical context where mathematics was a means to holistic human understanding. Quantitative epistemology in modern sport, by contrast, risks becoming an obsession—even a fetish—that desensitizes us to the qualitative knowledge (and much of the enjoyment) that can be gained from the sports experience.

Having cycled up the spectacular Gavia pass in the Italian Alps a few years back, I compared notes at dinner with a fellow cyclist. What I remembered was the beauty of the mountains and having overcome the doubt about whether I could make it to the top. His own experience was a product of the power and heart-rate monitors attached to his bike—he talked about watts, gear ratios, and heart-rate data, never mentioning the environment or even his state of mind. Because athletic performance is so readily quantified these days using electronic monitors and meters, even recreational

---

[10] S. Loland, "Olympic Sport and Sustainable Development," 144-156.

[11] For an overview of Pythagorean athletes' success and the role of technology in it, see J-M Roubineau, *Milon de Crotone ou l'invention du sport* (Paris: Presses Universitaires de France, 2017). Evidence that Pythagoreans took a scientific approach to training includes the story in Quintilian, *Institutes of Oratory*, I.9.5 about Milo lifting a calf above his head every day until it grew into a bull.

athletes risk the illusion that generating those numbers is *all that sports is about.* Quantitative epistemology tends to set aside, disregard, and sometimes even deny the existence of that which cannot be quantified—and so much of what is valuable in sport is qualitative rather than quantitative. A healthy sports ethos will take note of the quantitative, but will not let it squelch out the qualitative value of the sports experience.

Aesthetics

Our metaphysical and epistemological approaches to sport also generate an aesthetic—a sense of what is pleasing or beautiful within a given practice. The Olympic Hymn, written by the poet Kostis Palamas for the 1896 Athens Games aptly expresses the aesthetics of the Olympic Ethos:

> Immortal spirit of antiquity
> Father of the beautiful, good, and true
> Descend, appear, shine your light and glory
> On this earth and under this sky, so blue.

Here the poet actually invokes the god to appear in nature, to make an epiphany, and he characterizes, as ancient Greek philosophy did, beauty, goodness, and truth as being connected, three faces of a single idea. The thing that unifies them is their autotelicity; the fact that they constitute an end in themselves, requiring no further justification for their value. The Efficiency aesthetic, by contrast, is instrumental, it finds beauty in functionality, what serves a practical (often commercial) end. Modern sports equipment such as aerodynamic bicycles and carbon-fiber golf clubs is aesthetically fascinating because of its (real or perceived) ability to improve performance; a player's running or batting style is beautiful because it results in victory. Efficiency-beauty is contingent on its ability to produce results; Olympic beauty is good in itself.

The aesthetic contrast can be observed in the physical facilities of sport. Ancient Olympia, even today, is a naturally beautiful place, a green oasis of peace amid an often harsh and rocky landscape. In ancient times it was open-air museum, its sanctuary filled with statues, temples, monuments, and glowing altars.

Epilogue

During the festival, the performing art of poets, musicians, athletes, orators, and even philosophers enriched the atmosphere further. Sanctuaries like Delphi likewise boast a theater and odeon for musical contests. The stadium there is carved into the picturesque slopes of Mount Parnassos, near the top, beneath a brilliant blue sky, close to the gods. Modern sports grounds are more like laboratories, antiseptic and organized with clearly marked boundaries and perfectly level playing fields. The most celebrated tracks are the ones where athletes achieve their best times. The interference of natural elements like wind, rain, and uneven terrain are usually disdained as contaminating the purity of the contest. Even the dramatic natural scenery surrounding an alpine stage in the Tour de France is routinely ignored by athletes focused on the race and spectators running alongside them in silly costumes trying to get on TV.

If this last phenomenon seems to depart from the aesthetic point, consider the possibility that spectators using sport to serve their personal interests (goofy though they may be) simply reinforces the individualism and instrumentality of the Efficiency Ethos. Modern sport is most often consumed alone through visual media as personal entertainment, in contrast with the collective experience characteristic of spectatorship under the Olympic Ethos of sport. Likewise, the ethical-aesthetic concept of "fairness" is usually interpreted under the Efficiency Ethos legalistically as the protection of individual rights and the preservation of the rule of law (or perhaps the law of the rules in sport). Even such an aesthetically interesting technological development as slow-motion photography is valued under the Efficiency Ethos primarily for adjudicating rules disputes. Nevertheless, when one of those narcissistic spectators jumped out in front of a TV motorbike at the 2016 Tour de France, causing the leading riders to crash into it as it stopped, officials had to appeal to an aesthetic sense of fairness to adjudicate the result since there was no real precedent for dealing with it in the rules.[12]

I am not saying that rules and athletes' rights are not a concern under the Olympic Ethos, what I am saying is that they shouldn't squeeze out any appreciation of the sheer beauty of sport for its own sake and for the collective enjoyment of the larger community. Those amazing statues and songs that celebrated athletic victory in Classical Greece – the odes of Pindar and the sculptures of Praxiteles – were regarded not so much as proof of an individual athlete's excellence, but more of the athlete's, his family's, and his community's connection with the heroic past and with the realm of divine excellence. The epinician ode as an art form usually begins with some mythological story of universal glory, then tries to integrate the athlete and by extension his community into that paradigm; again, it is a bringing together rather than a singling out. Likewise, the athletic statues that Olympian victors set up in the *altis* are not individual portraits of the victors so much as idealized depictions of divine virtue (*aretē*). In effect, the sculptor tries to capture the moment of epiphany when the mortal athlete briefly embodied the hero or god; at rest the athlete probably looks nothing like his statue. The aesthetic of the athletic body in Classical Greek art is really an attempt to depict a perfected, divine soul.[13] The beauty of athletic bodies on the Efficiency aesthetic is more mechanical. The robotic football player used on National Football League broadcasts in America comes to mind, but so does Michael Johnson's duck-like stride, admired for its efficacy, and Dick Fosbury's "flop," which enables higher jumps.[14] Aesthetic value on the Efficiency Ethos derives from what can be achieved athletically, not what is represented

---

[12] The philosophical debate over how officials maintain fairness in cases where the rules are not clear is an important one. A good place to start is J.S. Russell, "Are Rules All an Umpire Has to Work With?," *Journal of the Philosophy of Sport* 27.1 (1999), 27-49.

[13] For the full argument, see Reid, "Athletic Beauty," 281-297.

[14] For a fuller discussion of sports aesthetics, see Reid, *Introduction to the Philosophy of Sport*, chapter 6, and Mumford, *Watching Sport*.

culturally and spiritually. To be sure, this aesthetic awareness of functionality has a place in sport, which by nature seeks and rewards efficiency. The danger is that we may lose the ability to recognize inefficient, autotelic beauty in sport.

Ethics

The contrast between idealized and mechanical depictions of the athletic body under the Efficiency and Olympic models is also reflected in their respective ethics. As I said, athletic statues and songs celebrate not so much individual achievement as an ideal of human virtue. The Greek word is *aretē*, a concept of personal excellence that applies to all aspects of a human being's life. In art, it is represented through athletic bodies (whether mortal or immortal) because athleticism had historically been associated with virtue and divine ancestry (not just in the Homeric epics, where Odysseus' athleticism proves his nobility, but also in the earlier civilizations of Egypt and Sumer).[15] *Aretē* was thought to be a matter of inheritance until relatively open contests like the Olympic Games showed that it could be trained at the gymnasium.[16] Crucially, though, it remained a quality of the *psychē*, and not only did philosophers appear in the gymnasium to train the intellectual aspect of the soul alongside the kinetic one, Xenophon (*Symposium* 9.1) posited the physically ugly philosopher Socrates as an ironic ideal of *kalokagathia* (beautiful goodness). Plato drives the same point home by having the conventionally athletic and beautiful Alcibiades extol Socrates' virtuous action and inner beauty (*Symposium* 216e). Under the Olympic Ethos, human virtue is expressed broadly, not just in athletics but in other pursuits as well.[17]

The Efficiency Ethos also has a virtue ethics, but its conception of excellence is narrowly focused on athletic performance and

---

[15] See "Pre-Olympic Heroes," in this volume.

[16] See "From Aristocracy to Democracy," in this volume.

[17] The 'transitivity,' if you will, of the virtues, is also insisted upon by MacIntyre. See *After Virtue* 189, and my analysis of the issue in *Introduction to the Philosophy of Sport*, 128-131.

involves few moral imperatives beyond adherence to the letter of the rules. Illegal doping, as we said, is not endorsed by Efficiency ethics – perhaps because it contaminates the scientific integrity of the contest – but almost every other means of gaining advantage is. In fact, a key part of athletic virtue in Efficiency ethics is being able and willing to adopt any scientific means necessary to win. The athlete's virtues on the Efficiency model are either out of his control (as in "choosing the right parents" and being born into the right economic situation), or subservient (as in trusting and being obedient to the coach) – they are not the kinds of things that appear on Aristotle's list.

Then again, Efficiency virtues do not need to appear on Aristotle's list because, unlike Olympic virtues, they are not expected to apply beyond sport. Under the Efficiency Ethos, virtues (including Aristotelian ones such as courage, self-control, and ambition) are put in the service of sport—specifically the improvement of athletic performance and the achievement of records. If we ask why these performances are meaningful or worthwhile, we might get a blank stare or some reference to their exchange-value, especially their monetary exchange value—how much the athlete and her entourage will earn from sponsors. That the primary exchange value of virtue should be monetary is too infrequently questioned in modern sport, including the modern Olympic Movement. I have no objection to athletic virtue having monetary exchange value. What I object to is the *reduction* of sport into a business or scientific experiment whose only recognized outcome beyond sport itself is the hoped-for production of unintended technological tools. The danger of the Efficiency Ethos is that it demands so little of sports and athletes in human terms. Athletics should be more than the production of data and athletes should be more than performance machines.

Under the Olympic Ethos, virtue does not serve sporting ends, sport serves the end of virtue. Its primary purpose (its Aristotelian final cause) is *paideia* – a word that encompasses (without distinguishing between) both culture and education. Gymnastic training is undertaken in order to cultivate the *aretai* (virtues) of heroes and gods from the distant past who were able to serve mankind with them. Although *aretē* was eventually believed to be trainable (not through athletics alone, but in combination with philosophy, rhetoric, and other intellectual activities), it was also understood to be in a state of decline. Hesiod (*Works and Days* V.106-201) tells of the gold, silver, bronze and iron races of mankind (long since lost), and Philostratus' ideal trainer exhorts his athletes to toil to be more like them (*Gymnasticus* 44). All of this was in the service of (and often financed by) the state. Remember, heroes won fame not for athletic feats but for service to humanity, which was performed not in expectation of reward but for its own sake, for its beauty. The ancient paradigm of decline inspires athletes to apply their virtues beyond sport and contrasts starkly with the Efficiency Ethos' paradigm of constant athletic improvement which focuses solely on sport. Nevertheless, the two are compatible because Efficiency ethics demands athletic excellence, and Olympic ethics simply expands that demand to civically beneficial *aretē*.

Politics

This last point brings us to politics, which for Aristotle is inseparable from ethics—even inseparable from human beings, which he understands to be essentially political animals (*Politics* 1253a). On the Olympic Ethos, sport serves, above all, common human interests. Even the military benefit of ancient athletic training (which is *vastly* overstated in the popular media) is ultimately a community service. On the Efficiency Ethos, by contrast, sport primarily serves individual interests. This should be obvious from what has been said already, but there are a few nuances to add. The Funeral Games for Patroclus in Homer's *Iliad* (a foundational text for all Hellenic Culture) have the dramatic function of reconciling the struggle between Achilles and Agamemnon—a reconciliation that leads to the Achaeans uniting to defeat their common enemy.[18] The Olympic Games in the

---

[18] The games take place in *Iliad* book 21. See also my analysis in Reid, *Athletics and Philosophy*, chapter 1.

Classical period were likewise credited with the unification of diverse Hellenic tribes that eventually led to the defeat of the their enemies. In any case, it is clear from archaeology as well as philology that Olympia provided common, neutral ground upon which even warring tribes could meet in peace and work out their differences. The truce was itself provided by a religious decree. Worship of common gods to achieve common benefits through propitiation was the primary, pre-athletic function of Olympia.

I have argued elsewhere that it was not the intention but the unexpected outcome of bringing people together for sport that led to ancient Olympia's association with peace.[19] The Modern Olympic Movement's attempt to adapt this political function to the contemporary cause of global peace seems dependent on a similar process of bringing diverse people together on common ground in an atmosphere of respect. Jim Parry recognizes this process as fundamental to the logic and structure of sport itself.[20] In a way, it is simply an expansion of the educational primacy of sport under the Olympic paradigm; by coming together for the games we are forced to treat each other with respect, as equals under the rules, and to submit to a cooperative negotiation for honor. It also reinforces the ancient understanding of sport as ritual. The Muslim ritual of the Hajj, by comparison, which brings pilgrims from around the world to worship together in Mecca, has such a unifying effect that it caused the erstwhile black separatist Malcolm X to "rearrange" his thought patterns about racial coexistence.[21] The point here is not that political goals are the "true purpose" of sport, but that putting sport into the service of humanity gives it special meaning in the Olympic Ethos.

It was appropriate, nevertheless, for Pierre de Coubertin, when reviving the Games on an international level in modern

---

[19] Reid, "Olympic Sport and Its Lessons for Peace," in this volume.

[20] J. Parry, "The Power of Sport in Peace-making and Peacekeeping," *Sport in Society*, 15:6 (2012), 775-787.

[21] Malcolm X qtd. in A. Haley, *The Autobiography of Malcolm X* (New York: Ballantine Books, 1999), 346.

times, to leave behind their ancient religious function; or, more precisely to turn sport itself into a kind of religion, what he called *religio-athletae*, in an effort to retain its political benefits without imposing one religion or attempting to reconcile all religions in an international gathering. I sometimes wonder, however, if the Efficiency Ethos doesn't represent an extreme kind of *religio-athletae*, in which sport itself has become such an obsession that all other human values – educational, political, and spiritual – are set aside. It is telling that Bradley Wiggins, Brailsford's first Tour de France victor, says that his old coach's team "dehumanizes" the sport and advises young riders to steer clear of it.[22]

Under the Efficiency Ethos, there is no goal other than increased performance. The Olympic motto, "Faster, Higher, Stronger" is interpreted quantitatively in terms of performance data and never poetically in terms of human character or aspirations. The political function of the games is seen as "war minus the shooting" – a political struggle among nations using athletes as proxies.[23] The modern Olympic medal count (something I personally oppose) affirms, with some reliability, the existing political hierarchy of the globe.[24] Beyond that, the community function of the Games is as a sports-entertainment product capable of attracting myriad viewers and the wealthy sponsors that prey on them at an opportune time in the television calendar. The monetary exchange value of this non-religious festival is huge (so, apparently, is the risk of bankruptcy). Not only is modern sport generally in need of the Olympic Ethos, the Modern Olympic Games have a special need to resist the potentially self-destructive obsession with efficiency.

---

[22] Bradley Wiggins, "Team Sky have dehumanized cycling," *The Bradley Wiggins Show*, Eurosport.com, 27/05/2019; Ian Tuckey, "From Brad to Worse," *The Sun*. 21 Feb 2018.

[23] Orwell's statement is endorsed by, among others, art historian Nigel Spivey, *The Ancient Olympics*.

[24] Bernard & Busse, "Who Wins the Olympic Games," 413-417.

Conclusion

It must be admitted that the basic structure of sport, which challenges us to overcome artificial obstacles, encourages and rewards an efficiency ethos. Ancient Olympic athletes sought efficiencies, too, but the relative absence of quantifying technology kept that search from crowding out other values (even in throwing and jumping events, the goal was simply to surpass the mark of one's immediate competitors—reliable means of measuring times and distances across competitions didn't exist). Now that sophisticated performance tools are available even to amateurs (Nike plans to retail a shoe with the performance-enhancing technology it developed for the sub two-hour marathon attempt for $150), the culture of sport seems to be forgetting about its ancient connection to human virtue.

Victory has always mattered in sport, and it always will. But in a cultural context where Milo's Olympic victories were thought to replicate the virtues of the mythological hero Heracles, who represented the virtues of Olympian Zeus, a victory attributable to technology, bribery, treachery, or anything other than virtue lacked meaning and worth. To be sure, the first athlete to run a sub two-hour marathon at the Olympic Games will need virtue – but his human achievement will be overshadowed by the technologies developed to make the feat possible. Human virtues are certainly involved in the development of this technology, but they are not the human virtues embodied in athletes like Milo and heroes like Heracles. The Efficiency Ethos does not focus on athletes' virtues; we may even contend that it dehumanizes them. Spectators are likely to notice the sponsor's name on the runner's uniform but unlikely to see reflection of Achilles or Hermes in his stride; either because they don't know who Achilles and Hermes are, or because they judge them to be irrelevant.

And this is precisely my point. In order to balance out the Efficiency Ethos in sport, we need to know the history, the mythology, the poetry, and most of all the philosophy that lies at the origins of our social practice. As MacIntyre says, "to enter into a practice is to enter into a relationship not only with its contemporary practitioners, but also with those who have preceded us in the practice, particularly those whose achievements extended the reach of the practice to its present point."[25] I would submit, whatever the particular sport engaged in, that we need to cultivate a relationship with our athletic ancestors of ancient Greece – not just the athletes, but all those who were inspired by the Olympic philosophy: its holistic metaphysics, its qualitative epistemology, its autotelic aesthetics, its idealized virtue ethics, and its unifying politics. The Efficiency Ethos tends to narrow down the purpose and meaning of sport where as the Olympic Ethos seeks to expand it. Once the new record is set, what will be sport's next meaningful goal? Once moral and educational ideals are stripped from athletic performance, what will give sport any meaning at all?

The answer, of course, is human beings—philosophers in particular. It is we who critically negotiate the ethos of sporting cultures. It is we who study and teach the metaphysics, epistemology, aesthetics, ethics and politics of sport—as well as its history. To understand Olympic philosophy, we should experience Olympia. We should not only look at the ruins, we should admire the art, and maybe run in the stadium. But we should also listen to the song of the Olympic earth...the cicadas, to be sure, but also the wind as it blows through the leaves of olives, pines, cypresses, and laurel—all ancient plants with mythological stories that connect them to the gods. Unlike the temples and monuments, they don't change (much) because they are alive, they know how to renew themselves, to speak in ancient voices and welcome us with their song. In Olympia we can remember what sport was once capable of, and perhaps we can discover the strength to renew its ancient power.

---

[25] MacIntyre, *After Virtue*, 181.

Glossary of Ancient Greek Terms

agōn - struggle or contest as in *Olympiakoi Agōnes*; also refers to the gathering or even the place of the games.

andreia – the virtue of courage, or bravery

aphthiton – imperishable, unwilting (especially of glory)

apodyterion – undressing room in a gymnasium or palaestra

aretē – excellence, virtue; applies to humans, gods, animals, objects.

aristeia – Homeric concept of being the best and outdoing others

catharsis – cleansing or clarification, especially of emotions or ideas

dēmokratia – democracy, government by the people

dikaiosynē – justice; as a personal virtue or political concept

Ekecheiria – Olympic truce; literally "hands off" of religious travelers

eleutheria – liberty, freedom; a key value

epiphania – appearance, coming into light or view – especially of gods

epistēmē – in-depth knowledge, understanding

ēthos – moral disposition or character; of persons or communities

ethos- custom, habit, training

eudaimonia – happiness, prosperity, good-fortune

eusebeia - reverence, piety, respect

gymnasion – parklike place for exercise and learning

gymnastikē – exercise and training

hērōs – hero, mortal with divine ancestry, extraordinary virtue

hexis – a state (moral or physical) produced by training and habit *hysplex* – a starting mechanism or gate on a race track

isēgoria – equal freedom of speech

isonomia – equality under the law

kalokagathia – being both beautiful good; a kind of super-*aretē*

kalon – beautiful, fair, good; also "the beautiful"

kleos – glory, renown, fame

koinon agathon – the common good

mimēsis – imitation, emulation, representation

olbios – blessed, happy

paideia – education, culture

palaestra – building in a *gymnasion* or city for wrestling, boxing, and other exercises, often private.

philonikia – love of victory

philosophia – love of wisdom

psychē – mind/soul; the part responsible for thought and movement

sōma – body; the material part of a being

sophia – wisdom, cleverness, skill

sōphrosynē – self-control, self-discipline, moderation, prudence

therapōn – ritual substitute, attendant, minister

xenia – hospitality shown to a guest, friendly relations between states

zanes – bronze statues of Zeus used to deter cheating at Olympia

Bibliography

ABC News. "Person of the Week: Joey Cheek." *ABC News.com*, February 24, 2006.

Adkins, Arthur W. H. *Merit and Responsibility: A Study in Greek Values.* Chicago: The University of Chicago Press, 1975.

Aristotle. *Complete Works*. Ed. Jonathan Barnes. 2 vols. Princeton, NJ: Princeton University Press, 1984.

Armstrong, J. "After the ascent: Plato on becoming like God." *Oxford Studies in Ancient Philosophy* 26.1 (2010): 171–83.

Arnold, Peter. "Democracy, Education and Sport." *Journal of the Philosophy of Sport* 16.1 (1989): 100-110.

Associated Press. "FINA Moves Up Bodysuit Ban." *ESPN Olympic Sports.* July 31, 2009. http://sports.espn.go.com/.

Associated Press. "Iranian judo competitor rewarded after failing to compete against Israeli," *USA Today*, September 8, 2004.

Associated Press. "Secret Ballot Eliminates Baseball, Softball." ESPN online, July 8, 2005.

Augustine. "City of God." Trans. G. Walsh. *Medieval Philosophy*, eds. F. Baird & W. Kaufmann, 95-123. New Jersey: Prentice Hall, 1994.

Bacchylides. *Complete Poems*. Translated by Robert Fagles. New Haven, CT: Yale University Press, 1998.

Baka, R. and R. Hess. "Doing a 'Bradbury'!: An analysis of recent Australian success at the winter Olympic Games." In *The global nexus engaged: Past, present, and future interdisciplinary Olympic studies,* eds. K. Wamsley, R. Barney and S. Marty, 177-184. London, ON: University of Western Ontario Press, 2002.

Bale, J. and M. K. Christensen. *Post Olympism? Questioning Sport in the Twenty-first Century*. London: Berg, 2004.

Barnes, J. *The Presocratic Philosophers* . New York: Routledge, 1993.

Barney, R. S. Wenn, and S. Martyn. *Selling the Five Rings: The International Olympic Committee and the Rise of Olympic Commercialism.* Salt Lake: University of Utah Press, 2004.

Bartsch, Shadi. *The Mirror of the Self: Sexuality, Self-Knowledge, and the Gaze in the Early Roman Empire*. U. of Chicago Press, 2006.

Beck, F. A. G. *Greek Education 450-350 B.C.* London: Methuen, 1964.

Benner, A and F. Fobes, translators, *The Letters of Alciphron, Aelian and Philostratus.* Cambridge, MA: Harvard University Press, 1949.

Bernard, A. and M. Busse. "Who Wins the Olympic Games: Economic Resources and Medal Totals." *The Review of Economics and Statistics* 86 (2004): 413-417.

Blundell, S. *Women in Ancient Greece*. Cambridge, MA: Harvard University Press, 1995.

Bok, Derek. "Can Higher Education Foster Higher Morals?" In *Social and Personal Ethics*, ed. W. H. Shaw, 494–503. Belmont, CA: Wadsworth, 1996.

Briggs, R., H. McCarthy, A. Zorbas. *16 Days: The Role of Olympic Truce in the Quest for Peace*. Athens: Demos, 2004.

British Broadcasting Corporation. "Italy-Iraq match marred by death," *BBC News*, August 27, 2004.

British Broadcasting Corporation. "Olympics badminton: Eight women disqualified from doubles," *BBC Sport*, 2012.

Brown, Ben. "Homer, Funeral Contests and the Origins of the Greek City." In *Sport and Festival in the Ancient Greek World*, eds. D.J. Phillips and D. Pritchard, 123-162. Swansea, The Classical Press of Wales, 2003.

Brown, W. Miller. "Ethics, drugs, and sport." *Journal of the Philosophy of Sport* 7:1 (1980): 15–23.

Brown, W. Miller. "Practices and Prudence." *Journal of the Philosophy of Sport* 17:1 (1990): 71-84.

Brownell, Susan. *Training the Body for China*. Chicago, IL: The University of Chicago Press, 1995.

Burckhardt, Jacob. *The Greeks and Greek Civilization*. Translated by Sheila Stern. New York: St. Martin's, 1998.

Burkert, Walter. *Greek Religion*. Trans. J. Raffan. Cambridge, MA: Harvard University Press, 1985.

Cary, T. "Sir Dave Brailsford faces mounting pressure as UK Anti-Doping chairman questions Team Sky chief's 'extraordinary' claims." *The Guardian*: 7 January, 2017.

Chariots of Fire. Directed by H. Hudson. 20th Century Fox, 1981.

Chatziefstathiou, D. *The Changing Nature of the Ideology of Olympism in the Modern Olympic Era*. Doctoral Dissertation, Loughborough University, U.K, 2005.

Chatziefstathiou, D. "Olympic education and beyond: Olympism and value legacies from the Olympic and Paralympic Games." *Educational Review*, 64.3 (2012): 385-400.

Chatziefstathiou, D. and Henry, I.P. "Hellenism and Olympism: Pierre de Coubertin and the Greek Challenge to the Early Olympic movement." *Sport in History* 27.1 (2007).

Cicero, M. T. *Tusculan Disputations*. Translated by J. King. Cambridge, MA: Harvard University Press, 1927.

Confucius. *Analects.* Trans. A. Waley. New York: Vintage, 1989.

Confucius. *Analects.* Trans. E. Slingerland. Indianapolis: Hackett, 2003.

Coubertin, Pierre de. *Olympism: Selected Writings.* Edited by Norbert Muller Lausanne: International Olympic Committee, 2000.

Coubertin, Pierre de. "Les sources et les limites du progrès sportif." *Revue Olimpique* 5 (1939), 1-2.

Cremer, Rodolfo. "Professionalism and its Implications for the Olympic Movement." *Olympic Review* 26:14 (1997), 23-24.

Crowther, Nigel. *Athletica: Studies on the Olympic Games and Greek Athletics.* Hildesheim: Weidmann, 2004.

Cruise Malloy, David, Robert Kell, and Rod Kelln, "The spirit of sport, morality, and hypoxic tents: logic and authenticity," *Applied Physiology, Nutrition and Metabolism* 32 (2007): 289-296.

Csíkszentmihályi, Mihály and Susan Jackson. *Flow in Sports.* Champaign, IL: Human Kinetics, 1999.

Curd, Patricia, ed., Richard McKirahan, trans. *A Presocratics Reader.* Indianapolis: Hackett, 1995.

DaCosta, L. "A Never-Ending Story: the philosophical controversy over Olympism." *Journal of the Philosophy of Sport* 33 (2006): 157-73.

Davidson, W. L. *The Stoic Creed*. Edinburgh: T. & T. Clark, 1907.

Davis, Paul. "Sexuality and sexualization in sport." In *Ethics and Sport*, eds. W. Morgan, K. Meier, and A. Schneider, 285–92. Champaign, IL: Human Kinetics. 2001

De Buck, A. Trans. "The Armant Stela of Tuthmosis III." *Egyptian Readingbook*. Chicago: Ares Publishers,1948. 64-65

Derrida, J. *On Cosmopolitanism and Forgiveness*. London: Routledge, 2001.

Descartes, R. *The Philosophical Writings of Descartes*, eds. J. Cottingham, R. Stoothoff, and D. Murdoch. 2 vols. Cambridge: Cambridge University Press, 1985.

Despland, Michael. *The Education of Desire: Plato and the Philosophy of Religion*. Toronto: University of Toronto Press. 1985.

DiDonato, Michele. "La Scuola Pitagorica e la Nascita della Ginnastica Educativa." *Alcmeone* 1(1977): 11-21

Dio Chrysostom. *Discourses* v. 2. Trans. J. W. Cohoon. Cambridge, MA: Harvard University Press, 1939.

Diogenes Laertius. *Lives of Eminent Philosophers*. Translated by R.D. Hicks. Cambridge, MA: Harvard University Press, 1950.

Dixon, Nicholas. "On Winning and Athletic Superiority." *Journal of the Philosophy of Sport* 26:1 (1999): 10-26.

Dodds, E.R.. *The Greeks and The Irrational.* Berkeley: University of California Press, 1951.

Drees L. *Olympia: Gods, Artists and Athletes*. New York: Praeger, 1968.

Epictetus. *Discourses, Fragments, Handbook*. Translated by Robin Hard. Oxford: Oxford University Press, 2014.

Epictetus. *The Handbook of Epictetus*. Translated by Nicholas White. Indianapolis: Hackett, 1983.

Erasmus. "The Complaint of Peace." *The Essential Erasmus*, Translated by J. P. Dolan, 174-204. New York: Mentor Books, [1510] 1963.

Erdbrink, Thomas. "FIFA bans headscarves for Iranian women's soccer team," *The Washington Post*, June 6, 2011.

Eshleman, Andrew. "Moral Responsibility, "*Stanford Encyclopedia of Philosophy* (Winter 2016 Edition).

Euripides. "Heracles." Trans. E.P. Coleridge. In *The Complete Greek Drama*, eds. Whitney J. Oates and Eugene O'Neill, Jr. New York: Random House, 1938.

Evangeliou, Christos C. *Hellenic Philosophy Origin and Character*. Burlington, VT: Ashgate, 2006.

Evangeliou, Christos C. "Philosophy, Human Wonder and Hellenic Logos." *Skepsis* II (1991): 29-41.

Evangeliou, Christos C. "Socrates on Aretic Athletics." *Phronimon* 11.1 (2010): 45–63.

Feezell, Randolph. "Celebrated athletes, moral exemplars, and lusory objects." *Journal of the Philosophy of Sport* 32.1 (2005) 2-35.

Finley, M. I., and H.W. Plecket. *The Olympic Games: The First Thousand Years*. New York: Viking, 1976.

Fischer, John Martin. "Free Will and Moral Responsibility." In *The Oxford Handbook of Ethical Theory*, edited by David Copp. Oxford: Oxford University Press, 2007.

Fisher, Marjorie. "Sport as an Aesthetic Experience." In *Sport and the Body: A Philosophical Symposium*, ed. Ellen Gerber, 315-321. Philadelphia: Lea and Febiger, 1974.

Fleming, S., A. Hardman, C. Jones, and H. Sheridan. "Role models amongst elite young male rugby league players in Britain." *European Physical Education Review* 11.1 (2005): 51–70.

Fotheringham, William. "Chris Froome given little sympathy as Team Sky get a sense of déjà vu." *The Guardian.* July 7, 2018.

Foundation for the Hellenic World, "The revival of the ancient Olympic Games." *From Ancient Olympia to Athens of 1896*, 2011.

Frankfort, H. and H.A. *The Intellectual Adventure of Ancient Man: An Essay on Speculative Thought in the Ancient Near East*. Chicago: University of Chicago Press, 1946.

Freeman, Kathleen, trans. *Ancilla to the Pre-Socratic Philosophers: A Complete Translation of Diels Fragmente der Vorsokratiker.* Cambridge, MA: Harvard University Press, 1948.

Gardiner, E. Norman. *Athletics in the Ancient World*. Oxford: Clarendon Press, 1955.

Geeraets, Vincent. "Ideology, Doping and the Spirit of Sport," *Sport, Ethics and Philosophy* 12.3 (2018): 255-71.

Georgiadis, K. *Olympic Revival: The Revival of the Olympic Games in Modern Times.* Athens: Ekdotike, 2003.

Girginov, V., ed. *Olympic Studies.* Abingdon: Routledge, 2014.

Gleaves, John, Matthew Llewellyn and Tim Lehrbach. "Before the Rules are Written: Navigating Moral Ambiguity in Performance Enhancement." *Sport, Ethics, and Philosophy* 8:1 (2014): 85-99.

Golden, L. "*Mimēsis* and *Katharsis*." *Classical Philology* 64.3 (1969): 145-53.

Golden, Mark. *Greek Sport and Social Status.* Austin: Univ. of Texas, 2009.

Golden, Mark. "Hierarchies of heroism in Greek athletics." In *Kulteren Formen des Alltaglishen in der Antike*, edited by P. Mauritsch and C. Ulf. Graz: Grazer Universitatsverlag, 2013. 349–356.

Golden, Mark. *Sport and Society in Ancient Greece.* Cambridge: Cambridge University Press, 1998.

Greenspan, Bud, director. *Bud Greenspan's Athens 2004: Stories of Olympic Glory*, Showtime Network, January, 2006.

Greenspan, Bud. *The 100 Greatest Moments in Olympic History*. Los Angeles: General Publishing Group, 1995.

Guttmann, Allen. *From Ritual to Record: The Nature of Modern Sports.* Columbia University Press, 1978.

Guttmann, Allen. *The Olympics: A History of the Modern Games*. Chicago: University of Illinois Press, 2002.

Haley, Alex. *The Autobiography of Malcolm X.* New York: Ballantine Books, 1999.

Halliwell, Stephen. *The Aesthetics of Mimesis: Ancient Texts and Modern Problems.* Princeton, Princeton University Press, 2002.

Hamilton, E. *Mythology: Timeless Tales of Gods and Heroes*. New York: Warner, 1942.
Havelock, Eric A. *Preface to Plato*. Cambridge, MA: Harvard University Press, 1963.
Heidegger, Martin. *Poetry, Language, Thought*. New York: Harper & Row, 1971.
Henne, K., B. Koh, and V. McDermott. "Coherence of drug policy in sports: illicit inclusions and illegal inconsistencies." *Performance Enhancement and Health* 2 (2013): 48–55.
Hermann, A. *To Think Like a God: Pythagoras and Parmenides The Origins of Philosophy*. Las Vegas: Parmenides Publishing, 2004.
Herodotus. *Histories*. Translated by. A. D. Godley. Cambridge. Harvard University Press, 1920.
Hesiod. *Works and Days*. Translated by H.G. White. Cambridge MA: Harvard U.P., 1978.
Hobbes, T. *Leviathan*. Indianapolis: Library of Liberal Arts, [1651] 1958.
Hoberman, John. "Toward a Theory of Olympic Internationalism." *Journal of Sport History*, 22:1 (Spring 1995): 1-37.
Holowchak, Mark A. and Heather L. Reid. *Aretism: An Ancient Sports Philosophy for the Modern Sports World*. Lanham, MD: Lexington Books, 2011.
Holowchak, Mark. "Fascistoid" heroism revisited: A deontological twist to a recent debate." *Journal of the Philosophy of Sport* 32.1 (2005): 96–104.
Homer. *The Iliad*. Trans. Robert Fagles. New York: Penguin, 1990.
Homer. *The Odyssey*. Trans. Robert Fagles. New York: Penguin, 1996.
Hyde, Walter Woodburn. *Olympic Victor Monuments and Greek Athletic Art*. Washington DC: Carnegie Institution, 1921.
Hyland, D. *Philosophy of Sport*. New York, NY: Paragon House, 1990.
Hyland, Drew A. "Competition and Friendship." *Journal of the Philosophy of Sport*, 5 (1978): 27-37.
Iamblichus. *The Pythagorean Life*. Translated by T. Taylor. London: Watkins, 1818.
Inoue, A. "Critique of Modern Olympism: A Voice from the East." In *Sports – The East and the West*, eds. G. Pfister and L. Yueye, 163-7. Sant Agustin: Academia Verlag, 1999.
International Olympic Committee. "Olympic Solidarity Commission." *Olympic.org*, 2012.
International Olympic Committee. "The Sport and Environment Commission." *Olympic.org*, 2009.

International Olympic Committee. *Code of Ethics and Other Texts*. Lausanne: IOC, 2012.

International Olympic Committee. *Evaluation Criteria for Sports and Disciplines*. Lausanne: IOC, 2012.

International Olympic Committee. *Factsheet on the Opening Ceremony of the Games of the Olympiad*. Lausanne: IOC, 2013.

International Olympic Committee. *Factsheet on Women in the Olympic Movement.* Lausanne: IOC, 2018.

International Olympic Committee. *Factsheet: the Sports on the Olympic Programme.* Lausanne: IOC, 2008.

International Olympic Committee. *Olympic Charter*. Lausanne: IOC, 2004-2018.

International Olympic Committee. *Olympic Movement's Agenda 21: Sport for Sustainable Development*. Lausanne: IOC, 1999.

Iowerth, H., C. Jones and A. Hardman. "Nationalism and Olympism towards a Normative Theory of International Sporting Representation." *Olympika* 14 (2010): 81-110.

Jackson, Phil. *Sacred Hoops: Spiritual Lessons of a Hardwood Warrior*. New York: Hyperion, 1995.

Jaeger, Werner. *Paedeia: The Ideals of Greek Culture*. 3 vols. Translated by Gilbert Highet. New York: Oxford University Press, 1939.

Jameson, Michael H. "Women and Democracy in Fourth-century Athens." In *Ancient Greek Democracy: Readings and Sources,* ed. E. Robinson. 281-91. Malden, MA: Blackwell Publishing, 2004.

Jones, C. "Drunken role models: Rescuing our sporting exemplars." *Sport, Ethics and Philosophy* 5.4 (2011): 414–432.

Kant, Immanuel. *Grounding for the Metaphysics of Morals*. Translated by James W. Ellington. Indianapolis: Hackett, 1981.

Kant, Immanuel. *Perpetual Peace and Other Essays*. Tranlated by T. Humphrey. Indianapolis,: Hackett, [1795] 1983.

Kennell, Nigel M. *The Gymnasium of Virtue: Education & Culture in Ancient Sparta*. Chapel Hill: U. of North Carolina Press, 1995.

Kidd, Bruce. "Taking the Rhetoric Seriously: Proposals for Olympic Education," *Quest* 48 (1996): 82-92.

King, Winston. *Zen and the Way of the Sword*. New York: Oxford University Press, 1993.

Kirk, G.S., J.E. Raven, and M. Schofield. *The Presocratic Philosophers*, Cambridge: Cambridge University Press, 1983.

König, Jason. *Athletics and Literature in the Roman Empire.* Cambridge: Cambridge University Press, 2005.

Kornbeck, J. "The Naked Spirit of Sport: A Framework for Revisiting the System of Bans and Justifications in the World Anti-Doping Code." *Sport, Ethics and Philosophy* 7.3 (2013): 313-330.

Kramer, S. K. "Hymn of Praise to Shulgi." In *History Begins at Sumer*. 285-288. Philadelphia: U. of Pennsylvania Press, 1981.

Kyle, Donald G. *Sport and Spectacle in the Ancient World*. Malden MA: Blackwell, 2007.

Lamont, D.A. "Running Phenomena in Ancient Sumer." *Journal of Sport History*, vol. 22, n. 3 (1995).

Lao-Tzu. *Tao Te Ching*. Translated by S. Addiss and S. Lombardo. Indianapolis, IN: Hackett, 2003.

Laozi. "Daodejing." In *Readings in Classical Chinese Philosophy*, eds. P. Ivanhoe and B. Van Norden. Indianapolis: Hackett, 2001.

Lasch, C. "The degradation of sport." In *The Ethics of Sports: A Reader*, ed. Mike McNamee, 369–381. Abingdon: Routledge, 1977.

Lehman, Craig. 1981. "Can Cheaters Play the Game?" *Journal of the Philosophy of Sport* 8 (1981): 38-45.

Lenk, Hans. "Towards a Philosophical Anthropology of the Olympic Athletes and the Achieving Being." Ancient Olympia, Greece: *International Olympic Academy Report*, 1982. 163-77.

Levy, Glen "British Athletes Told to Avoid Shaking Hands at the Olympics," *Time Newsfeed*. March 6, 2012.

Liddell, H. G., and R. Scott. *A Greek-English Lexicon*. Oxford: Clarendon Press, 1940.

Llewellyn, Matthew P. and John Gleaves. *The Rise and Fall of Olympic Amateurism*. Urbana: University of Illinois Press, 2016.

Lloyd, G. *Ancient Worlds, Modern Reflections*. London: Oxford UP, 2004.

Lloyd, G. and N. Sivin. *The Way and The Word: Science and Medicine in Early China and Greece*. New Haven, CT: Yale U. P., 2002.

Lloyd, G.E.R. *Adversaries and Authorities: Investigations into Ancient Greek and Chinese Science*. Cambridge University Press, 1996.

Loland, S. "Coubertin's Olympism from the Perspective of the History of Ideas." *Olympika* 4 (1995): 49-78.

Loland, S. "Olympic Sport and the Ideal of Sustainable Development." *Journal of the Philosophy of Sport*, 33 (2006): 144-56.

Loland, S. "Performance-enhancing drugs, sport, and the ideal of natural athletic performance." *The American Journal of Bioethics* 18.6 (2018): 8–15.

Loland, S. "Record Sports: An Ecological Critique and Reconstruction." *Journal of the Philosophy of Sport* 28 (2001): 127-139.

Loland, S. and M. J. McNamee, "The 'spirit of sport', WADAs code review, and the search for an overlapping consensus." *International Journal of Sport Policy and Politics* (2019): 9.

Loland, S. *Fair Play in Sport: A Moral Norm System*. London: Routledge, 2002.

Loland, Sigmund and H. Hoeppler. "Justifying Anti-doping: The Fair Opportunity Principle and the Biology of Performance Enhancement. *European Journal of Sport Science* 12:4 (2012): 347-353.

Lopez Frias, Francisco Javier. "Unnatural Technology in a "Natural" Practice?: Human Nature and Performance-Enhancing Technology in Sport." *Philosophies* (2019): 4-35.

MacAloon, John J. "Religious Themes and Structures in the Olympic Movement and the Olympic Games." *Philosophy, Theology and History of Sport and Physical Activity*, eds. F. Landray and W. Orban. Quebec: Symposia Specialists, 1978.

MacAloon, John J. *This Great Symbol: Pierre de Coubertin and the Origins of the Modern Olympic Games*. London: Routledge, 2007.

MacIntyre, A. *After Virtue*. University of Notre Dame Press, 1981.

Mallawitz, Alfred. "Cult and Competition Locations at Olympia." *The Archaeology of the Olympics*, ed. W. Raschke, 79-109. Madison: U. of Wisconsin Press, 1988.

Marrou, H. I. *A History of Education in Antiquity*. Translated by George Lamb. Madison, WI: University of Wisconsin Press, 1956.

Martinkova, I. "*Kalokagathia:* How to understand harmony of a human being." *Nikephoros* 14 (2001): 21–8.

Martinkova, I. "Three Interpretations of Kalokagathia." *Korper in Kopf*, ed. P. Mauritsch, 17-28. Graz: Grazer Universitatsverlag, 2010.

Mayr, Erasmus. *Understanding Human Agency*. Oxford: Oxford University Press, 2011.

McFee, G. *Sports, Rules and Values: Philosophical investigations into the nature of sport*. Abingdon: Routledge, 2004.

McNamee, Mike, C. Jones, and J. Duda. "Psychology, ethics and sport: Back to an Aristotelian Museum of normalcy." *International Journal of Sport and Health Sciences* 1.1 (2003): 15–29.

McNamee, Mike. "Olympism, Eurocentricity, and Transcultural Virtues." *Journal of the Philosophy of Sport* 33 (2006), 174-87.

McNamee, Mike. "The spirit of sport and anti-doping policy: an ideal worth fighting for." *Play True: An Official Publication of WADA* 1:1 (2013): 14-16.

McNamee, Mike. "Whither Olympism." *Sport, Ethics, and Philosophy* 8:1 (2014): 1-2.

McNamee, Mike. *Sports, Virtues and Vices: Morality Plays*. Abingdon: Routledge, 2008.

Metheny, Eleanor. "The Symbolic Power of Sport." In *Sport and the Body: A Philosophical Symposium*, edited by Ellen Gerber., 231-236. Philadelphia: Lea & Febiger, 1979

Mikalson, Jon D. *Ancient Greek Religion*. Malden, MA: Blackwell, 2005.

Miller, Stephen G. *Ancient Greek Athletics*. New Haven, CT: Yale University Press, 2004.

Miller, Stephen G. *Aretē: Greek Sports from Ancient Sources*. 2nd ed. Berkeley: University of California Press, 1991.

Miller, Stephen G. "Naked Democracy." In *Polis and Politics*, eds: P. Jensen, T. Nelson, and L. Rubenstein, 277-295. Copenhagen: Museum of Tusculanum Press, 2000.

Mogens, Herman Hansen. *Polis: An Introduction to the Ancient Greek City State*. Oxford: Oxford University Press, 2006.

Morgan, W.J. "Cosmopolitanism, Olympism, and Nationalism: A Critical Interpretation of Coubertin's Ideal of International Sporting Life." *Olympika* IV (1995): 79-91.

Morgan, W.J. "Multinational Sport and Literary Practices and Their Communities: The Moral Salience of Cultural Narratives." In *Ethics and Sport*, eds. M. McNamee and J. Parry, 184-204. London: E & FN Spon, 1998.

Morgan, W.J. "Sport as the Moral Discourse of Nations." In *Values in Sport*, eds. T. Tannsjo & C. Tamburrini, 59-73. Oxon: Spon, 2000.

Morgan, W.J. *Why Sports Morally Matter*. Abingdon: Routledge, 2006.

Morris, "Ian. "Equality and the origins of Greek Democracy." In *Ancient Greek Democracy*, ed. E. Robinson. Malden, MA: Blackwell, 2004.

Mouratidis, John. "Heracles at Olympia and the Exclusion of Women from the Ancient Olympic Games." *Journal of Sport History* 11 (1984), 41-55.

Mumford, S. *Watching Sport: Aesthetics, ethics and emotion*. Abingdon: Routledge, 2012.

Nagy, Gregory. *Pindar's Homer: The Lyric Possession of an Epic Past*. Washington DC: Center for Hellenic Studies, 1980.

Nagy, Gregory. *The Ancient Greek Hero in 24 Hours*. Cambridge: Harvard University Press, 2013.

Nakamura, J. and Csikszentmihalyi, M. (2001). "Flow Theory and Research". In *Handbook of Positive Psychology* C. R. Snyder Erik Wright, and Shane J. Lopez, 195–206. Oxford University Press.

Nanayakkara, S. "Olympism: A Western Liberal Idea That Ought Not to Be Imposed on other Cultures?" In *Pathways: Critiques and Discourse in Olympic Research*, ed. K. Wamsley,. 351-358). London, Ontario: University of Western Ontario, 2008.

National Collegiate Athletic Association, "Estimated Probability of Competing in Athletics Beyond the High School Interscholastic Level," *NCAA.com*, 2011.

Neubauer, Deane. "Modern Sport and Olympic Games: The Problematic Complexities Raised by the Dynamics of Globalization," *Journal of Olympic History* 19:1 (March, 2011).

Nicholson, Nigel James. *Aristocracy and Athletics in Archaic and Classical Greece*. Cambridge: Cambridge University Press, 2005.

Nissiotis, N. "The Olympic Movement's Contribution to Peace." *International Olympic Academy Proceedings*, 1985. 54-63.

Nissiotis, N. "The Philosophy of Olympism." *Olympic Review* 13.6 (1979), 82-85.

O'Leary, J. *Drugs and Doping in Sport*. London: Routledge, 2013.

Obree, Graeme. *Flying Scotsman: Cycling to Triumph Through My Darkest Hours*. Boulder, CO: Velo Press, 2005.

Olympic Solidarity. *Where the Action is: 2009-2012 Quadrennial Plan*. Lausanne: IOC, 2009.

Parke, H.W. *Festivals of the Athenians*. Ithaca, NY: Cornell U. Press, 1977.

Parry, J. "Globalization, Multiculturalism and Olympism." *Proceedings of the International Olympic Academy* (2000): 86-97.

Parry, J. "Olympism at the Beginning and End of the Twentieth Century." *Proceedings of the International Olympic Academy* (1998): 81-94.

Parry, J. "Sport and Olympism: Universals and Multiculturalism." *Journal of the Philosophy of Sport* 33 (2006):188-204.

Parry, J. "The Power of Sport in Peace-making and Peacekeeping." *Sport in Society* 15:6 (2012): 775-787.

Pausanias. *Guide to Greece: Volume 2: Southern Greece*. Translated by Peter Levi. London: Penguin, 1971.

Pawlenka, C. "The Idea of Fairness: A General Ethical Concept or One Particular to Sports Ethics." *Journal of the Philosophy of Sport* 32 (2005): 49-64.

Penner, Terry. "The Unity of Virtue," *The Philosophical Review* 82 (1973), 35-68.
Pereboom, Derk. *Living without Free Will.* Cambridge, UK: Cambridge University Press, 2001.
Peters, F.E. *Greek Philosophical Terms: A Historical Lexicon.* New York: New York University Press, 1967.
Petersen, T.S. "Good athlete—bad athlete? On the 'role-model argument' for banning performance enhancing drugs." *Sport, Ethics and Philosophy* 4.3 (2010): 332–340.
Pfister, G. "Outsiders: Muslim Women and Olympic Games – Barriers and Opportunities." *The International Journal of the History of Sport* 27.16-18 (2010): 2925-2957.
Philostratus, Flavius. *Heroicus, Gymnasticus, Discourses 1 and 2.* Edited and translated by Jeffrey Rusten and Jason König. Cambridge, MA: Harvard University Press, 2005.
Philostratus, Flavius. *On Heroes.* Translated by Ellen Bradshaw Aitken and Jennifer K. Berenson Maclean. Washington DC: Center for Hellenic Studies, 2012.
Pindar. *Olympian Odes, Pythian Odes.* Translated by William H. Race. Cambridge, MA: Harvard University Press, 1997.
Pindar. *Nemean Odes, Isthmian Odes, Fragments.* Translated by William H. Race. Cambridge, MA: Harvard University Press, 1997.
Pindar. *The Complete Odes*. Translated by Anthony Verity. Oxford U.K.: Oxford University Press, 2007.
Pindar. *The Odes of Pindar.* Translated by Richard Lattimore. Chicago, 1959.
Plato. *Complete Works.* Edited by J. Cooper. Indianapolis: Hackett, 1997.
Plutarch. *Lives.* Trans. Bernadotte Perrin. Cambridge, MA. Harvard University Press. London. William Heinemann Ltd. 1919.
Poliakoff, M. *Combat Sports in the Ancient World.* New Haven, CT: Yale U. Press, 1987.
Pound, Dick. *Inside the Olympics.* New York: Wiley & Sons, 2004.
Preuss, Holger. *Economics of the Olympic Games.* Petersham, NSW: Walla Walla Press, 2000.
Prouty, D. *In Spite of Us: My education in the big and little games of amateur and Olympic sports in the U.S.* Brattleboro, VT: Velo-News, 1988.
Raubitschek, A.E. "The Panhellenic Idea and the Olympic Games." *The Archaeology of the Olympics*, ed. W. Raschke. Madison, WI: U. of Wisconsin Press, 1988.

Rawls, John. *A Theory of Justice*. Cambridge, MA: Harvard University Press, 1971.
Reid, Heather and M. Austin. *The Olympics and Philosophy*. Lexington, KY: University Press of Kentucky, 2012.
Reid, Heather L. "Amateurism is Dead: Long Live Amateurism." In *The Olympic Idea Nowadays,* eds. D. Chatziefstathiou, X. Ramon and A. Miragaya. 61-63. Barcelona: Centre d'Estudis Olímpics i de l'Esport Universitat Autònoma, 2016.
Reid, Heather L. "Aristotle's Pentathlete." *Sport, Ethics and Philosophy*, 4: 2 (2010): 183-194.
Reid, Heather L. "Athletes as heroes and role models: an ancient model." *Sport, Ethics and Philosophy* 11.1 (2016): 40-51.
Reid, Heather L. "Athletic Beauty as *Mimēsis* of Virtue: The Case of the Beautiful Boxer." In *Looking at Beauty in Western Greece*, eds. H. Reid & Tony Leyh. Sioux City: Parnassos Press, 2019. 77-91.
Reid, Heather L. "Athletic Beauty in Classical Greece: A Philosophical View." *Journal of the Philosophy of Sport* 39 (2012): 281-97.
Reid, Heather L. "Athletic Competition as Socratic Philosophy." *AUPO Gymnika* 35:2 (2006): 73-77.
Reid, Heather L. "Athletic Virtue and Aesthetic Values in Aristotle's Ethics. *Journal of the Philosophy of Sport* 47:1 (Spring 2020).
Reid, Heather L. "East to Olympia: Recentering Olympic Philosophy between East and West." *Olympika: The International Journal of Olympic Studies* 19 (2010): 59-79.
Reid, Heather L. "Eros vs. Ares" In *Cultural Relations Old and New: The Transitory Olympic Ethos*, eds. K.B. Wamsley, S.G. Martyn, and R.K. Barney, 231-9. London, Canada: International Centre for Olympic Studies, 2004.
Reid, Heather L. "Heroes of the Coliseum." *Football and Philosophy*, ed. M. Austin 28-140. Lexington: Univ. Press of Kentucky, 2008.
Reid, Heather L. "Olympic Epistemology: The Athletic Roots of Philosophical Reasoning." *Skepsis* 17:1-2 (2007): 124-132.
Reid, Heather L. "Olympic Sport and Its Lessons for Peace" *Journal of the Philosophy of Sport* 33:2 (2006): 205-214.
Reid, Heather L. "Performing Virtue: Athletic *Mimēsis* in Platonic Education," *Politics and Performance in Western Greece*, eds. H. Reid, D. Tanasi, S. Kimbell. 265-277. Parnassos Press, 2017.
Reid, Heather L. "Racing for truth: Sport, religion, and the scientific spirit in ancient Olympia." *Stadion: International Journal of the History of Sport*, 33 (2009): 211-20.

Reid, Heather L. "Responsibility, Inefficiency, and the Spirit of Sport." *American Journal of Bioethics* 18.6 (2018): 22-23.
Reid, Heather L. "Sport as Moral Education in Plato's *Republic*." *Journal of the Philosophy of Sport* 34:2 (2006): 160-175.
Reid, Heather L. "Sport, Philosophy, and the Quest for Knowledge." *Journal of the Philosophy of Sport* 36:1 (2009): 40-49.
Reid, Heather L. "Was the Roman Gladiator an Athlete?" *Journal of the Philosophy of Sport* 33.1 (2006): 37–49.
Reid, Heather L. *Athletics and Philosophy in the Ancient World: Contests of Virtue.* Abingdon: Routledge, 2011.
Reid, Heather L. *Introduction to the Philosophy of Sport.* Lanham, MD: Rowman and Littlefield, 2012.
Reid, Heather L. *The Philosophical Athlete.* Durham, NC: Carolina Academic Press, 2002. Second revised edition, 2019.
Ren, Hai. *A Comparative Analysis of Ancient Greek and Chinese Sport.* Doctoral Thesis, University of Alberta, 1988.
Right to Play. "Right to Play at a Glance" *Right to Play.com*. 2006.
Roubineau, J-M. *Milon de Crotone ou l'invention du sport.* Paris: Presses Universitaires de France, 2017.
Russell, J.S. "Are Rules All an Umpire Has to Work With?" *Journal of the Philosophy of Sport*, 27:1 (1999) 27-49.
Samaranch, Juan A. "Foreword," *Olympic Movement's Agenda 21* ed. IOC Sport and Environment Commission. Lausanne: IOC, 1999.1-7.
Sandars, N.K., translator. *The Epic of Gilgamesh.* London: Penguin, 1960.
Sansone, David. *Greek Athletics and the Genesis of Sport.* Berkeley: University of California Press, 1988.
Sartre, Jean-Paul. "The Humanism of Existentialism." In *Existentialism from Dostoevsky to Sartre*, ed. Walter Kaufman, 345-368. New York: Meridian Books, 1975.
Savulescu J., B. Foddy; M. Clayton, "Why we should allow performance enhancing drugs in sport." *British Journal of Sports Medicine* 38 (2004): 666–670.
Scanlon, Thomas F. *Eros and Greek Athletics.* Oxford: Oxford University Press, 2002.
Scanlon, Thomas F., ed. *Sport in The Greek and Roman Worlds*, 2 vols. Oxford: Oxford University Press, 2014.
Scheuerman, William. "Globalization." In *The Stanford Encyclopedia of Philosophy* (Summer 2010 Edition). Ed. Edward N. Zalta.
Schlosser, Markus. "Agency." In *The Stanford Encyclopedia of Philosophy* (Fall 2015 Edition), ed. Edward N. Zalta.

Schneider, A. and R. Butcher. "Fair Play as Respect for the Game." *Journal of the Philosophy of Sport* 25:1(1998): 1-22.

Schneider, A. and R. Butcher. "Why Olympic Athletes Should Avoid the Use and Seek the Elimination of Performance-Enhancing Substances and Practices From the Olympic Games." *Journal of the Philosophy of Sport* 20-21 (1994): 64-81.

Segrave, J. "Toward a Definition of Olympism." In *The Olympic Games in Transition*, eds. J. Segrave and D. Chu, 149-161. Champaign, IL: Human Kinetics, 1988.

Simon, Robert L. "Good Competition and Drug-Enhanced Performance." *Journal of the Philosophy of Sport*, 9.1 (1984): 6-13.

Simon, Robert L. *Fair Play: The Ethics of Sport*, 2nd Ed. Boulder, CO: Westview Press, 2004.

Smith, Nicholas D. "Plato and Aristotle on the Nature of Women." *Journal of the History of Philosophy* 21:4 (1983): 467-478.

Snell, Bruno. *The Discovery of the Mind in Greek Philosophy and Literature.* New York: Dover, 1982.

Spivey, Nigel. "Meditations on a Greek Torso." *Cambridge Archaeological Journal*, 7:2 (1997) 309–17.

Spivey, Nigel. *The Ancient Olympics: A History*. Oxford, U.K.: Oxford University Press, 2004.

Stocking, Charles. "Ages of Athletes: Generational Decline in Philostratus' Gymnasticus and Archaic Greek Poetry." *CHS Research Bulletin* 1.2 (2013).

Stoll, Sharon K. and J. M. Beller. "Do Sports Build Character?" In *Sports in School: The Future of an Institution,* edited by John Gerdy. New York: Columbia University Press, 2000. 18-30

Suits, Bernard. *The Grasshopper: Games, Life, and Utopia.* 2nd ed. Peterborough, ON: Broadview Press, 2005.

Swaddling, J. *The Ancient Olympic Games*. London: British Museum 1980.

Sweet, Waldo E. *Sport and Recreation in Ancient Greece*. Oxford University Press, 1987.

Tacitus. *Annals: Books 13-16.* Trans. John Jackson. Cambridge, MA: Harvard University Press, 1937.

Tamburrini, Claudio. "Sports, Fascism, and the Market." *Journal of the Philosophy of Sport* 25.1 (1998): 35-47.

Tannsjo, T. "Is our admiration for sports heroes fascistoid?" *Journal of the Philosophy of Sport* 25.1 (1998): 23–34.

Teja, A. and S. Mariano, eds. *Agonistica in Magna Grecia: La Scuola Atletica di Crotone*. Calopezzati: Edizioni del Convento, 2004.

Terry Fox Humanitarian Award Program. 2015. http://terryfoxawards.ca/

The Nielsen Company, "Beijing Olympics Draw Largest Ever Global Television Audience," *Nielsenwire,* September 8, 2008.

Tillet, S. "Jesse Owens, a Film hero once again." *New York Times,* February 12, 2016.

Topfer, K. "Foreword." In *Olympic Movement's Agenda 21,* ed. IOC Sport and Environment Commission, 9-10. Lausanne: IOC, 1999.

Torres, Cesar "What Counts as Part of a Game? A Look at Skills." *Journal of the Philosophy of Sport* 27.1 (2000): 81-92.

Torres, Cesar. "Results or Participation? Reconsidering Olympism's Approach to Competition." *Quest* 58, (2006): 242-254.

Tuckey, Ian. "From Brad to Worse." *The Sun.* 21 Feb 2018.

Valavanis, P.. "Thoughts on the Historical Origins of the Olympic Games and the Cult of Pelops in Olympia." *Nikephoros* 19 (2006): 137-152.

Valavanis, Panos. *Games and Sanctuaries in Ancient Greece.* Translated by David Hardy. Los Angeles: Getty Publications, 2004.

Vergil. *The Aeneid.* Trans. W.F. Jackson Knight. London: Penguin, 1956.

Waddington, Ivan, A.V. Christiansen, J. Gleaves, J. Hoberman, and V. Moller "Recreational drug use and sport: Time for a WADA rethink?," *Performance Enhancement & Health* 2.2 (2013): 4 1-47.

Waley, Arthur. *Three Ways of Thought in Ancient China.* Stanford, CA: Stanford University Press, 1939.

Weaving, C. "Smoke and Mirrors: A Critique of Women Olympians' Nude Reflections." In *Olympic Ethics and Philosophy,* eds. M. McNamee and J. Parry, 130-148. Abingdon: Routledge, 2013.

Weaving, Charlene. *"The Burning Flame Within*: The Sexualization of Women Athletes in Beach Volleyball." In *The Olympics and Philosophy,* eds. Austin and Heather L. Reid. 228-41. Lexington: University of Kentucky Press, 2012.

Wiggins, Bradley." Team Sky have dehumanized cycling." *The Bradley Wiggins Show.* Eurosport 27/05/2019.

Wing, John Ian. "Letter saved the Games." *National Library of Australia, Papers of Sir Wilfred Kent Hughes,* NS 4856/series 19.

Woodruff, Paul. *First Democracy.* Oxford: Oxford University Press, 2005.

Woodruff, Paul. *Reverence: Renewing a Forgotten Virtue.* Oxford: Oxford University Press, 2002.

World Anti-Doping Agency. *World Anti-Doping Code: 2015 with 2018 Amendments.* Montreal: WADA, 2018.

World Commission on Environment and Development. *Our Common Future.* Oxford: Oxford University Press, 1987.

Xenophon. *Xenophon in Seven Volumes.* Translated by E.C. Marchant. Cambridge: Harvard University Press, 1923.

Young, D. *The Modern Olympics: A Struggle for Revival.* Baltimore: John Hopkins University Press, 1996.

Young, David C. "How the Amateurs Won the Olympics." In *The Archaeology of the Olympics*, ed. W. Raschke. Madison: University of Wisconsin Press, 1988. 55-78.

Young, David C. *The Olympic Myth of Greek Amateur Athletics.* New York: Ares, 1984.

Young, David. "*Mens Sana in Corpore Sano*? Body and Mind in Greek Literature." *North American Society for Sport History*, 1998.

Index

Achilles, 12, 29, 30, 50-54, 56, 59-62, 120, 131, 148, 153, 155-159, 178, 211, 367, 428, 431.

Aesthetics, 160, 181, 182, 201, 238, 372, 417, 423, 425, 432.

Agency (moral), 290, 293, 297-306.

Agenda 21, 329, 357, 358, 398. *See also*: Environment

Agōn, 6, 8, 29, 43, 50, 55, 57, 123, 124, 152, 156, 184, 193, 369, 370, 433.

Amateurism, 104, 442.

Anti-doping, 239, 291, 296. *See also*: doping

Aretē (excellence) 2, 7, 29, 36, 40, 49-51, 53, 62, 71, 80-82, 87, 90, 93, 94, 116-136, 140, 145, 147, 148, 152-159, 169-175, 178-182, 189, 191, 192, 196, 198, 211, 229, 230, 233, 249, 251, 252, 254, 266, 282, 318, 320, 365-368, 370, 372-425, 426, 428, 433, 434.

Aristotle, 2, 10, 11, 36, 43, 44-45, 52, 54, 69, 71, 72, 80, 83, 88, 92, 118, 123, 126, 145, 155, 156, 166, 169, 179, 195-203, 215, 229, 237, 239, 243, 251, 265, 267, 272, 276, 282, 320, 323, 367, 368, 398, 417, 421, 427, 428.

Athena, 9, 42, 100, 168, 177.

Athens 2004 (Games), 109, 122, 439.

Athla (feats), 38, 51, 53, 155, 171

Autotelicity, 154, 160, 197, 202, 423

Bacchylides, 62, 151, 177, 435.

Badminton, 202, 240, 436.

Beauty, 22, 64, 117, 147-151, 154, 155, 163-175, 181-203, 230, 233, 237, 274, 353, 372, 374, 399, 412, 422-428. *See also*: *Kalokagathia*

Bobsleigh, 286, 304, 305.

Boxing, 13, 15, 31-33, 75, 82, 84-86, 89, 90, 91, 95, 97, 99, 119, 124, 156, 158, 166, 170, 270, 274, 319, 328, 334, 378.

Boycott, 79

Buddhism, 148

China, 333, 350, 367, 375, 379, 380, 382, 387, 388, 403, 404, 406, 409, 410, 411. *See also*: Beijing 2008

Commercialism, 104, 106, 249

Confucianism, 208, 218, 231, 236, 366, 367, 372, 395, 404

Confucius, 214, 215, 248, 365, 368, 374, 379, 384, 385, 388, 391-400, 404, 409, 410.

Cosmopolitanism, 17, 219, 241, 344, 345

Coubertin, Pierre de 5, 17, 103, 116, 208, 209, 211, 212, 219, 222, 223, 225, 229, 232, 234, 243, 345, 348, 429.

Csikszentmihalyi, Mihaly *see*: Flow

Cycling, 47, 61, 226, 249, 256, 259, 260, 285, 286, 297, 300,

302-305, 357, 376, 405, 411, 415, 430.
Daoism, 148, 208, 210, 218, 231, 236, 366, 367, 372, 375, 395, 404, 407. *See also*: Laozi
De (virtue), 17, 51, 57, 103, 116, 173, 186, 189, 208, 209, 222, 223, 232, 243, 303, 345, 348, 365-368, 371-388, 391, 397, 415, 422, 424, 429.
Delphic Oracle, 14, 332
Democracy, 2, 13, 79, 82-84, 85, 87-90, 94-96, 103, 227, 269, 270, 271, 314, 318, 340, 350, 356, 433.
Descartes, Rene 209, 228, 236, 350, 380, 386, 390, 418, 437.
Diversity, 5, 13, 16, 17, 60, 95, 207, 211, 213, 227, 235, 243, 258, 260, 285, 287, 325, 344, 349, 352, 354, 357, 362, 383, 399.
Doping, 48, 202, 233, 238, 254, 255, 279, 284, 288, 289-296, 302, 303, 305, 419, 427. *See also*: Anti-doping
Education, 13, 49, 50, 54, 63, 117, 128-132, 136, 139, 140, 156, 172, 179, 180, 181, 194, 202, 207, 209, 221-223, 229, 232, 245, 251, 252, 271, 277, 282, 291, 293, 323, 329, 355, 356, 359-361, 365, 389, 427.
Efficiency Ethos, 290, 306, 415, 418, 426-432.
Enlightenment, 2, 208, 209
Environment, 74, 126, 148, 150, 220, 226, 260, 311, 326, 329, 351, 357, 398, 400, 408. *See also*: Agenda 21, Sustainability.
Epic poetry, 53, 60, 62, 63, 152
Epictetus, 184, 191-193, 230, 344, 365, 370, 374, 392, 438
Equality, 13, 79, 87, 89, 90, 96, 143, 200, 213-215, 243, 244, 265, 268-271, 275-277, 287, 301, 303, 313, 325, 335, 340, 341, 343, 346, 434. *See also: Isonomia*
Erasmus, 299, 336, 342, 345, 438.
Ethics, 7, 10, 49, 160, 167, 169, 181, 182, 195, 201-203, 211, 213, 215, 216, 231, 236, 245, 255, 260, 286, 291, 294, 295, 338, 351, 366, 371, 391, 394, 399, 417, 426, 428, 432, 443.
Ethos, 43, 80, 90, 156, 207, 234, 235, 248, 249, 261, 319, 416, 423, 431, 432, 433
Eurocentrism, 5, 242
Fair play, 12, 195, 199, 202, 203, 215, 220, 221, 232, 236-239, 244, 245, 250, 254-256, 262, 265-268, 270, 276, 280, 283-285, 288, 291, 335, 351, 360, 384, 398.
Flow, 41, 127, 147, 154, 374, 387, 393.
Gilgamesh, 22, 23, 24, 130.
Globalization, 220, 222, 240, 241, 242, 245, 317, 325, 328, 347, 349, 350, 352, 353, 355, 359, 361, 366, 379, 383
Heracles, 8, 35-46, 50-53, 62, 68, 93, 130, 131, 155-158, 168, 171, 192, 211, 243, 322, 333, 419, 431.

Heraclitus, 72
Hermes, 156, 166, 337, 431
Heroes, 2, 8, 17, 21-34, 47, 48-63, 109, 131, 147-159, 282, 324, 343, 420, 428, 431.
Hesiod, 59, 60, 157, 336, 337, 393, 428.
Hinduism, 148.
Homer, 11, 12, 21, 22, 28-31, 34, 43, 57-62, 69, 70, 74, 79, 99, 101, 116, 119, 120, 148, 151-153, 155, 159, 170, 252, 282, 313, 318, 319, 337, 367, 372, 388, 428.
Honor, 12, 29-31, 38-40, 61, 69, 70, 75, 94, 101, 120, 121, 140, 141, 144, 175, 177, 185, 197, 198, 201, 217, 225, 226, 238, 244, 273, 293, 313, 376, 380, 429
Humanism, 6, 9, 10, 12, 18, 110, 266, 293, 300, 405

Idealism, 6, 9, 18, 260
Impartiality, 11, 73, 238, 265, 268, 271-273, 275-277, 321.
Individualism, 198, 200, 365, 366, 424.
Instrumentalism, 160, 197, 198, 365
IOC, 7, 104-107, 195, 198, 202, 216, 218, 220, 224, 225, 235, 237, 238, 242-244, 248, 250, 253, 255, 256, 259, 274, 284, 286, 289, 316, 317, 325, 329, 335, 350-352, 354, 356, 358, 390, 393, 398, 400
Isocrates, 14, 9.2, 327, 334
Isonomia, 13, 87, 89, 270, 271, 274, 340, 434

Jackson, Phil, 441
Justice, 6, 7, 9, 12, 13, 16, 18, 55, 87, 97, 110, 117, 119, 121, 125, 126, 132, 133, 135, 137, 142, 143, 144, 202, 221, 236-239, 245, 251, 254, 260, 262, 265-277, 288, 351, 353, 368, 433
Juvenal, 212, 229

Kalokagathia, 117, 155, 163, 164, 168, 174, 181, 182, 195-198, 201, 203, 366, 426.
Kant, Immanuel, 213, 441
Kantianism, 208, 215
Kidd, Bruce, 441

Laozi, 214, 215, 365-379, 381, 383, 384, 391-396, 400, 404, 405, 407, 408, 409, 410, 411, 412. *See also:* Daoism
Leadership, 21, 28, 30, 82, 88, 139, 329, 394, 404, 405
London 2012 (Games), 202, 240, 244.
Lysias, 14, 327, 334.

Magna Graecia, 318, 320.
Medal count, 203, 234, 385, 430.
Mencius, 369, 385, 391, 400, 401.
Metaphysics, 119, 196, 211-213, 267, 272, 275, 385, 389, 390, 417.
Milo of Croton 157, 158, 320, 419, 422, 431.
Mimēsis, 53, 54, 57, 59, 156, 188, 419, 434.
Multiculturalism, 5, 219, 222, 225, 242, 353, 354, 379, 395.
Muscular Christianity, 212, 229.

Nationalism, 200, 250, 332.

Nomos, 85, 397, 398.

Obree, Graeme, 445

Odysseus, 31, 32, 43, 57, 62, 131, 158, 170, 211, 252, 319, 337, 426.

Officials, 15, 74, 76, 84, 85, 110, 137, 143, 201, 202, 237, 238, 240, 262, 272-274, 328, 334, 347, 354, 359, 385, 400, 424, 425. *See also*: referees.

Olympic Creed, 197-8, 224, 232, 234, 252, 253.

Olympic Hymn, 423

Olympic Motto, 1, 195, 224, 232-234, 252-3, 389, 301, 356, 433.

Olympic Solidarity, 227, 284, 325, 351, 352, 440, 445

Olympic Spirit, vii, 67, 195, 384

Olympic Truce (*ekecheiria*), 110, 219, 257, 258, 315, 331, 339, 355, 433.

Olympism, 2, 5, 7, 17, 103, 116, 117, 129, 197, 199, 205, 208-245, 248, 251-256, 259, 261, 262, 276, 279, 282, 283, 286, 287, 293-297, 300-305, 311, 315, 316, 329, 335, 351, 354-356, 363, 365, 379-391, 394, 398-401.

Pankration, 15, 75, 84, 90, 158, 166, 174, 334

Pausanias, 14, 15, 76, 81, 86, 267, 318, 323, 332, 333, 334, 445

Peace, 6, 8, 9, 14-16, 18, 67, 77, 95, 97, 110, 128, 152, 184, 199, 217-219, 224, 250, 251, 256-58, 260, 262, 265, 266, 276, 286-288, 311, 315, 326- 328, 330, 331-345, 355, 358, 359, 361, 362, 389, 395, 400, 403, 410, 424, 429.

Pelops, 8, 151, 217, 450

Pharaohs, 26

Philonikia, 118, 373, 434

Physis, 397, 417

Pindar, 2, 8, 58, 62, 68, 71, 72, 78, 80, 95, 147, 150, 151-155, 159, 160, 169, 175, 177, 233, 319, 333, 334, 425.

Pistorius, Oscar, 233

Plato, 2, 7, 8, 18, 36, 39-43, 52, 54, 56, 63, 69, 72, 75, 88, 94, 101, 105, 118-126, 129, 132, 134-144, 148, 154, 156, 169-176, 179, 180, 186, 187, 190, 199, 215, 229, 230, 233, 237, 243, 265-267, 275, 282, 320, 321, 323, 327, 333, 342, 365, 367, 368, 370- 374, 378, 383, 388, 392, 393, 398, 418, 426.

Politics, 16, 216-217, 240, 244, 311, 315, 326, 347, 361, 394, 398-399, 428-432.

Ponos, 77, 102, 169, 170, 191

Prometheus, 9, 10, 41, 42, 373

Protesilaos, 150, 151, 419.

Protest, 219, 328, 405.

Pythagoras, 72-74, 132, 210, 230, 319, 320, 323, 383.

Qi, 260, 374, 387, 400, 408.

Referees, 95, 272. *See also*: Officials

Religio-athletae, 430

Religion, 9, 10, 15, 41, 67-78, 98, 101, 103, 105, 122, 152, 212, 231, 240, 244, 255, 311, 327,

337, 360, 430. *See also specific religions.*

Rules, 11, 12, 14, 84, 85, 95, 124, 125, 127, 135, 137, 142, 143, 164, 195, 198, 200, 202, 203, 214, 216, 218, 226, 228, 237-239, 247, 250, 254-256, 261, 262, 268-272, 275-277, 280, 281, 284, 286, 287, 289, 291, 292, 297, 301, 302, 304-307, 314, 325, 335, 339, 340-342, 353, 354, 359, 377, 389-394, 399, 404, 424, 425, 427, 429.

Shulgi, 22, 24, 25, 26, 130, 442
Simonides, 177
Social exclusion, 324, 326, 358
Social responsibility, 109, 117, 195, 196, 199, 201, 251, 259, 293
Socrates, 8, 10, 39, 41, 59, 69, 72, 75, 94, 105, 106, 115, 118, 122-124, 126, 134-144, 171-176, 179, 193, 194, 199, 215, 229, 233, 251, 265, 282, 320, 327, 368, 370, 373, 376, 383, 384, 392, 393, 394, 426.
Suits, Bernard, 55, 86, 120, 280, 301, 419.
Sustainability, 220, 326, 329, 330, 356-358, 398. *See also*: Agenda 21, Environment.
Swimming, 109, 259, 261, 274, 279, 285, 288, 302

Technology, 200, 228, 240, 279-281, 285-288, 293, 300, 301, 348, 409, 410, 412, 415, 422, 431.

Vergil, 97, 99, 100
Virtue, 7, 10, 12, 21, 22, 27-34, 35-46, 49, 53, 56, 59-63, 69-75, 82, 87, 90, 92, 96, 108, 123, 128, 130- 144, 156, 158, 166, 177, 179, 183-194, 196, 200, 215, 216, 230, 231, 245, 251, 253, 266, 281, 283, 288, 299, 302, 303, 306, 313, 318, 320, 323, 324, 365-377, 384, 388, 391-400, 405, 409, 410, 416, 417, 419, 421, 425-427, 431-433. *See also*: *aretē*.

WADA, 239, 252, 290, 291, 293, 295, 306, 443, 450.
Wing, John Ian, 450
Women, 87, 93, 178-180, 202, 243, 244, 256, 325, 352, 354, 362.
Wrestling, 12, 22, 27, 31, 32, 75, 81, 90, 119, 125, 155, 156-158, 166, 176, 192, 227, 270, 287, 305, 320, 419, 434.
Wushu, 258, 378.

Xenophanes, 67, 72-77

Youth Olympic Games, 258, 259, 260

Zeus, 9, 14, 35, 41, 42, 50, 51, 68, 75, 76, 102, 103, 131, 147, 149, 152, 156, 160, 163, 238, 249, 314, 315, 323, 333, 337, 343, 418, 431, 434.
Zhuangzi, 374, 375, 382, 388.

About the Author

Heather L. Reid is Professor of Philosophy at Morningside College in the USA and Scholar in Residence at Exedra Mediterranean Center in Siracusa, Sicily. She is a 2015 Fellow of the American Academy in Rome, 2018 Fellow of Harvard's Center for Hellenic Studies, and 2019 Fulbright Scholar at the Università degli Studi di Napoli Federico II. As founder of Fonte Aretusa, she promotes conferences and research on Western Greece. She has also published books and articles in ancient philosophy, philosophy of sport, and Olympic Studies, including *Introduction to the Philosophy of Sport* (2012) *Athletics and Philosophy in the Ancient World: Contests of Virtue* (2011), and *The Philosophical Athlete* (2002, 2nd. ed. 2019).

Printed in Poland
by Amazon Fulfillment
Poland Sp. z o.o., Wrocław
26 January 2024

711b9959-ee0b-4fe7-85ec-3aaff1c2487fR01